Czech Songs in Texas

AMERICAN POPULAR MUSIC SERIES

AMERICAN POPULAR MUSIC SERIES

CZECH SONGS IN TEXAS

FRANCES BARTON
JOHN K. NOVAK

FOREWORD BY JAMES P. LEARY

UNIVERSITY OF OKLAHOMA PRESS : NORMAN

This book is published with the generous assistance of the McCasland Foundation, Duncan, Oklahoma.

Library of Congress Cataloging-in-Publication Data

Names: Barton, Frances A., 1946– author. | Novak, John K. author. | Leary, James P., 1950–writer of foreword.

Title: Czech songs in Texas / Frances Barton and John K. Novak ; foreword by James P. Leary.

Description: [First.] | Norman : University of Oklahoma Press, 2021. | Series: American popular music series ; volume 7 | Includes bibliographical references and index. | Summary: "An annotated songbook and music history of 61 songs that have remained popular for generations in the Texas Czech ethnic community. Each song has Czech lyrics, side-by-side English translations, music notation, and an analysis exploring the European roots, American evolution, lyric meaning and significance, and notable performances and recordings" —Provided by publisher.

Identifiers: LCCN 2020054663 | ISBN 978-0-8061-6887-6 (hardcover)

Subjects: LCSH: Czechs—Texas—Music—History and criticism. | Folk songs, Czech—Texas—History and criticism. | Popular music—Texas—History and criticism. | Czechs—Texas—Music. | Folk songs, Czech—Texas. | Popular music—Texas.

Classification: LCC ML3560.C93 B37 2021 | DDC 782.42162/91860764—dc23

LC record available at https://lccn.loc.gov/2020054663

Czech Songs in Texas is Volume 7 in the American Popular Music Series.

The paper in this book meets the guidelines for permanence and durability of the Committee on Production Guidelines for Book Longevity of the Council on Library Resources, Inc. ∞

1 2 3 4 5 6 7 8 9 10

To those who keep the songs alive

CONTENTS

MAJEKS-ORCHESTRA
CAMERON TEX

ILLUSTRATIONS

FOREWORD

Czech Songs in Texas reveals the historical origins, enduring complexity, and immense allure of an immigrant/ethnic group's tradition. Situated firmly in the Lone Star State, the songs of Texas Czechs nonetheless brim beyond borders, enchanting others aplenty, while expanding our appreciation of America's musical diversity.

Settlers from the Czech lands, prominent in Central Texas, likewise established vibrant farming communities in Nebraska, Iowa, Minnesota, and Wisconsin. Their songs, cast in jaunty polka and stately waltz tempos, became an integral part of the rooted soundscape throughout that mid-continental swathe where the Great Plains and the Midwest merge. Reverberating from kitchens, dance halls, radios, and record players throughout the twentieth century, they propelled couples, captivated listeners, and made memories for Czech Americans and many neighbors irrespective of ethnic origins.

In the early 1940s, outlaw country icon Willie Nelson famously launched his career by playing with Czech polka bands in Texas beer joints around Abbott and West. Leighton "Skipper" Berg, leader of the Viking Accordion Band, ventured beyond Nordic standards like the singing toast "Skål, skål, skål" and "Livet i Finnskogarna" (Life in the Finnish Woods) to charm a duke's mixture of Minnesota dancers with such Czech favorites as "Švestkova alej" (Prune Song) and "Prsi, Prsi" (Rain, Rain). In Omaha my Irish American mother, Patricia Berigan—daughter of a livestock broker raised on a Nebraska Sand Hills ranch—learned to hum the tune and sing the chorus of "Baruška" (Barbara), a lively risqué song acquired from a classmate who frequented the fraternal Sokol Auditorium in South Omaha's "Little Bohemia." About the same time but 500 miles to the northeast, my dad, Warren Leary, hung out with Czechs from the hamlet of Haugen, Wisconsin, where their local ZCBJ hall, affiliated with the Zapadni Cesko Bratrske Jednota/Western Czech Fraternal Union, was facetiously dubbed the lair of Zebras, Cats, Bears, and Jackasses. Years later I heard squeezebox players hold forth in that very hall, including "Uncle Joe" Tomesh, a genial piano accordionist known for "Louka zelená" (Green Meadow Waltz), a tune we associated with his farm's back forty and surreptitious mid-1960s high school beer parties.

Similar stories and a great deal more enliven every page of *Czech Songs in Texas*. Co-authors Frances Barton and John K. Novak impressively combine decades of dedicated research, Czech and English fluency, command of published and archival sources, ethnomusicological expertise, sophisticated understanding of esoteric symbols suffusing older folk songs, and rich relationships with Texas Czech communities, singers, dance bands, and DJs to situate and illuminate sixty-one vibrantly circulating songs. An instant classic, *Czech Songs in Texas* merits inclusion on a scant yet expanding roster of comparable works by folklorists and cultural historians.

Discontented with reliance on the dead testimony of texts preserved solely in songbooks, Barton, Novak, and kindred scholars have centered instead on living lyrics actively performed over time by particular participants in shifting styles and settings. Walter Boyer, Albert Buffington, and Don Yoder showed the way with *Songs along the Mahantongo: Pennsylvania Dutch Folksongs* (1951). Harriet Pawlowska's field research in Detroit gave us *Merrily We Sing: 105 Polish Folksongs* (1961). Subsequent fine-grained studies include Américo Paredes's *A Texas-Mexican Cancionero: Folksongs of the Lower Border* (1976); Joshua Clegg Caffery's *Traditional Music in Coastal Louisiana: The 1934 Lomax Recordings* (2013); my own *Folksongs of Another America: Field Recordings from the Upper Midwest, 1937-1946*; and *Songs of the Finnish Migration* (2020) by Simo Westerholm, Thomas DuBois and Marcus Cederström.

Collectively such efforts offer an inclusive understanding of America's many-splendored grassroots song traditions that transcends language barriers, embraces cultural pluralism, and recognizes that immigrant/ethnic communities in our nation creatively fuse Old and New

World experiences, while persistently influencing and intermingling with sounds of various neighbors. The latest but, let us hope, not the last in a succession of comprehensive song chroniclers, Barton and Novak take us on a poetic, historical, and ethnographic excursion deep into a community's expressive heartland. Their *Czech Songs in Texas* just might be the finest extant annotated anthology of any American immigrant/ethnic group's regional song tradition.

James P. Leary
University of Wisconsin–Madison

ACKNOWLEDGMENTS

The authors are grateful to the many individuals and groups in the United States and the Czech Republic who helped with research, technical assistance, and provision of documents.

First, we wish to thank those who preserve this music most directly by performing it, thereby encouraging people to dance, to sing, and to want more! These musicians and music appreciators shared their time and experiences with us: Alfred Vrazel, Matt Strmiska, Jerry and Martha Ann Majek, Joe Ray Krenek, Martha Viktorin, Darwin Machu, Diane Volek, Father Paul Chovanec, Danny Zapletal, Fritz Hodde, Cenobio "Bubba" Hernandez, Mark Hermes, Daniel Klapuch, John Dujka, Mark Halata, Jeff Brosch, Chris Rybak, Jerry Haisler, Irene Sulak, Christopher Urban, Gracie Hatten, Nica Pyron, Vencil Broz, Margie Hanslik, Dixie Rhoades, Bertha Sefcak, and the late Ray Krenek and Vernon Drozd. We also thank Czech musicians Jiří Unruh, Zdeněk Tofel, and Ondřej Tofel.

We thank these private collectors who generously provided recorded and printed music: George Koudelka, Dennis Svatek, Dave Bedrich, Thomas Durnin, Gary Krupala, Donna Kaspar, Ginny Prasatik, and James B. Koehler. We thank the following for help with photographs: Freddie Krc, Rudy Patek, Glen Chervenka, Gary E. McKee, Alfred Vrazel, Rick Patrick, and Czech Daniela Stavělová. Likewise, we are obliged to historians, folklorists, ethnographers, and journalists who shared their knowledge with us: James P. Leary, Clinton Machann, Josef Barton, Gary E. McKee, Theresa Cernoch Parker, Carolyn Heinsohn, Mike Gest, Lori Najvar, Dawn Orsak, Roger Kolar, and Czechs Lubomír Tyllner, Eva Paulová, and Filip Šir.

Of tremendous importance were those who corrected the Czech texts and English translations and taught us nuances of the rich and beautiful Czech language: Lida Cope, Alena Fiala, Jubilee Barton, and Czechs Ivana Bozděchová and Věra Chovancová. We thank those who helped with the music notation: William A. Koehler, Brian Penkrot, and Tim Blickhan.

These institutions provided invaluable assistance: Fayette Heritage Museum and Archives in La Grange, Fayetteville Area Heritage Museum, Williamson Museum in Georgetown, Texas Polka Music Museum in Schulenburg, Texas Czech Heritage and Cultural Center in La Grange, Czech Heritage and Genealogy Center in Temple, the Czech Center Museum Houston, Arhoolie Foundation in El Cerrito, California, Texas State Library and Archives in Austin, Texas A&M University Press in College Station, Briscoe Center for American History at the University of Texas at Austin, Cushing Memorial Library and Archives at Texas A&M University in College Station, and the Vitak-Elsnic Collection at Bowling Green State University in Ohio.

Frances Barton is especially indebted to Felix Barton-Ganem, Jubilee Barton, Jacob Leverich, Dick Leverich, Josef Barton, Mary Durfor, and the late Lonn Taylor. John Novak wishes to thank Brian Hart, David Beveridge, and Czechs Otto Růžička and Petra Růžičková for their unique support.

The authors are grateful to Steve Harris of Music Publishers of America, LLC, and the Vitak-Elsnic Company for authorization to use copyrighted music in this work.

Finally, we thank the following organizations for their generous contributions toward publication of this book: the Austin Czech Historical Association, Northern Illinois University, PolkaWorks.org of Austin, the SPJST (Slavonic Benevolent Order of the State of Texas), the Victoria County Czech Heritage Society, and an anonymous donor. We also thank the University of Oklahoma Press and its great staff for publishing *Czech Songs in Texas*.

Frances Barton and John K. Novak

CZECH PRONUNCIATION GUIDE

When one views Czech and English in comparison with other Indo-European languages, the rules of pronunciation appear to be quite different, but when the two are seen from a world language perspective, they appear to have much in common. The following is not a complete guide to Czech phonetics; rather it is intended to help speakers of American English to pronounce the words of the Czech songs such as those in this book.

The Diacritical Markings

The primary accent in Czech is always on the first syllable. A ***čárka*** (′) is a mark placed over a vowel to lengthen it. Thus, in the word *voják* [soldier], the accent is on the first syllable, but the vowel **á** is prolonged. Athough the musical settings of the language determine both accent and vowel length, the *čárka* remains important in discerning the meaning of the word.

The ***kroužek*** is the small circle seen over certain **u** letters (**ů**).The symbol is equivalent to **ú** in its indication to prolong the vowel.

The ***háček*** [hook] may be placed over the consonants **c**, **r**, **s**, **z** or the vowel **e**, thus appearing as **č**, **ř**, **š**, **ž**, and **ě**. The ***háček*** also may appear as a "half ***háček***," which looks like an apostrophe placed immediately after the consonants **d'**, **n'**, and **t'**. In both guises, the *háček* changes the pronuciation of these letters as shown below.

Vowels

The vowels of Czech are comparable to the pure vowels of Italian and Spanish. Here they are compared to their sound in American English.

a as in *tall*

e as in *pencil*

ě is palatal and is pronounced as "ye" in ***yes***

i as *visa*

o as in *tone*

u as in *lunar*

y as in *lucky*

Consonants

b as in ***bath***

c is a "ts" sound as in *hats*. It is identical to the German **z**.

č as *ch* in ***ch**ange*

d as in ***d**im*

d' is palatal as in the British pronunciation of ***duty***

f as in *feather*

g is always hard as in ***g**uy*, never soft as in *gin*

h as in ***h**ope*

ch has no English equivalent. It is guttural and like the **ch** in German *na**ch**t*.

j is as the "y" sound in ***y**ellow*

k as in ***k**ettle*

l as in ***l**emon*

m as in ***m**other*

n as in ***n**ice*

n'or **ň** is palatal like "ny" in *ca**ny**on*

p as in ***p**encil*, but, as in Spanish, lacks explosion (aspiration).

q is found in foreign words and is pronounced "kv" as in the Yiddish ***kv**etch*

r is either flipped or rolled, never "chewed" as in the American **r**.

ř is a combination of a rolled **r** and and **ž** (see below). It is the only sound in Czech that does not exist in other languages and is usually the last to be learned by Czech children.

s as in ***s**and*

š as "sh" in ***sh**ine*. Also remember that the combination **sh** in Czech is not **š**, but is two separate sounds **s** and **h**.

t is similar to ***t**ime*, but as in Spanish lacks explosion. The sound is made with the middle of the tongue against the roof of the mouth, not the tip of the tongue against the upper teeth.

t' is palatal as in the British pronunciation of ***tune***.

v as in **v**est

w is found in foreign words and is equal to the **v** sound
x is found in foreign words and is pronounced as in *exit*
z as in *zoo*
ž as **s** in *leisure*

Other Rules

A common consonant-vowel combination is the letters **di**, **ni** and **ti**. These sounds are always palatal, meaning that they are pronounced as though there were an English **y** between the letters. Thus, **di** is pronounced **dyi**, **ni** is **nyi**, and **ti** is **tyi**. For a non-palatal vowel pronunciation, these same consonants are followed by **y** or **ý**, such as in **tý** [you], which is pronounced as the English **tea.**

Vowel combinations result in diphthongs such as **ou**. The sounds of both vowels must be clear, one following the other.

The letters **l** and **r** can serve as schwa-like vowels such as in the Czech words *vlk* [wolf] and *prst* [finger]. This property accounts for several words in the Czech language which seem to have no vowels, or not enough vowels.

There are more rules for certain words and of certain letter combinations, including those that govern alteration of sounds depending in part on the usage of the word in a sentence. However, readers who master the above sounds are well on their way to an authentic pronunciation of the Czech language.

INTRODUCTION

Frances Barton

On any weekend, musicians sing and play Czech music for a dance somewhere in Texas. Yet, despite this musical liveliness, the Texas Czech ethnic community has reached a crucial moment in its history. The last generation of musicians who learned Czech as their first language are leaving the stage. This book offers a treasure of Czech-language songs that generations of the Texas Czech community—its singers, instrumentalists, dancers, listeners, dance hall managers, and collectors—have nurtured and performed. *Czech Songs in Texas* is an annotated collection of sixty-one songs, mostly polkas and waltzes. More especially, the book includes music notation, Czech lyrics, their English translations, and interpretative text. It is a work of both recovery and celebration: recovery of forgotten histories and stories that document a rich musical tradition, and celebration of lively musical performances still heard around the state.

This introduction outlines the story of Czech migration to Texas and characterizes the history and meaning of the songs the immigrants brought and the ones they added after they arrived. The two following chapters describe the role music has played in the Texas Czech community and survey the history of Czech folk and popular music in its European home.

Czech Immigration to Texas

In the 1850s, drawn by the availability of farmland, immigrants from the Habsburg provinces of Bohemia, Moravia, and part of Silesia, now the Czech Republic, began to settle in Texas. They flowed in until the 1920s, when the United States severely restricted immigration. By the time the gates closed, roughly 50,000 foreign-born Czechs and their children had settled in the state.[1]

The first group of Czech immigrants to Texas, which counted sixteen families of seventy-four people, began their journey in November 1851 after they had harvested the crops. They left the area around the village of Čermná on the northern border of the Habsburg province of Bohemia. Conditions on the boat were so terrible that only thirty-eight survivors of the original seventy-four reached Austin County, Texas, in January 1852. From the tragic mistakes made by the first group, the groups that came after learned important lessons, such as which ship companies were not to be trusted and which routes were to be avoided.[2] By the 1920s, when immigration was curtailed, almost 10 percent of Texas Czechs had arrived from the Čermná area and a smaller number from southern Bohemia. But by far, most Texas Czechs had emigrated from Moravia, the province just east of Bohemia.[3]

Texas Czechs started out as family and neighbors in Europe. The majority of the Czechs who immigrated to Texas—over 80 percent of them—came from just three clusters of villages in the mountainous region of northeastern Moravia centered around the towns of Vsetín, Zádveřice, and Frenštát pod Radhoštěm. Once they were in Texas, they stayed close to one another and soon sent for other family members and neighbors to join them. Three miles from Frenštát, for example, five hundred inhabitants of the little Moravian town of Trojanovice came to Texas between 1856 and 1895. Many of them established roots in three small settlements in east-central Texas—Fayetteville, Dubina, and Hostýn, all in Fayette County, all within thirty miles of one another.[4]

These kindred immigrants were not only closely bound by intimate personal ties but were also linked by having come from a larger district that contained many interwoven families and villages. One linkage was religion. The Czechs who came to Texas were overwhelmingly Catholic, perhaps as high as 75 percent. A smaller proportion were Protestant, about 20 percent; and a few identified as freethinkers who were skeptics of organized religion.[5] Another affinity was education and language. Most of them were literate, and most spoke distinctive Moravian dialects. Yet a third was occupation and status. With few exceptions, their roots were rural. The largest number were small farmers who had owned ten acres or less. But there were also farm laborers and a lesser number of shepherds and servants. A large group of weavers, whose cottage industry had been replaced by textile factories, came from the Frenštát area. Other skilled craftspeople were shoemakers and blacksmiths. Also in their ranks were teachers, writers, editors, priests, and ministers, as well as musicians and their instruments if they had room in their trunks.

All these people had been subjects of the Austrian Habsburg Monarchy. From 1620 until the end of World War I, the Austrian branch of the House of Habsburg controlled the historic lands of the Bohemian Crown—Bohemia, Moravia, and Silesia. Centuries of occupation by the imperial power suppressed Czech culture: German was the language of administration, education, and business; young males had to serve in the Austrian army; and religious freedom was greatly curtailed. Furthermore, these Texas immigrants had also lived through the disintegration of feudalism and the emergence of industrialism and a capitalist economy, dramatic changes that transformed nineteenth-century traditional agrarian society. For most, the economic upheaval had been devastating.

The 1848 political uprising in Prague presented a possibility of relief from a hopeless situation. The revolt, like many similar midcentury revolutions in Europe inspired by liberal Enlightenment thought, was quickly suppressed. Nevertheless, it resulted in reforms that were especially life-changing for peasants: the abolition of the last burdens of feudal bondage and the loosening of restrictions on emigration. The new freedom to relocate provided an escape as well as an opportunity. The distressed peasants could start over, sell what they had, and try to find work in a town or city. Another option was to immigrate to Texas, a place that wanted immigrants, and get a farm of their own.[6] This is how that first group of seventy-four people came to leave Čermná for Texas in 1851.

Czech Songs in Texas is a collection of the secular songs the descendants of these immigrants still sing, play, and dance to. The majority of the songs echo the music popular at the time of emigration. They are mostly in the style of two remarkably adaptable European dance forms, both couple dances. The first is the waltz. Initially scandalous because the couple held each other so closely, the waltz grew out of several central European dances in 3/4 time and became popular in the eighteenth century. The second is the polka, a vigorous couple dance in 2/4 time that came out of rural northern Bohemia in the 1830s. It soon spread like wildfire through the ballrooms and taverns of Prague. By the 1840s, polka had entered the salons of high society in Paris and London and even made it all the way to the Americas.

These two couple dances expressed the new revolutionary ideas of individualism and equality then taking hold in Europe. The ethnomusicologist Charles Keil links the waltz, with its break from traditional peasant and aristocratic group dances—its shocking individualism—to the revolutions that swept Europe in the late eighteenth-century Enlightenment era. Keil links polka, a generator of joy with its infectious energy and exuberant movements—and its roots in peasant life—to the Romantic-era revolutions of the mid-nineteenth century and the longing for freedom, equality, and self-determination they embodied.[7]

Polka and Nineteenth-Century Social and Musical Upheaval

Polka flourished in the Czech lands concurrent with the birth of several other cultural and social phenomena of the nineteenth century, as the folklorist James P. Leary has pointed out.[8] These phenomena included the collection and publication of folk songs, the use of folk material and themes by Czech classical composers, the availability of new instruments, the growth of civilian brass bands, and the influence of František Kmoch's march compositions. For the Czechs who were chafing under Habsburg rule, polka became a powerful expression of the growth of their own quest for an independent nation and democratic government. The music the Czech immigrants brought to America was in many ways shaped by these forces and ideas.

The Habsburgs, by policy and by force, suppressed the Czech language and elevated German as the language of the state, the law, and education. But after over two centuries of enforced Germanization, Czech was revived in the first half of the nineteenth century through what became known as the *Národní obrození,* or the National Revival.[9] One of its major endeavors was the collection of folk songs, which were a large repository of the Czech language.

Czech intellectuals, enthused by Romantic-era ideas, began to study the customs of peasant life and to document and publish traditional agrarian folk songs in collections. This largely linguistic endeavor was contemporary with similar efforts elsewhere in Europe and influenced by the writings of the German theorist Johann Gottlieb Herder.[10] The Revival served as the foundation of the movement that eventually led to the return of a vigorous, literary Czech language and, ultimately, in 1918, to an independent Czech nation. The songs that were collected became part of the national vocabulary. Some of the songs, for example, appeared in one of the seminal novels of this period, Božena Němcová's wonderful *Babička* (Grandmother). Furthermore, about one-half of the songs in *Czech Songs in Texas* were first documented by those early folklorists. A few are "Louka zelená" (Green Meadow Waltz; Song 37), "Kdybych byla ptáčkem" (If I Were a Bird; Song 29), "Pivo červené" (Red Beer; Song 46), and "Zahučely hory" (Roaring Mountains; Song 61).

Influenced by the Revivalists, Czech classical composers began to write chamber music, orchestral works, and operas with national subjects, characters, and folk-inspired music. The titles of these works, as well as the lyrics to the operas, were—importantly—in the Czech language. Bedřich Smetana introduced polka to the classical world in *Prodaná nevěsta,* known in English as *The Bartered Bride*, his 1866 comic opera set in a rural Czech village. A few years later, Antonín Dvořák wrote several polkas for the piano and also featured a number of folk-dance rhythms and styles in his *Slavonic Dances*. These compositions gave a stamp of legitimacy to the use of the Czech language and peasant folk music in high art. Several of these pieces entered the popular repertory. For example, the opening chorus from *The Bartered Bride* was one of the first recordings made by an early Texas Czech band, Bačova Česka Kapela (Baca Czech Band) of Fayetteville. They recorded it for Okeh Records in a 1929 session in San Antonio.[11]

Technological innovations during the first half of the nineteenth century brought forth the newly invented accordion and improved brass instruments as well as better manufacturing techniques to produce them more quickly. The accordion was first patented in Vienna in 1829 and was being mass-produced in Europe by 1850.[12] The best-known and most successful Czech brass instrument manufacturer was Václav František Červený, who started his company, called V. F. Červený, in Hradec Králové in 1842. Červený's many improvements and innovations to brass instruments made his horns popular all over Central and Eastern Europe, and his firm became the main producer of instruments for the Austrian army.[13] His horns could also be found in the Americas. One example is an 1878 order placed to the company for instruments by a newly forming Texas Czech brass band connected to a theater club in Velehrad, a farming settlement in Lavaca County named after a Moravian pilgrimage site.[14]

The introduction of these new instruments affected traditional Czech rural and village music during the same time that the music of an earlier era was being documented by the Revivalists. Bagpipes, hammered dulcimers, violins, and other traditional instruments began to be supplemented or even replaced as improved horns and accordions were introduced into village ensembles. As people of peasant origins migrated from villages to work in the towns and cities, the songs they brought along changed in the new environment. Irregular rhythms gave way to more driving, danceable beats, such as that of the popular polka. Major-scale patterns became dominant as well as melodies with wider, more dramatic intervals.[15] A few examples of village songs that migrated to urban centers and were changed there are "Sirotek" (Orphan Waltz; Song 51), "Spadl lístek z javora" (Falling Leaf; Song 53), and "Julajda/Julida" (Song 26).

Polka became popular at the same time that the organization of civilian brass bands surged. By the 1860s, the civilian bands, playing a mix of traditional folk songs and new, sometimes locally composed pieces, could be heard even in the remote mountainous regions of Moravia where many of the Texas immigrants had lived. The bands played in processions, at religious events, at popular local festivals, in taverns and small pubs, and at village fairs.

Made up primarily of amateur musicians, many such ensembles were attached to local organizations of firefighters, miners, sharpshooters, veterans, factory workers, and athletes from the numerous Sokol clubs. All these local bands played an important role in promoting the growing sentiment for national independence. Ironically, service in the Austrian military, required of Czech young men, had proven to be an excellent training program for band musicians. Upon returning home, former military musicians were able to continue using their skills by playing in local community bands.[16] One fine example of a brass band piece composed by a local musician that is now a popular Czech polka in Texas is "Nemelem" (Grinders Polka; Song 43). It was written in the early twentieth century by Jan Čermák, an influential schoolteacher and youth band director in the eastern Bohemian town of Vysoté Mýto.

František Kmoch, a popular civilian band conductor and composer but also one of the leaders of the politically significant Sokol athletic movement, began writing a different kind of band music in the latter part of the nineteenth century. His genius was to subvert the Austrian military march and put it to use for Czech unity and identity purposes. He used the musical form of the march, but within some of his marches he placed, in the lyrical middle section called the trio, a familiar folk song. The lyrics to the song were not in the official German language but in Czech, rooting the music in traditional peasant life. Many of the folk songs in his trios came from the collecting efforts of the early Revivalists. Kmoch's danceable marches, or polka-marches, as the historian Victor Greene has described them,[17] are still popular in Texas. The full composition is performed as a stirring march, or the trio is played alone as a great polka and lyrical song. Six can be found among the pages of this book: "Andulko šafářova" (Annie the Foreman; Song 3), "Co ten ptáček jarabáček?" (Bird of Spring; Song 16), "Kolíne, Kolíne" (Song 32), "Muziky, muziky" (Song 39), "Pod našima okny" (Under Our Windows; Song 47), and "Pode mlejnem" (At the Mill; Song 48).

Czech immigration to Texas peaked during the years 1870–1920 when these pivotal ideas, events, and changes were taking form in the homeland. Despite the uncertainties of a strange new land, the immigrants brought with them the comforts of a familiar body of music, including the very popular polka. This lively dance carried a load of meaning, for it had emerged as a potent national expression of freedom, of revival of the suppressed Czech culture, and of hope for national self-determination. That the polka survives and thrives all these years later testifies to the power of song and dance to evoke this ethnic community's foundational story: that the immigrants came to America because they wanted freedom, democracy, and a better life.

1 MUSIC AND THE TEXAS CZECH COMMUNITY

Frances Barton

In May 1844, word arrived in New York City of a new dance from Europe called the polka. A month later, two couples danced "La Polka" in a Broadway show.[1] By the 1850s, polka had spread to Mexico, not only to the urban salons but also out to the villages.[2] In Galveston, Texas, in 1857, a dancing master was honored at a party given by his students where European dances, including the polka, were performed.[3] A scandalous couple dance much like the waltz before it, polka had settled in the New World.

As the folklorist Richard March has pointed out, when polka became part of mainstream American popular culture in the mid-nineteenth century, it carried no ethnic identification or cultural connection—it was a broadly popular phenomenon. That began to change as immigration from Central, Eastern, and Southern Europe intensified after the Civil War. Non-Anglo Europeans, who spoke languages other than English, were becoming a larger and more visible component of American society.[4]

After the war, when the ports reopened and new arrivals began to land on these unfamiliar shores, polka and brass bands—the dance style and type of music ensemble immensely popular in the European soundscape—were already established in the United States. For the newcomers, hearing these familiar, old-country sounds in the new land may have been a surprise and a great comfort. Even as polka's general popularity began to wane, it grew stronger in many of the immigrant communities that were beginning to form.[5] Within certain of them, it remained and developed into recognizable styles. Today the term "polka" refers to the fast couple dance in 2/4 time as well as to a genre that includes several other nineteenth-century couple dances, such as the waltz, schottische, ländler, redowa, mazurka, quadrille, and others that are still regularly performed.

There are now at least six polka traditions in the United States, each one nourished and developed for a century or more. All strongly rooted in ethnic and working-class enclaves of dancing cultures, the six include Mexican conjunto, Arizona O'odham (the People) *waila* or "chicken scratch," and the various polka styles of Polish, Slovenian, German, and Czech ethnic communities.[6] Four of these polka traditions—Mexican, German, Czech, and Polish—are part of the wonderfully diverse music that can be found in Texas.

Early Texas Czech Settlements

Cat Spring, a small settlement in Austin County, was founded by German immigrants in the early 1830s. It was just a few miles west of San Felipe, the headquarters for Stephen F. Austin's Anglo-American colony established on the Brazos River beginning in 1823. Both settlements began when Texas was part of Mexico, prior to independence in 1836. After Texas was admitted to the United States in 1845, Cat Spring became the first destination of most early Czech emigrant groups after they started arriving at the Port of Galveston in the early 1850s.[7]

The colonization of Texas began to take place in the middle part of Austin Colony, between the Colorado River to the west and the Brazos to the east. The colonists were made up of Anglo migrants bringing cotton plantation culture and African slaves from the southern states, and of non-English-speaking emigrants bringing rural village culture from Central and Eastern Europe. The settlements were part of the larger nineteenth-century westward expansion of the frontier that by the 1870s either annihilated or relocated the native American Indian inhabitants of Texas to reservations, most of them in Oklahoma.[8] Migration from the southern states moved in first, followed by immigration from Europe. The Germans began settling the Brazos-Colorado area in 1831; the Czechs in 1850; the Sorbs, also called Wends, in the mid-1850s; and the Silesian Poles in the 1870s. Austin Colony and the surrounding Central Texas region became the most diverse in the state.[9]

Like the Germans who had settled in Texas prior to their arrival, the Czech emigrants had been profoundly influenced by letters received from an early settler. In the case of the Germans, the letters were from Friedrich Ernst of Oldenburg, Germany, who in 1831 began to farm land in the Mill Creek valley, located in northwestern Austin County. He wrote glowingly about his life in Texas to friends back home in Germany.[10] Twenty years later, the Protestant minister Rev. Ernst Bergmann, originally of Zápudov in northern Bohemia, settled in Cat Spring and repeated this scenario. His letter, describing his family's journey to Texas, was published in a Moravian newspaper in 1851 and influenced subsequent waves of Czech immigration.[11]

Bergmann and his family landed in Galveston in early 1850 and made their way to Cat Spring, where they bought land. Bergmann, fluent in both German and Czech, taught school and preached while farming on the side. Inspired by Bergmann's letter about Texas, two parties of emigrants set out from the Lanškroun region of northeastern Bohemia, in 1851 and 1853, bound for Galveston. Those who survived the trip finally made it to Houston, then to Cat Spring, and from there moved on to nearby German communities, including New Ulm and New Bremen.[12]

As Czechs continued to arrive, they followed this same pattern, first staying in Cat Spring long enough to get supplies and information about jobs or land for sale or rent, then moving on. But when nearby land was no longer available, they looked farther into adjoining counties, always in search of good farmland. By the start of the Civil War, there were over seven hundred Czechs in the state. The majority of them were Catholic, and the largest number found land in Fayette County. They had learned to farm cotton and had inserted themselves into the rural economy as farm owners, renters, laborers, or servants. They had also established a few rudimentary social institutions: intermittently scheduled religious services conducted in private homes or small chapels and several makeshift schools for their children. But they were too few in number and living too far apart to create a cohesive ethnic culture to secure their loyalty and root them to their new home.[13] Kateřina Herrmann, who arrived in Cat Spring from Bohemia with her husband and children in 1851, wrote back home about the isolation she felt in Texas: "Those used to social life and activities outside their household feel very lonely here because there are no pubs or other public places."[14]

Scattered on isolated farms that by this time were spread out within an area of over two hundred square miles,[15] the early Czech immigrants made their own entertainment. They visited neighbors and relatives when possible; attended occasional weddings; met one another at services led by either visiting clergy or a lay person; and danced at house parties to music of a violin, guitar, accordion, hammered dulcimer, or *flašinet,* a hand-cranked barrel organ imported from the old country.[16]

Civil War and Ethnic Identity

Except for a few individuals who came to Texas before group immigration began, most Czechs missed the upheavals caused by the Texas Revolution of 1835–1836 or the U.S.-Mexican War of 1846–1848.[17] The early groups of settlers, however, arrived just in time for the Civil War. The eligible citizens of Texas voted to secede from the Union on February 23, 1861, by a vote of 46,129 to 14,697. Nineteen Texas counties voted against secession, including Fayette, which had a "large German population and a Czech minority."[18]

The Czech settlers were immediately affected by secession. All foreign immigration came to a halt while the Union blockaded southern ports to eliminate the South's source of wealth, the international cotton trade. The Czechs were also forced to confront the issue of military service. Remarkably, some of them managed to avoid conscription by either leaving the state or by hiding out in the woods or river bottoms. Most chose more conciliatory routes. They enlisted in local or reserve units, served their time typically within the state, and then went back to farming. Some hauled Confederate cotton on oxen-pulled wagons from the end of the railroad in Colorado County to the Mexican port of Matamoros, an alternative service that provided an exemption from conscription. About forty served in the Confederate Army, and a few joined the Union forces.[19]

The war experiences amplified the differences between the Anglo-Americans and the Europeans who lived together in the area near the Brazos and Colorado Rivers. They both raised cotton for a living. The Anglo plantation owners used slaves for labor, as did small farmers who could afford them, while the Europeans, with rare exceptions, depended on their families to work the fields. The two groups lived in close proximity, but they "remained apart in language, religion, and intimate society."[20] On the other hand, the war strengthened Czech and German ties. Among the Czechs, it stoked a growing recognition of their need to form community institutions for mutual protection, aid, and comfort. In 1866, when immigration started up again, the growing Czech community took "the first steps toward becoming an ethnic group," as Phil Hewitt describes it.[21] They established churches with their own buildings, cemeteries, and resident pastors. They organized schools where their children could learn. And within a few years they began to read Czech language newspapers published in Texas.

Churches and Schools

An estimated 75 percent of the Czechs in Texas were Catholic, and about 20 percent were Protestant.[22] The early Czech Catholics built at least four small chapels or churches, initially served by missionary priests: at Ross Prairie in 1855, Hostýn in 1856, Praha in 1865, and Fayetteville in 1870. The first permanent Czech priest in Texas, Father Josef Chromčík from the Frenštát area of Moravia, arrived in 1872, just in time to conduct Christmas Mass at the Fayetteville church with some of his former parishioners. He ministered to many of the Catholics in Fayette County, and by 1890, three other Czech priests also served in the county. A Catholic school was built in Hostýn in 1868, and a Czech-English school was established in Praha in 1870. In 1875, Father Chromčík established and taught at the Fayetteville Catholic School.[23]

In 1864, in the Washington County Czech settlement of Veselí (Happiness), now called Wesley, the Protestant minister Rev. Josef Opočenský helped his congregation establish a permanent home. The Wesley Brethren built a church in 1866, and thus began the Texas revival of the ancient *Jednota bratrská* (Unity of the Brethren), a Protestant body that originated in the fifteenth-century Czech Reformation but had been suppressed in its homeland since 1620. Wesley was also the site of an early school organized by the teacher Josef Mašík in 1859. Mašík taught in a private home and, from 1866 to 1872, in the Wesley Brethren church building. The school closed about 1900.[24]

Newspapers

Before the first Texas Czech newspaper began publishing in 1879, early settlers relied on the Czech American press, with its first newspaper established in 1860, for news in their own language. Texas reading clubs used these early newspapers in their libraries and meetings, and some schoolchildren were taught to read from them. One Texan was part of the national press. Josef Lešikar, an early settler who lived in New Ulm, had been a founder and served as correspondent and distributor for the pro-Union *Národní noviny,* a St. Louis paper. In 1861, he was threatened with hanging by pro-slavery vigilantes and forced to send back a shipment of papers. The Czech press in America was outspoken, lively, and prolific—over three hundred newspapers were introduced between 1860 and 1911.[25]

The first Texas paper in the Czech language was the weekly *Texan,* published in La Grange in 1879 and then sold that same year. Its successor, *Slovan* (Slav), moved to Bryan and closed in 1890. Another La Grange weekly, called *Svoboda* (Freedom), was founded in 1885 by the highly respected county judge Augustin Haidušek and was "the most influential Czech newspaper ever published in Texas."[26] It focused on state and local matters such as political developments; farmland for sale and advice on crops and markets; announcements on births, deaths, and weddings; community news of dances and other social events; helpful information about emigration; and letters from readers. Its editorials called for civic participation and education, and urged Czechs to learn English along with their mother tongue, a controversial opinion at the time. Haidušek published the paper and was its editor from 1886 to the mid-1920s. After his death in 1929, *Svoboda* later was issued as a supplement to *El Campo News* and closed in 1966.[27]

In the pre–World War II years, as many as thirty Czech-language newspapers, journals, and supplements to other papers were published in Texas. Some of these were church-affiliated, others were official organs for fraternal and community organizations, and a few, such as *Svoboda,* were independent. *Našinec* (Fellow Countrymen), published since 1912 and affiliated with Katolická jednota Texaská (Catholic Union of Texas), known as the KJT, bowed out in 2018. It was the last Texas paper in the Czech language. A few others still exist, all published in English, including the church-affiliated *Bratrské listy,* established in 1902 and now known by its translated title *Brethren Journal.* Another is *Věstník* (Gazette), the official organ of Slovanská podpurující jednota státu Texas (Slavonic Benevolent Order of the State of Texas), commonly called SPJST. Věstník was founded in 1912 and still bears its Czech name.[28]

The press played an important role in the establishment of a Czech musical culture in Texas. While it conquered the distances between the rural settlements and provided its readers with continuous practice in the use of the Czech language, it also offered a publicity medium for musicians, advertising their upcoming events as well as reporting on performances after they occurred.

Brass Bands, Dulcimers, Accordions, and Fraternal Organizations

By the 1880s, almost every town and hamlet in America had at least one brass band.[29] The English-language *La Grange Journal* included many local reports on Fayette County's musical life. One story from La Grange in the May 5, 1880, issue announced that "our town is soon to have a brass band, and we will have all the fun of hearing the boys practice for three or four months."[30] For the 1883 Fourth of July celebration in the German settlement of Round Top, two brass bands were chosen to lead a large procession from the center of town to a park half a mile away. This was followed by a dance on a platform that evening.[31] And in the town of Ellinger, a band led fifteen hundred people in a procession in 1886 to dedicate the opening of the Czecho-Moravan school.[32]

Processions, parades, dances, concerts—these activities were common for brass bands of the time. A band in Fayetteville, organized in the mid-1880s, is shown on page 9. The caption identifies the eleven members. The trombone player, second from left in the back row, is Frank Baca, who also composed music for the band. Frank had been an infant in 1860 when his father, Joseph Baca, and his family emigrated from Bordovice in Moravia. They arrived in Galveston in September and traveled by ox-drawn wagon to Fayetteville, where they settled on a nearby farm in an area that became known as Bordovice.[33]

Frank showed early musical talent, taught himself clarinet at age nine, later picked up trombone, taught music, and studied arranging and composition. He married Marie Kovar, an emigrant from Hovězi in Moravia who was a midwife. They had thirteen children between the years of 1882 and 1899, all musicians who were taught by their father. In 1892, Frank founded the first of the various Baca family bands and orchestras that followed, which over the years included his children as well as other family members and local musicians.[34]

Old World Dulcimers

Though brass bands were notably ascendant during this time, instruments of rural Moravian folk music could also be found in Texas. One of these folk instruments, the *cimbál,* called a hammered dulcimer or cimbalom in English, was given to Frank's oldest son, Joe, by his uncle Ignac Krenek, who had made it in 1892.[35] When Frank died in 1907, Joe became bandleader. One year later, Joe and his siblings, aged nine to twenty-six, posed for a formal band portrait. There on the bass drum is their name: "Baca's Family Orchestra." The instruments displayed or held by the members include the large dulcimer, sitting on its

Fayetteville, Texas, band, mid-1880s. *Left to right from rear:* ___ Orsak, Frank Bača, John Jiřik, Ernest Knežek, J. R. Kuběna, John Řek. *Front:* John Bartoň, Vince Šulak, Joe Bartoň, Joseph Janak, J. S. Zvesper. Image and names from Hudson and Maresh, *Czech Pioneers of the Southwest,* 316. *Photo courtesy of Dick Leverich.*

Baca Family Orchestra, circa 1908. *In no order:* Joe O. Baca (director), John R. Baca, Rudolph A. Baca, Frank A. Baca Jr., Raymond "Ray" Baca Sr., Ludwig B. Baca, Mary Baca Kubena, Betty Baca Tschiedel, Jennie Baca Scherpick, Frances Baca Zapalac, Annie Baca Stastny, Emilie Baca Kulhanek, Julia Baca Chalupa (one member not shown, names from Cleo R. Baca, *Baca's Musical History*). *Photo courtesy of Dick Leverich.*

Krenek Orchestra, late 1910s–early 1920s. *Fourth from left:* Josef Krenek, violin; Frank Krenek, hammered dulcimer; Edward Krenek, violin; others unknown. *Photo courtesy of Freddie Krc.*

side to show all its strings, three violins, two clarinets, two cornets, trombone, string bass, and snare drums, reminiscent of a Moravian village band.[36]

Joe died in 1920, and his brother John R. Baca became bandleader. By this time, the group was known as Baca's Band and Orchestra and included family members as well as local musicians. Under John's leadership, the band played on several radio stations in the mid-1920s and also, in 1929, became the first Czech band in Texas to make records.[37] A photo from about 1925 documents the core members from this period: the five living Baca brothers, a son of their deceased brother Joe, and two local musicians. The hammered dulcimer is displayed in front of the band and can be heard on their recordings.[38] The instrument also featured in several other groups organized by Baca family members. Anna Baca Stastny, who had played dulcimer with the first family orchestra, performed with her husband and sons from the 1930s until the start of World War II. Her brothers Ray and Ludwig were also skilled players, and Ray continued to play dulcimer with his son Gil's band into the 1970s.[39]

The Kreneks were another family of musicians who featured the hammered dulcimer in their music. Michael, the patriarch of the Krenek family, and his wife Rosina left their home in Vigantice, a village in the Moravian region. They arrived in Galveston in 1855 and settled in Pisek, near Fayetteville, where they raised seven sons. Family stories say that the first Krenek band formed in Europe in 1846 with sixteen-year-old Michael on violin. When he and Rosina came to Texas, Michael formed a new band and began playing, most likely for house dances and other private affairs. Michael's son Josef took over as the bandleader in 1881, and a photograph, taken in the late 1910s or early 1920s, shows the instrumentation of the Krenek Orchestra: hammered dulcimer, two violins, small horn, and string bass.[40] The photo could pass for a

Ilse Orchestra, circa late 1920s. *Left to right:* Elo Ilse, Arnold Ilse, Lee Ilse, Hugo Ilse, Milton Ilse. *Photo courtesy of Fayette Heritage Museum and Archives, La Grange, Texas.*

band in a Moravian village—if the men were not wearing American-style clothing, that is.

The next leader of the Krenek Orchestra was Josef's son Edward, who was at the helm for thirty-five years, starting in 1911. Edward made seven or eight dulcimers, played one himself, and made one especially for his son Ray, who took over his dad's band in 1946. Ray, who settled in Wallis with his family, played dulcimer, fiddle, clarinet, and saxophone and was bandleader for the next sixty-odd years. In 2008, Ray's son Joe Ray of Sealy assumed leadership, and the band can still be heard at church picnics and dances. Members of this large musical family—which includes many descendants, such as Texas favorites Al Sulak of Orchard and Freddie Krc of Austin, among others—have been performing in Texas for an astonishing length of time.[41]

One final dulcimer band example is the Ilse Orchestra of La Grange, formed in 1905 by baritone player George Ilse with three of his sons: Elo on string bass, Arnold on clarinet, and Hugo on trumpet. Two other sons joined them as soon as they were old enough, Lee on hammered dulcimer and Milton on drums. A photo, probably from the late 1920s, shows Lee standing behind the dulcimer that he made, holding the wooden hammers in his left hand, with his brothers and their instruments on either side, yet another example of Texas Czechs maintaining their old-world customs. In 1947, Lee became bandleader and changed the name to the Lee Ilse Orchestra.[42] It continued to perform until 1964, when he retired and band member Lee Roy Matocha, who had joined in 1952, formed his own band with several of the Ilse Orchestra musicians.[43]

Accordions

Mass manufacture of accordions, a new type of free-reed instrument, began in 1850s Europe, when the continent's immigrants were streaming into the United States.[44] The relatively lightweight, portable squeezebox that could simultaneously play bass, rhythm, and melody at a

Majek's Orchestra, 1930s. *Left to right:* Leo Majek Sr., John Majek, Julius Majek, Joe Balusek. *Photo courtesy of Texas Polka Music Museum, Schulenburg, Texas.*

robust volume made it versatile enough to be part of an ensemble or function as a one-man or one-woman band. The account records of the Ondrej Gallia general store in Praha, Texas, show that the store had accordions in stock in the 1870s and was selling them for $6.40.[45] These would have been small diatonic button accordions, the kind Leo Majek learned to play as a young boy.

Leo Majek began to play professionally in 1897 in his hometown of Slavkov, Moravia, just east of Brno. He was twelve years old and played his button accordion for parties and dances after he got home from work at a sugar factory. In 1908, Leo married Rosie Pruch, and in 1913, with prewar tensions high in Europe, he emigrated to Texas, where he joined his wife's brother in Granger. Rosie and their two children followed later, on the last boat to leave Europe before the beginning of World War I. They moved to Marak, a community near Cameron, where Leo and Rosie lived on a rented cotton farm and

Granger Picnic Band on main street of Granger, Texas, circa 1907. *First row:* George Matyscak, ___ Hruska, Frank Martinets, Emil Wentercek, Jim Martinets. *Second row:* Charles Vitek, Karel Strmiska, Joe Vitek, Frank Kerbala, Joe Rozacky. *Third row:* Tom Martinets, William Vitek, Roman Zatozek, Frank Drozd. *Photo courtesy The Williamson Museum, 2001.001.1028, Georgetown, Texas.*

raised their seven children.[46] But Leo always found time to play his accordion. According to his wife, Rosie, in a 1961 interview, he rode a horse to the jobs and made "as much as $1 for a night's playing."[47]

Leo's six sons learned to play instruments when they were young, and by the 1930s, the two oldest, Julius and John, were part of Majek's Orchestra, the band their father led. The instrumentation consisted of Leo's button accordion, saxophone, clarinet, and drums. In 1940, the family moved to Corpus Christi, where Leo found work in the shipyards. Five of the sons served in World War II, and all returned, inspiring Rosie and son John to write the beautiful song "Vzpomínka na Cameron" (Memories of Cameron; Song 59), which is included in this book. The six sons eventually joined their father on stage, thus adding piano, cornet, and the piano accordion of Leo Jr. to the group's lineup. Leo Sr. died in 1976, but third-, fourth-, and fifth-generation Majek descendants, led by Leo's grandson Jerry, still play for festivals, weddings, anniversaries, reunions, and other local events in the orchestra Leo founded.[48]

Platforms, Dance Halls, and Fraternal Organizations

All these musicians needed places to play, preferably with band stages and smooth, indoor dance floors. The construction of many of these venues was taken on by the fraternal and mutual aid organizations, the Catholic parishes, and Sokol clubs, which also used the halls for their own activities.

The predecessors to dance halls were outdoor dance platforms. Those constructed for a one-time event, like a home wedding celebration, were often built with boards rented from a local lumberyard.[49] Other platforms were more permanent. Frank Lotto, in his 1902 history of Fayette County, mentions one located on the town square of

Praha, a community he describes as "entirely Bohemian." The platform was owned by the saloon proprietor Frank Vyvjala.[50] A photograph from about 1900 shows a crowd of maybe two hundred well-dressed people dancing on another platform, this one in Dubina, the first Czech settlement west of the Colorado River.[51] About 1905 in Williamson County, an area of rich blackland soil where Czech settlement began in the 1870s, the Granger Picnic Band regularly played for events held at platforms, including two located by the San Gabriel River.[52]

The first hall built by a Czech fraternal organization in Texas was a small, rectangular building with a gable roof constructed in Praha in 1894. It was built by a local lodge of the national Czech fraternal benefit society known as the Český-Slovanská podporující společnost (CSPS, or Czecho-Slovak Benevolent Society) that had been organized in Texas in 1884. The national organization was replaced in 1897 by a new independent state fraternal called the SPJST (Slovanská podpurující jednota státu Texas, or Slavonic Benevolent Order of the State of Texas). With the organizational change, the Praha hall became the property of the SPJST. Though it had been designed as a meeting place, it also served as a dance hall.[53] The Cottonwood SPJST lodge, close to the Czech town of West, located between Austin and Dallas, built a similarly modest-sized hall in 1902, using the same basic design as the one in Praha. Through the years, the Cottonwood lodge added a stage, a kitchen, additional floor space, and air conditioning. Its members still use the comfortable facility today.[54]

Just east of Temple, the Buckholts SPJST Lodge built a hall in 1911, but it was destroyed by a storm in 1915. The members replaced it with a second, more elaborate hall, but in 1936 it was burned by bank robbers who set the fire as a distraction. The members were not to be deterred. They constructed a new hall that same year, and it is still in use today. Like some of the early German halls, it was built on an octagonal plan, sometimes called a round hall, a design conducive to moving a crowd of dancers in a circular pattern around the room.[55] Another Czech octagonal hall was built in Fayetteville in 1912 by the Katolická jednota Texaská, known as the KJT, or Catholic Union of Texas. The KJT, a Catholic men's fraternal society, was organized in 1889, and the KJZT, a Catholic women's counterpart, began in 1894. Before the Fayetteville hall was torn down in the late 1970s, the architect Roger Kolar wrote that the "steeply pointed roof of the building gives a sort of circus tent effect and imposes a festive feeling on the structure."[56]

Two recent large-scale halls, both in the town of Ennis, a Czech settlement located in the fertile farmlands just south of Dallas, have long histories. The KJT hall, first built in 1924, had a dance floor surrounded on three sides by a balcony. It was replaced in 1982 by a structure that can hold about one thousand people.[57] An even larger hall, built by Ennis Sokol, houses not only a dance floor, large kitchen, museum, and library, it is also a well-equipped gymnasium. Sokol, from the Czech word meaning "falcon," was founded in 1862 in Prague, when it was still under Austrian rule. An athletic organization, Sokol was dedicated to the moral and physical renewal of the Czech people. In 1908, Texas Sokol formed in Ennis, and the large structure, built in 1991, is the sixth to stand on the property since 1911. Three burned, and two were replaced because they were too small.[58] The KJT and Sokol halls plus the local Knights of Columbus hall are part of the annual National Polka Festival, one of the largest in the nation, held in Ennis each year since 1967.[59]

These groups created an impressive circuit of versatile lodges throughout Czech Texas where they could hold meetings, serve massive feasts, provide an array of youth services and lessons, teach Czech culture and customs, coach and practice gymnastics, set up small libraries, and, of course, host bands and crowds of dancers. In an article on Czech music in Texas, Clinton Machann estimates that by the 1980s, 250 Czech fraternal dance halls had been built in the state, 150 by the SPJST and 100 by the KJT.[60] These numbers do not include halls built by private owners or by other community groups.

In 1900, there were over nine thousand European-born Czechs in Texas plus their Texas-born descendants.[61] The establishment of their own churches, schools, newspapers, music ensembles, and fraternal organizations with community halls allowed these foreign immigrants to create a substitute community for the homes and villages they had left behind. Here they could not only speak their familiar language, eat together, sing their songs, dance, and worship but also learn how to grow better crops, how to navigate a new political and social system, and how to become Americans.

World War I and Czech Unity

Like the Civil War, World War I marked an important turning point in Texas Czech history. New immigration to the state again came to a halt, as it did during the first conflict. But in other ways the experience was very different. In contrast to the reluctance of Texas Czech immigrants to participate in the Civil War, over two thousand served in World War I.[62] The Czechs had two reasons to become involved in this conflict. First, as Americans, their response was unambiguously patriotic. Second, as Czech Americans, they were committed to the idea of liberating the Czech lands from Austrian oppression. These passionately held dual reasons to support the war united the Texas Czechs—the Catholics, Protestants, and freethinkers, the fraternal and Sokol club members, the newspaper editors, the seasoned settlers, and the recent arrivals. They put aside their differences and worked together as a united ethnic community in concert with Czech Americans in other states.[63]

In 1914, a few months after the war began, the Nebraska newspaper *Osvěta americká* (American Culture) reported on the Czech soldiers, known as the Czech Legionnaires, who were deserting the Austrian army and joining the Allied forces. The newspaper issued a call for all Czech Americans to help their former countrymen. This triggered the formation of České národní sdružení, also known as the Czech National Alliance, or CNS, with headquarters in Chicago. The organization's purpose was to support the Czech provisional government, a group in exile led by Tomáš Garrigue Masaryk, as it sought Allied support for an independent Czech nation.[64]

Texas began to organize chapters of CNS during the 1916 SPJST state convention held in Galveston. Soon, local organizations formed in communities, starting with Ennis in the northern reaches of Czech settlement, near Dallas, and extending about 350 miles down to Robstown at the southern edge of the Czech belt, close to Corpus Christi. Two Louisiana locals also joined the Texas group. The locals threw their efforts into raising money and did so in a variety of ways. They passed the hat at socials and lectures, sold tickets for special events, and held bazaars that auctioned items contributed by members. Donated cotton bales were especially successful money makers. The largest event was a 1918 statewide bazaar held in Taylor, 40 miles northeast of Austin, that raised about $54,000. Overall, almost $100,000 was raised and sent to the national office from Texas.[65]

After the war ended, Tomáš Masaryk was elected first president of the newly formed Czechoslovakia. Czechs all over America celebrated. In Fayetteville, a 1919 tribute to returning soldiers was written up in the *La Grange Journal*: "The largest crowd in years gathered to express their welcome. Returned soldiers, wearing uniforms, marched in the big parade." The Baca band led the marchers around the town of Fayetteville and then on to the SPJST hall. Commenting on the music, the *Journal* reporter wrote, "It seemed to me that Baca's Band, ever ready and willing, had never played better."[66]

Music Publishers, Records, and Radios

The world of music was both challenged and stimulated by new social and technological developments that were introduced at the turn of the century. Phonographs, invented in 1877, began to penetrate the market in the early 1900s. Motion pictures became available in the 1910s, as did automobiles and, eventually, better roads. Radio broadcasting was widely accessible starting in the 1920s, when it began to reach the rural population.[67] Marshall B. Davidson, a writer on American culture, called the rise of these industries the "industrial revolution of recreation."[68] These changes opened many opportunities for ethnic artists and business entrepreneurs.

Music Publishers

A handmade Baca Orchestra band book, part of the collection of the Czech Heritage Museum and Genealogy Center in Temple, contains early twentieth-century sheet music published by companies founded by Czech Americans.[69] These companies were the first to recognize the potential market within their own communities for published music. In the nineteenth century, most American music publishers were "non-ethnic in nature," as the historian Victor Greene describes them.[70] They were not familiar with and did not publish the kind of music the immigrants wanted—familiar tunes in their own language. Musicians who performed for these communities had to either import music, write out their own scores, or play by memory. In the early twentieth century, the void in sheet music for the ethnic-music market came to be filled by entrepreneurs who were immigrants themselves.[71]

Four Czech Americans played a leading role in the development of the ethnic music industry as they began to publish orchestral arrangements, music books, and sheet music for this specialized market. The four were Joseph Jiran of Chicago; Louis Vitak, also of Chicago, who was joined by his nephew Joseph P. Elsnic in 1924; and Anthony Maresh of Cleveland. They were all musicians and familiar with the commercial music industry that developed in Europe in the latter 1800s, especially with one of its major centers located in Prague, the capital of Bohemia. They all had retail music stores that became the headquarters of their successful importing, composing, arranging, and publishing businesses. Though other ethnic music publishers also began to thrive, the firms of these businessmen, especially Vitak-Elsnic, grew to dominate the ethnic field by the 1930s.[72]

Records

The recording industry was the first of the nonethnic businesses to understand the buying potential of the ethnic communities. By the beginning of the 1900s, some 150,000 phonographs had been sold in the United States as well as about three million records. Soon the early 1920s record sales had accelerated to almost one hundred million annually.[73] A healthy part of these sales was made to the immigrant community, catered to early on by the record companies.[74]

The three major American companies in the early days, Victor, Columbia, and Edison, noticed the popularity of European classical vocalists, such as the Italian opera singer Enrico Caruso, the first recording superstar. Columbia, in 1906, issued an elaborate catalogue aimed at the foreign-language audience, listing records in twelve languages.[75] Most of these were reissues of European origin, but a few were recordings of US residents made in New York City studios.[76] In 1909, Columbia distributed a policy instructing its sales force to focus on their foreign customers because "records in their own language have an irresistible attraction and they will buy them readily."[77]

The outbreak of World War I forced the record companies to find recording talent in established ethnic communities within the United States rather than rely on musicians in Europe. Columbia opened a studio in Chicago in 1915 and began recording groups such as František Przybylski and his Polish village orchestra and Anton Brousek and his Bohemian brass band. Brousek, for example, recorded almost two hundred songs between 1915 and 1926.[78] By the early 1920s, the record companies had also recognized that there was a market for the vernacular music of both blacks and rural whites, and they developed a classification system for catalog and distribution purposes based on race and ethnicity. The sociologist William G. Roy described the system as "organized around a dominant mainstream of classical and popular music plus a margin of race records, hillbilly music and foreign language music."[79] Finding music that would appeal to the groups on the margins led to field recordings, when engineers set up equipment in hotel rooms, churches, or other venues throughout the country and recorded regional artists, including many they found in Texas.[80]

Starting in 1929, national labels recorded several Texas Czech bands. Almost all the recordings were made in San Antonio and Dallas. The Baca Orchestra of Fayetteville recorded for Okeh/Columbia/Vocalion, initially at a 1929 session in San Antonio and then again in 1930 and 1935. The 78s from these sessions were released under the name Bačova Česka Kapela (Baca Czech Band).[81] Another Texas Czech band, Adolf and the Bohemians of Schulenburg, recorded for Columbia/Vocalion in San Antonio sessions in 1936 and 1937.[82] The Patek Orchestra of Shiner, under the name Joe Patek's Bohemian Orchestra, recorded for Decca at a Dallas session in 1937.[83] One more band, led by a polka/western swing crossover musician, Adolph Hofner of San Antonio, was recorded in 1936, 1938, 1940, and 1942 by Bluebird and Okeh/Columbia in San Antonio and Dallas, with the last session taking place in Hollywood, California.[84]

Radios

The recording industry was badly hurt by the economic depression of the 1930s. In 1932, for example, only 6 million records were sold, whereas 104 million had been sold just five years earlier, in 1927.[85] The growing broadcast industry, on the other hand, flourished. Radios, a more affordable means of home entertainment, sold steadily. In 1931, 40 percent of American homes had radios, and by 1938, that number had increased to over 80 percent.[86]

When radio broadcasts first began, in the early 1920s, people who lived in rural America composed about half of the country's total population. For the first time, technology was able to bring isolated farms and far-flung settlements into daily contact with the rest of the nation. The radio provided news, weather forecasts, crop prices, sports, religion, comedy, and music.[87] Bill C. Malone, in his massive study on country music, illustrated some of the excitement felt by people who first listened to a 1923 rural-oriented radio program broadcast by Fort Worth station WBAP. Like most early stations, according to Malone, WBAP played mainstream popular, jazz, sacred, and semiclassical music that would appeal to the urban middle class. But after just a few months of being on the air, the station scheduled a live program of square dance music performed by an old-time fiddler directing a string band. The first hour-and-a-half show aired the night of January 4, 1923. Audience response—by telephone and telegraph—was astonishing. Within a short time, the show inspired a multitude of what came to be known as hillbilly barn dance programs, the most famous being Nashville's Grand Ole Opry, which started in 1925.[88]

Listener response was similarly supportive when Texas Czech bands began to be heard on the air. In 1926–27, the Baca Orchestra of Fayetteville played on KPRC, the Houston station. According to Baca family history, the band received "hundreds of telegrams—some in Czech, from all parts of the state."[89] The Texas A&M sociologist Robert Skrabanek wrote about how happily his parents listened to Czech polka programs after they bought a radio in 1929. Since they were the first family in the Snook community to own a radio, friends and neighbors often came over to listen. Some of the early stations they listened to broadcast from Houston, Dallas, and Mexico and then later from Temple, Texas, and Nebraska. Czech music programs were his parents' favorites.[90] An example of a band that generated a large following within the Texas Czech community due to their radio appearances is Adolf and the Gold Chain Bohemians of Schulenburg. How they managed to get their own program is an unusual story.

In 1935, the musician Julius Pavlas of Engle entered his Czech polka band in a San Antonio band contest and won first place. They were invited to return the next week and audition for Universal Mills, the Fort Worth company that made Gold Chain flour. The company was looking for a band to represent its product. The band members were unwilling to return for the audition, so Pavlas pulled together a new group of musicians, including several who played with Lee Prause, also of Schulenburg. For an announcer, Pavlas recruited Johnny Luecke of the local low-wattage station CTSB, which stood for Come to Schulenburg. The newly formed Pavlas band not only passed the audition, it was rewarded with a contract and a new name. The leader, Julius Pavlas, became Adolf, and the band became the Gold Chain Bohemians.[91]

The band broadcast its first radio program on November 3, 1935, from Schulenburg's Cozy Theater located in the Von Minden Hotel. The live show ran from 8 to 8:15 every weekday morning and from 3 to 3:45 every Sunday afternoon. It was carried over Texas Quality Network, formed by four of the state's largest stations, including WOAI, San Antonio; KPRC, Houston; and WFAA and WBAP of Dallas/Fort Worth. The band also maintained a full schedule playing dance jobs. Henry Kubala, the band's clarinetist, remembered that in 1936 they played seventeen nights in a row but always returned to Schulenburg for the morning radio program. "We never missed," he said.[92] The band played its last radio show on May 31, 1937, and broke up shortly thereafter.[93]

During the 1920s and 1930s, radio brought the music of the nation's dominant culture into the homes of rural and ethnic Americans. But the reverse is also true. The proliferation of race, hillbilly, and foreign language records and radio programs introduced the music of these groups to one another and also to the dominant culture. For European ethnic communities, one particularly satisfying outcome of this cultural exchange was the phenomenal national rise of two recordings in the late 1930s. Both of these records were made by the Andrews Sisters, the close-harmony trio from Minnesota whose

Adolph and the Gold Chain Bohemians, circa 1935. *Photo courtesy of Gary E. McKee.*

father was Greek and mother's family was Norwegian. The first recording was their 1937 hit with the Yiddish song "Bei Mir Bist Du Shön," composed by an immigrant from Ukraine. The second recording was their big hit in 1939 with "Beer Barrel Polka," a reworking of the Czech song "Škoda lásky" (Wasted Love), which had been composed by Jaromír Vejvoda in Prague in 1927. The new upbeat English words were written by two other American immigrants, Russian-born Lew Brown and Greek-born Wladimir Timm.[94] These two Andrews Sisters' hits were jaunty, swinging, danceable American songs, combining elements of multiple music cultures.

Changing Times, Changing Music

In 1935, a few years before the outbreak of World War II, most Texas Czechs farmed for a living, and cotton was the major cash crop, as it had been for the early settlers. The mother tongue was still strong—the 1940 census counted 62,680 Texans whose first language was Czech, and of these, 84 percent lived in rural areas. Prohibition had been repealed in 1933, beer was flowing again, and the dance floors were crowded.[95] But several dramatic forces in the 1930s and 1940s ended the isolation of the tightly knit Texas Czech community. The Great Depression, the commercialization of agriculture and consequent loss of family farms, and World War II uprooted and rearranged populations. The occupation of Czechoslovakia by first the Nazis and then the Soviets shut off relations with the homeland. Texas Czechs were challenged and exposed to experiences that broadened their views and diminished their cultural and regional differences.[96]

The stories of six prominent Texas Czech musical figures—Joe Patek, Adolph Hofner, Bill Mraz, Lee Roy Matocha, Alfred Vrazel, and Alice Sulak—illustrate how

Joe Patek Orchestra, 1940s. *Left to right:* Jerome Patek, Jim Patek, Charlie Patek, John Patek, Ladie Patek, Joe Patek. *Photo courtesy of Rudy Patek.*

the changing times affected the character of the community's music. Joe Patek played brass-band polka influenced by early jazz; Adolph Hofner played string-based western swing; Bill Mraz, Lee Roy Matocha, Alfred Vrazel, and Alice Sulak all played a mix of polka and country and swing that combined accordion with a varied instrumental lineup of brass, reeds, piano, strings, drums, and country-style electric bass and guitar. These and many more musicians developed their styles and played their hearts out during an energetic and creative era for Czech polka in Texas—from about the mid-1930s through the 1950s and even beyond. This golden age coincided with the general popularity of polka in the United States that was ultimately eclipsed by the arrival of rock and roll.

Joe Patek

Chris Strachwitz, the founder of Arhoolie Records, a California company, started coming to Texas in the early 1960s to record bluesman Mance Lipscomb. For many years after, Strachwitz continued to produce records documenting the state's vernacular music. He described his introduction to Texas Czech music this way: "It was John Lomax Jr., Alan's brother in Houston, who told me once, 'Chris, on your way back to California, drive through the area around Shiner and Gonzales and you will hear radio stations there that play all this Czech music.' So I took his advice, and sure enough I heard this wonderful swinging polka music on the radio. It was not like it sounded in Europe; this had much more of the Southwest swing to it. A year later I heard the Joe Patek Orchestra in person at a dancehall in north Houston. There were many of these bands in the area, but Patek's was the best of them."[97]

Seventy years earlier, in 1889, twenty-year-old John Patek, a baritone horn player and bandleader, immigrated to Texas with his parents. They came from the small village of Mahouš, located in southern Bohemia near the town of České Budějovice, which is famous for beer. In Texas, the Patek family lived on a rented farm near Moulton. John met Veronika Mauric, and the two were married in 1893. They settled near Shiner, farmed, and raised six sons. John played in community bands, where he was joined by the boys, usually when they reached the age of twelve. In 1920, he formed an eight-piece brass band that included three of his older sons and called it the Patek Band of Shiner, Texas. His two youngest, Jerome and Joe, joined the band within a few years. Jim became bandleader in the 1930s; Joe took over in the early 1940s and changed the name to the Joe Patek Orchestra. John continued to play with his son's band until retiring in 1950.[98]

Joe, born in 1907 and the youngest, grew up speaking Czech and also learned to read and write Czech in his Catholic elementary school.[99] He and Emilie Novosad married in 1934, raised a large family, and operated a grocery and meat market in Shiner for about fifty years, starting in 1937.[100] When Joe took over leadership of the Patek band, the members were his father, four of his brothers, and three musicians from the community. The instrumentation consisted of tuba, baritone horn, piano, drums, trombone, cornet, trumpet, and two saxophone/clarinet players.[101] Though his father's band often played concert music, by the time Joe took over, audiences preferred what the folklorist James P. Leary describes as "dancing, singing, and a little beer drinking to sitting still."[102]

The Joe Patek Orchestra of the 1940s and early 1950s is recognizable for its "barrelhouse piano, hot drums, and, above all, its jazzy saxophones," wrote the German record producer Thomas Meinecke in his liner notes for the 1994 CD *Texas Bohemia*.[103] Joe himself, the band's saxophone player, said: "I like jazz."[104] Emil Coldway, the piano player, retired in 1952, and the electric guitarist Robert Werner Jr. replaced him, solving the problem of the broken-down pianos they encountered in Texas dance halls.[105] Through the years, the band maintained what has often been described as polka with a "harder sound, with more swing."[106] That "hard sound" came from Charlie's always lively tuba and the entire band's uninhibited enthusiasm. The music featured Joe's vocals, with his brother Jerome singing a high part, sometimes harmony and sometimes melody. The timbre of their voices and their animated but sincere delivery rival that of many high lonesome harmonies of early country music. Jerome died in 1972, but other singers in the band continued to emulate his vocal style.

Mark Rubin, who played tuba with the Texas Czech band Mark Halata and Texavia, highlighted Patek's important contribution to Texas polka when he wrote, "The Pateks established the material that is today the canon of Czech tunes in Texas."[107] The band's music became well known through the songs it performed and through the ones it introduced into the shared repertory, such as the beloved "Shiner Song" (Song 31), "Hora Shinerská" (Hill of Shiner; Song 23), and "Sirotek" (Orphan Waltz; Song 51). These songs and others spread quickly due to the band's busy schedule, its many recordings for several independent Texas record companies, and its weekly radio show on station KCTI in Gonzales called *The Patek Hour*. The show was broadcast live, starting in the late 1940s, and later continued with recordings until closing down in 1985. The band played its last dance in 1982, at an emotional Fireman's New Year's Eve celebration, an annual Shiner event the Pateks had played since 1939.[108]

Adolph Hofner

Most early Texas Czech bands were town or family bands that played brass and reed instruments and broke down into smaller ensembles to play for dances. But there were also dulcimer bands with fiddle, string bass, and horn or clarinet, very much like the string bands of eastern Moravia. As we have seen, Joe Patek created his own unique take on brass band and polka music. Adolph Hofner introduced a new sound in his string band that smoothly combined western swing, itself a hybrid Texas dance-hall style, with Czech polkas and waltzes.

Adolph Hofner and the Pearl Wranglers, circa 1950s. *Left to right:* Eddie Bowers, J. R. Chatwell, Charlie Harris, Adolph Hofner, Emil Hofner, Leon Merritt, Charlie Poss. *Photo courtesy of the Chris Strachwitz Collection at the Arhoolie Foundation.*

Adolph Hofner, whose mother was Czech and father was Czech and German, was born in 1916 in the small town of Moulton in Lavaca County. He and his younger brother, Emil, later nicknamed Bash for bashful, learned Czech as their first language. The boys were exposed to music by hearing their mother play concertina and sing Czech songs, by listening to the radio, and by going to dances where they heard polka music. Attracted to Hawaiian music, which was nationally popular at the time, the boys began lessons on string instruments after the family moved to San Antonio in 1928. Adolph learned standard guitar, and Emil chose lap steel guitar. In 1933, they started their own band, called the Hawaiian Serenaders, with the musician Simon Garcia. Another musician, Floyd Tillman, who later became a honky-tonk star, also played and sang with the Hofners during this time.[109]

In the mid-1930s, a new music style developed in Texas dance halls and honky-tonks, and the Hofner brothers became early practitioners, giving the new style their own interpretation. The music was later called western swing, but at the time it was labeled "hot dance" by the record companies. It was a hybrid style that reflected the times and its birthplace—a cross between hillbilly string bands, jazz orchestras, and the music of the diverse cultures found in Central Texas.[110] Adolph told an interviewer that he liked western swing because "it had the steel there, it had the rhythm there, the drive and it had the instrumentation."[111]

Starting in 1935, the Hofner brothers toured and recorded with Jimmie Revard and His Oklahoma Playboys. By the late 1930s, Adolph began to record for Bluebird Records under his own name and organized a band with himself as leader, singer, and guitarist. Emil played steel guitar and sang vocal harmony. Besides Adolph on guitar and Emil on steel guitar, the band most often included fiddle, string bass, drums, piano, and occasionally an accordion. Notable members were the fiddler J. R. Chatwell and the pianist/accordionist Walter Kleypas. As Adolph Hofner and His Texans, and then as His San Antonians, they performed and recorded a mix of western swing, honky-tonk, Mexican songs, pop tunes, blues, and Czech polkas and waltzes. Emil was drafted in 1942, but Adolph never was. Adolph took the band to Los Angeles, where they recorded and performed under the name Dolph Hofner and the San Antonians to avoid comparison to Adolf Hitler. They remained in California and played for GIs who were coming home from the war, but in about 1947 they returned to Texas.[112]

In 1950, Pearl Beer became the longtime sponsors for the radio show of Adolph Hofner and the Pearl Wranglers, the name the band eventually retired with. They broadcast on station KTSA in San Antonio for some thirty-odd years and recorded singles for Luling independent label Sarg Records, thus producing a discography that amounts to "a glossary of Texas music: waltzes and hoedowns, regional standards and rockabilly."[113] On Saturday nights, in the crowded dance hall called the Farmer's Daughter in San Antonio, they "served their polka-country-swing mix"[114] to the dancers. The band retired in 1993 after Adolph suffered a stroke. The British music writer Tony Russell summed up Hofner's career in an obituary published in 2000, the year of the musician's death: "In a career extending over more than half a century, he produced a unique, all-American alloy of country crooning, polkas, and western swing."[115] And the historian Victor Greene, in his book *A Passion for Polka,* says "the musician who best synthesized European and contemporary American music genres was Adolph Hofner of San Antonio."[116]

Bill Mraz

After World War II, many Texas bands began to regroup as brass, string, and accordion combinations that played polka, swing, or country music and sometimes all three. The chromatic piano accordion, with its expanded capabilities, had become popular in polka bands by this time, even though the diatonic button accordion continued to be played. The piano accordionist Bill Mraz led a brass, reed, and accordion group that played ballroom-style Czech polka and big band swing. He also owned, managed, cooked, hosted, and played at the legendary Bill Mraz Ballroom, a large dance hall he built in Houston.[117]

Born in 1907, Bill Mraz grew up on a farm in the Moulton-Shiner area of Lavaca County. Bill and his younger brother, Mills, were taught accordion by their father, Louis, and first played for nearby private parties and house dances. Bill moved to Houston, where he became a daytime bricklayer and home builder under his uncle's tutelage. Come nighttime, he was a musician, again playing house dances with his brother Mills, who had also moved to Houston. Bill married Anna Motl of Moulton in 1928. In 1936, with Mills as one of the six members, Bill organized the band Bill Mraz and the Novelty Boys. The band played regularly for nine years at Miller's Dance Hall, a few blocks from the Heights neighborhood near downtown Houston. Mills left the band when he was drafted, but he never returned; he was killed in Italy in 1944. In 1945, Bill bought Miller's Dance Hall and, after two years, built a new one across the street because he needed a bigger place. The Bill Mraz Ballroom opened on August 15, 1948. It had a 9,500-square-foot dance floor; 4,527 tickets were sold for the celebration, and about that many people were outside, according to the writer Theresa Cernoch Parker, "stomping their feet to the upbeat music provided by Bill Mraz and his Orchestra."[118]

Mraz knew how to keep things exciting in his new place. He brought in huge crowds by booking big-name polka bands like the Six Fat Dutchmen of Minnesota, Frankie Yankovic of Cleveland, Romy Gosz of Wisconsin, and Ernie Kucera from Nebraska. Bringing in these bands exposed many Texas musicians to a wide variety of polka styles. Mraz also regularly booked popular Texas bands like Joe Patek, Lee Roy Matocha, Alfred Vrazel, Jimmy

Lee Roy Matocha Orchestra, late 1960s–early 1970s. *Left to right:* Kenneth Renger, Harold Ilse, Ivan Fajkus, Charlie Rainosek. *Seated:* Lee Roy Matocha. *Photo courtesy of Fayette Heritage Museum and Archives, La Grange, Texas.*

Brosch, and Harry Czarnek. When Mraz died in 1975, the mayor of Houston officially proclaimed it Bill Mraz Day. Bill's wife and children kept the hall going but closed it in 1986, a run just shy of forty years. It reopened briefly in 2002 but burned in 2004.[119] For the years it was open, the Bill Mraz Ballroom provided an important service. For many people who had left the farm after the war and moved to the city to find work, the hall was a place to engage in familiar and comforting pleasures: dancing the polka, hearing and speaking Czech, drinking beer, visiting, and eating barbecue. It became an anchor, a place to experience home and community in the big city.

Lee Roy Matocha

Lee Roy Matocha of Fayetteville, born in nearby Plum in 1932, was "the leading propagandist of Texas polka music," according to Tony Russell, a writer and historian of American popular music.[120] Russell was referring to Matocha's hearty promotion of polka music on the multiple radio shows he hosted for over forty years. Starting in 1960, Matocha's Czech music programs eventually entertained thousands of fans, as he could be heard in "nearly 50 counties" at the peak of the shows' distribution. Matocha's first program, hosted weekly in Czech on station KVLG in La Grange, Texas, soon became a daily show, encouraging other stations to put him on the air. He developed an impressive radio presence of over twenty different hour-long programs broadcast on stations located within the Czech centers of La Grange, Brenham, Gonzales, El Campo, Kenedy–Karnes City, Cameron, and Columbus.[121] Even in the late 1990s, he could still be heard announcing in both Czech and English on thirteen different shows.[122]

Matocha recorded in a twelve-by-twelve-foot room he built onto his house that was filled with records and included his extensive collection of 78s, reel-to-reel tapes, and band photographs.[123] He was widely admired for his homey radio style and generous support of new Texas polka bands, those just learning how to perform. "Everyone got the same royal treatment and promotion from Lee Roy," wrote the musician and online polka show host Dennis Svatek of Taylor.[124] Matocha recorded his last show in 2003, just before he died.[125]

Lee Roy and Doris Malota married in 1955, and together they raised five children. He was a full-time musician who supported his family with advertising commissions from his radio shows and as a longtime bandleader, piano accordionist, and singer. His father taught him to play, and Matocha's first job, in 1947 when he was fifteen, was replacing his father in his uncle Frank Zbranek's Accordion Band. In 1952 he joined the Lee Ilse Orchestra, managed it for four years, and in 1964 formed his own group, the six-piece Lee Roy Matocha Orchestra. The band played all over Texas and traveled to shows in a bus named the Golden Eagle. Matocha's daughter Janice, who sang harmony and played keyboards in the band, said her father acquired the nickname the Fayetteville Flash because if "you saw the Golden Eagle coming down the road in a flash, you'd better get out of the way." The band recorded profusely, mostly in Houston for the independent Guide label.[126]

Alfred Vrazel

Vrazels' Polka Band, led by Alfred Vrazel and managed by his older brother, Anton, combined Czech polka and Texas country. Their father Florian's family was from Zděchov, Moravia, a village in the Beskid foothills close to the Slovakian border. In 1903, when Florian was still a baby, the family immigrated to Texas, sharecropped, and eventually bought their own farm near Buckholts. Florian, who became known as Lawrence, stayed on this farm. He married Albina Sustek, and their children grew up on the farm, speaking only Czech until they learned English in school. When Alfred, one of Lawrence and Albina's children, was ten years old, he talked his father into buying him a two-row Hohner button accordion from Sears Roebuck. Soon Alfred's brother, Anton, began learning to play piano accordion, and Alfred picked up saxophone and guitar. Their music teacher was the radio, and the shows they listened to were the Grand Ole Opry, the *Czech Melody Hour* from Temple, Joe Gavronovic from Rosenberg, and Adolph Hofner from San Antonio.[127]

In 1953, Alfred and three of his cousins started a band called Vrazels' Playboys, playing for tips at nearby stores, hamburger joints, and halls. When Anton joined them on piano accordion, the name became Vrazels' Polka Band. Two years later, they had a Sunday afternoon radio program, hosted by Alfred, on the newly established radio station KMIL in Cameron. In 1959, they recorded the first of their thirteen LPs. The band's membership changed throughout the years, but Alfred and Anton were regulars. For fifty-five years they farmed during the week, played most weekends, and released a slew of recordings, including albums, tapes, videos, and CDs, most under their own label called VPB.[128] Though the band retired in 2008, Alfred still has the weekly radio program. In 2014, he became the first Texan inducted into the International Polka Hall of Fame in Cleveland, honored as a Polka Pioneer.[129]

Carl Finch, leader of the rock-inspired polka band Brave Combo, had this to say about the Vrazels' music: "They really brought about some modern innovation with the instrumentation, their arrangements and their drummer."[130] Their instrumental lineup consisted of piano accordion, drums, trumpet, saxophone/diatonic accordion, electric guitar/steel guitar, and electric bass, a mix of polka and country. Alfred's warm and clear vocals, his and Anton's Czech fluency, and the band's easy rapport with its audience helped them become a popular group on the Texas polka circuit.

Vrazels' Polka Band, 1996. *Left to right:* Alfred Vrazel, George Strmiska, Albert Heselmeyer, Thomas Strmiska, Anton Vrazel. *Photo courtesy of Alfred Vrazel.*

Alice Sulak

The dancing audience at a Texas dance hall is usually equally male and female, but Texas Czech polka musicians have largely, but not exclusively, been men. The hardworking, talented women of Texas polka have had an outstanding trailblazer in Alice Sulak. She exemplifies the contributions of these special women because she does it all—she is a longtime instrumentalist, vocalist, and owner-manager of a revered country dance hall. Alice, born in 1931 to Tom and Terezie Rose Sefcik, grew up in the Czech farming community of Seaton, just east of Temple, which had been settled by Czech families in the early 1880s. Her father, Tom, a farmer and musician, built the two-story Sefcik Hall in 1923 and ran it for almost fifty years. Still open for business, the tavern is downstairs, where there also used to be a general store, and the dance floor, which holds about three hundred people, is above.

In the early 1940s, when she was ten, Alice began playing in her older sister's band, called Adela and the Music Masters. Adela played accordion while Alice played drums and saxophone; Julius Dubcak on trumpet and Jerry Adamek on guitar rounded out the band. Adela left the music business about the late 1950s.[131] In the early 1960s, Alice formed a trio with the farmer and accordionist

Bob Haisler and his son, Jerry, who played accordion and saxophone and later learned guitar, too. They served as an unofficial house band for Sefcik Hall. In 1966, the three joined a dance band called the Melody 5 led by Otis Beck. It became the crowd-pleasing Jerry Haisler and the Melody 5 in 1971. The band continues to play polka, country, variety songs, and old rock and roll. All along, Alice played saxophone and sang in Czech, her first language.[132]

Since 1970, Alice has been working not only as owner-manager of Sefcik Hall but also as bartender and, despite her modest size, occasional bouncer. Besides her musical skills, she is known as an "even better business woman, before business women became popular," according to Jerry Haisler.[133] Like her father, he said, she booked acts that would bring in the crowds. That included polka bands, of course, but also the hard-rocking, genre-bending polka band Brave Combo; Austin bands with a hippie vibe like Greezy Wheels; and country/Tejano star Johnny Rodriguez.

Alice still lives in the house next door to the hall where she grew up and raised her three sons as a single mom. Now a late octogenarian, she stopped playing with the band in 2014. She no longer climbs what Gary McKee describes as the "dozen well-trodden steps at a 45-degree incline" up to the dance hall, and instead perches comfortably in the bar downstairs. There she visits with customers on the weekends while her son Kenny and his wife, Irene, help run the business.[134] But on November 17, 2019, she did go upstairs, riding the hall's outside equipment lift, to accept a Lifetime Achievement Award. She was recognized by Texas Dance Hall Preservation as, among other things, possibly the longest-running female dance hall owner and manager in Texas history.[135]

Assimilation, Preservation, and the Future

Joe Patek, Adolph Hofner, Bill Mraz, Lee Roy Matocha, Alfred Vrazel, and Alice Sulak all grew up speaking Czech. It was the way they regularly communicated with their families and often with their friends and relatives, too. Many of them learned English in elementary school. This intergenerational transmission of the Czech language in Texas ended after World War II. That it lasted almost one hundred years within "a linguistically alien environment," as the linguist Eva Eckert describes it, is a remarkable feat of language maintenance.[136] After the war, according to the book *Krásná Amerika,* "Not only was the Czech language heard less frequently on the streets of Czech towns and in Czech homes, but it was phased out as the official language of Czech fraternal organizations, the language of the Brethren Church, and the language of some Texas Czech journals."[137] With this key part of their ethnic culture in decline, Texas Czechs turned to other ways to affirm and preserve their identity.

Church Picnics and Festivals

Annual rural church picnics, some of them long-standing, have a homecoming quality as former residents return to renew friendships and participate in cultural rituals such as polka dancing and eating traditional foods. They are also important fund-raisers, especially for Catholic parishes. In 2019, of about one hundred picnics in the state hosted by historically Czech Catholic parishes and a few Protestant churches,[138] one of the best known is the Pražská Pout' (Praha Fair), always held on August 15. The tiny Central Texas community of Praha, often referred to as Matička Praha (Mother Prague), is home to St. Mary's, one of the state's most beautiful painted churches. Praha's yearly mid-August picnic typically sells around five thousand dinner plates of fried chicken, beef stew, sauerkraut, green beans, pickles, and kolaches.[139] The day begins with a Mass followed by several polka bands playing from 11 A.M. until late at night. The 2019 Pražská Pout' was advertised as its 164th.

Twenty or more festivals take place in the state each year to celebrate good things, ranging from polka, sausage, kolaches (pastries), klobase (sausage rolls), and May Day to Czech-German friendship at Flatonia's Czechspiel. The National Polka Festival, held annually on Memorial Day weekend in Ennis since 1967, hosts a large and lively turnout. In 2019, it featured a parade, thirteen bands, three dance halls, and about 50,000 attendees.[140] Westfest, which started in 1976 in West to fund community projects, is held on Labor Day weekend. By 2019, it had raised a cumulative amount of $986,000. It typically attracts 20,000 attendees and features, among other things, a polka Mass, parade, and continual polka music.[141] In Caldwell, vendors sell over 100,000 Czech kolaches while polka bands play, quilt makers demonstrate their skills, and kolache bakers gather to compete for the title of state champion. The Caldwell Kolache Festival has been held the second weekend in September since 1984 and regularly attracts up to 15,000 attendees.[142]

At the festivals, church picnics, and other similar celebrations, Czech words and short phrases can be seen on T-shirts and other merchandise associated with these gatherings. The language can also be heard in the amplified Czech song lyrics of the polka bands.[143] These events provide opportunities for choral groups and dance troupes to perform folk songs and dances as well as provide a showcase for traditional arts and crafts. And, importantly, they attract attendees of all ages, including young people.

Preservation

That the Czechs would approach the task of preserving their culture by enthusiastically establishing numerous organizations is yet another confirmation of the old saying, "Where there are two Czechs, there are three clubs."[144] There are at least twenty heritage societies, educational associations, museums, and libraries with the mission of preserving the state's Czech culture. A few date from the early 1900s, but many began in the 1970s and 1980s. Besides the heritage groups, other organizations include cultural preservation as one of their several commitments, namely, the fraternal and mutual aid societies and the parishes and churches. There are also arts ensembles, such as choral clubs, orchestras, dance troupes, and dance clubs. These groups support and create newsletters, journals, and books as well as meetings, exhibits, workshops, symposiums, performances, and conventions.

One area of Texas Czech traditions that has benefited from this preservation urge is the documentation of its music and, more specifically, of the songs that have lyrics in the Czech language. Two types of collectors need to be recognized for their contribution to this effort: the collectors of recordings and the curators of song lyrics.

Much of recorded Texas Czech music is not easy to find. Most of the original recordings were issued on independent or private labels and sold by the bands at their performances. The number of recordings held by state and national libraries and institutions is relatively small; their holdings are incomplete; and many of the older, more fragile artifacts have not been digitized. Fortunately, a committed group of private collectors have worked for decades to accumulate and protect the delicate 78s, 45s, LPs, tapes, and CDs that preserve the sounds of Texas Czech music past and present. Several of these archivists have made recordings available to *Czech Songs in Texas.* They are acknowledged below both to highlight their contributions to preservation and, by extension, to recognize all the other such collectors in the state.

Probably the best known is George Koudelka of Flatonia, a music educator and longtime drummer who has played with numerous bands, including Adolph Hofner's. Koudelka has a prodigious memory and knowledge of Texas polka history. His stellar and enormous polka music collection, which includes recordings from both Europe and America but focuses on Texas, is well organized. Other knowledgeable collectors who provided recordings for this book include Dennis Svatek, Dave Bedrich, and Thomas Durnin, bandleader and musicians, respectively, with the Czech Melody Masters of Taylor and Austin; Gary Krupala, a member of the Taylor Czech Singers; and Mike Gest of the Houston area, a tuba and bass player with Mark Halata and Texavia as well as several other bands. Koudelka is a former radio polka show host, Durnin currently has a show on KOOP radio in Austin, and Svatek is the DJ for his long-running online polka program called *Czech Classics—Then and Now* at czechpolka.com.

The second group of collectors is responsible for three large Texas lyric collections that were published in book form between the 1960s and 1985, when most of the bands detailed in this chapter were still active. The first was produced by one of the fraternal societies, the second was a private endeavor undertaken by two sisters, and the third was a choral group project. Though none of the books have music notation, they are an invaluable historical source.

The first book, *Sbírka českých písní* (Collection of Czech Songs), was published in the mid-1960s by Katolická jednota Texaská (Catholic Union of Texas), commonly known as the KJT. It contains Czech lyrics to 175 songs. The material most likely grew out of the song sheets that facilitated group singing at the yearly KJT and KJZT conventions. The song lyrics seem to have come from various sources, and no editor is named. Information obtained at the KJT state office in La Grange in 2014 indicates that the lyric book was printed by the newspaper *Našinec* in Granger "probably in the 1960s."[145] The spiral-bound book is out of print but still held in a few libraries connected to Czech heritage centers.

The second collection, the 1976 *Spivejme pisničky* (Let's Sing Songs), was privately printed and published in Rosenberg by two sisters, Evelyn Bartosh Rainosek and Agnes Bartosh Broz. The two sisters are listed on the book's title page as Evelyn and Aneška, and they dedicate the book to their parents, Vladimir and Marie Bartoš. It contains Czech lyrics to 227 songs. The sisters grew up in the 1920s and 1930s on a farm near Needville, about twenty-five miles southwest of Houston's current outskirts. Evelyn's granddaughter Nica Pyron said that Evelyn loved to sing and first fell for her husband, Jerome Rainosek, when she heard the music from his distant accordion drifting over their farm. In the early 1970s, when Evelyn lived in Fairchilds and Agnes in West, the sisters started working on their lyric collection. One of their goals was to find as many verses to each song as possible, grouping them together as one long song.[146] The spiral-bound book had limited distribution and is preserved in a few Czech heritage center libraries.

The last book is called *Písničky České: Czech Folk Song Collection,* published by the Dallas Czech Singers in 1985. Often referred to as the "Blue Book" because of its sturdy blue cover, it contains lyrics to 315 Czech songs and was edited by Henrietta Schindler, who, at the time, was in charge of the choir's song sheets. To gather the songs for the proposed book, she "invited the public to contribute their favorites[,] and the response was great."[147] The acknowledgments page lists fifty-three people who contributed "the words of their favorite songs."[148] The Dallas Czech Singers began in the 1920s as a choral club associated with SPJST Lodge 84. After some dormancy, the club reactivated in the 1960s and again in the 1980s. It had eighty members when the songbook was published in 1985.[149] The hardbound book, currently held by several libraries, was reprinted in 2020 and is again available.

Into the Future

It is now about 170 years since the first Czech groups settled in Texas. Like many immigrants before and after them, they built an ethnic community that cushioned their adjustment to the new land as well as eased their gradual participation in the marvelous cultural diversity inherent in American life. Generations have passed, and Texas Czech culture has not stood still. This evolution can be seen in new media and publications, the addition of new songs to the repertory, the birth of new ensembles, and renewed exchange with the Czech Republic.

Most notable among the local and statewide media that currently promote Texas Czech music is the monthly *Texas Polka News,* founded in 1987 by the musician and writer Julius Tupa of Houston. After Tupa passed away in 2002, his wife, Marie, continued as publisher along with the writer and field correspondent John Rivard. In 2014, the Houstonite Theresa Cernoch Parker, whose roots are in Dubina, took over as owner-publisher with Gary E. McKee of Fayette County as editor-photojournalist. Currently, *Texas Polka News*, available in both print and digital versions, covers polka music primarily but also closely related styles like Cajun, zydeco, Tejano, conjunto, western swing, country, and other dance-hall favorites. In an essay called "About Texas Polka News," Parker says the paper is "a tribute to Texas Roots Music."[150] Interviews, features, and historical articles are mixed with stories on heritage festivals, church picnics and feasts, and music performances. For the last few years, the paper also seems to be a lively training ground for young and old music reporters and photographers as well as an exciting experiment in rural journalism. It is allied with the website polkabeat.com founded by Parker in 2010 in honor of Willie Cernoch, her polka-loving father. The site and its Facebook page publicize polka and other music and include photos of recent events. Parker retired in 2020, and the nonprofit Texas Czech Heritage and Cultural Center in La Grange assumed ownership of the paper and its digital platforms and continues with the same format and purpose.[151]

Texas musicians have not simply kept the old songs alive—they have been writing new songs with English lyrics and thus expanding the living songbook. Among these new songs are the popular "Polka Time in Texas" by Bob Suttie and "Church Picnic Polka" by Donnie Honz, who also has a Czech-language song in the works. Another is the English-language "Moon over Moravia"

(Song 38) by Daniel Klapuch and Mark Hermes, which has a chorus translated into Czech by Martha Viktorin. One other example is a song from the Dujka Brothers, their bicultural tribute called "Pivo and Kolaches, Cerveza and Tamales."

New and energetic young bands keep forming as well, such as the Ennis Czech Boys, the Moravians of Ennis, and the All Around Czechs of West. The Ennis Czech Boys began as a garage band and first performed in the 2005 National Polka Fest parade, when they only knew nine songs. Band member Corey Mikula says the experience inspired them to keep performing.[152]

The Moravians put together a polka band in 2009 so they could enter their Ennis High School talent show. They played the one song they quickly managed to learn, won the contest, and have been together ever since.[153] Most of the members of All Around Czechs of West played in family bands before they were even teenagers. As the young boys got to know one another through the dance circuit, they decided in 2014 to form a band themselves.[154] All three of these popular groups play and sing Czech polkas and waltzes as well as other dance-hall favorites.

And finally, after the peaceful Velvet Revolution of 1989, when the Czech Communist Party was forced out of power, the Czech borders were opened once again. Since then, a growing stream of Texans have visited the Czech Republic either privately, as part of a heritage group tour, or as members of one of the tours led by Texas polka bands. The visits have helped generate something of a new cultural and musical exchange. These are all signs of continuing community cohesion and vigor as well as suggestions of future improvisations and adaptations to come.

The distinctive Texas evolution of Czech music was evident to Zdena Salivarová, a prominent Czech émigré in exile. Salivarová fled communist Czechoslovakia in 1968 with her husband, Josef Škvorecký, a well-known dissident and novelist. The couple went on to found the exile press 68 Publishers in Toronto, Canada. When Salivarová spoke at the 1986 "Sesquicentennial Symposium on Czech Music in Texas" at College Station, she said: "I admire the stubbornness with which the Czech, the Moravian, and the Slovak folk songs survive in this country. Here in Texas you may sing our common-heritage songs in a slightly different way. There are little charming misunderstandings of the lyrics, delightful mispronunciations of words, but I feel this is nothing else but the little pebble being polished by the Brazos River to a new beauty."[155]

2 CZECH FOLK AND POPULAR SONGS

From Their Roots to the Lidovka Tradition

John K. Novak

The Czech Lands: The First Millennium

The three regions that are both historically and currently known as the Czech lands are Bohemia (Čechy in the Czech language) to the west, Moravia (Morava) to the east, and Czech Silesia (Slezsko) to the northeast. These regions have been linguistically and politically unified for the better part of the last millennium. The neighboring states of the Czech lands are Poland and Germany to the north, Germany and Austria to the west and south, and Slovakia to the east.

The history of the Czech lands is characterized by constant changes of power, politics, and religion. In the ninth century A.D., Prince Mojmír of Moravia brought about unification of the region in what became the Great Moravian Empire, a Christian nation that, at that time, was the third-largest empire in Europe. Between A.D. 907 and 910, the Great Moravian Empire fell to the Hungarian Magyar armies. At the same time, the Přemyslid dynasty in Bohemia (A.D. 900s–1306) promoted cultural development in that region and, toward the end of the dynasty, ushered in a time when art and science flourished in Prague.

During the ensuing Luxemburg dynasty (A.D. 1310–1437), Prague became the seat of the Holy Roman Empire; however, the last twenty-five years of this dynasty were severely marred by wars between Catholics and Hussite Protestants. After King Louis II of Hungary was killed by Ottoman Turks in 1526 during the Battle of Mohács, Archduke Ferdinand I of Austria became the new king of Bohemia (which comprised all the Czech lands, not just Bohemia proper). Bohemia was now one of several dozens of territories that made up the Austrian Habsburg Monarchy.

Early in the Austrian Habsburg Monarchy, Bohemia was given certain religious and linguistic freedoms. In 1576, Holy Roman Emperor Rudolf II was crowned king of Bohemia. He moved the seat of the empire from Vienna back to Prague in 1583, and the "Mother of Cities" once again became a peaceful center of art, science, and even alchemy. However, the succeeding emperor, Matthias, who ruled from 1612 to 1619, proved fanatically opposed to Protestantism. His laws led to protests, and eventually to the Battle of White Mountain in 1620. The battle was a great loss for Czech Protestants, whose faith would be oppressed for the next 150 years. Moreover, it also began the Thirty Years' War, a debacle that led to the death of eight million Europeans.

In the eighteenth century, the reforms of Empress Maria Theresa, who ruled the Austrian Empire from 1740 to 1780, and her son and successor, Joseph II, who reigned from 1780 to 1790, expelled the right-wing Jesuits from the empire and began a law of religious tolerance for all of Austria. Language was a separate issue, however, as Joseph II proclaimed German the official language of the entire empire. Schools in major cities of the Czech lands were forced to be German speaking only. This pattern of vacillation between freedom and oppression in the Czech lands was not to be broken until modern times.

The year 1848 marked the first Pan-Slavic Congress, which considered the political consolidation of many of the Slavic nations of Europe, including the Czech Republic, Poland, Ukraine, Slovakia, Croatia, and Serbia. Although Austria was strong after the fall of Napoleon in 1815, the Austro-Prussian War of 1866 led to the expulsion of Austria from the German Confederation. The Compromise of 1867 created the Austro-Hungarian Empire, a politically complex marriage during which Hungary remained partly autonomous. The Czechs were still ruled from Vienna and had very little political power.

Collecting the People's Songs

By a request from Count Furstenberg, the president of the Vienna Society of Friends of Music (Die Gesellschaft der Musikfreunde), the first systematic collection of songs from the various nations within the Austrian Empire, including the Czech lands, began in 1819 (four years after Napoleon's defeat) as an attempt to validate the diverse nations and cultures within the realm. Thus, the Austrian Ministry of the Interior and Supreme Chancellor Count František Saurau (1760–1832) ordered a gubernatorial campaign for constituent Czech nations to make official collections of their peoples' folk songs. Although the order was bureaucratic in nature, it sparked interest within the Czech lands in the living tradition of folk music in Bohemia and Moravia that existed before nonfolk influences altered this body of music.

An important and early collector of Bohemian song and dance music was Ludvik Ritter von Rittersberk (also spelled Rittersberg; 1780–1841), who in 1825 published *České národní písně—Böhmische Volklieder* (Bohemian national songs—Bohemian folk songs). Prodigious collectors and editors followed Rittersberk's lead, but perhaps the most important was the poet and archivist Karel Jaromír Erben (1811–70), who collected and published Bohemian folk music during the years 1852 to 1864. Erben's greatest folk song collection is *Prostonárodní české písně a říkadla* (Czech folk songs and nursery rhymes). In addition to his musicological contributions, Erben's original poetry, especially his famous *Kytice* (A bouquet), a volume of Czech fairy tales and legends set in verse, became instrumental in the regeneration of both the Czech language and Czech cultural legends.

Traditional Bohemian folk songs can be similar to German folk songs due to both geography and political history. Although one finds differences within the folk music of the various regions of Bohemia, the following characteristics are common to most of them: Bohemian folk songs tend to be in either major or minor modes. They may be in duple, triple, or quadruple meters, with triple meter the most common.[1] (Of the folk songs in Rittersberk's collection, 80 percent are dance tunes, which accounts for the characteristics of their structure.[2]) They tend to be based on one or two motifs and feature repetitions and sequences. The number of measures per phrase varies from four, five, or six to eight measures per phrase, although a minority of songs have uneven phrases. Most songs tend to end on the first scale degree (the tonic).

The collectors of Moravian folk songs dealt with music of even greater stylistic diversity from that of Bohemian music. František Sušil (1804–68), a professor in Brno, collected nearly 2,500 Moravian folk songs in his *Moravské národní písně s nápěvy do textu vřaděnými* (Moravian folk songs with melodies inserted into the texts). Following in Sušil's footsteps were two important ethnomusicologists: the Lachian-born preeminent composer Leoš Janáček (1854–1928) and František Bartoš (1837–1906), a schoolteacher with an interest in Moravia. Together they coedited three volumes of Moravian folk songs in the years 1890 to 1901.

Moravian folk songs contrast with the folk songs of Bohemia. Although Moravian songs may also be in major or minor modes, some are in older modes with raised fourth degrees (Lydian), lowered seventh degrees (Mixolydian), and lowered second degrees (Phrygian). Some songs are built on scales of fewer than the typical seven degrees—some contain as few as four or five unique notes. A large group of Moravian folk songs end on the fifth scale degree (the dominant).

Prominent dance features in Moravian folk songs are dotted rhythms and accents. While some Moravian meters are the same duple, triple, and quadruple meters of Bohemian music, Moravian folk music may also be in quintuple and septuple meters. In the music of the region known as Moravian Slovakia (Slovácko), a certain style of music that is considered by the performers to be in quadruple meter is performed with prolongations of the second and fourth beats. The resulting irregular pulse is unlike any meter mentioned above. In contrast, certain folk songs intended for unaccompanied solo outdoor singing may have no meter at all. The diversity of musical styles within Moravia is greater than that of Bohemia because of the relative seclusion of the regions, which are isolated by Moravia's mountain ranges and valleys.

The early collections remain vital to the preservation of Bohemian and Moravian music. However, other styles from within the Czech lands, within other nations in Austria, and from foreign nations such as Italy and Germany resulted in the creation of newer styles of popular songs that range in time from the seventeenth century to the present. These styles include operetta couplets, shopkeepers' songs, and so-called half-folk songs.

Operetta Couplets

One significant influence on the direction of Czech popular music was operetta couplets. (For the genre of operetta, Czech uses both the word *zpěvohra* [sung play] and the word *opereta*.) The Italian word *operetta* (the diminutive of *opera*) indicates a drama or comedy characterized by spoken words combined with songs, duets, choruses, and other vocal genres, often in dance rhythms. Couplets were songs and arias that originated in seventeenth- and eighteenth-century Baroque and classical operas, as well as in ceremonial religious plays. The couplets made their way into the sung plays of the nineteenth century. By their very nature, couplets are strophic (i.e., they have a verse that repeats with different texts, but they have no chorus). Grammatically speaking, couplets are a plural entity because they are typically made up of two pairs of lines of text and music.

Throughout their history, the texts of couplets became increasingly prevalent in sung plays that were comic or satirically witty in nature. A verse of a couplet text often ended with wordplay or catch phrases, and some became increasingly hilarious with each new verse. Singers with wit and charisma were known to improvise verses of couplets to the delight of audiences.

The work considered to be the greatest of all sung plays, *Die Zauberflöte* (*The Magic Flute*; 1791), is at once a morality play and a comedy. With text by Emanuel Schikaneder (1751–1812) and music by Wolfgang Mozart (1756–91), who died three months after its premiere, this magnificent work pleased audiences throughout Austria and abroad. The citizens of Prague were in love with Mozart even before the premiere of *Don Giovanni* (1787), which he composed for the Estates Theater in that city. Prague was the third city to stage a production of *Die Zauberflöte*. Many of its songs, both serious and comic, are in couplet form. Some Czech operettas from this era were clearly modeled on this work.[3]

Although the earliest couplets in Bohemia were in the German language, Czech composers, librettists, and playwrights frequently employed couplets as the Czech language made its way to the stage. František Škroup (1801–62), an important Bohemian composer, wrote the music of his stage works to Czech librettos. His musical play *Dráteník* (The tinker), with libretto by Josef Krasoslav Chmelenský (1800–39), is usually considered the first opera in the Czech language.[4] Škroup actually performed on stage the title role of the tinker, who ironically is a Slovak character and is the only character who speaks and sings Slovak in the otherwise Czech operetta! Additionally, Škroup is best known for composing the song "Kde domov můj?" (Where Is My Home?; Song 28) for the play *Fidlovačka* (The shoemakers' fair; 1834). This song, with words by Josef Kajetán Tyl (1808–56), became one of the most important national songs for the Czechs, and was later joined with a Slovak song, "Nad Tatrou sa blýska" (It's Lightning over the Tatras), to become the official national anthem of Czechoslovakia when the country was formed in 1918.

Tyl, the author of the libretto of *Fidlovačka*, wrote important Czech plays both with and without music. The ethnomusicologist Josef Kotek writes about him:

Example 2.1

> Josef Kajetán Tyl, who can rightly be called the father of Czech couplets, was not the first to employ this kind of genre in the country. Certainly, however, he became not only the most acute cultivator [of couplets] of all local composers in the first half of the 19th century, but also the most capable. The results of his work, backed by a commitment and ability to respond boldly and profoundly to the political, national, social, and cultural problems of the revivalist society, the richness of means of expression, and musicality itself, Tyl's verses outdid even the couplets' most successful period, which occurred at the meeting of the 19th and 20th centuries.[5]

Example 2.1 is the first verse from a song from the Czech operetta *Princ a had* (The prince and the snake; 1835), with text by Chmelenský and music by Škroup. In addition to its usual couplet form a a^1 b b^1, other characteristics of this song are typical of the genre.[6] The range of the vocal line is within one octave. The two-measure introduction and interlude were likely filled with instrumental vamps, motifs, or riffs. (This final characteristic becomes prevalent in the *lidovka* style to come.)

Shopkeepers' Songs—Kramářské písně

Shopkeeper's songs, also known as broadside ballads,[7] began to circulate in Bohemia in the eighteenth century and declined in the late nineteenth century. They ceased to exist by World War I. The popularity of these songs of single sheets and folios, which were sold both at markets and in stores and by traveling salesmen and pitchmen, was nothing short of phenomenal. The sellers, who were often the authors as well, would sing the songs in the open air to lure buyers. They often accompanied themselves with a hurdy-gurdy, barrel organ, harp, violin, or concertina.

The alternative term for shopkeepers' songs, "broadside ballads," denotes the same phenomenon in different countries such as England or the United States, where the entire song and illustration was printed only on one side of the paper (the "broadside"); the other side was usually blank. Some of the shopkeepers' songs in the Czech lands were produced broadside and others folded, with the words on the inside of the paper. They were printed in more than fifty Czech cities and townships.[8] Tens of thousands were made and sold; 25,000 alone are housed in the National Museum in Prague.[9]

Most of the sellers of the ballads were from lower social classes and included war veterans with disabilities. The songs attracted the eyes of potential buyers by their variety of woodcut prints (later, steel prints) that typically adorned their covers. Shopkeepers' songs seldom included any musical notation. Rather, they contained just the words of the song and a reference to a tune to which the words should be sung. These tunes were familiar to the buying public, and included folk songs, Baroque hymns (usually German in origin), and newer songs that were popular at the time. Unfortunately, historians have found it difficult to recover many of these tunes, but the Czech ethnomusicologists Josef Kotek and Lubomír Tyllner have both determined that the songs typically ended on the third scale degree, as opposed to the more conclusive first scale degree. These two historians, however, disagree on the learnedness of the composers. Kotek believes the authors were "from the lowest social classes and with only the most basic school education."[10] Tyllner contends that "the authors of the broadside ballads were educated people, often teachers or priests."[11]

The authors of the lyrics were seldom included in the folios. The first of these songs were of a religious nature and were intended to propagate the Catholic Church. Some told stories of the lives of saints, while others warned of the perils that await nonbelievers. These songs were, in fact, religious tracts, which began with lines such as "Christians, pause! Hear things unheard of!" Typically, these songs were composed of many stanzas. In fact, one of them contained ninety-eight stanzas![12] Kotek describes the songs as follows:

> Shopkeepers' ballads had attracted popular strata both as a mediator of current reports on political, military and criminal events, of natural disasters and public affairs in general, but especially as an attractive addition to church singing, mainly in the form of sensational religious legends and miracles (songs with religious themes accounted for around three-quarters of all shopkeeper's prints). Shopkeeper's ballads are famous for their nature as news bearers, since they promptly filled [the public] in on current topics to which the folk song was not able to respond quickly.[13]

By the beginning of the nineteenth century, the texts of shopkeepers' songs were much more diverse in topics. Thus, in addition to devout or admonishing texts, there were also texts that were romantic, historical, patriotic, bawdy, satirical, comic, nonsensical, and even bizarre and terrifying. Approximately one-quarter of the songs housed in the National Museum are of a secular nature.[14] Moreover, the songs acted as newspapers that published current events quickly in lyrical format. Tantalizing scandals were set to music and sold immediately. It is astonishing that a genre that began as a tool for religious evangelism became the Czech peoples' social tabloid!

Historians attribute the populace's obsession with the shopkeepers' songs to three main causes. First, the songs usurped interest in traditional folk songs. Second, the mere notion of writing new texts to old music impeded any reciprocity of melody and text. Finally, the texts themselves lacked artistry in comparison with other, older sources of Czech literature and poetry.[15] However, quality aside, the shopkeepers' song might well be appreciated for contributing to the perpetuation of the written Czech language. Moreover, in the twentieth century, broadside ballads were performed on the burlesque stage and were later spoofed in musical plays.

The Half-Folk Song (Pololidové píseň)

The third type of Czech popular song began in the nineteenth century and is the most important type in the formation of a body of Czech music in Texas. This is what is called the *pololidové píseň*, or the "half-folk song." Lubomír Tyllner admits that, as a concept, the half-folk song is not clearly defined.[16] Some of the songs of this category are simply variants of folk tunes, while others are new songs that possessed characteristics of folk songs. Still others fit somewhere between these two categories. In both melody and text, half-folk songs are often considered "folksy" rather than true "folk." As with operetta couplets, these songs tended to divert the interest of the populace away from original folk songs. Some half-folk songs contained traditional folk lyrics, but the style of their melodies ranged from containing just a few simple alterations of the original melody to being completely newly written tunes.

Regarding their musical style, half-folk songs lack the diversity of phrasing and the use of both major and minor keys found in Czech folk songs as well as the modal elements of Moravian folk music. Instead, their meters are usually either in waltz-like 3/4 or polka-like 2/4. Their phrasing is often a strict, regular four measures each, a quality that we also see in operettas and shopkeeper's songs. The sole scale resource was the major mode. Their texts, if new, were markedly sentimental. Typical topics included hard times, longing for youth or days of old, lost or unrequited love, a loved one going off to war, exaltation of nature over community life, and dark, morbid tragedies. The half-folk song writers borrowed symbols from true folk songs, such as animated elements of nature (e.g., birds, brooks, and trees) that have the power to speak and advise. References to drunkenness or other types of debauchery were among the new developments of this style. Sometimes the verses do not tell a complete story, but they seem to be conglomerates of texts torn from different songs.

The features of half-folk songs can usually be distinguished from those of older folk songs. For example, half-folk songs can be more chromatic than folk songs. They commonly end on the third scale degree like the shopkeeper's songs, as opposed to ending on the first scale degree (the tonic).[17] The typical tendency of the seventh scale degree (i.e., the leading tone) is not fulfilled by motion to the tonic.[18] The half-folk song may contain longer note values and vocal silence between phrases, the latter of which is often filled by short instrumental passages. All of these features are seen as well in operettas and shopkeeper's songs, which further demonstrates the influence that all of these styles had on the direction of popular music.

By the mid-nineteenth to the early twentieth century, the half-folk song had replaced the folk song in most regions of the Czech lands, especially in the larger cities. However, Kotek points out that certain regions remained more faithful to tradition and were not as prone to being influenced by the other styles. These regions included, but are not limited to, Chodsko (in southwest Bohemia), Slovácko (which includes Dolňácko), and Podluže (in southeast Moravia).[19]

The manuscript collections stored in archives and museums in the Czech Republic that were originally thought of as folk songs contain a great proportion of half-folk songs. In field investigations in the early twentieth century (with the exception of the mentioned areas where folk music was strongly held on to), the total number of half-folk songs in the Czech lands actually was a massive 80 percent of all songs.[20]

Example 2.2 shows two versions of the song "Pod našima okny" (Under Our Windows; Song 47). Version A is from Erben's collected folk songs, and version B is a

Example 2.2

later half-folk song version from about 1870.[21] Version B remains more popular even today. Note first the length of the two songs; the B version repeats "Já se koně bojím" (I am afraid of the horse), which turns fourteen measures into sixteen. This "squares off" the melody into two even couplets. The leading-tone F-sharp is the apex of the first half of version B; the Czech musicologist Vladimír Karbusický finds this tendency note (the note a half-step below the tonic note that makes the latter sound like the tonal center) in this place to be "exposed" and "sentimental."[22] The song also ends lower than a standard plagal range (whose lowest note should be the fifth degree—from the dominant below the tonic to the dominant above the tonic). The end of version A is on the tonic note G; the ending of version B is a third above, on the note B. This end of the third indicated the influence of both operetta couplets and shopkeeper's songs.

The Inception and Irresistible Rise of the Polka

Although more than one history of the invention of the polka exists, it is quite certain that both the dance and its name are from Bohemia, and therefore are Czech. The word "polka" is said to derive from *půlka,* which means "little half," which probably refers to the quicker, smaller step taken between the main steps.[23] Additionally, the word "polka" can also be a Czech noun referring to a Polish girl or woman. Let us first investigate the most widespread and famous legend of the dance's history, which, though romantic, could actually be true.

The historian Čeněk Zíbrt (1864–1932) collected this story from an unnamed witness.[24] A young girl named Anna Slezáková (her married name was to be Chadimová), who was the daughter of a brewery and restaurant owner in the Bohemian town of Kostelec nad Labem, "came up" with the dance on a Sunday afternoon at the brewery. The tune she danced to was a musical setting of the familiar nursery rhyme *Strejček Nimra koupil šimla* (Uncle Nimra Bought a White Horse). The witness stated: "Around 1830 on a Sunday afternoon, a maiden on duty was singing and dancing. Everyone in the house watched her, as it was an unusual dance that she offered to my former teacher Josef Neruda."[25] Later in the century, Zíbrt followed up on the story and wrote that "the girl named Anna Slezáková is married, lives in Konětopy, is 60 years old and is the mother of four sons."[26] Alternate early synonyms for the polka include two words from the original rhyme: šimla (white horse) and *maděra* (madeira wine).

An alternative history of the polka comes from a 1935 article by J. Langer. According to him, certain Polish dance styles, such as the *Krakowiak* and the related *strašák* and *břitva, had become popular in* Hradec Králové (in eastern Bohemia, fifty-five miles from Kostelec nad Labem), but were danced differently than in Poland. Thus the dance style was called "polka" in honor of the dance music's origin.[27] Langer also adds that František Hilmar (1803–81) composed the first piece of music that was called a polka. The three most significant early polka composers were Hilmar, Josef Neruda (1807–75), and Josef Labický (1802–81).

The polka was first danced in Prague in 1835 and quickly captivated both dancers and spectators in other countries and continents. The year 1837 marked the first published collection of polkas: *Prager Lieblings-Galopen für Pianoforte (Prague darling-gallops for piano).* It included polkas by Neruda, Hilmar, and Labický. In 1939, regimental bands brought the polka to both Vienna and St. Petersburg. Many accounts recall how the Prague dancer master Jan Raab brought the polka to Paris the following year, and in a few short years it was the most popular dance of Paris society.[28] In fact, the word "polkamania" was coined there to describe its sweeping popularity. The year 1844 proved a critical one for the polka, as this was when it reached London via the French as the Parisian ballet stars Carlotta Grisi and Jules Perrot performed it on the stage of Her Majesty's Theatre. That same year, the polka was introduced to America (in Chatham Hall in New York City) and India (in Calcutta, in honor of a visit by Queen Victoria).

However, not all who witnessed the polka were enthusiastic. In April of 1844, *The Illustrated London News* stated: "It is a waste of time to consider this nonsense. The weathercock heads of the Parisians have been delighted always by any innovation, but they never imported anything more ridiculous or ungraceful than this Polka. It is a hybrid confusion of Scotch lilt, Irish jig and Bohemian waltz, and need only to be seen once to be avoided forever."[29]

Regarding the polka, *The New Grove Dictionary of Music* states: "It attained extraordinary popularity, and clothes, hats, streets and even puddings were named after it. Magazines and newspapers of the time were full of news items, descriptions, illustrations and advertisements referring to the dance."[30]

Although early instructions and illustrations indicate that the polka was danced in a variety of manners, the directions to dance common standard dance steps to the polka are quite simple. "[The polka] consists of a hop right, in place; an immediate slide to the left, along the line of direction; a step left, to close the right foot to the left; and a slide or spring with the left foot to the side, with a half turn clockwise. After a pause, the step is repeated on the opposite foot, along the same line of direction, to complete a full turn. The partner performs the counterpart step on the opposite foot."[31]

The middle step in each measure is the *půl, pol,* or half-step mentioned above. During the steps, the pair is to be turning (and when the tempo is fast enough) twirling in a clockwise fashion. All the while the pairs on the dance floor are moving counterclockwise in a circle. These last two elements are typical of most round dances, such as the waltz. The individual pairs turn on their own axis as planets, while they simultaneously revolve in a greater circle as the planets do around the sun.

Example 2.3 presents three rhythmic sets found in polka.[32] Despite being here in the second position, Rhythm B is the most authentic. Note the absence of anacruses (pick-up notes). Since the Czech language always stresses the first syllable of each word, the short, unaccented syllables only seldom appear at the beginning of a sentence. This long-short, long-short (dactylic), and long-short-short (trochaic) manner of speech is essential to the way most Czechs speak their language, and it is also expressed in the rhythms of their music.

Beyond the dance floors of countless nations, the polka became an important signifier of Czechness and was incorporated into the concert music of the nineteenth century. Bedřich Smetana (1824–84), who was especially fond of the genre, composed polkas for the piano and incorporated them into his chamber works, suites, and operas. One famous example is the second section of the *Moldau* (*Vltava*) movement of his *Má vlast,* where the river is passing an outdoor wedding dance. Smetana, Dvořák, Zdeněk Fibich, Josef Suk, and Bohuslav Martinů, all composed concert music in the polka style and with the name "polka." Martinů's (1890–1959) "Etudes and Polkas" (1945) for piano solo is an attempt to bring the polka to the artistic status held by the prelude or fugue. Speaking of the fugue, the most famous piece by far by the Czech composer Jaroslav Weinberger (1896–1967) is the jaunty "Polka and Fugue" from his opera *Švanda Dudák* (Švanda the bagpiper; 1926). Looking beyond Bohemia for the polka, we find Johann Strauss Jr. and Josef Strauss, in nearby Vienna, composing polkas that were second only to their waltzes in popularity. Johann Jr. even wrote a polka that he called "Czechen-polka" and another "Heski-holki," which is a transliteration of *Hezké holky* (Pretty girls). Popular Viennese composers Franz von Suppé and Franz Léhar featured the polka in their operettas. Russian composers penned original, creative polkas, including an "Italian Polka" for piano by Sergei Rachmaninoff, a prominent theme of Dmitri Shostakovich's Fourth Symphony, and Igor Stravinsky's "Circus Polka" for band (or two pianos).

The Ever-Essential Waltz

The precursors to the waltz were several couple's dances, all in 3/4 time, from southern Germany, Bavaria, Austria, and Bohemia. (Similar pieces at the time were also danced in Italy, France, and Hungary.) The dances' names were: *Walzer, Spinner, Dreher,* and *Weller* (all of which imply the act of turning) or names like the *Ländler,* all in German and referring to a geographic location (here, the town of Land ob der Enns). These dances were more intimate than the older minuet, which had more complicated steps and kept the bodies of the dancing pair at a distance from one

Example 2.3

another. In 1780, about the same time that the term *Walzer* (waltz) became standard, Emperor Joseph II, a great supporter of music and dance, officially recognized the waltz at the Viennese court, only to proclaim it verboten five years later.

What provoked the emperor to withdraw his approval? It appears that many critics were denouncing the waltz in newspapers and journals as indecent, lustful, and even erotic. The factor of touch was too much for these opponents, and reports were made of embracing and even kissing on or near the dance floor. Second, since the dance was ushered into fashion by the bourgeoisie, it was seen as a type of rebellion against the rule-bound dances that traditionally kept the dancers apart, as well as the stifling mores and prejudices of the Austrian Empire.

The dance survived outside the court, and after the Congress of Vienna of 1815, the waltz became an international favorite, much as the polka would become thirty years later. In the Czech lands, the waltz was the favorite dance that did not arise from Czech origins. In fact, the proto-nationalist author and impresario Jan Neruda hoped to popularize his own Czech word for the dance. Alas, the *houpavá* (swaying dance) didn't catch on, but the *valčík* (a diminutive of *Walzer*) did.[33] Czechs loved both the waltzes of the great Vienna composers such as Josef Strauss and Johann Strauss Jr. and the domestic waltzes by Josef Labický and Julius Fučík, as well as arrangements of half-folk songs in three-quarter time.

The footwork of the waltz is a larger step on the downbeat, and two shorter steps on beats two and three. This allows each alternative downbeat to be marked by alternating right and left feet. "The Viennese waltz is a rotary dance where the dancers are constantly turning either toward the leader's right (natural) or toward the leader's left (reverse), interspersed with non-rotating *change steps* to switch between the directions of rotation. Furthermore, in a properly danced Viennese waltz, couples do not pass but turn continuously left and right while traveling counterclockwise around the floor following each other."[34]

Czech Ballroom Dances and the Beseda

Essential to the growth of Czech nationalism after the 1848 revolution was the development of Czech ballroom dances. These formal dances became especially popular beginning in the 1860s. They distinguished themselves from the Austrian balls of the major cities in Bohemia and Moravia in three ways. First, the predominant language of the participants was Czech. (To speak Czech at an Austrian state ball, or any other nonspecific Czech ball, was considered highly uncouth.) Second, most of the dances played and danced were either of Czech origin or bore new Czech names. Third, and of special importance, the literature for the balls (posters and dance cards) were printed exclusively in Czech. These documents were a rarity for the Czechs, whose language had fallen into disuse in the cities of the Czech lands and existed largely in oral tradition. To see everything at an illustrious ball written in Czech was a rare treat and source of pride. Figure 2.1 is a photograph of an ornate dance card from a Czech ball showing the Czech dances in order of performance.[35]

Participating in a Czech ball was a way for Czechs to rediscover their own culture and speak freely with persons of like minds. Moreover, a dance or ball of any type was a significant symbol of social status. The existence and popularity of Czech balls implied that to be Czech was no longer contrary to being educated, cultured, and sophisticated. And although ethnic Czechs in the nineteenth century were still second-class citizens on their own territory, they proved that they were a richly cultured nation with a formidable history and composed of individuals who never ceased to contribute to all aspects of life for Austria and beyond, including but not limited to their ingenuity in science and brilliance in the arts.

An important development in Czech dance occurred in 1862: the *beseda*. The Czech *beseda* is a quadrille, or ordered group of dances, some of which are Czech folk dances in origin, while others were already popular in urban dance settings. Daniela Stavělová describes the *beseda* as

> a suite of dance movements from ten folk dances, whose steps and figures were combined to form something of a ballroom quadrille. Initiated by the poet Jan Neruda—and performed by him first at the Konvict Inn in Prague on November 13th, 1862, the beseda was co-created by the dance teacher

Karel Link (1823–1911) and the composer Ferdinand Heller (1824–1912). The first printed version of the dance was published in France in 1863, followed by numerous Czech editions that saw various changes and revision[s] (e.g., the original instrumental accompaniment was later expanded with song lyrics, overtures and intermezzos). The name of the suite itself changed as well, from "the Czech ballroom dance beseda" to: "the Czech beseda."[36]

One listing of the dances (albeit nine instead of ten) goes as follows: *sousedská, furiant, rejdovák, polka, dvojpolka, kalamajka, obkročák, hulán,* and *řezanka.*[37] Most of these were danced at balls as early as the 1830s; they were to dance what half-folk songs were to song: revamped and urbane versions of older art forms.

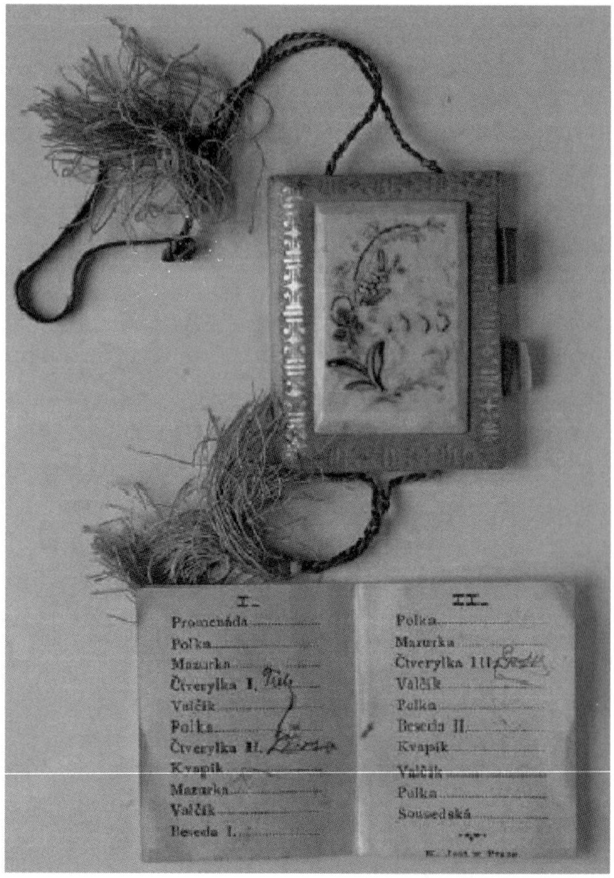

An ornate dance card from a Czech ball, second half of the nineteenth century. *Photo courtesy of the Czech National Museum.*

Wind Bands: Disseminating Czech Music to the Populace

The principal musical vehicle for the rise in nationalism in the Czech lands under the auspices of Austria-Hungary was ironically the military wind bands that were formed by the state and placed in its service. Gradually, and through a series of events, one can trace the progression of the band's place in Austrian nationalism to its place in Czech nationalism.

Although versions of bands featuring brass or wind instruments have existed in the Czech lands since at least as early as the Renaissance, the first bands of importance were associated with the military during the Thirty Years' War (1618–48). This grisly conflict, which claimed the lives of more than eight million people, actually began in Bohemia and spread through all of Central and Northern Europe. The military bands at this time consisted of trumpets, oboes, bassoons, and whistles. The next major event to influence the instrumentation of the military bands occurred in the following century: the Austro-Turkish War (1788–91). It was during this war that the Turkish sultan's Janissary bands brought unprecedented music and instruments to Austria within ensembles containing the oboe-like zarna, new bugles, and many types of percussion instruments, such as eight small timpani, a bass drum, and bells.

At the beginning of the eighteenth century, the typical military band in both Austria and Prussia consisted of two oboes, two clarinets, two bassoons, two horns, and eventually a tuba, one large drum, and one small drum. In 1860, with the invention of new instruments and the improvement of existing ones, the Austrian military band became much larger and contained one piccolo, one flute, one A-flat clarinet, four F clarinets, four E-flat clarinets, nine C clarinets, nine B clarinets, two bassoons, one contrabassoon, four horns, four bugles, one bass bugle, one tenor horn, two euphoniums, six trumpets, one bass trumpet, three trombones, one bombardon, two bass tubas, two small drums, one large drum, and one pair of cymbals.[38] By 1890, new tubas and "sub-contrabasses" replaced the bassoons altogether.

By the end of the nineteenth century, the Austrian Empire boasted more than one hundred military bands. Most bandleaders were highly educated in music in conservatories in Prague, Vienna, Leipzig, Budapest, and elsewhere. Many of the directors and players throughout Austria-Hungary were ethnic Czechs. Twenty-two of the bands were formed and located in the Czech lands themselves: four in Prague, two each in Terezín, Brno, Olomouc, and Josefov, and one each in Těšín, Liberec, Jindřichuv Hradec, Jihlava, Opava, Kutná Hora, České Budějovice, Plzen, Hradec Králové, and Znojmo.[39]

These bands played much more than military music. They frequently performed arrangements of popular Viennese waltzes and operetta numbers by composers such as Johann Strauss Jr. and Josef Lanner. Many military bands played a repertoire that included arrangements by Classic and Romantic masters such as Mozart, Beethoven, and Mendelssohn. The bands played at official balls; in the Czech lands, the patrons of the balls were an ever-growing bourgeoisie of Czech nationals.

Led by Czech intellectuals such as František Palacký (1798–1876), the second quarter of the century saw an increase in Czech literature and art, especially in the cities. Likewise, the music of balls, although officially Austrian, became increasingly more ethnically Czech in origin. However, the year 1848 was fraught with national revolutions throughout the European continent. In the end, the Czech cause for social, political, and artistic freedom failed. Instead, the reactionary policies of the Austrian prime minister Prince Felix of Schwarzenberg and the minister of the interior Baron Alexander von Bach limited the freedom of the press and gave the Roman Catholic Church control over education and public life. This period from 1849 to 1860 is known both as the era of Neo-Absolutism and "Bach's Absolutism."

In 1860, the "October Diploma" was adopted by Emperor Franz Josef. It was the first of several constitutions that allowed private societies to be established again. The cultural life of the Czech bourgeoisie quickly grew and exhibited specific national genres. From 1860 to 1880, public Czech activities such as choirs, theater troupes, dance and dances, opera, and folk art grew rapidly, and a great number of Czech wind bands formed independently of the military. These civilian bands were made up of firemen, miners, sharpshooters, and veterans, and, perhaps of greatest importance to the expression of Czech culture, they included the bands that accompanied the Sokol. The Sokol (Falcon) Gymnastics club was a fraternal nationalist organization that promoted physical fitness, especially through their group displays of gymnastics, often performed to music. Also central to the revival of Czech culture was the formation in 1861 of the Prague Hlahol (Joyful Noise), a Czech choral society. Shortly afterward, Hlahol groups were formed in other Czech and Moravian cities and towns.

František Kmoch (1848–1912), the most influential of the nineteenth-century bandleaders, was also a composer and arranger with a gift for scoring for band. He was born in Zásmuky near Kolín. In 1868, he became the conductor of the Sokol Wind Orchestra in Kolín. Kmoch is especially important for his incorporation of folk and half-folk melodies in his marches. His first experimentation with the incorporation of folk music was the inclusion of Serbian melodies. A high point in Kmoch's career was when he directed the music of the opening ceremony of the 1873 Gymnastics Festival in Prague. Kmoch's Sokol Band played to enthusiastic audiences in Krakow, Vienna, and Budapest, and it even spent three months in 1862 in Novgorod, Russia.

The form of a Kmoch march is similar to that of the marches of the late eighteenth century. It is in three sections. The first section is in the tonic key, and the second section is usually in the dominant key. After a return to the first section, the section known as the "trio" is then played in the subdominant key. (The trio gets its name not from being the third section of the work, but because the corresponding section of a march or a minuet was originally played by only three members of the ensemble.) Kmoch trios are the most melodic sections of his marches and typically feature the woodwinds rather than the brass. Many of the trios are settings of folk songs and half-folk songs from Bohemia. In fact, Kmoch encouraged the members of the band who were not playing the trio to sing it instead. At Kmoch's concerts and other performances, the Czech audiences heard folk tunes that they may not have heard in years—or perhaps ever. Some critics considered this use of these tunes with some melodic, metric, and rhythmic alterations to be contrary to the preservation of Czech folk music. However, Kmoch himself and his supporters contended that in these arrangements he was simultaneously reviving and popularizing the songs. Certainly, if Kmoch had not set these melodies into his famous marches, the songs themselves would not be as ubiquitous as they are today. At the beginning of the twentieth century, Kmoch's marches in editions published by Mojmír Urbánek flew off the shelves. The march "Muziky, muziky" (Song 39) alone sold more than 120,000 copies.[40]

Kmoch's raising of national pride through furtive borrowing from folk music did not end with the Czech lands and Czech melodies. He incorporated Serbian melodies for performances in Serbia and Polish melodies for his acclaimed performances in Poland; moreover, he demonstrated pan-Slavic fervor with the incorporation of "Hey, Slavs!" and other songs that extolled the Slavic nations as one family.

Lidovka

The original meaning of *lidovka* is a song or musical work composed in the manner of folk songs and folk music.[41] Etymologically, it is a noun that suggests the music is "a bit folk." Of course, this definition is also true of half-folk songs; actually the two genres overlap significantly. *Lidovka* is not a folk song, although much of the general populace remains unaware of the distinction.[42]

The term *lidovka* became popular around the time of World War I. The golden era of *lidovka* coincided with the span of the two World Wars. *Lidovka* music contained sentimental folk-like melodies that grew out of folk song and were filtered through genres such as couplets, shopkeepers' songs, and urban songs such as Prague street songs (*Pražské písničky*) and cabaret songs (šantány). Thus the characteristics associated above with these music types are prevalent features in *lidovka* songs as well. These include major keys, regular phrasing, melodic cadences on the third scale degree, and texts with symbols from nature. The form of a *lidovka* song often had the same three sections as those in early marches. Kmoch is seen as the father of the genre; indeed, the wind band was the preeminent vehicle for the performance of *lidovka* songs, yet string and mixed ensembles also played *lidovka*. Polkas, marches, and waltzes dominated the genre, but it also included tangos and some foxtrots.

A significant and new trait of *lidovka* music was the public awareness of the songs' composers. Throughout the twentieth century, many *lidovka* composers reached star status, such as Karel Hašler (1879–1941), Jaromír Vejvoda (1902–88), Karel Vacek (1902–82), and Ladislav Kubeš (1924–98), among others. These composers followed the style of half-folk songs in both music and lyrics.

Lubomír Tyllner summarizes the content of their lyrics:

> They are commonly sentimental lyrical and lyrico-epic lyrics, kitsch renderings of idyllic pictures of the village churches or regions (Šumava, Bohemia, Vysočina), churches, streams, rivers (Lužnice, Vltava), valleys, olden times, travels abroad, the homestead, groves, little roses in the garden. At other times, the texts point to old Prague themes, forsaken love, or departure to war. The poetics are rich in diminutives (*háječek* [little grove], *vesnička* [little village or dear village], *chaloupečka* [little cottage or dear cottage], *kaplička* [little chapel, etc.]), and constant epithets . . . *láska horoucí* ([burning love], *láska nehynoucí* [undying love], *rodná víska* [the hometown]).[43]

The invention of the gramophone and the radio enabled *lidovka* music to enter Czech homes in an unprecedented manner. The sheet music industry continued to flourish as well, as it published band arrangements and folios for piano or accordion, usually with words for the sung trio sections of the music. Although large wind and brass ensembles were the golden standard for recorded music throughout the twentieth century (including after the Velvet Revolution of 1989), *lidovka* is played by an infinite combination of instruments and singers. Smaller groups suffice for taverns or smaller parties. In addition, some folkoric bands included authentic instruments such as bagpipe-led ensembles in Chodsko or cimbalom-led ensembles in Slovácko; these are groups whose main fare is true folk music indigenous to their respective regions.

After the Habsburg dynasty was defeated at the end of World War I in 1918, the sovereign state of Czechoslovakia was formed. For the Czechs and Slovaks, the first taste of freedom from Austrian oppression was made sweeter still by the excellent economy enjoyed by the new nation. Music of all kinds flourished, including brass bands, *lidovka*, and the new Czech cabaret.

Technology Broadens Lidovka's Exposure

It is not an overstatement to declare that the manufacturing of gramophones and gramophone discs was the most significant contribution to the dissemination of music of all time. Although the methods by which we record, store, and play sound now in the twenty-first century are more efficient, the gramophone was nevertheless the first mass-produced instrument of recorded sound, making it the ancestor of all aural media that was to follow. Thomas Edison (1847–1931) invented the phonograph in Menlo Park, New Jersey, in 1877. With wax cylinders as the medium, his "favorite" invention did not have optimal sound quality, nor was it practical to mass-produce recordings. Ten years later in Washington, D.C., German-born Emile Berliner (1851–1929) invented the flat gramophone recording disk (later simply known as the "record") as well as processes of mass recording capable of reproducing and disseminating music and the spoken word.

The gramophone gradually became popular in the Czech Republic in the early twentieth century. However, until 1923, all makers of gramophones and disks were foreign. Still, these companies made recordings of various Czech musicians, singers, and comedians. For example, František Kmoch's Kolín Band was recorded and published in 1904, as was opera star Emmy Destinnová and violin virtuoso Jaroslav Kocián. The first three Czech record companies were Homocord (1924), Esta, and Ultraphon (the latter two were established in 1929).

The first Czech radio station began broadcasting in Prague in 1923. At its inception, radio was funded by listeners who paid a subscription. In that first year, there were just forty-seven official listeners.[44] By late 1931, there were six stations in Bohemia and Moravia, and six years later there were more than a million registered listeners of Czech radio.[45]

The synthesis of Czech published music, records, and radio combined with the creative talents in the First Republic brought about the Golden Era of Czech music, a period that ranged from 1920 to 1939. The radio played massive quantities of domestic and foreign classical, folk, cabaret, and *lidovka* music. *Lidovka* music was usually performed by proficient domestic brass bands or other instrumental and vocal combinations.

Lidovka and Dechovka in the Twentieth and Twenty-First Centuries

The twentieth century gave the Czechs and Slovaks many hugely talented and unique musical artists. A seminal figure in music of the First Republic was the multitalented Karel Hašler (1879–1941). Hašler wrote more than twenty plays and movies. He also acted and sang in more than twenty movies, both silent and "talkies." In fact, Hašler thoroughly immersed himself in every genre of the entertainment field, to the great delight of audiences. His most famous song, Česká písnička (Our Czech Song; Song 12), is included in this collection. Hašler spoke his mind in his lyrics, which made them direct and engaging. However, he endeavored to criticize and lampoon the Third Reich in his lyrics. For this act of "treason," Hašler was sent to the Mauthausen concentration camp, where he was tortured and murdered. His songs remained largely out of favor for most of the rest of the century due to anti-communist sentiments also present in his lyrics.

A contrasting figure in the history of *lidovka* was Jaromír Vejvoda, who was born into a line of musicians dating back to the eighteenth century. He learned several instruments in his youth and eventually became a bandleader. He was equally at home playing or conducting, but he never considered composing music until the job was thrust upon him due to his band's need for new repertoire. In 1927, at age twenty-five, Vejvoda composed his first song at the piano, the "Modřanská Polka," named for Modřany, a district of Prague. It was recorded on the Esta label and became an immediate hit. However, this was only the beginning of the amazing journey of this song. In 1934, the popular lyricist Vašek (Václav) Zeman (1899–1987) wrote words to the polka and called it "Škoda lásky" ("Love's Pity" or "Wasted Love"). Recordings of the song with the new words were even more successful. Soon it became an international hit and was recorded under many different names and with different lyrics in a host of countries. In June 1939, Will Glahé's American recording of "Beer Barrel Polka," as it was now titled by the American lyricists Lew Brown and Wladimir Timm, rose to number one on the Hit Parade. The popular 1939 American release of "The Beer Barrel Polka" by the Andrews Sisters made an unprecedented $780,000 for the Decca label.[46] Vejvoda continued to play, conduct, and compose throughout much of his life until he was fired for not being loyal to the Czechoslovak Communist Party. The lyricist Zeman emigrated to Canada in 1948, a move that caused him to lose all royalties from his songs.

Another vital voice in *lidovka* repertoire was Václav Bláha (1901–59), who was born in Křečov, fifty kilometers north of Pilsen. He learned trumpet as a boy and soon was sought after for his unique style both on that instrument and the flugelhorn. After serving in World War I, Bláha replaced trumpeter Karel Vacek in the famous R. A. Dvorský Orchestra in Prague. After World War II, Bláha conducted his own band until his death in 1951.

Bláha was prodigious as a songwriter in the *lidovka* style, penning both the words and music. Although criticized in modern times for being frivolous and sentimental, his songs were true to the *lidovka* style and have had enormous staying power at home and abroad. His polkas include "Jetelíček u vody," "Kdo tě bude milovat," "Muzikanti pojďte hrát," and "Včera jsem tě čekala." His most famous waltz, "Červená sukýnka," was recorded on the Esta label and sung by the Bajo Trio with the Esta Orchestra conducted by Sláva Mach (1902–70). Slovenian-American Frankie Yankovic recorded it in the United States for Columbia Records in 1949. The retitled "Blue Skirt Waltz," with words by Mitchell Parish, was a best-seller in the United States for six months and the biggest hit for the American accordionist and bandleader.

Other pioneers of *lidovka* include Václav Vačkár (1881–1954), whose nickname was the "Daddy of Czech Musicians";[47] Antonín Borovička (1895–1968), called one of the "Three Kings of Brass Band Music" (together with Josef Poncar and Jaromír Vejvoda);[48] and Karel Valdauf (1913–82), whose original career was as a police inspector, and whose large body of songs reached many countries through recordings.

Another genre that began in the 1910s and featured frequently on the radio was *trampská muzika* ("tramping" or "scouting" music). Close to *lidovka* in melody and sometimes in text, the roots and instrumentation of this music were in North American western and rural ballads. The "Tramps" or "Scouts" even had a headquarters community, Ztracenka (Lost Hope), which was situated at the St. John's Currents of the Vltava River. Important songwriters in this style included Jaroslav Mottl (1900–86) and Karel Vacek (1902–82), formerly of the R. A. Dvorský Orchestra.

In September 1938, Nazi Germany annexed the Sudetenland, and the following year it annexed the rest of Bohemia. Moravia became a protectorate of Germany. To quote the author Milan Koukal, "For most of the duration of the occupation, wind bands, mostly rural, continued to play at balls and various legal festivities . . . without [wind bands] one could not cope with funerals, weddings and the like."[49] However, the German agents in charge of such festivities often controlled the music and prohibited songs written by Jews. Surprisingly and fortunately, the brass band and *lidovka* music were never officially condemned outright by the occupation forces and continued to be played frequently on the radio. Perhaps the style of the music was close enough to that of German popular music that no denunciation seemed necessary. Whatever the reason, the prevalence of *lidovka* was invaluable for the morale of the imperiled Czechs. Furthermore, as grandiosity was standard for the Third Reich, it made sure that the wind band concerts in Prague's Lucerna Theatre continued to grow, until one concert was played by a band of two hundred members and conducted by twenty different composers![50] Just as surprising, the prisoners of several infamous concentration camps, including Dachau, Terezín (Theresienstadt), Mauthausen, and Sachsenhausen, were allowed to form bands and play *lidovka* and other types of music. At times, the prisoners even succeeded in playing prohibited music such as melodies associated with the *verboten* Sokol organization. In 1945, all of Czechoslovakia was freed from German occupation by the Allied forces, namely Russian and American troops. On May 8, 1945, the Axis powers in Europe surrendered.

After World War II, Germans in Czechoslovakia, including German musicians, were forced to leave. This left a demand for musicians; however, most of them could not return to their old bands, since in the new Czechoslovak Socialist Republic, the Communist Party did not allow for the privatization of bands, publishing, or recording. Jaroslav Vejvoda's fate during this era was mentioned above. The Communist Party also impacted and eventually ended the career of the modern Renaissance figure Rudolf Antonín Dvorský (1899–1966). The much-loved Dvorský started in the cabaret circuit and soon became a star and national treasure as a singer, motion-picture actor, composer, conductor, and publisher. (Recall that both Karel Vacek and Václav Bláha got their start in Dvorský's Prague orchestra.) Dvorský's later band, the Melody Boys, met with even greater success than his orchestra despite the control of communism. In 1950, Dvorský and members of his band attempted to emigrate from Czechoslovakia. The effort failed, and Dvorský was imprisoned for three years. Afterward, he was officially an enemy of the state, and his career became a mere shadow of his earlier greatness.

Still in the communist era, other musicians and brass bands with the necessary ties to the Communist Party prospered and continued the *lidovka* tradition in grand style. Ladislav Kubeš (1946–2017), a classically trained musician, conducted the seemingly eternal band Veselka. His father handed the baton to Ladislav, and at the end of his career, he handed it down to his own son. Jan Slabák (born 1941) was a weekly television presence who conducted the highly popular *dechovka* band Moravanka. He also left a tremendous discography. Václav Hybš (born 1935) and his orchestra were even more prolific, as their recordings spanned the years 1971–2007. Hybš played many styles of music and a broad range of dance music, including *lidovka*. He frequently featured the most famous Czech vocalists from several generations and genres as well as the violinist Josef Suk.

After the Velvet Revolution of 1989, all types of music were exchanged into and from the reformed democratic Republic of Czechoslovakia (later the Czech Republic and the independent democratic Republic of Slovakia). Many musicians who lived near the German and Austrian borders played a wide variety of music in those countries, including *lidovka*. The neighbors were happy to get excellent Czech musicians at bargain prices. New brass bands emerged, including ensembles of great quality. Unfortunately, lesser musicians also began to appear regularly on the Czech cable channel Šlágr TV as well. This much-reviled channel still exists and amounts to an endless infomercial that feebly attempts to lure older generations to purchase *lidovka* recordings. Fortunately, the artists represented have significantly improved in recent years. Despite the jeers that Šlágr TV receives from Czechs as they flip through their television channels, the tradition of the brass band and *lidovka* is alive and well in the twenty-first century. This was especially evident at Prague's Sazka Arena in a *dechovka* festival of October 7, 2006, which featured sixteen Czech and Slovak brass bands and was witnessed by an audience of 10,000 fans.[51]

3 CZECH SONGS IN TEXAS

1. A já sám *All by Myself*

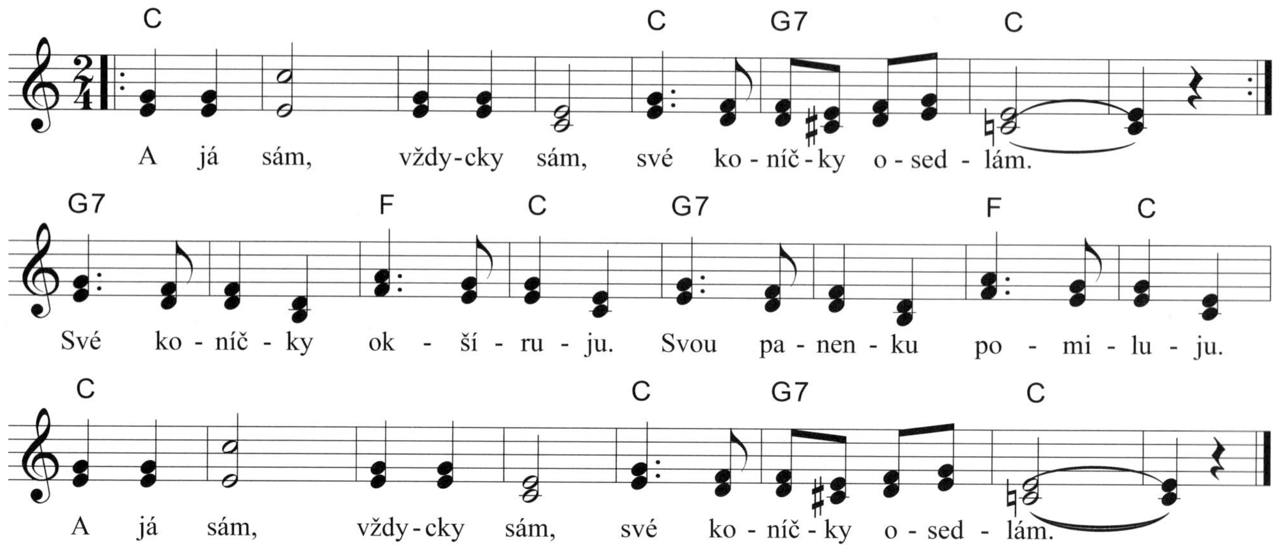

A já sám

1. A já sám, vždycky sám,
své koníčky osedlám.
A já sám, vždycky sám,
své koníčky osedlám.
Své koníčky okšíruju.
Svou panenku pomiluju.
A já sám, vždycky sám,
své koníčky osedlám.

2. Co je moc? To je moc,
čtyři koně na starost.
Co je moc? To je moc,
čtyři koně na starost.
Čtyři koně okšíruju.
Svou Mařenku pomiluju.
Co je moc? To je moc,
čtyři koně na starost.

And I Alone

1. And I alone, always alone,
saddle my horses.
And I alone, always alone,
saddle my horses.
I comb my horses,
I love my sweetheart.
And I alone, always alone,
saddle my horses.

2. What's too much? It's too much,
four horses to care for.
What's too much? It's too much,
four horses to care for.
I comb my four horses,
I love my Mary.
What's too much? It's too much,
four horses to care for.

English Lyrics

All alone, by myself,
with my horse and no one else.
All alone, by myself,
just my horse and no one else.
First you loved me, then you left me.
Where did you go to forget me?
All alone, by myself,
just my horse and no one else

Folk origins; Erben, *Prostonárodní české písně a říkadla* (1864), 415, and Novotný, *Bechyňské písně*, 53. Words and music from Taylor Czech Chorus, "A já sám," *Songs of Our Heritage* (Taylor: 2007), CD. Music (trio only) from "A já sám Pochod" by F. Krejčík, arranged by Maresh (Cleveland: Maresh Music Co., 1914). English lyrics by Cenobio Xavier "Bubba" Hernandez, used with permission.

This traditionally one-verse song from southern Bohemia about a young man who cares for his horses and misses his sweetheart is an old Czech folk song. Part of its appeal lies in the mystery of why the man is alone, a puzzle that invites speculation. The author of one Czech folk song collection provides an answer by categorizing it as a song about the life of a soldier.[1] Another includes it in his section on agriculture and rural life.[2]

The text to the first verse of "A já sám" was published in 1864 by the Bohemian Czech poet and folklorist Karel Jaromír Erben.[3] The lyrics have remained the same, with minor word changes, from that time. Several melodies are associated with the song, but the best known was collected by Václav Juda Novotný in Bechyně, a small town about seventy-five miles south of Prague.[4] This folk tune, which is the basis for the melody known in Texas, can be found in many songbooks in the Czech Republic, including textbooks for elementary school students.

In Texas, "A já sám" is most at home in dance halls and at other social gatherings, played as a rousing polka. This energized arrangement of the Novotný melody comes from a nineteenth-century march composed by František Krejčík from near Prague in which "A já sám" functions as the lyrical trio.[5] The Ennis band Czech and Then Some recorded the several-part composition on their 2009 CD, *A Tribute: 10 Years of Polka Music*,[6] but most groups perform the trio section only. When the polka musician Alfred Vrazel from Buckholts was asked how many times he had played "A já sám," he just laughed and said, "A whole lot. It's the standard polka."[7]

Vrazels' Polka Band, founded and led by brothers Alfred and Anton Vrazel, retired in 2008 after a fifty-five-year run. Alfred is one of the Texans who sings the second verse in which the young man confides how much he loves his Mary but also complains about how much work it is to care for horses. The Vrazels recorded both verses in 2003 on their fiftieth-anniversary CD, a track that was reissued by Jimmy Brosch on the CD that accompanies the book he and Theresa Cernoch Parker published in 2011, called *Jimmy Brosch Remembers Twenty Legendary Texas Czech Polka Bands*.[8] The Taylor Czech Chorus, which has been together since 1967, included both verses on its 2007 CD called *Songs of Our Heritage*.[9]

The English lyrics are by Cenobio Xavier "Bubba" Hernandez, a former bassist and singer for Brave Combo, the self-identified "nuclear polka" band from Denton founded in 1979 by bandleader Carl Finch. The band recorded "A já sám" in both Czech and English on its twenty-fifth-anniversary album *Let's Kiss*, winner of the Grammy award for best polka album in 2005. Hernandez gives another reason for the young man's solitude—his sweetheart has run off and left him alone, with only his "horse and no one else."[10]

2. Aj, lučka, lučka *Green Meadow Polka; Oh, Meadow Polka*

Aj, lučka, lučka

1. Aj, lučka, lučka široká!
Roste na ní tráva, roste na ní tráva.
Aj, lučka, lučka široká!
Roste na ní tráva vysoká. Hej!
Chorus:
Teče voda z hora, čistá je jako já.
Točí se dokola okola javora.
Teče voda z hora, čistá je jako já.
Točí se dokola okolo mňa.

2. Žaly tam na ní dvě panny,
obě žalostně, obě žalostně.
Žaly tam na ní dvě panny,
obě žalostně plakaly. Hej!

Oh, Meadow, Meadow

1. Oh, meadow, meadow wide!
The grass grows in it, the grass grows in it.
Oh, meadow, meadow wide!
The tall grass grows in it. Hey!
Chorus:
Water flows from above. It is pure as I am.
It turns around, around the maple tree.
Water flows from above. It is pure as I am.
It turns around, around me.

2. Two ladies were harvesting there;
both were in grief, both were in grief.
Two ladies were harvesting there;
both in grief were crying. Hey!

3. Díval se na ně z hradu pán,
na své pachole, na své pachole.
Díval se na ně z hradu pán,
na své pachole zavolal. Hej!

4. Vstávej pachole, stroj koně,
pojedeme spolu, pojedeme spolu.
Vstávej pachole, stroj koně,
pojedeme spolu do boje. Hej!

5. A co tam budem dělati?
Nemáme flinty, nemáme flinty.
A co tam budem dělati?
Nemáme flinty nabitý. Hej!

6. Budem tam honit děvčata,
osmnáctiletá, osmnáctiletá.
Budem tam honit děvčata,
osmnáctiletá poupátka. Hej!

3. The nobleman was watching his servants
from the castle, from the castle.
The nobleman was watching his servants
from the castle, he called to them. Hey!

4. Get up, servant, harness the horses,
We'll go together, we'll go together.
Get up, servant, harness the horses,
we'll go together to battle. Hey!

5. And what are we going to do there?
We don't have guns, we don't have guns.
And what are we going to do there?
We don't have loaded guns. Hey!

6. We'll chase girls there,
eighteen-year-olds, eighteen-year-olds.
We'll chase girls there,
eighteen-year-old flower buds. Hey!

Unknown origins. Words from Bartoš and Bartoš, *Spivejme pisničky*, 112–14. Music from Atherton, *Oblíbené písně*, 1–3.

"Aj, lučka, lučka" is one of forty-five songs published in a 1921 songbook called *Oblíbené písně našich hochů v Česko-Slovenské armádě v Rusku* (Favorite songs of the Čecho-Slovak Army in Russia).[1] This songbook commemorates the experiences of World War I Czech and Slovak soldiers who deserted the Austrian army and joined Allied military units, known as the Czech Legions, and fought against Austria-Hungary. They were organized under the leadership of the Czech exile Tomáš G. Masaryk. When the independent nation of Czechoslovakia was formed after the war, many of the Legionnaires took leading roles in the new country. Masaryk became the nation's first president, and the Czech Legions became the basis of its national army.[2]

The songbook was compiled by Charles Atherton, music director of the Jan Hus Bohemian Presbyterian Church in New York City. In 1917, Atherton joined the Legionnaires in Russia as a volunteer with the international Young Men's Christian Association (YMCA), an aid group. In the book's foreword, he says the soldiers sang these songs day after day, in their camps and also on their fraught journey across Siberia as they made their way to the Western Front.[3] Atherton's "Aj, lučka, lučka" also became a favorite choral piece with glee clubs in America such as Yale University's Whiffenpoofs and other choirs and singing societies.

The song, of unknown origins, is widely known in Slovakia and the Czech Republic as a folk song. It begins with a description of a pristine meadow but turns into a vignette of two servants being ordered by their master to accompany him to a battleground. Two weeping women watch this scene unfold while the servants respond by joking about what awaits them at the battle. We are left to wonder if this is naive behavior on the servants' part or subversive slapstick, the kind of Czech humor exemplified by Jaroslav Hašek's book *The Good Soldier Švejk*. This darkly satirical war novel from the early 1920s chronicles the life of the Czech soldier Josef Švejk, who was drafted into the Austrian army in World War I, as the novelist himself had been. The book is credited with inspiring Joseph Heller's *Catch 22* among other classics.[4]

The Joe Patek Orchestra of Shiner, Texas, released the first two verses and chorus of "Oh! Meadow" as a 45 rpm in 1963.[5] The Jodie Mikula Orchestra of Ennis released "Meadow Polka" on its 1973 LP, *From the Good Old Days*.[6] Dujka Brothers of Brenham, Texas, sang "Oh, Meadow Polka" in Czech and English on their 2008 CD, *Shining Up Old Favorites*.[7] "Green Meadow Polka" was released by the All Around Czechs, a young band from West, on their first CD in 2016 called *Where It Began*.[8]

3. Andulko šafářova *Annie the Foreman; Annie the Foreman's Daughter; Caretaker's Annie*

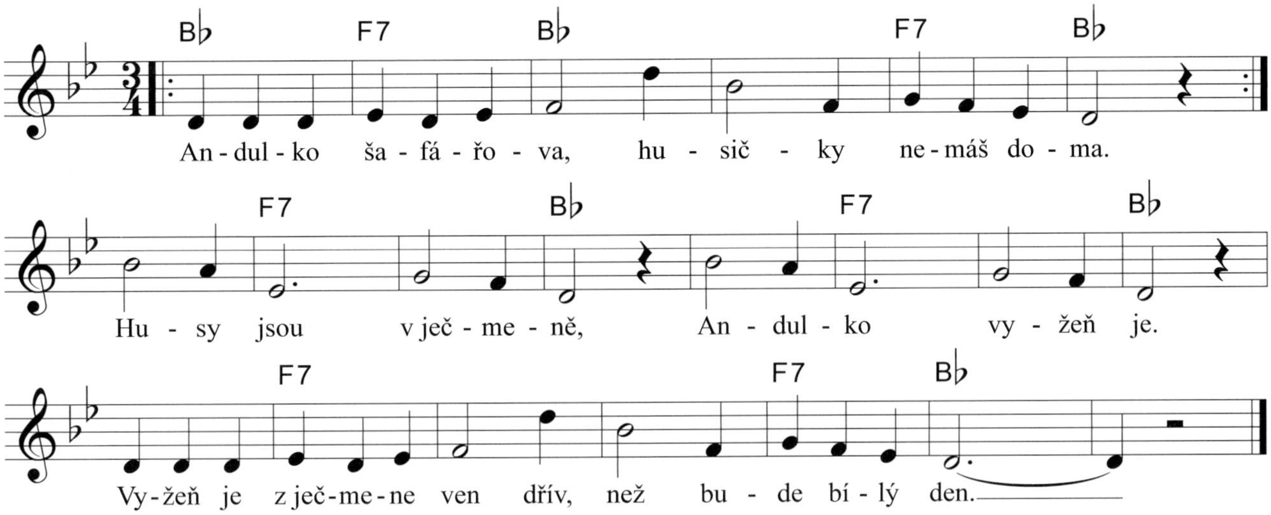

Andulko šafářova

1. Andulko šafářova,
husičky nemáš doma.
Husy jsou v ječmeně,
Andulko vyžeň je.
Vyžeň je z ječmene ven
dřív, než bude bílý den.

2. Já bych je ven vyhnala,
jen kdybych se nebála.
Paňmáma lehce spí,
jak vstanu, se vzbudí.
Já nesmím z komůrky ven
dřív, než bude bílý den.

3. Andulko šafářova,
jen nebuď' tak bláhová.
Z paňmámy neměj strach,
musíš jít po špičkách.
Vyklouzneš z komůrky ven,
dřív, než bude bílý den.

Annie of the Foreman

1. Annie of the foreman,
you don't have the geese at home.
The geese are in the barley.
Annie, drive them away.
Drive them out from the barley
before the break of day.

2. I would drive them out
if only I weren't afraid.
My mistress sleeps lightly,
she knows my every move.
I am not allowed to leave my room
before the break of day.

3. Annie of the foreman,
just don't be so naive.
Don't be afraid of your mistress.
You must go up the stairs.
You will slip out from your chamber
before the break of day.

4. Jeníčku můj, rozmilý,
nemohu ni na chvíli.
Tam ti je pantáta.
Leh' si hned za vrata.
Vrznou-li ty vratka jen,
hned na nás přiběhne sem.

5. Andulko šafářova,
pantáta není doma.
Ten sedí u džbánu,
vrátí se až k ránu,
z hospody nepůjde ven,
dřív, než bude bílý den.

6. Jeníčku můj rozmilý,
já přijdu ven na chvíli.
Paňmáma tvrdě spí.
Ta se již nevzbudí.
Bude mít nejhezčí sen
dřív, než bude bílý den.

7. Andulko šafářova,
neříkej ani slova
že jsme se líbali,
ve tmě se scházeli.
Neříkej, že jsem vinen,
že jsem tě vylákal.

4. My dear Johnny,
I can't do so, not even for a moment.
The master there
is lying right behind the gate.
If the gate squeaks
he will run here right away.

5. Annie of the foreman,
the master is not home.
He is sitting with a pitcher,
he will return at dawn.
He won't leave the tavern
until the break of day.

6. My dear Johnny,
I'll come out for a moment.
My mistress sleeps lightly.
It won't wake her.
She'll have the most beautiful dream
before the break of day.

7. Annie of the foreman,
don't say a word
that we kissed,
in the dark we met.
Don't say I am to blame
for luring you out.

Folk origins; Novotný, *Bechyňské písně*, 6. Words from Bartoš and Bartoš, *Spivejme pisničky*, 110–11. Waltz music from Novotný, *Bechyňské písně*, 6.

In the late 1800s, Václav Novotný, a Prague composer and influential music journalist, spent a summer holiday in Bechyně, a small town in southern Bohemia. One evening, a friend took him to a local pub to hear a folksinger. Novotný, enchanted by the songs, wrote down the words and music to fifteen of them that evening. A few days later, he followed the folksinger to a small village a few miles south called Hodonice. There he transcribed more songs, including the endearing "Andulko šafářova." Novotný published *Bechyňské písně* in 1900, a book of fifty songs that had its start at that pub in Bechyně.[1]

The title "Andulko šafářova" is literally translated as "Foreman's Annie" or "Annie of the Foreman." The possessive grammatical construction describes Andulka's subservient status, that she "belongs" to the šafář or foreman.[2] The song has acquired several English titles, including "Annie the Foreman" and "Annie the Foreman's Daughter." Another English title, from Vitak-Elsnic, is "Caretaker's Annie."[3]

Two versions of the melody are known in Texas. The waltz is the one Novotný learned from the singer in Hodonice and is well known in the Czech Republic today. Novotný published two verses, the same as the first two in this songbook. But several other verses, of unknown origins, are also found in Texas. They all tell the story of Annie, a girl who herds the geese and lives in a farmhouse. A boy named Johnny calls for her to come outside, saying that the geese are in the barley. Annie replies that she cannot leave the house before daybreak because her mistress watches her closely. Eventually, Annie does go outside. But she goes to see Johnny, not to chase the geese out of the barley.

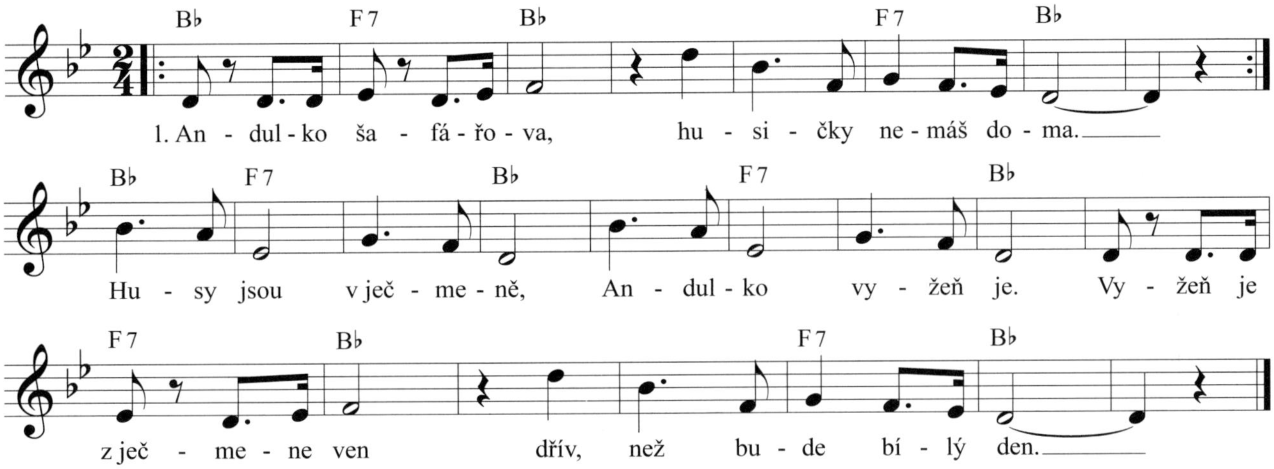

Music, trio only, by František Kmoch (Prague: Mojmír Urbánek, 1903).

In Texas, "Andulko šafářova" is usually sung as a polka or played as an instrumental march. This version comes from the brass band composition by František Kmoch first published in Prague in 1903. Kmoch changed the waltz to march time and used it as the trio, or lyrical section, of his band composition.[4] The trios were also easily adapted to accompany the dance that was widely popular at the time—the polka.

"Andulko šafářova" was one of the first recordings made by a Texas Czech band. In San Antonio on June 19, 1929, the Baca Orchestra of Fayetteville, under the name Bačova Česka Kapela (Baca Czech Band), recorded an instrumental version of the Kmoch march for Columbia Records.[5] The recording includes musical flourishes played on a string instrument called a *cimbál*.[6] The cimbalom, or hammered dulcimer, two English terms for the instrument, was popular in nineteenth-century Moravia, and a number of Texas polka bands included it in their instrumental lineup.[7] Ray Krenek of Wallis, another Texas dulcimer player, recorded the song under the title "Happy Annie." It was released on a late-1960s album and featured the Kmoch version played by Krenek's nine-piece dance orchestra, with Krenek on dulcimer.[8] Two other recordings are by Houston's SPJST Lodge 88 Choral Group and Orchestra on their 1978 album, *Czech Folksongs*,[9] and Lee Roy Matocha Orchestra of Fayetteville on its 1982 cassette tape, *Red Hot and Rolling*.[10]

4. Baruška *Barbara Polka*

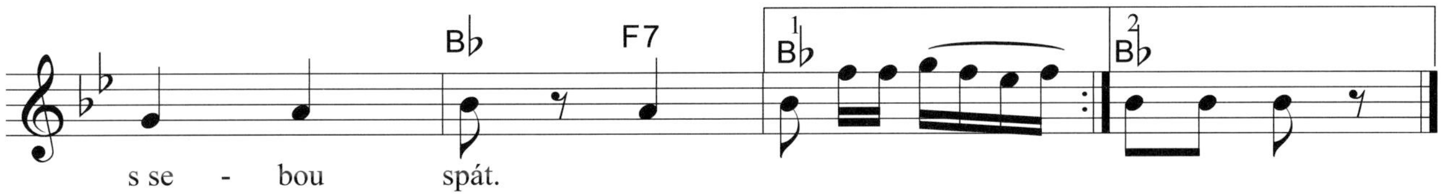

Baruška

1. Když jsem já šel do Vršovic na posvícení,
na posvícení, na posvícení,
potkal jsem tam hezkou divku, líbila se mi.
Ona byla celá bílá, ona se mi líbila.
Ona byla celá bílá, ona se mi líbila.
Chorus:
Má roztomilá Baruško,
vem mě s sebou na lůžko.
Má roztomilá Baruško,
vem mě s sebou spát.

2. Ona na to povídala, to nejde tak hned,
to nejde tak hned, to nejde tak hned,
ty jsi hoch jak malovaný snadno bys mne sved,
což jest tobě kdybych robě kolíbala na klíně.
což jest tobě kdybych robě kolíbala na klíně.
Chorus:
Můj roztomilý Pepíčku,
dej mně sladkou hubičku.
Můj roztomilý Pepíčku,
dej mně hubičku.

Barbara

1. When I came to Vršovice to go to the fair,
to go to the fair, to go to the fair,
I met there a pretty girl. I liked her.
She was all fair, I liked her.
She was all fair, I liked her.
Chorus:
My lovely Barbara,
take me to bed with you.
My lovely Barbara,
take me to sleep with you.

2. To that she replied, it can't happen that quickly,
it can't happen that quickly, it can't happen that quickly.
You're such a sweet boy, perhaps you would easily seduce me.
What is it to you if I have to rock a baby in my lap?
What is it to you if I have to rock a baby in my lap?
Chorus:
My charming Joey,
give me a sweet kiss.
My charming Joey,
give me a kiss.

Words and music from "Barbara Polka, Baruška," by František Kovářík (Chicago: Georgi and Vitak, 191?).

In "Baruška," also known as "Barbara Polka," two young people meet at a fair in Vršovice, a lively, very old section of Prague. Joey expresses his immediate and intense attraction to Barbara. She responds with a mix of practical cautiousness and clear desire, a tension that enlivens the song. "Baruška" appeared in America as early as 1905 in *Bohemian Melodies,* a book of four songs arranged for two violins and piano by Anthony L. Maresh, owner of Cleveland's Maresh Music Company.[1] A popular polka, it was also published in the 1910s by Chicago music companies Joseph Jiran, Aloysius J. Turek, and Georgi and Vitak, the latter citing František Kovářík as songwriter.[2]

Kovářík (1858–1936) was a bandleader and composer from Čelakovice, a town located about twenty-five miles northeast of Prague. A self-taught musician, he began composing popular songs and marches at age twenty-nine. At some point, Kovářík spent two years in Baltimore before returning to Bohemia, where he lived the rest of his life.[3] His son, also named František Kovářík (1899–1948), began to publish sheet music in 1922. The Kovářík firm, along with those of Mojmír Urbánek and R. A. Dvorský, became the three largest popular music publishers in Prague during the 1930s and 1940s.[4]

Adolph Hofner and His Bohemians of San Antonio recorded "Baruška Polka" for Columbia Records in a 1942 session in Hollywood that was released after World War II.[5] The band later recorded another take that was released by Imperial under the name "Barbara Polka." This version is well known, especially after being reissued in a 1993 Arhoolie collection called *Texas-Czech, Bohemian, and Moravian Bands: Historic Recordings 1929–1959*.[6] The Arhoolie CD included another swinging version of "Barbara Polka," this one a fiddle-heavy instrumental from West Texas by Benny Brosh and His Orchestra. Brosh was from Rowena, a small town about halfway between Lubbock and Austin. This area hosts a number of people with Czech and German ancestry who came in the early 1900s in search of farmland.[7] The Brosh recording was first released about 1950 by Humming Bird Records, a Waco company.[8]

The Galveston-based Czech Heritage Singers, directed by Fr. Paul Chovanec and accompanied by four accordions, clarinet, bass horn, and drums, included all the "Baruška" lyrics on their 1981 self-titled LP.[9] Ray Zapletal, one of the founders of the Ennis National Polka Festival, recorded an instrumental in the 1960s.[10] Julius Tupa, who established the monthly *Texas Polka News* in 1987, included an instrumental "Barbara Polka" on his band's LP *Songs I'll Always Remember* from the 1970s.[11]

5. Bolí, bolí *Headache Waltz*

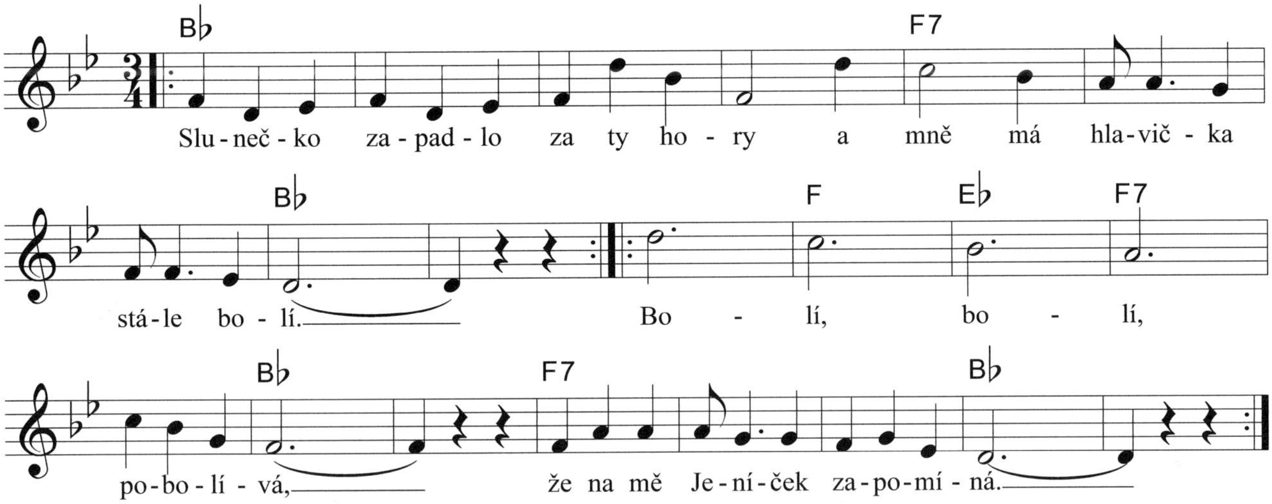

Bolí, bolí

1. Slunečko zapadlo za ty hory
a mně má hlavička stále bolí.
Bolí, bolí, pobolívá,
že na mě Jeníček zapomíná.

2. Když tvoji rodiče takoví jsou,
bohatou nevěstu pro tebe chcou.
Bohatou a tu si vezmeš
a na mě chudobnou zapomeneš.

3. Když jsem tě, nedostal za manželku,
tak si tě vyvolím za družičku.
Za družičku nejprvnější,
protože's mi byla nejvěrnější.

4. To se ti Jeníčku nemůže stát,
nemohla bych pro pláč v kostele stát,
v kostele stát, k oltáři jít.
Nemohla bych pro pláč věneček mít.

It Hurts, It Hurts

1. The sun set behind the mountains
and my head is still hurting me.
It hurts, it hurts, it keeps on hurting
because my Johnny is forgetting me.

2. Since your parents are so particular
they want a rich bride for you.
She'll be rich and you'll choose her
and you'll forget about poor me.

3. Since I didn't get you as my wife
I choose you to be a bridesmaid,
to be the first bridesmaid
since you were the truest to me.

4. This, Johnny, cannot happen.
I couldn't stand in church because of my crying,
stand in church or go to the altar.
I couldn't hold a wreath because of my crying.

Unknown origins. Words to verses 1 and 3 and music from Jimmy Brosch and His Happy Country Boys, "Bolí, bolí" (Houston: Guide, circa 1968), 45 rpm; reissued on *Jimmy Brosch's Collection* (Houston: 2000), CD. Verses 2 and 4 from Bartoš and Bartoš, *Spivejme pisničky*, 31.

Jimmy Brosch and His Happy Country Boys were known for playing this sad song, one of the standard Czech waltzes in Texas, which they recorded in the late 1960s. Brosch first heard the song in his Fayette County hometown of Praha at Firasek's Store. His wife, Lucy, said the store was behind the cotton gin and was a place that sold general merchandise and cold beer. The store also had tables where people would meet, visit, play dominoes, sing songs, and sometimes listen to records that Mr. Firasek would play. It was in this environment that Brosch learned the song.[1]

"Bolí, bolí" is also known as "Headache Waltz." A young woman says that her head hurts because her Johnny has forgotten her. The form is a dialogue between a girl and a boy that reveals the reason for her broken heart. She says his parents will not allow them to marry because she comes from a poor family and they want "a rich bride" for him. Johnny is resigned to his fate and asks her to be "the first bridesmaid" at his wedding to someone else. The song ends with the poor girl in misery as she lists the reasons why she cannot join his wedding party.

One can find a number of songs in early Czech and Slovak folk collections that use images of the sun setting behind the mountains to signify the end of a relationship and a headache to describe the pain such a break causes. Olga Pazdral, who was a high school history teacher in West, Texas, includes one of these songs, collected by the Bohemian folklorist Karel Jaromír Erben, in her 1942 master's thesis titled "Czech Folklore in Texas." In this song, which Pazdral calls "Why My Poor Head Aches," the girl is the one who forgets the boy, and it is he who has a headache.[2]

Jimmy Brosch and His Happy Country Boys of Houston recorded the first and third verses of "Bolí, bolí" about 1968.[3] Brosch sings the first two lines of each verse and the whole band sings the last two lines. The call-and-response vocal arrangement is appropriate for the dialogue song as is the plaintive wail of the steel guitar. Two other arrangements are by the Ray Krenek Orchestra of Wallis, featuring the sounds of Ray's hammered dulcimer,[4] and one from the 1960s by the Leo Majek Orchestra of Corpus Christi.[5] The Lee Roy Matocha Orchestra of Fayetteville included "Headache Waltz" on its late-1960s album *By Special Request* and then again on a 1997 live recording called *50 Years of Accordion Music*.[6] Ray Zapletal and His Music Masters included "Headache Waltz" on their 1960s LP called *Bluebonnet Czech*.[7] A few more examples are the 2001 CD *Grandpa's List* by the Dujka Brothers of Brenham,[8] the 2012 CD *Play Old Time Music* by Czech and Then Some of Ennis,[9] and the 2015 CD *Czech, Please* by the Czech Melody Masters of Taylor and Austin.[10]

6. Brána malovaná *Painted Gate Polka; Garden Gate Polka*

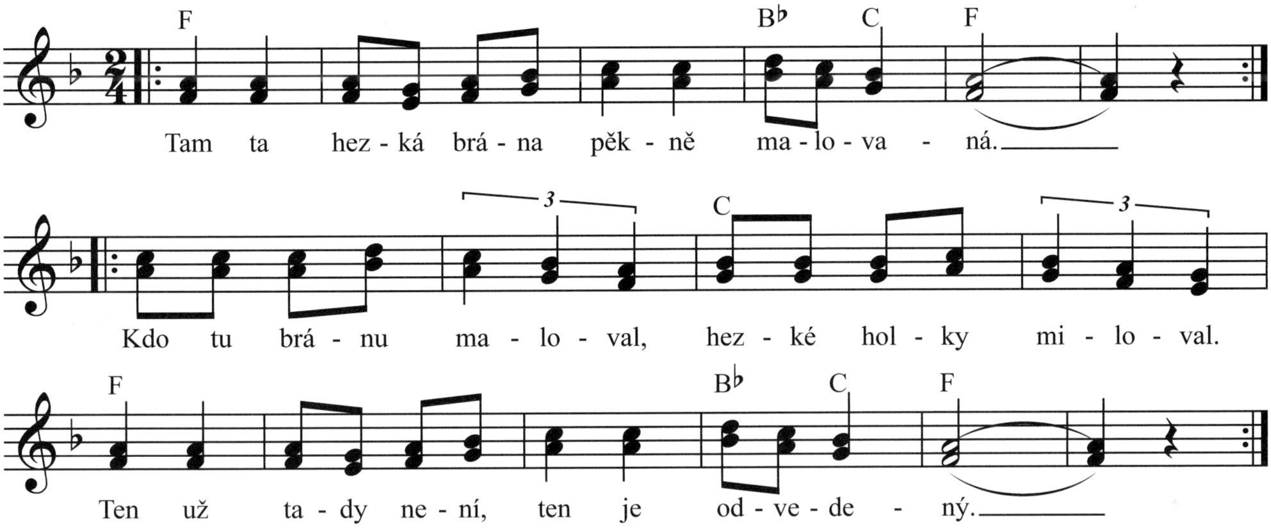

Brána malovaná

1. Tam ta hezká brána pěkně malovaná.
   Kdo tu bránu maloval, hezký holky miloval.
   Ten už tady není, ten je odvedený.

2. Ten je odvedený, na to nezapomeň.
   Ty budeš Anduličko, ty budeš Anduličko,
   plakati pro něho, plakati pro něho.

3. To ti nepomůže plakati pro něho.
   Ty budeš Anduličko, ty budeš Anduličko,
   jak ta zvadlá růže, jak ta zvadlá růže.

Painted Gate

1. There is a pretty gate, nicely painted.
   Whoever painted that gate loved pretty girls.
   He is no longer here, he has been recruited.

2. He has been recruited, don't ever forget.
   You will, Annie, you will, Annie,
   you will cry for him, you will cry for him.

3. It will not help you to cry for him.
   You will be, Annie, you will be, Annie,
   you will be like a wilted rose, like a wilted rose.

Folk origins. Erben, *Pjsně národnj w Čechách,* 1:208, and Sládek, *Náš poklad*, 126. Words from Taylor Czech Chorus, *Still . . . Carrying on the Tradition* (Taylor: 2018), CD. Music from Vrazels' Polka Band, *Greatest Hits: Vol. 2* (Buckholts, TX: VPB 517, 2002), CD.

In "Brána malovaná," or "Painted Gate Polka," a young man who has painted a pretty gate has been recruited as a soldier, but he leaves behind someone special, Annie. The lyrics tell us that she will cry for him and be "like a wilted rose." The melody of this sad soldier's song is an upbeat polka.

The song is one of a large group of related Czech songs that feature a pretty painted gate and a soldier parting from loved ones. Many of these songs feature the name of a town or region, for example, "Ta moravská brána" (That Moravian Gate), published by Karel Jaromír Erben in 1842.[1] Another variant, called "Domažlická brána," referring to the western Bohemian town of Domažlice, is one of several songs featured in Jaroslav Hašek's World War I novel *The Good Soldier Švejk.*[2]

The melody for "Brána malovaná" is derived from "Poděbradská brána" (The Gate of Poděbrady), published in the 1890s by Ferdinand Sládek.[3] Professor Svatava Pírková Jakobson, a University of Texas at Austin Czech teacher and folklorist in the 1970s, describes the Poděbrady version of the song in her 1943 work with Alan Lomax on World War II songs. She calls it "a soldier folk song from the town where the most famous king of Bohemia was born—George of Poděbrady." She goes on to explain the lyrics: "There are horses painted on the gate of Poděbrady. The man who did the job loved the girls, but he is no longer here. He's been drafted and he's saying, 'Have a good time, beautiful girls; when you go to the dance, remember the gay times we had.'"[4]

Under the title "Garden Gate Polka," the song was released by the Red Ravens of El Campo in 1981 on their cassette tape *Polka Better.*[5] Wence and Helen Shimek sang a duet on their 1984 cassette tape, *Wence and Helen Present More Polkas and Waltzes.*[6] Mark Halata and Texavia of Houston included "Painted Gate Polka" on the 2003 CD *Moon over Moravia.*[7] Leroy Rybak's Swinging Orchestra of Hallettsville included "Painted Gate Polka" on the 2006 CD *Polka and Waltz Classics.*[8] Vrazels' Polka Band of Buckholts reissued an earlier recording of the song on their 2002 CD, *Greatest Hits, Vol. 2.*[9] Taylor Czech Chorus, founded in 1967, included "Malovaná brána" on its 2018 CD, *Still . . . Carrying On the Tradition.*[10]

7. Červená a bílá *Red and White*

Červená a bílá

1. Vždycky se mně líbívalo
   tvé jméno Mařenka.
   Za rok se změnily časy,
   ty už jsi maminka.
   Chorus:
   Červený, bílý, to se mně líbí,
   to já, to já mám rád.
   Červený, bílý, to se mně líbí,
   to já, to já mám rád.

2. Vždycky se mně líbívalo
   tvé jméno Pepíček.
   Za rok se změnily časy,
   ty už jsi tatíček.

Red and White

1. I always have liked
   your name, Mary.
   After a year times have changed you,
   you're already a mother.
   Chorus:
   Red and white, I like that,
   I do, I do like it.
   Red and white, I like that,
   I do, I do like it.

2. I always have liked
   your name, Joey.
   After a year times have changed,
   you're already a father.

3. Vždycky se mě líbívala,
červená mašle v hlavě.
Za rok se změnily časy,
kluk ji má v poviáně.

3. I always have liked
a red ribbon in hair.
After a year, the times have changed,
The boy has swathed her.

Folk origins. Erben, *Prostonárodní české písně a říkadla* (1864), 140. Words and music (trio section only) from "Červená a Bílá," arranged for voice and piano by Louis Vitak (Chicago: Georgi and Vitak, 1922).

The words of the chorus to "Červená a bílá" are derived from a folk text collected in southern Bohemia and published in Karel Jaromír Erben's 1864 folk song collection.[1] The song has long been associated with what is now SK Slavia Praha, one of the major *fotbal* (soccer) teams in the Czech Republic. Slavia, known as the Červenobílí (Red and Whites), was founded in 1893 during a period of heightened nationalism. The song, with chorus and only one verse, is an old unofficial anthem of the team.[2]

From Erben's earliest version, the song has featured two colors, red and white. These are the colors of the Bohemian coat of arms from the twelfth century, a two-tailed white lion against a red background. The lion symbol is still used today, both officially and as a stand-in for Czechness, and the red and white colors are featured on the current national flag. After World War I, the first flag adopted by the new nation of Czechoslovakia was a white stripe over one of red. The current flag, a triangle of blue that intersects the white and red stripes, was settled on in 1920.[3] The song, because of these colors, can carry additional connotations of identity.

In America, Joseph Jiran music publishing company of Chicago copyrighted an orchestral arrangement of the song by Anton Grill in December 1921. A few months later, it was recorded by Victor Orchestra and released as a 78 rpm record.[4] In 1922, Louis Vitak of Chicago brought out the version with the three verses widely known in Texas. In the Vitak verses, a young couple reviews the changes brought about by their first year of marriage, especially their new role as parents of a baby. In the last line, the boy has wrapped their baby in a swaddling blanket.

Baca Orchestra of Fayetteville, under the name Bačova Česka Kapela, recorded an instrumental version of "Červená a bílá" for Columbia Records in 1930.[5] The performance features Ray Baca weaving ethereal strains of his hammered dulcimer, also called cimbalom, through the brass instruments. Gary Krupala, a member of the Taylor Czech Chorus, says he decided to build his own dulcimer after he heard Ray's playing on the Baca Orchestra's recording.[6]

The Bill Mraz Orchestra included an instrumental "Red and White Waltz" on its first LP, *Festival Album*, released sometime in the 1950s. Mraz owned, managed, cooked, and performed in the Bill Mraz Ballroom in Houston, one of the most popular polka hot spots in the state, from 1948 until his death in 1975.[7] The Lee Roy Matocha Orchestra of Fayetteville released "Red and White" on its mid-1960s LP, *Let's Dance with Lee Roy*. This was the first album Matocha made after organizing his own orchestra in 1964. Alfred Vrazel says the Matocha recording largely popularized the tune in Texas.[8] The East Bernard Czech Singers, the female choir from the farming community close to Houston, sang "Red and White Waltz" on their 2000 CD, *Our Best to You*.[9] The Bellville Lazy Farmers included "Red and White" on their 2008 CD, *New Sounds*. It was recorded live in Coshatte Agricultural Society Hall, the historic octagonal structure built in 1928, located outside of Bellville in the Coshatte community.[10] The Czech Melody Masters of Taylor and Austin sang two verses on their 2015 CD, *Czech, Please*.[11]

8. Červená růžičko *Red Rose Polka*

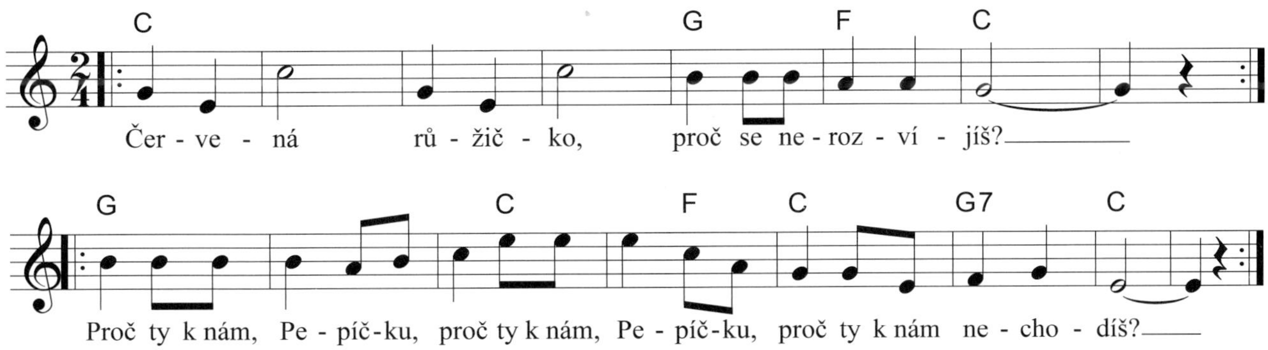

Červená růžičko

1. Červená růžičko,
proč se nerozvíjíš?
Proč ty k nám, Pepíčku, proč ty k nám, Pepíčku,
proč ty k nám, nechodíš?

2. Kdybych já k vám chodil,
ty by jsi plakala.
Červeným šátečkem, červeným šátečkem,
oči utírala.

3. Proč bych já plakala,
když mě nic nebolí?
Milovali jsme se, milovali jsme se,
jako dva holubi.

4. Jako dva holubi,
jako dvě hrdličky
dávali jsem sobě, dávali jsem sobě
slad'ounké hubičky.

5. Upřímné hubičky,
falešná tvá láska.
Nebudu ti věřit, nebudu ti věřit,
až bude ohláška.

6. Až bude ohláška,
na té naší faře.
Tenkrát budu říkat, tenkrát budu říkat
bratru tvému švagre.

Red Rose

1. Red rose,
why don't you unfurl?
Why, Joey, don't you come? Why, Joey, don't you come?
Why don't you come by anymore?

2. If I were to come to your place,
you would cry.
With a red handkerchief, with a red handkerchief
you would wipe your eyes.

3. Why would I cry
when nothing hurts?
We loved each other, we loved each other,
like two doves.

4. Like two doves,
like two turtledoves
we gave one another, we gave one another
sweet kisses.

5. Sweet kisses,
untrue your love.
I won't believe you, I won't believe you
until there are banns of matrimony.

6. Until there are banns of matrimony
at our church.
Then I will call, then I will call
your brother my brother-in-law.

7. Bratru tvému švagre, matce panimámo. Budu jí líbávat, Budu jí líbávat ruce každé ráno.	*7.* To your brother my brother-in-law, to your mother my mother-in-law. I will kiss, I will kiss her hands every morning.
8. Ruce každé ráno, nohy každý večer, a to všecko proto, a to všecko proto, že jsi ty můj přece.	*8.* Her hands every morning, her feet every evening, and all of this because, and all of this because you are mine after all.

Folk origins. Erben, *Pjsně národnj w Čechách,* 1:90–91, and Vycpálek, "Vozičko v písni," 217. Words from KJT, *Sbírka českých písní,* 107–8. Music from Vycpálek, "Vozičko v písni," 217.

In "Červená růžičko," a young woman indirectly begins a conversation about matrimony with her young man by asking a red rose why it does not open. These eight verses of "Červená růžičko," with slight differences, were published in 1842 by the folklorist Karel Jaromír Erben.[1] The melody generally known today was documented by another Czech folklorist about one hundred years later, in a 1950 article in *Český lid* (Czech people).[2]

The Erben lyrics could be found in Texas at least by 1916, in a lyric booklet called *Česko-americký zpěvník* (Czech-American songbook), published by the Houston Czech-language newspaper *Texan.*[3] But the song as we know it today, with the lively polka tune, apparently came to the state in the 1970s.

Harry Czarnek and the Texas Dutchmen from Houston, who recorded "Red Rose Polka" around 1976, tell the story of how they came to know the song in their album's liner notes. At a festival in Shiner, a couple from San Antonio enthused about a song they had heard on a recent trip to what was then Czechoslovakia. The Dutchmen learned it and began playing it at their performances. They found that some audience members could sing the words because they had known them in "childhood days." The song became so popular that a 1976 dance ad in *Věstník,* the SPJST newspaper, described the Texas Dutchmen as "The Red Rose Polka Band."[4]

Vrazels' Polka Band of Buckholts included "Red Rose Polka" on their 1976 album commemorating their appearance that year at the Smithsonian Folklife Festival in Washington, D.C.[5] The Bill Mraz Orchestra of Houston recorded the song in 1977 on its LP *Polka Heritage—Made Famous.*[6] The Joe Patek Orchestra of Shiner released "Red Rose Polka" on the 1970s LP, *The Magic of Joe Patek.*[7] Mark Halata and Texavia of Houston included it on their 2007 CD, *Amerika.*[8] The Moravians of Ennis sang two verses on their 2013 CD, *Czech Spirit Will Live On.*[9]

9. Červená růžičko *Red Rose Waltz*

Červená růžičko

1. Za lesem, za vodú,
   měsíček se bělá.
   Kdybych já věděla, co můj milý dělá.
   Kdybych já věděla, co můj milý dělá.

2. Včera mi povídal,
   že dnes večer přijde,
   abych ho čekala, až měsíček vyjde,
   abych ho čekala, až měsíček vyjde.

Red Rose

1. Across the woods, across the water,
   the moon shines white.
   If only I knew what my dear one is doing.
   If only I knew what my dear one is doing.

2. Yesterday he told me
   that he will come this evening,
   that I should wait till the moon comes out,
   that I should wait till the moon comes out.

3. Měsíček již vyšel,
   můj milý nepřišel.
   Snad se mu zas jiná, lepší zalíbila.
   Snad se mu zas jiná, lepší zalíbila.

4. Červená růžičko, co se nerozvíjíš?
   Co k nám už Jeníčku, co k nám už nechodíš?
   Kdybych já k vám chodil, ty by si plakala,
   červeným šatečkem oči utírala.

3. The moon is already out,
   but my darling didn't come.
   Perhaps he took a liking to another, better than me.
   Perhaps he took a liking to another, better than me.

4. Red rose, why don't you unfurl?
   Why, Johnny, don't you come, why don't you come by anymore?
   If I were to come to your place, you would cry,
   with a red handkerchief you would wipe your eyes.

Folk origins. Erben, *Pjsně národnj w Čechách,* 1:90–91, and Slavia, *Národní pohádky,* Series 1, part 2, 31–33). Words from KJT, *Sbírka českých písní,* 106–7. Music from Dujka Brothers, "Red Rose Waltz," *The Tradition Continues* (Brenham, TX: JED Musical Prod., 1999), CD.

In his 1968 book on Czech popular music, called *Mezi lidovou písní a šlágrem* (Between folk song and smash hit), the Czech ethnomusicologist Vladimír Karbusický calls this waltz version of "Červená růžíčko" a popular half-folk song from the nineteenth century.[1] By half-folk, Karbusický means the song uses part of an old folk text but has additional or changed verses plus a new or updated melody.

Half-folk songs are part of the development of Czech popular music: new songs, often of unknown origins, were grounded in older songs. The last verse of "Red Rose Waltz," for example, is the same as the first two verses of "Red Rose Polka," Song 8 in this volume. As pointed out there, the words of the polka were collected in the early part of the nineteenth century by the Czech folklorist Karel Jaromír Erben.[2] The first three verses of the waltz are taken from a different book of folk songs, published in 1873, that were collected by students who belonged to the literary society Slavia.[3] The newer waltz tune is different from the older folk melody. The Texas recordings of "Red Rose Waltz" typically feature the lovely melody and only the Erben verse, the fourth one. But all four verses of the waltz are included here because they appear in several lyric collections of Texas Czech songs.[4]

The Jodie Mikula Orchestra of Ennis released "Red Rose Waltz" on its 1973 album, *From the Good Old Days.*[5] Jodie, the founder of the family orchestra, learned to play accordion from a great-uncle while growing up on the family cotton farm near Ennis. He left to serve in World War II and married in 1947, soon after returning home from the war. The couple raised three sons—Ken, Nick, and Andy— all of whom became musicians. When Jodie started his orchestra in 1967, his sons were members, along with his wife, Rosie, and his brother Frank. Jodie died in 1987, but the sons assumed leadership, and the band plays on. They celebrated their fiftieth anniversary in 2017.[6]

Other recording examples include one from the Joe Patek Orchestra of Shiner on their 1970s LP, *The Magic of Joe Patek.*[7] The Dujka Brothers of Brenham reissued one of their earlier recordings, which includes an English verse, on their 1999 compilation CD, *The Tradition Continues.*[8] The Czechmates of Dallas released "Red Rose Waltz" on their cassette tape called *20th Anniversary Live.*[9] The Lee Roy Matocha Orchestra of Fayetteville played the song as an instrumental on its mid-1970s LP, *The King of Polka.*[10]

10. Červené víno, bílé koláče *Red Wine Polka*

Červené víno, bílé koláče

Chorus:
Červené víno, bílé koláče,
najíme se, napijem, to se dobře skáče.
Červené víno, bílé koláče,
najíme se, napijem, to se dobře skáče.

1. Sloužila jsem u Glubáka, není to tak dávno.
Učili mne na mašině, jak se šije plátno.

2. Sloužila jsem u sedláka, není to tak dávno.
Učili mne večerama, jak se dělá víno.

Red Wine, White Kolaches

Chorus:
Red wine, white kolaches,
we eat and we drink, they go well together.
Red wine, white kolaches,
we eat and we drink, they go well together.

1. I worked at Glubák not that long ago.
They taught me how to sew linen on a machine.

2. I worked at the farmer's not that long ago.
They taught me how to make wine in the evenings.

Unknown origins. Words from KJT, *Sbírka českých písní*, 26–27. Music from Dujka Brothers, "Red Wine Polka," *The Tradition Continues* (Brenham, TX: JED Musical Prod., 1999), CD.

Though Czechs are known the world over for brewing and drinking beer, the country is also home to the vineyards and wine cellars of southern Moravia, the country's wine-producing region. Popular with tourists, the region lies in the Morava River basin, extending south from Brno to the borders with Austria and Slovakia.[1] The song "Červené víno, bílé koláče," under the title "Víno sem, víno tam," is also known in Slovakia near the Moravian border.[2] During the many festivals and fairs held in this folklore-rich area,[3] one can easily find both *víno* and *koláče,* the semisweet pastry with fruit or poppy seed filling that is also popular in Texas.

The word for *koláč* comes from *kolo*, meaning "wheel" or "round." The final letter, with the diacritical mark above it, is pronounced like the "ch" in "church." Thus *koláč* became "kolach," and *koláče*, the plural form, became "kolaches" in America. Another interesting Czech word in the song is *mašině*, which translates as "machine," an example of a borrowed word.[4] *Mašina* can be found in Czech dictionaries but also in the "first known Czech-English dictionary," completed in 1876 by the journalist and linguist Karel Jonáš of Racine, Wisconsin.[5]

In the song, a worker describes two of his recent jobs. At the first, he learned how to sew linen fabric on a machine. At the second, he was taught to make wine. Robert Skrabanek, who taught sociology at Texas A&M from 1949 till 1984, wrote about making wine on his family's farm near Snook during Prohibition, when he was a boy. The family would gather wild mustang grapes from their pasture, put them in washtubs, and it was Skrabanek's job to stomp them. After he had juiced the grapes, his father would transfer the liquid to a crock, add sugar, and leave it in the smokehouse to ferment. When ready, the wine was stored in a wooden keg with a spigot. It was served diluted with water, depending on the age and sex of who was drinking it. As a youth, Skrabanek's favorite way to consume the watered-down version was to eat "homemade bread dunked in a mild wine drink" as a mid-morning or mid-afternoon snack while working in the fields.[6]

The Joe Patek Orchestra of Shiner recorded "Red Wine Polka" in the late 1950s for TNT, a San Antonio independent label.[7] Vrazels' Polka Band of Buckholts released the song about 1959, also on a TNT 45.[8] The Telstars of Schulenburg, a band that was founded in 1962, recorded "Red Wine Polka" in the 1970s on their first album, *The New World of Polka*, featuring a trio of saxophones. The band continues to play a popular mix of polkas and waltzes, country, pop, and rock and roll.[9] John and Mark Dujka included "Red Wine Polka" on their 1999 compilation CD, *The Tradition Continues*. The Czechaholics of La Grange released the song on their CD *Certified P.O.L.K.A.* in 2017 to celebrate their fifteenth anniversary."[10]

11. Červený šáteček *Red Handkerchief Waltz*

Červený šáteček

1. Červený šátečku, kolem, kolem se toč,
má milá se hněvá, já ne, já nevím proč.
Když se chce hněvati at' se, at' se hněvá,
jen když jí přede mnou jiný neobjímá.

2. Když si chce choditi at' si, at' si chodí,
jen když to nevidí moje černé oči.
Jen ty mně šenkýřko, pivo, pivo nalej,
nic na to nekoukej, že jsem, že jsem malej.

3. Když jsem šel cestičkou lesem,
lesem jsem šel,
usedl jsem si tam pod ja-, pod jalovcem.
Zelený jalovec libě, libě voní,
že za mou milou již jiný, jiný chodí.

Red Handkerchief

1. Red handkerchief, circle, circle around,
my darling is cross, I don't know why.
If she wants to be cross, let her be cross
as long as no one else hugs her in front of me.

2. If she wants to go, let her go,
as long as my dark eyes don't see it.
Just pour me a beer, innkeeper gal,
don't gawk at me because I am short.

3. When I walked down the path through the woods,
through the woods I came.
I sat down under the, under the juniper tree.
The green juniper smells very nice,
telling me that another is seeing my girl.

Folk origins. Bartoš, *Národní písně moravské*, 2:878, and Erben, *Prostonárodní české písně a říkadla* (1886), 241–42. Words and music from "Červený šáteček," arranged for voice and piano by Anton Grill (Chicago: Joseph Jiran Music, 1917).

"Červený šáteček" was collected by František Bartoš and Karel Jaromír Erben, folklorists from Moravia and Bohemia, respectively, as well as by numerous other nineteenth-century song collectors. The version well known in the Czech Republic combines the Bartoš melody and the one verse he collected with two verses from Erben.[1] This combined version is often sung and danced by children and ends with a spirited chorus of "tra la la la las."[2] It is part of *Hanácká beseda* (Hana Beseda), one of several patriotic and regional folk dance quadrilles that gained popularity beginning in the 1860s.[3]

The song most known in Texas, usually under the title "Red Handkerchief Waltz," starts with the Bartoš verse. A new melody and the other two verses, perhaps based on folk origins, were added when it was published in 1917 by Joseph Jiran Music Company of Chicago. The song opens with what seems to be a dancer going around in a circle, flourishing a red handkerchief. The lyrics focus on a sad, jealous boy who cannot understand why his girlfriend is mad at him. He orders a beer and snaps at the waitress. Later he walks along a path in the woods until he comes to a juniper tree and sits down. The pleasant fragrance from the tree carries the somber message that his girl is with someone else.

The Texas polka musician George Koudelka says his father first heard "Red Handkerchief Waltz" in the 1920s, in the small farming community of Engle, located in Fayette County.[4] The song has long been taught in dance classes for young people sponsored by fraternal and heritage organizations as well as by schools. During Czech Day at the 1974 Dallas State Fair, for example, young children from SPJST Lodge 84 in Dallas performed "Červený šáteček" along with "Šla Nanynka do zelí," also in this book.[5]

Adolph Hofner and His San Antonians recorded "Cerveny satachek" during a session for Columbia Records in Hollywood on March 1, 1942. It was never released, but in 2010, a British country-music heritage group issued it on a Hofner collection called *Swing with the Music*. "Cerveny satachek" features Adolph and his brother Emil's vocals as well as the accordion styling of Walter Kleypas.[6] Frank Migl and His Orchestra of Hallettsville released a 78 rpm of "Red Handkerchief" on the Humming Bird label in the early 1950s. They played an orchestral arrangement and sang the first verse. Frank began playing trumpet in 1926 in the band of his brother, the Adolph Migl Orchestra, but started his own group in the mid-1930s. Frank and his orchestra were regular performers in the Hallettsville area until the early 1960s.[7] The Joe Patek Orchestra of Shiner released an instrumental on a TNT 45 in the mid-1950s.[8] Harry Czarnek and the Texas Dutchmen of Houston included the song on their 1970s LP, *A Polka Picnic*.[9] In 1997, the Donnie Wavra Orchestra celebrated twenty-five years of performing by releasing an album recorded live at a picnic in Weimar; it includes an instrumental of the song.[10] The Shiner Hobo Band, about thirty musicians strong, produced a big sound for its version of "Red Handkerchief Waltz" on the band's 2007 CD, which includes vocals.[11]

12. Česká písnička *Song of Bohemia; Our Czech Song*

Česká písnička

1. Ty naše písničky jsou jak ty perličky
na sňůrce navlečené.
Tolik je krásy v nich, a je to velký hřích,
že jsou tak utlačené.

Czech Song

1. Our Czech songs are like little pearls
strung on a thread.
There is so much beauty in them and it's a great sin
that they are so oppressed.

Chorus: Ta naše písnička česká, ta je tak hezká, tak hezká, tak jako na louce kytička vyrostla ta naše písnička. Až se ta písnička ztratí, pak už nic nebudem mít. Jestli nám zahyne, všechno s ní pomine. Potom už nebudem žít.	Chorus: Our Czech song is so pretty, so pretty, like a blossom in the meadow our song grew. When our song is lost then we will have nothing. If it dies all will pass with it. Then we will no longer live.
2. Zpívejte, lidičky, ty naše písničky z Moravy, Slovenska, z Čech, ta naše písnička je sice prostičká, ale je nejhezčí všech.	2. People, sing our songs from Moravia, Slovakia, and Bohemia. Our song is very simple, but it is the prettiest of all.

Words and music from "Česká písnička," sheet music by Karel Hašler (Prague: Hašlerových písniček, 1933).

A statue of a man singing and playing guitar greets people as they walk up the steps to the old castle in the historic center of Prague, capital city of the Czech Republic. The sculpture was erected and dedicated in 2009. The man is Karel Hašler, who wrote a song about the castle steps but who is best known for his song "Česká písnička," usually called "Song of Bohemia" or "Our Czech Song" in English.

Hašler, who was born in Prague in 1879, was a songwriter, cabaret singer, film star, director, and, from 1919 to 1935, also a music publisher. He wrote over three hundred songs, a number of them political in nature. Like František Kmoch, he is an important figure in the early development of Czech popular music. Hašler appeared in the 1932 film *Písničkář* (Balladeer) singing "Česká písnička." The song became a symbol of hope and persistence after Nazi troops occupied Czechoslovakia in 1939. While filming a movie in 1941, Hašler was at a pub with friends and performed "Česká písnička" with alternate anti-Nazi lyrics that he had written. Someone reported him to the Gestapo, and he was soon arrested. He was taken to the concentration camp in Mauthausen, where he was tortured to death a few months later.[1]

In Texas, "Česká písnička" is often performed as a choral piece by choirs or, in the past, as a group song to open lodge and fraternal meetings.[2] It was a favorite of the Rev. John Vaniček, a Czech native who served as priest of Sts. Cyril and Methodius Catholic Parish in Granger from 1927 to 1965. Loretta Skrovan Mikulencak remembers Father Vaniček teaching classes at the parish school and especially his use of patriotic Czech songs to teach the children about Czech history. One of the songs she remembers learning was "Česká píšnicka."[3]

Bačova Česka Kapela (Baca Czech Band) of Fayetteville recorded "Pisnička Česká" at the Gunter Hotel in San Antonio on August 28, 1935. Columbia Records released a 78 rpm record, subtitled "Song of Bohemia," of the band playing the verses as instrumentals and singing on the chorus. The hammered dulcimer in the instrumental mix shines through and gives this version a unique sound. Arhoolie Records reissued "Song of Bohemia" in 1993 on the CD *Texas-Czech, Bohemian, and Moravian Bands.*[4] Kovanda's Czech Band included "Our Czech Song" on its 1994 cassette tape, *Our Czech Music.*[5] The East Bernard Czech Singers recorded the song, under the title "Our Czech Songs," in 1992,[6] and the Taylor Czech Chorus recorded "Pisnicka Ceska" in 2007.[7] Other recordings are by the Hallettsville accordionist Chris Rybak in 1996[8] and the Ennis-based band Czech and Then Some in 2005.[9]

13. Cestička k Mayrovce *Path to Moravia; Road to Moravia*

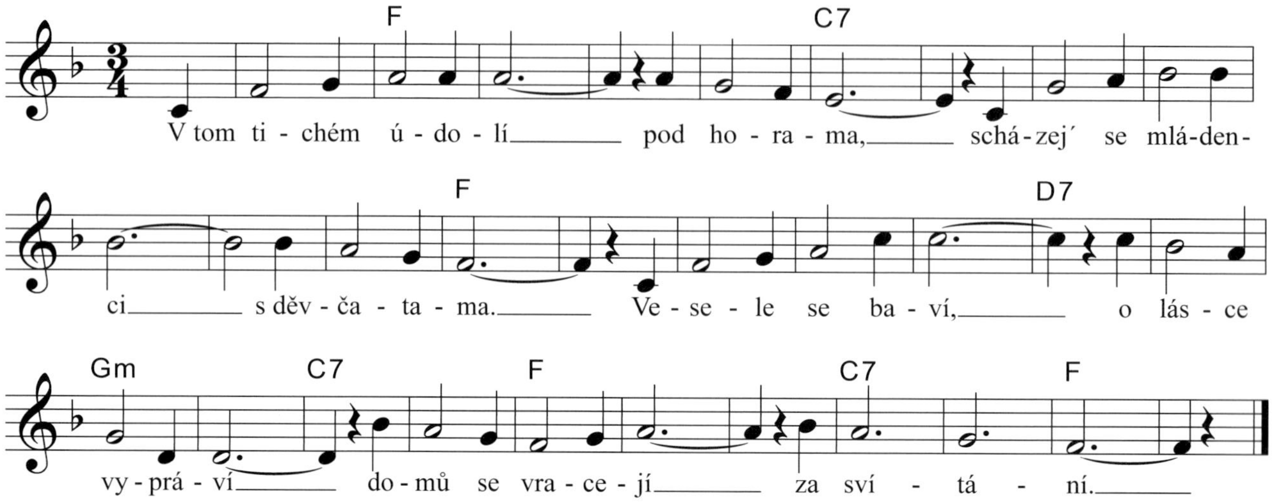

Cestička k Mayrovce

1. V tom tichém údolí pod horama,
   scházej' se mládenci s děvčatama.
   Vesele se baví, o lásce vypráví
   domů se vracejí za svítání.

2. Cestička k Mayrovce ušlapaná,
   šla po ní dívenka uplakaná.
   Včera si zpívala, miláčka líbala,
   dnes už je od něho odloučená.

3. Čekala miláčka po celý den,
   až on jí vyfárá z Mayrovky ven.
   Vyšlehly plameny nad černé kameny
   a v nich je miláček zavalený.

4. Cestička k hřbitovu uježděná,
   odvážej' tam těla, zohavená.
   Zavřel se navždy rov,
   zanechal tisíc slov,
   v mém srdci rána je otevřená.

Path to Mayrovka

1. In that still valley, below the mountains,
   the young boys are meeting the girls.
   They're happily enjoying themselves, speaking of love.
   They go home when the sun rises.

2. The path to the mine, well trodden,
   a girl walked along it and cried.
   Yesterday she sang, she kissed her lover,
   today she is parted from him.

3. She waited for her lover all day long,
   for him to come up from the mine.
   Flames lashed out over the black rocks
   and in them her lover is buried.

4. The path to the cemetery is beaten down,
   the mutilated bodies are taken there.
   The tomb has been shut forever,
   leaving a thousand unspoken words,
   in my heart a wound is opened.

Unknown origins. Words and music from Taylor Czech Chorus, "Cestička k Mayrovce," *Still . . . Carrying On the Tradition* (Holland, TX: Awesome Works Recording, 2018), CD.

The mining ballad "Cestička k Mayrovce" refers to the Mayrau coal mine, located on the outskirts of Vinařice u Kladna, a village about twenty miles northwest of Prague. The mine, owned by Prague Ironworks Company, was named after the company chairman, Kajetán Mayer von Mayrau. It is also widely known by the informal Czech name Mayrovka. Excavation of the pit began in 1874, and the mine operated for about a hundred years, until its closure in 1998. It has been preserved as a large open-air museum that also doubles as a site for concerts and other community events.[1]

One type of popular song that arose in Czechoslovakia during the years between the two world wars focused on personal tragedies and catastrophic events. The mining song "Cestička k Mayrovce" is one of several songs that seemed to bring expression to a generalized anxiety within the culture, especially before the outbreak of World War II.[2] The singers Karel Ctibor and František Poupě recorded a popular duet of the song in 1940. The accompaniment was understated—just Poupě on accordion and Antonín Pauch on violin. This same arrangement came out in sheet music a year later. The song is generally still performed this way, as a simple, heartfelt ballad.[3]

The story opens in a valley beneath the mountains where a group of young people are visiting and having a good time. The next day, one of the girls from the group is crying as she walks the path to Mayrovka. Her boyfriend had been working in the mine when an explosion caused a cave-in that killed him. In the last verse, she walks the path to the local cemetery where they bury his body.

Though it was not a widely known chapter in Texas Czech history, Czech-speaking coal miners worked in the state at the turn of the nineteenth century. In the late 1800s, the discovery of coal deposits in Erath and Palo Pinto Counties, between Fort Worth and Abilene, drew workers to several boomtowns in North Texas. By 1910, Thurber, the largest of these towns, had a population of 3,805, a 49 percent increase from 1900. It was home to coal miners from eighteen different nationalities—84 percent of the workforce was immigrants, mostly from Eastern and Southern Europe, especially Italy and Poland; roughly 5 to 7 percent were Czech.[4] Several of the Czech miners and their families lived in nearby Lyra, where they organized a local branch of the SPJST fraternal organization, a branch of the national organization to support Czechoslovak independence, and a Sunday school to teach their children religion and Czech heritage.[5] After the largest coal company struck oil in 1915 in nearby Strawn, the once-thriving coal industry became secondary. By the 1930s, most of the mines were closed.[6]

"Cestička k Mayrovce" became one of the Czech songs known in Texas in the 1970s, long after the coal mines of North Texas had shut down. The song is typically titled "Path to Moravia" or "Road to Moravia." One reason it may have been given those names is that the Mayrau mine was probably unfamiliar to Texas Czechs, whereas they knew about Moravia. They were also more likely to know about the coal mines near Ostrava in northern Moravia than those of western Bohemia, where Mayrau is located.

Vrazels' Polka Band of Buckholts performed "Path to Moravia" at the 1976 Smithsonian Folklife Festival in Washington, D.C., and included it on their live album from that performance.[7] The Joe Patek Orchestra of Fayetteville released "Road to Moravia" on the 1976 album *The Magic of Joe Patek*.[8] Czech and Then Some of Ennis included "Path to Moravia" on the 2005 CD *Polkas for Everyone* in an arrangement by Sonny Patalik. David Slovak skillfully weaves his rich accordion fills through the full sound of the band and also plays a lovely solo.[9] Mark Halata and Texavia of Houston recorded the song twice, first as an accordion instrumental in 2001 and then again as a duet with Halata and Greg Machac on the band's 2018 CD. Like the Vrazels, the Halata band also performed "Path to Moravia" at their appearance at the Smithsonian Folklife Festival in 2008.[10] The Taylor Czech Chorus sang all four verses of "Cestička k Mayrovce" on their 2018 CD, *Still . . . Carrying on the Tradition.*[11]

14. Chaloupky pod horami *Cottages under the Mountains*

Chaloupky pod horami

1. Hřálo slunko, hřálo krásně,
hřálo na horách.
Pod tím slunkem chaloupka má
stála jako v snách.
Tam jsem prožil svoje mládí,
celý život svůj.
Tam jsem už jak dítě zpíval:
"Kde domov můj?"

2. Svítí hvězda, svítí jasně,
svítí v oblacích.
Proč ti, děvče moje milé,
na rtech zmlknul smích.
Musíš celý život bráti
tak, jak se to dá.
Kdo má srdce plné lásky,
ten nezoufá.
Chorus:
Chaloupky pod horami,
co se to stalo s vámi?
Byly jste takové hezké,
vy naše chaloupky české.
Smutně teď' jdeme světem,
štěstí je zvadlým květem.
Ale vy budete jednou
patřit zas našim dětem.
Last chorus ending:
O vás vyprávíme s láskou
pohádky našim dětem.

Cottages under the Mountains

1. The sun warmed, it warmed beautifully,
it warmed the mountains.
Under the sun my cottage
stood as if in dreams.
There I spent my youth,
my whole life,
there I as a child sang:
"Where is my home?"

2. The star shines, it shines clearly,
it shines in the clouds.
This is why, my dear girl,
laughter has fallen silent on your lips.
You have to take your whole life
as it comes.
Whoever has a heart full of love
does not despair.
Chorus:
Cottages under the mountains
what has become of you?
You were so nice,
our little Czech cottages.
Now we go through the world sadly,
happiness is a wilted flower.
But one day you will
belong again to our children.
Last chorus ending:
We will lovingly tell fairy tales
about you to our children.

From "Chaloupky pod horami," words by Josef Dalecký, music by František Voborský, arranged by Joseph P. Elsnic (Chicago: Vitak-Elsnic, 1940), used with permission by Vitak-Elsnic Company, a Division of Music Publishers of America, LLC.

Chalupa is a Czech word for farmhouse, but in more recent times it has taken on the meaning of a vacation or weekend cottage in a rural location. Many of these vacation houses are owned by city dwellers who have either bought or inherited them. Organized campsites and modest get-away places in the Czech countryside began to appear in the 1920s with the scouting and tramping phenomena, the latter a movement among young people who idealized the mythology of the American West. But having a *chalupa* or a one-room *chata* grew into a more general way to endure the years of occupation, first by the Nazis and then by the Soviets. As one scholar put it, by 1989, "the most tangible expression of any private ownership that was left in communist Czechoslovakia became the ownership of weekend homes ranging from little wooden cabins to substantial cottages and farmhouses."[1]

Chaloupky is the plural diminutive of the word *chalupa* and is often translated as "small"— in this instance meaning small cottages. But Czech diminutives also convey a quality of sweetness, one that permeates the song and creates the main impression: a sense of wistful endearment.

"Chaloupky pod horami" was composed by František Voborský, and J. Dalecký is credited for the words. Voborský was a cartoonist and musician. He wrote the song in response to the 1938 Munich Agreement between Germany, France, Great Britain, and Italy ceding the Czech/German borderlands, called the Sudetenland, to Nazi Germany. As the Czech music historian Josef Kotek explains, it is often a popular song such as "Chaloupky pod horami" that can best describe the emotional response of a nation's people to such a shock.[2] The lyrics of the song focus on a love for the land and even quote the Czech national anthem, "Kde domov můj?" (Song 28).

The song was published in 1939 in Prague and became a hit. Voborský, however, was arrested by the Nazis for anti-German activity. He was forced to cooperate with his captors and served a prison sentence after the war for collaboration. He died in obscurity, another compromised victim of those hard times, but his song survived.[3]

"Chaloupky pod horami" was picked up quickly, in 1940, by American ethnic music publisher Vitak-Elsnic of Chicago. In Texas, the song can be found in lyric books and choir folders and on song sheets and recordings. The SPJST Choral Group of Lodge 88 in Houston included "Chaloupky pod horami" on its 1978 LP, *Czech Folksongs.* The choir was accompanied by the lodge's full orchestra.[4] Harry Czarnek and the Texas Dutchmen played the song, with Czarnek singing the chorus, on their mid-1980s cassette tape, *Polka Hit Parade.*[5] The Travelers, so named because the members live some distance from one another and travel to meet for rehearsals and gigs, recorded a sharp instrumental version of "Cottages under the Mountains" on their 1992 CD.[6] George Koudelka, the drummer for the Travelers and a private record collector, says a notable early Texas recording of the song, an instrumental, was made by the Lee Ilse Orchestra of La Grange on the Bess label in the early 1960s.[7]

15. Co jste hasiči? *Fire Brigade Polka*

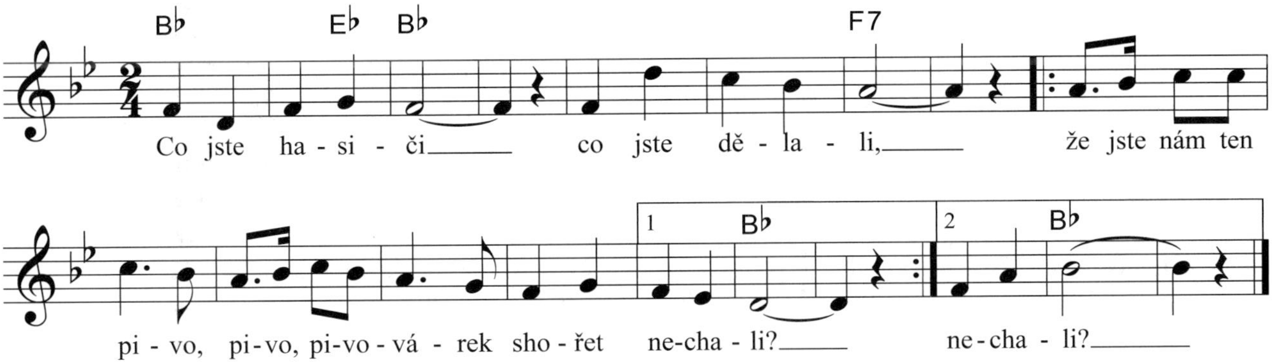

Co jste hasiči?

1. Co jste hasiči, co jste dělali?
   že jste nám ten pivo, pivo, pivovárek
   zhořet nechali?

2. Zhořet nechali i tu hospodu.
   My staří mazáci, staří úlejváci,
   máme pít vodu.

3. Vodu nepijem, my pijeme rum.
   My vínečko pijem, vesele si žijem,
   za pár jdem domů.

4. Paní Blažková hezkú dceru má.
   Já tam za ní půjdu, milovat ji budu.
   Za to bude má.

What, Firemen?

1. What, firemen, what have you done
   that you have let our brewery
   burn to the ground?

2. You even let the pub burn.
   We old hands, old slackers,
   have to drink water.

3. We don't drink water, we drink rum.
   We drink wine and live happily,
   after a few we go home.

4. Mrs. Blažek has a pretty daughter.
   I'll go to see her, I will love her.
   She will be mine.

Unknown origins. Words and music from Vrazels' Polka Band, *Golden Sounds: 50th Anniversary* (Buckholts, TX: VPB 518, 2003), CD.

During a dance, the drummer will often introduce "Co jste hasiči?" by ringing a bell or playing a triangle—sounds to imitate those made by a fire truck. The song begins as a playful rebuke of firemen for letting a brewery and tavern burn down, but this jovial drinking song cheerfully moves on to praise the pleasures of drinking rum and wine. Known in Texas as "Fire Brigade Polka," it can be found in songbooks in the Czech Republic and heard as a sing-along in Czech pubs.[1]

A popular Czech "rum," which has been produced there for about two hundred years, is not made from sugarcane, like Caribbean and other traditional rums, but rather from sugar beets. The reason is simple: sugarcane does not grow in Central Europe, but beets grow there abundantly. However, using this source to make rum amounts to a deceptive trade practice, according to European Union standards. Prior to the Czech nation's admission to the Union in 2004, flexible Czech distillers changed their labeling category. The liquor is no longer sold as rum but is typically labeled *tuzemák,* which means "domestic." Various brands of "domestic" spirits continue to be highly popular, both in the Czech Republic and in Slovakia, served in a shot glass, in a hot toddy called *grog,* and as an ingredient in Christmas cookies.[2]

Zetka's Polka Band of El Campo recorded "Fire Brigade" for their 1994 cassette tape, later reissued on a compilation CD by the Texas Polka Music Museum in Schulenburg.[3] Vrazels' Polka Band of Buckholts included "Fire Brigade Polka" on their fiftieth-anniversary compilation CD, *Golden Sounds.*[4] The Shiner Hobo Band recorded an instrumental "Fire Brigade Polka" for their 2004 CD, *Ještě jednou (One More Time).*[5] The Dujka Brothers of Brenham reissued an earlier recording of "Fire Brigade Polka" for their 2001 compilation CD called *Grandpa's List.*[6]

16. Co ten ptáček jarabáček? *Jarabáček; Bird of Spring*

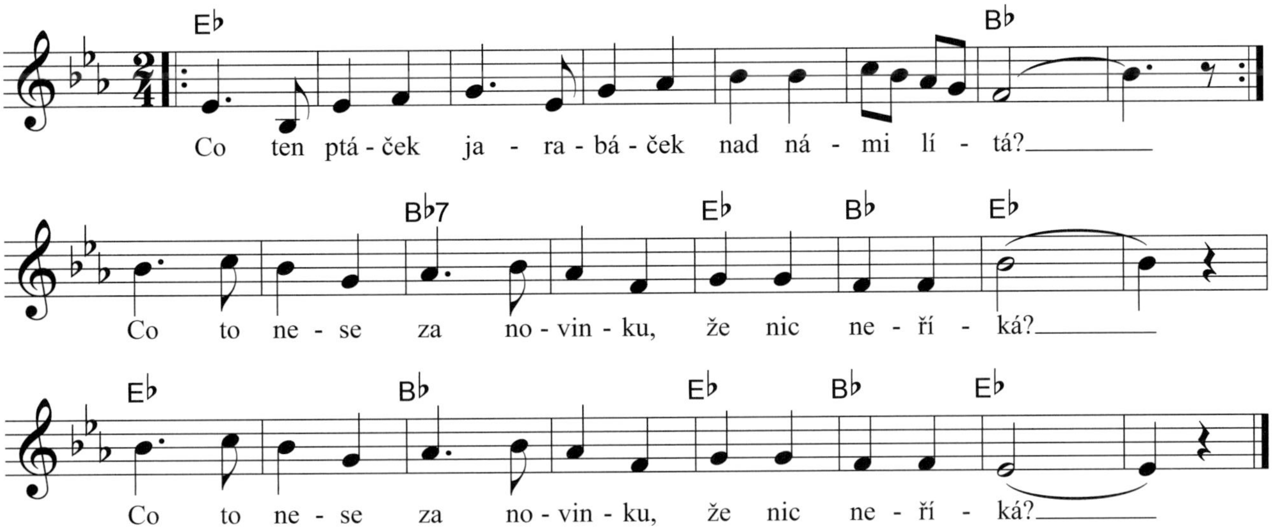

Co ten ptáček jarabáček?

1. Co ten ptáček jarabáček
nad námi lítá?
Co to nese za novinku,
že nic neříká?

2. Nese, nese novinečku,
ale takovou,
že mi ze všech nejmilejší
chodí za jinou.

3. Když si chodí, ať' si chodí,
já o něj nedbám.
Pro něj smutek neponesu,
ani ho nemám.

4. Proč bych měla smutek nosit,
vždyť' je hochů víc?
Za jednoho mládenečka,
najdu jich tisíc.

5. Kdyby jich tak tisíc přišlo,
co bych dělala?
Jednomu jak druhému
košem bych dala.

What about That Speckled Bird?

1. What about that speckled bird
flying over us?
What news does it carry,
that it doesn't tell?

2. It carries, it carries news
but of the kind
that my dearest boy
is stepping out with another.

3. If he does, let him,
I do not care about him,
I will not carry sadness for him
for I have none.

4. Why would I grieve
when there are more boys?
For one young man
I will find a thousand.

5. What if a thousand of them came,
what would I do?
One after another
I would jilt them.

Folk origins. Sušil, *Moravské národní písně*, 198. Words for verses 1–3 from Sušil, verses 4–5 from KJT, *Sbírka českých písní*, 2–3. Music from "Jarabáček," by František Kmoch (Prague: Mojmír Urbánek, 1893).

"Co ten ptáček jarabáček" appears, with the same melody and first three verses, in the collection of Moravian folk songs by František Sušil.[1] A priest who taught theology in Brno, Sušil spent his spare time in the 1840s and 1850s collecting songs in all parts of Moravia, which he published in a massive collection in 1860.[2] A later version of the song is a popular march by František Kmoch, sometimes called the "Bohemian March King." Kmoch used both the lyrics and melody collected by Sušil as the trio in his 1893 march that he called simply "Jarabáček."[3]

"Co ten ptáček jarabáček" begins with the common folkloric use of an animal messenger that brings news to the world of humans. In this case, the news is carried by a speckled bird, a *ptáček jarabáček*. This bird with speckled, mottled feathers has been interpreted as a bird of spring, perhaps a young bird with its protective, camouflaged coloring still intact. "Bird of Spring" is the English title of Louis Vitak's arrangement of the Kmoch march, published by Georgi and Vitak of Chicago.[4]

A young woman who sees the speckled bird flying high above interprets this as a sign that her "dearest boy is stepping out with another." She responds with exaggerated defiance, saying that she does not care because there are so many other boys to be had. "I will find a thousand," she says, and if a thousand of them show up? "I would jilt them" is her response.

Round Top Brass Band performed "Bird of Spring March," Kmoch-style, arranged for the band by its cofounder and drummer George Koudelka of Flatonia, on their 1981 self-titled LP. The seventeen-member band was organized in 1971 and typically performs Czech and German polkas, waltzes, and marches at festivals and fairs.[5] Wence Shimek and the All Star Sounds of Hallettsville included "The Bird (Jerabacek) Polka" on their 1982 LP, *You Asked for It*, with Shimek on vocals.[6] Gene Lichnovsky, a pianist who also plays trumpet and has performed with many Central Texas polka bands since the age of fourteen, included "Jarabacek (Bird of Spring) March" on one of his piano solo CDs called *Gene Lichnovsky: Piano Solos, Polkas, Waltzes, Marches*, released about 2010.[7]

17. Čtyři koně *Four Horses*

Čtyři koně

1. Čtyři koně ve dvoře,
žádný s nima, má zlatá Mařenko,
čtyři koně ve dvoře,
žádný s nima neoře.

2. Oře s nima Pepíček,
červený byl, má zlatá Mařenko,
oral s nima Pepíček,
červený byl jak rohlíček.

3. A když pole dooral
na svou milou, má zlatá Mařenko,
a když pole dooral
na svou milou zavolal.

4. Pojd' má milá, pojd' ke mně,
já ti povím, má zlatá Mařenko,
pojd' má milá, pojd' ke mně.
já ti povím, co je mně.

Four Horses

1. Four horses in the yard,
no one with them, my dear Mary,
four horses in the yard,
no one is plowing with them.

2. Joey is plowing with them,
he was red, my dear Mary,
Joey plowed with them,
he was red like a bread roll.

3. And when he finished plowing the field,
he called his darling, my dear Mary,
and when he finished plowing the field,
he called his darling.

4. Come, my darling, come to me,
I will tell you, my dear Mary,
come my darling, come to me,
I will tell you what's bothering me.

5. Bolí mne má hlavička, pobila mne, má zlatá Mařenko, bolí mne má hlavička, pobila mne, má matička.	5. My head hurts, she beat me, my dear Mary. my head hurts, my mother beat me.
6. Nech tě pro mne nebijú, můžeš chodit, můj zlatý Pepíčku, nech tě pro mne nebijú, můžeš chodit za jinú.	6. Don't let them beat you because of me, you can go, my dear Joey, don't let them beat you because of me, you can go with another.
7. Já za jinů nepůjdu, radši se dám, má zlatá Mařenko, já za jinů nepůjdu, radši se dám na vojnu.	7. I won't go with another, I'd rather join, my dear Mary, I won't go with another, I'd rather join the army.

Folk origins. Erben, *Pjsně národnj w Čechách,* 3:14–15, and Bradáč, *Plzeňské písně*, 70. Words from KJT, *Sbírka českých písní*, 103. Music from Joe Patek Orchestra, "Four Horses" (San Antonio: TNT 5064, 1963), 45 rpm.

Several variants of "Čtyři koně" have been collected and published by early Czech folklorists. Bohemian Karel Jaromír Erben published fourteen verses to "Čtyři koně" in his 1845 book of folk songs and also in his later collections. Both František Sušil and František Bartoš published variants they found in Moravia, under the title "Štyry koně."[1] The words sung in Texas are closest to the one Erben collected. The melody widely known in Texas was published in Prague in a 1906 songbook by Jaroslav Bradáč called *Plzeňské písně* (Pilsen Songs).[2]

In "Four Horses," as it is known in English, a young couple is confronted with the objections of the boy's mother to their relationship. The repetitive structure of the lyrics creates a chant-like rhythm that underlies this story of thwarted love. The first two lines of the verses are an abbreviated version of the last two lines. The second line, furthermore, is always addressed to a specific person, most often to "má zlatá Mařenko." *Zlatá*, which is the Czech word for "gold," means "dear" or "dearest" as well.

In the opening scene, four horses stand idly in the yard, but Joey is soon out plowing with them. He is described as being "red like a bread roll." The lyrics from both Erben and Bartoš compare his redness not to a bread roll but to a "hřebíček," which can mean either the aromatic spice clove or a carnation flower.[3] The Leo Majek Orchestra of Corpus Christi sings the lyrics with this word. Whether compared to bread, clove, or carnation, Joey's skin is a ruddy, reddish color. We do not find out if his color is from working in the sun, from anger, or from his mother's beating, but we do know this song marks a time of crisis for him. By the song's end, Joey's sweetheart has given him permission to go with another girl, but Joey has refused, saying he would rather join the army.

Joe Patek Orchestra of Shiner released their recording of "Four Horses" in 1963.[4] The Pateks added an instrumental section that is also popular with other groups. The Leo Majek Orchestra recorded "Four Horses Waltz," released as a 45 rpm record, in about the mid-1960s.[5] The Rudy Kurtz Orchestra included a slightly different variation of the instrumental section on its 1964 45 rpm.[6] All three of these early bands sing the same first two verses, Rudy Kurtz as a solo, whereas the Pateks and the Majeks perform duets. Two later Texas recordings included one by the Czech Harvesters of Ennis, who sang the first five verses on their 1988 *10th Anniversary* album.[7] Another is by the Czechaholics of La Grange, who included two verses and their variation of the instrumental on the band's 2006 CD titled *Spreadin' the Tradition*.[8]

18. Dobrú noc, milko má *Good Night, My Darling*

Dobrú noc, milko má

1. Dobrú noc, milko má, už dobrú noc,
dobrú noc ti vinšuju.
Dobrú noc, milko má, už dobrú noc,
dobrú noc ti vinšuju.
Ty jsi jak ta vodní rosa v louce.
Miluju tebe z celého srdce.
Dobrú noc, milko má, už dobrú noc,
dobrú noc ti vinšuju.

Good Night, My Darling

1. Good night, my darling, already good night,
good night I wish you.
Good night, my darling, already good night,
good night I wish you.
You are like the moist dew on the meadow,
I love you with my whole heart.
Good night, my darling, already good night,
good night I wish you.

2. Good night, my darling, yes, good night,
good night and sweet dreams to you.
Good night, my darling, už dobrú noc,
good night and sweet dreams to you.
You are like a rose in the morning sunshine.
I love you and hope you'll always be mine.
Good night, my darling, už dobrú noc,
good night and sweet dreams to you.

Broadside origins (Augusty, 1855). Words and music from Vrazels' Polka Band, "Good Night My Darling Waltz," *On the Road* (Buckholts, TX: VPB-112, 1981), LP. Czech words to verse 1, lines 5–6, and English words, verse 2, by Alfred Vrazel, used with permission.

Alfred Vrazel's grandson Matthew Strmiska says the first Czech words he learned were *dobrú noc,* meaning "good night." His father, Thomas, sang and played drums with Vrazels' Polka Band of Buckholts for thirty-five years. Matt's mother, Cindy, daughter of Alfred and Bernice Vrazel, would often take Matt and his sister, Jessica, to the band's performances. As a young boy, Matt remembers his mother waking him up as he lay sleeping on the dance-hall floor, a quilt serving as his bed. When he came awake, he could hear his father and grandfather singing "Dobrú noc," the last song of the dance.[1] The salutation "good night" in standard Czech is *dobrou noc,* but in northeastern Moravian dialects, it is *dobrú noc.* Both forms can be heard in Texas.

Vrazels' Polka Band recorded "Good Night, My Darling" in 1981 for their LP *On the Road.* Alfred says he cannot recall how he learned the song but that he remembered the melody and a few of the words, so he filled in the Czech blanks himself and also wrote an English verse. The band gave the song a Texas sound with its dance-hall rhythm, electric bass, and the two saxophones playing harmony. Vrazels' Polka Band played it to end their shows during the 1980s and 1990s.[2]

The words Alfred had trouble remembering descended from a *kramářská píseň* (shopkeepers' song). These songs were part of a style widely found in Europe starting in the sixteenth century, generally known as broadside ballads. They were song lyrics printed on a sheet of paper and sold to the public, usually by a performer, at fairs, markets, and other public trading areas. "Dobrou noc, dobrou noc, milko má, dobrou noc ti winssugi," in old orthography, was printed in Litomyšl, a town close to the Bohemian-Moravian border, in 1855. A copy can be found in the regional museum in nearby Vysoké Mýto.[3] "Dobrou noc, milko má" is well known in the Czech Republic by the melody Alfred remembers; it can be found in numerous songbooks and on several recordings.[4] The lyrics there closely follow the ones from the broadside print and compare the sweetheart to a white dove.

The Red Ravens of El Campo sang a lovely three-part harmony rendition of "Good Night My Darling" on their 1981 cassette tape, *Polka Better.*[5] The Ellinger Combo included "Goodnight My Darling Waltz" on its LP *A Little Bit of the Best* in 1984.[6] The Bobby Jones Czech Band sang "Good Night My Darling" for Splash Day at SPJST Lodge 88 in Houston in the mid-1980s, captured on a recording by Dennis Svatek of Taylor.[7] The Ennis Czech Boys included "Good Night My Darling Waltz" on their 2016 CD, *Cheers to 10 Years.*[8] All these bands performed Alfred's lyrics.

19. Dráteník *Tinker Polka*

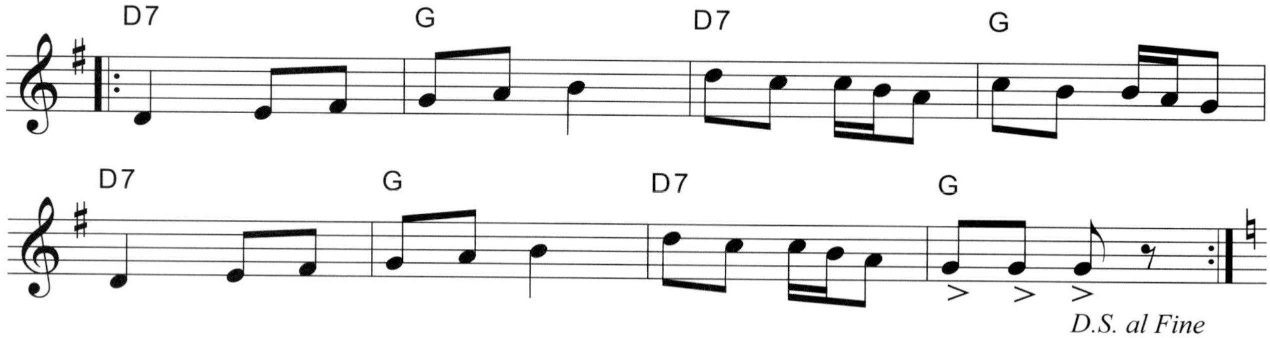

Dráteník

1. Šel dráteník po ulici.
   Selka na něj volala,
   aby jí šel zadrátovat,
   hrnec s dvouma ušima.

2. Drátoval jsem půl hodiny,
   drátoval jsem hodinu,
   zítra koval jsem si děvče,
   měla černou ofinu.

Tinker

1. A tinker walked along the street,
   a farmer's wife called to him
   to come repair
   a pot with two handles.

2. I tinkered for half an hour,
   then I tinkered for an hour,
   the next day I forged me a girl,
   she had black bangs.

Unknown origins. Words from Dancehall Boys, *An Evening in Dubina* (Taylor: C.M.M. Records CD5/A, 1998), CD. Music from "Dráteník," arranged by Louis Vitak (Chicago: Vitak-Elsnic, 1927), used with permission by Vitak-Elsnic Company, a Division of Music Publishers of America, LLC.

The Czech word *dráteník* comes from the word *drát,* meaning "wire." *Dráteník*, usually translated as "tinker," refers to the historical trade of itinerant wire workers, peddlers who repaired broken clay pots by skillfully weaving a tight wire net around them. One writer claimed that a carefully wired clay pot "rang like a bell" when the repair was finished.[1]

Tinkers were once common in Europe. An 1826 comic operetta called *Dráteník*, the first native Czech-language opera, features the hero disguised as a wandering tinker, a disguise that gives him access to his sweetheart.[2] Old-time tinkers could be found plying their skills on the streets of Prague as late as 1945.[3] The earthy song "Dráteník" has folk roots and in the Czech Republic is often performed as a sing-along, usually in a pub.[4]

The first recording of "Dráteník" in the state was a 1929 instrumental of the Louis Vitak arrangement by Bačova Česka Kapela (Baca Czech Band) of Fayetteville, recorded in San Antonio.[5] The Ray Krenek Orchestra of Wallis recorded an energetic instrumental with two clarinets soaring on the trio. It was reissued in 2006 on a CD called *Top Hit Tunes,* coproduced by Krenek and the musician John Dujka of Brenham.[6] The Shiner Hobo Band also recorded an instrumental on its 2007 CD, *Frankie and Johnny Hobo Style.*[7]

The lyrics typically performed in Texas are similar to those of the Czech pub song. They fall within the genre of suggestive jokes that feature another kind of itinerant worker, the traveling salesman. It is not clear who first introduced the words, but they have been sung here for many years. The Joe Patek Orchestra of Shiner released a 78 rpm record of the song with the two verses, probably in the late 1940s or 1950s.[8] The Dancehall Boys of Austin and Taylor, now the Czech Melody Masters, sang the verses and played the full Vitak arrangement on a live recording released on their 1998 CD, *An Evening in Dubina*.[9] The Czechaholics of La Grange included both verses on their 2014 CD, *Cause for Celebration*.[10] The Lee Roy Matocha Orchestra included the first verse and a different second, similar to one of the Czech pub verses, on the band's compilation CD *Muziky, Muziky*.[11] The Leo Majek Orchestra of Corpus Christi recorded the same two verses as Matocha for its 1992 LP, *Memories*.[12]

20. Haj, husičky, haj *Gander Polka*

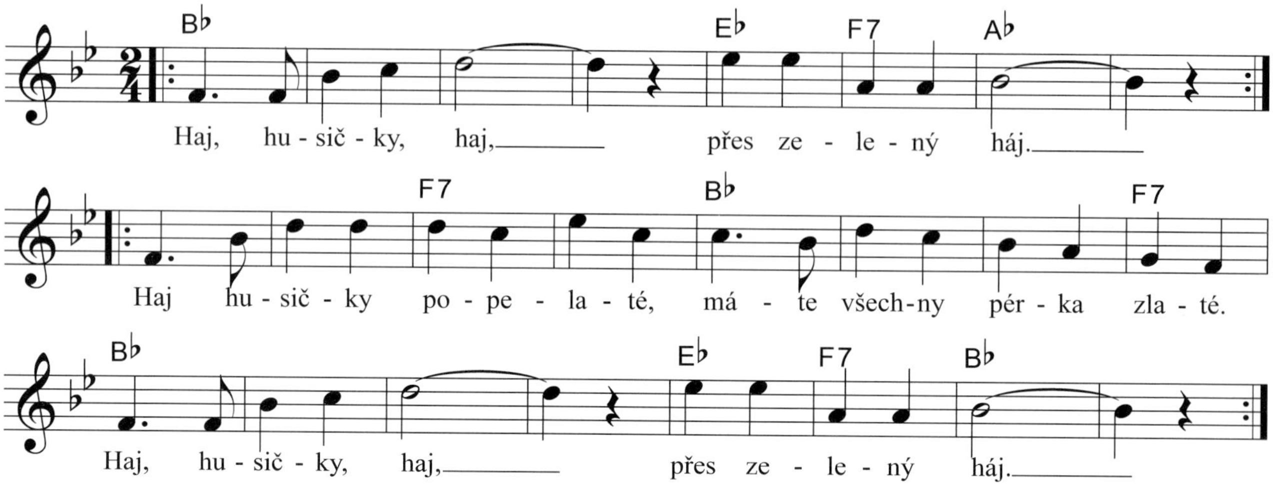

Haj, husičky, haj

1. Haj, husičky, haj, přes zelený háj.
Haj, husičky, haj, přes zelený háj.
Haj husičky popelaté,
máte všechny pérka zlaté.
Haj, husičky, haj, přes zelený háj.

2. Haj, husičky, haj, pod zelený máj.
Haj, husičky, haj, pod zelený máj.
Haj, husičky, k té voděnce
a já půjdu k mé panence.
Haj, husičky, haj, pod zelený máj.

Go, Geese, Go

1. Go, geese, go, through the green grove.
Go, geese, go, through the green grove.
Go, ash-gray geese,
all of your feathers are golden.
Go, geese, go, through the green grove.

2. Go, geese go, under the green maypole.
Go, geese, go, under the green maypole.
Go geese, go toward the water
and I will go to my girl.
Go, geese, go, under the green maypole.

Folk origins (Moravia). Bartoš, *Naše děti*, 200–1, and Svoboda, *Věnec lípový*, 175–76. Words from Svoboda, *Věnec lípový*, 175–76. Music (trio only) from Kovanda's Czech Band, "Haj, husičky, haj," *Authentic Czech Polka and Waltz Music* (Omaha: 1999), CD.

František Bartoš (1837–1906), a Moravian folk-song collector, published "Haj, husičky, haj" in his 1898 book called *Naše děti* (Our children). This book contains all kinds of songs, poetry, amusements, and games, but one section is about young shepherds, the children who herd flocks of geese, goats, and cattle. Bartoš introduces this part by explaining that the lives of children "are not just fun and games."[1] Rural children were expected to help in the household and around the farm from an early age. Two anthropologists who wrote a case study about village life in Komárov, a farming area in southern Bohemia, described the children's work this way: "Usually among their first chores was herding the geese, and later, at about the age of ten, the cattle."[2]

The description certainly fits the experience of Anna Žárský, who emigrated from Huslenky, a small village near the town of Vsetín in northeastern Moravia. Anna came to Texas in 1892 at the age of twenty-four and married Josef Mikulenčak of Corn Hill in Williamson County. The couple raised ten children on their farm and, after 1907, in the town of Granger. Before coming to Texas, Anna began herding the family's flock of geese when she was six years old. She walked them to the sloping meadows above the Huslenky valley and brought them back home for the night. At about age eight, she started grazing the family's fifteen to thirty sheep, and within a few years she assumed responsibility for the cattle. In her late years, she spoke warmly about the beautiful outdoors of that mountainous region but regretted her limited formal education, curtailed by farm duties.[3]

In the first line of the song, two words appear that look alike—*haj* and *háj*. This playful use of language is often found in children's songs. The first word, *haj*, is an archaic Czech command meaning "go!" which was once used exclusively for herding geese but now applies generally. The word *háj*, spelled with an accent—called *čárka*—is a different word that refers to a grove of trees.

The lyrics to "Haj, husičky, haj" are simple and lively, focused on the geese and the green grove. The first verse is the one Bartoš published in his children's book. The second verse, from a small, much-used songbook that belonged to another Moravian immigrant in Texas,[4] adds colorful details with the mention of a maypole and a sweetheart. This second verse describes the grove and likens one of the trees to a maypole, a *máj*. This kind of maypole, still customary in the Czech Republic, is a tall tree that young men chop down and bring to the village for May Day festivities, its top still bearing fresh spring leaves.[5] One can imagine a young shepherd noticing a tall, straight tree and thinking it would make a fine maypole, the same way some Texas children learned to evaluate a nicely shaped cedar as a potential Christmas tree.

The tune we sing in Texas is derived from the one Bartoš published. In Central Europe, "Haj, husičky, haj" is widely known. The song attained general popularity in an arrangement for brass band by Alois Čuma of Brno, Moravia. Columbia Records released a 1925 Czech-language recording by the Frank Linhart Orchestra with vocal chorus by Česko-Americké Kvartet.[6]

Texas bands usually sing the first verse only and sometimes add one or more parts of the Čuma band arrangement. Vrazels' Polka Band of Buckholts included "Gander Polka (Haj, husičky, haj)" on the LP *Polka Sounds from the Country*, released about 1970, with Alfred on vocals.[7] Harry Czarnek and the Texas Dutchmen of Houston included "Haj, husičky, haj Polka" on their 1975 LP, *Red Rose Polka*. This popular album features old Czech favorites on side one and country music on the other, with Gene and Sonny Patalik singing the Czech songs.[8] Kovanda's Czech Band of Fayetteville released the song on their CD *Authentic Czech Polka and Waltz Music*.[9] The East Bernard Czech Singers made a medley of three goose songs, all in this book, which they included on their 1988 cassette tape, *Czech Listening and Dancing Favorites*. The first song of the medley, "Pode mlejnem" (Song 48), is about a boy who refuses to shoot trespassing geese. The second is "Haj, husičky, haj," and the third is "Letěla husička" (Song 34), the tale of a goose flying overhead who suddenly falls into a creek.[10]

21. Hastrman *Hasterman; Water Sprite Waltz*

Hastrman

1. Byla jednou jedna panna,
   milovala hastrmana. Hopsa!

2. Ty můj milý hastrmane,
   jak to spolu uděláme? Hopsa!

3. Ty nemůžes bez vody žít,
   já nemůžu bez piva být! Hopsa!

Water Sprite

1. There once was a maiden,
   she loved a water sprite. Hopsa!

2. You, my dear water sprite,
   how will we get along? Hopsa!

3. You cannot live without water,
   I cannot live without beer! Hopsa!

Folk origins. Slavia, *Národní pohádky*, Series 1, part 2, 39. Words from Jerry Haisler and the Melody 5, "Hasterman," *Favorites, 1978–1992* (Temple: 2006), CD. Music from Jodie Mikula Orchestra, "Hastrman," *A Toast to Czech Music* (Ennis: 1985), Vol. 7, LP.

The *hastrman*, also known as *vodník*, is a supernatural being said to inhabit the waters of Moravia and Bohemia. The Czechs brought this superstition with them to Texas and applied the old idea of the *hastrman* to the creeks, wells, tanks, and other wet places of their new home.

Hastrman is a Czech word that evolved from the German *Wassermann*, which means "water-man."[1] A popular character in stories and fairy tales, he is sometimes described as a man with a green coat and webbed feet. Other times he is said to look human, but he can be recognized by the water that drips from the left tail of his long coat. Some say he can change into a fish, a snake, a frog, a horse, or even other forms. Most agree that he lives in a palace submerged in deep water, often near mills, where his rooms are covered with crystals. Here he keeps drowned souls in pots. If the lids of the pots are raised, the souls escape as bubbles to the surface. He lures his prey to the water, especially young women and children, but anyone who comes under his spell is in great danger of being dragged under.[2]

The Czech writers Božena Němcová and Karel Jaromír Erben both wrote poems with the title "Vodník." In Němcová's 1844 poem, a mother warns her beautiful daughter not to swim in the lake because the *vodník* will pull her down. Erben's poem, published in 1853, tells the frightful story of a woman who marries a *vodník* and lives in his underwater palace with their child. When she leaves to visit her mother and refuses to return, the *vodník* kills the child. Antonín Dvořák's great opera *Rusalka* premiered in Prague in 1901. It draws on these poems for the character of Rusalka's father, Vodník. The doomed Rusalka falls in love with a human prince who breaks her heart but ultimately pays with his life.[3]

The song known in Texas humorously subverts the folk storyline of a young woman entrapped by a *hastrman*. In this song, the woman and the *hastrman* want to be together but cannot figure out how it will work. The woman states the problem simply: "You cannot live without water, I cannot live without beer! Hopsa!" Following the shout, the musicians often play some version of the lively instrumental notated in the score. The three verses most performed in the state are from a longer folk song. One published version was collected in the eastern Bohemian town of Litomyšl and included in an 1873 book of folklore by Slavia, a Czech literary society.[4] The lyrics evolved into the humorous version before coming to Texas, possibly in Czech pubs where "Hastrman" became a popular sing-along.[5]

The *hopsa!* at the end of each second line is an informal Czech interjection, a call or shout that translates as "hop."[6] The usage suggests the kind of movement that has a lot of joy. Variations on *hopsa* are common in Central and Northern European languages, where they are used in folk dances and songs, including children's songs. The Texas "Hastrman" recordings document several calls that polka bands shout out while singing the song. These include Lee Roy Matocha's "ha ha!," the Fabulous Six's and Mark Halata's "zase!," meaning "once again!" and Wence and Helen Shimek, Leroy Rybak, and Alice Sulak of Jerry Haisler's band all shouting the always popular "hopsa!" on their recordings.

The title "Hastrman," sometimes spelled "Hasterman," is the most familiar name given to the song. Wence and Helen Shimek of Hallettsville sang a duet of the song on their 1984 cassette tape, *Presents More Polkas and Waltzes*.[7] The Jodie Mikula Orchestra of Ennis, with Jodie on accordion solo, released "Hastrman" on the album *Toast to Czech Music* in 1985.[8] The 1987 LP *Jerry Haisler and the Melody 5, Volume 3*, included "Hasterman Waltz" with saxophonist Alice Sulak on vocal, reissued on their CD *Favorites* in 2006.[9] The Lee Roy Matocha Orchestra included "Hastrman Waltz" on its 1987 LP *By Popular Demand*,[10] and Leroy Rybak's Swinging Orchestra recorded "Hasterman" for its circa-1980s cassette tape *Don't Mess with Texas Polkas and Waltzes*.[11] More recent recordings are from the 2003 CD *40 Years* by Fritz Hodde and the Fabulous Six of Hutto,[12] the 2003 *Moon over Moravia* by Mark Halata and Texavia,[13] and the 2014 *Cause for Celebration* by the Czechaholics of La Grange.[14]

22. Hledám galánečku *Looking for My Sweetheart*

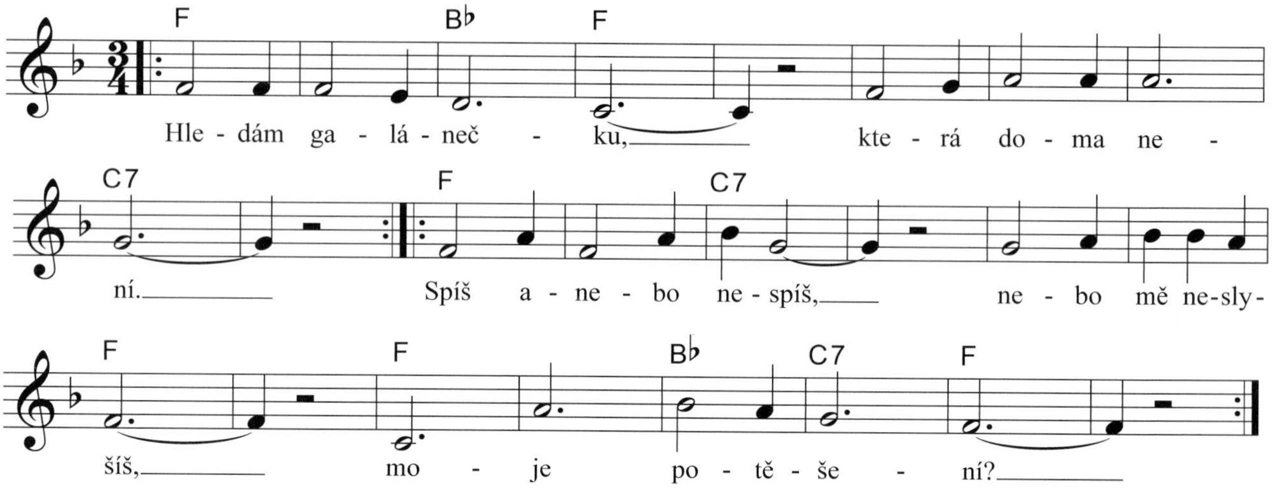

Hledám galánečku

1. Hledám galánečku,
   která doma není.
   Spíš anebo nespíš,
   nebo mě neslyšíš,
   moje potěšení?

2. A já ještě nespím,
   já tě dobře slyším.
   Jenom že já tobě
   v této noční době
   otevříti nesmím.

I'm Looking for My Sweetheart

1. I'm looking for my sweetheart,
   who is not at home.
   Are you asleep or awake,
   or do you not hear me,
   my darling?

2. And I am not yet asleep,
   I hear you well.
   Only that I am not allowed
   at this time of night
   to open the door for you.

> Unknown origins. Words from KJT, *Sbírka českých písní*, 112–13. Music from University Czech Singers, *Czechoslovakian Folksongs* (Houston: EMPAC-1212, 1977), LP.

The word for sweetheart, *galánečka*, came into Czech from the Spanish *galán*, meaning either a handsome, well-dressed man or a man who is wooing a woman—similar to the word "gallant" in English.[1] In Moravian dialects, the word evolved to simply mean "sweetheart" or "boyfriend/girlfriend." Studies of Czech dialects going back to the 1880s localize this affectionate "sweetheart" meaning as unique to the eastern Moravian regions of Lašsko and Valašsko.[2] The origins of the song are unknown, but the use of "galánečka" implies that the song's characters are eastern Moravian.

"Hledám galánečku" is well known in the Czech Republic, a sing-along and dance number that also appears on several recordings of popular pub songs.[3] The lyrics describe a man who is looking for his sweetheart, though it is never quite clear where the action takes place. We do know that he is on one side of a door wanting to get in and that she is on the other side, determined to keep him out. In Texas, the song has inspired light-hearted interpretive fun.

Texas Polka News photojournalist Gary E. McKee has taken a number of photographs that show male band members wearing calico sun bonnets while playing—and interpreting—the story told in "Hledám galánečku." This playful spirit seems to spill out into the audience, where couples can be seen dancing together, the men decked out in bonnets and the occasional skirt. John Dujka, of the Brenham band Dujka Brothers, says this kind of cross-dressing was fairly common with some of the older bands, that they would "have fun and dress up in a bonnet or even a dress" while playing "Hledám galánečku."[4]

The song is known in Texas as "Looking for My Sweetheart." Johnny Mensik and Orchestra of Ennis included it on their 1972 album, *Required of Us a Song.* In their rendition, a male duet sings the first verse and is answered by a female duet on the second.[5] The orchestras of Lee Roy Matocha of Fayetteville and Joe Patek of Shiner also included it on record albums from the early 1970s.[6] The University Czech Singers, the choral group associated with Czech language classes at the University of Texas at Austin during the 1970s and 1980s, included "Hledám galánečku" on their 1977 album, *Czechoslovakian Folksongs.*[7] The Czech Melody Masters of Taylor and Austin included the first two verses on their 2000 CD, *Czech Melody Masters Play Old Tyme Radio Favorites,* reissued on Volume 4 of *Bands of Texas,* published by Schulenburg's Texas Polka Music Museum.[8]

23. Hora Shinerská *Hill of Shiner; Hills of Shiner*

Hora Shinerská

1. Hora Shinerská,
   krásné městečko.
   Jest tam pivovar,
   dobré pivečko.

Hill of Shiner

1. Hill of Shiner,
   a beautiful little town,
   there is a brewery there
   and good beer.

2. A co jste sedláci, co jste dělali,
že jste pivovar nepodporovali?
A co jste sedláci, co jste dělali,
že jste pivečko nepili?
Chorus:
Pijem, pijem, pivováři,
protože jsme kamarádi.
Pijem, pijem, pivečko pospolu.
A ne, a ne, a nebudem se ženiti,
ani do městečka choditi.
A ne, a ne, a nebudem se ženiti,
ani do městečka choditi.

2. And what, farmers, what were you doing
when you weren't patronizing the brewery?
And what, farmers, what were you doing
when you weren't drinking beer?
Chorus:
We drink, drink, brewers, because we are friends.
We drink, drink beer together.
And no, and no, we won't get married,
nor will we go into town.
And no, and no, we won't get married,
nor will we go into town.

Unknown origins. Words from KJT, *Sbírka českých písní*, 84. Music from Joe Patek Orchestra, "Shiner Beer Polka" (Rosenberg, TX: FBC Records 122-1, 1949), 78 rpm.

The town of Shiner lies in the coastal plains of the Gulf of Mexico. It occupies a stretch where the grasslands are relatively flat but broken up by creeks and rolling hills.[1] Just east of Shiner, on Hilltop Road, is the town's water tower. If you drive this road toward town, it goes directly to Spoetzl Brewery, a distance of about half a mile. The terrain forms a shallow basin as it approaches Boggy Creek. The brewery sits next to the creek, facing the higher ground reached by Hilltop Road. Perhaps this is the hill of Shiner memorialized in "Hora Shinerská."

The brewery has been there since 1909, operating continuously ever since a group of Shiner businessmen formed the Shiner Brewing Association. Their purpose was to produce beer in the Central European style for the many Czechs and Germans who lived in Lavaca County, one of the original four Central Texas counties with early Czech settlements. A German immigrant and brewmaster, Kosmos Spoetzl, bought the brewery in 1915. Kosmos and then his daughter Cecelie managed the brewery until the late 1960s. Known as "Miss Celie," she was the only female brewery owner in the country at the time. The present owner, Mexican immigrant Carlos Alvarez, CEO of the family-owned Gambrinus Company based in San Antonio, bought the brewery in 1989. Spoetzl Brewery continues its tradition of producing Czech- and German-style Shiner Beer.[2]

"Hora Shinerská" was first introduced into the Texas Czech playlist by the Joe Patek Orchestra of Shiner, a band that was sponsored by Shiner Beer for many years. Fort Bend County Records (FBC), partially owned by the polka musician Ray Krenek, released the 78 rpm Patek recording of the song in 1949 with the English title "Shiner Beer Polka."[3] This was a fruitful moment for songs with Shiner in the title; the Pateks released their version of the enduring "Když jsme opustili Shiner" (Song 31), also called "Shiner Song," about this same time. But the Patek title "Shiner Beer Polka" did not stick to "Hora Shinerská." The song is most commonly known by the translation of its first line, "Hill of Shiner," or sometimes "Hills of Shiner." Confusing matters, or perhaps making them more interesting, Lee Roy Matocha of Fayetteville calls it "Texas Special" on his 1970s LP, *The Country Boy Is Back*.[4]

Vrazels' Polka Band of Buckholts reissued a 1981 recording of "Hills of Shiner" on their second greatest-hits CD in 2002. It features Alfred Vrazel on vocals with the addition of George, Patrick, and Thomas Strmiska on a hearty male chorus.[5] John and Mark Dujka of the Brenham-based Dujka Brothers included "Hill of Shiner Polka" on their 1999 CD, *The Tradition Continues*.[6] The Czechaholics of La Grange released "Hills of Shiner Polka" on *Ještě jednou (One More Time)*, their 2007 CD.[7]

24. Já mám tragač nový; Já mám trakař novej *Wheelbarrow Polka*

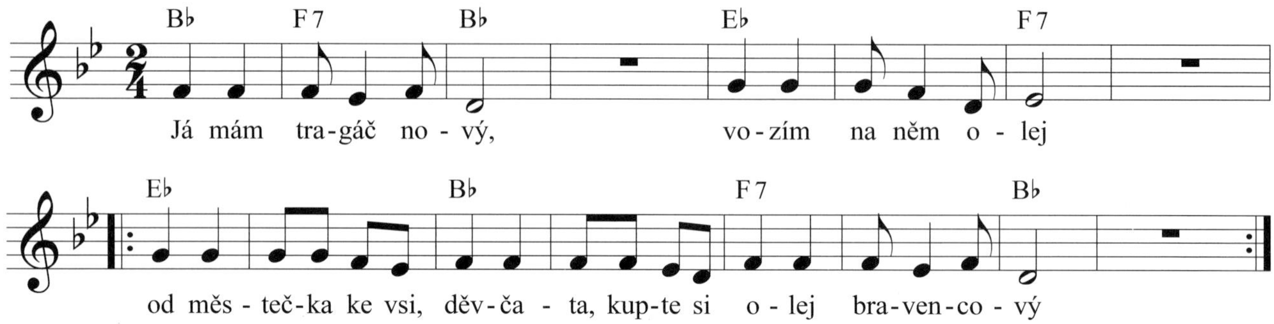

Já mám tragač nový

1. Já mám tragač nový, vozím na něm olej
od městečka ke vsi, děvčata, kupte si
olej bravencový.

2. Holky vybíhaly, olej koupovaly.
By si namazaly panty od komůrky,
by jim nevrzaly.

3. Která holka je bledá, ta se vdávat nemá.
Která je jak růže, ta se vdávat může.
Zde je hezká žena!

4. Já jsem bledá byla, já jsem se vdávala.
Vzala jsem si muže, ten byl jako růže.
Já jsem zčervenala!

I Have a New Wheelbarrow

1. I have a new wheelbarrow, I carry oil in it
from town to village. Girls, buy some
Bravenec oil.

2. The girls came running, they bought some oil.
They'll grease the chamber's hinges
so that they won't squeak.

3. Whichever girl is pale won't get married.
Whichever is like a rose can get married.
Here's a pretty woman!

4. I was pale, I did marry.
I chose a man who was like a rose.
I blushed!

Folk origins. Peck, *Valašské národní písně*, 36. Words from Bartoš and Bartoš, *Spivejme pisničky*, 49. Music from Joe Patek Orchestra, "Wheel Barrow Polka" (San Antonio: Martin M104, circa 1949), 78 rpm.

Já mám trakař novej

1. Já mám trakař novej, vozím na něm olej.
Od vesnici ke vsi děvčata jsou hezký.
Já mám dobrý olej.

2. Jám mám doma kvočnu, co já si s ní počnu?
Snesla je tu vejce, sedět na nich nechce,
ja mám hloupou kvočnu.

I Have a New Wheelbarrow

1. I have a new wheelbarrow, I carry oil in it.
From village to village the girls are pretty.
I have good oil.

2. I have a hen at home, what am I going to do with her?
She laid eggs there, she doesn't want to sit on them.
I have a stupid hen.

3. Já mám taky prase, stojím za nim zase,
celou noc se toulal, toulal že "to rána
budu jitrnice."

3. I also have a pig. I stand behind him again.
He wandered all night long, wandered that "come morning
I'll be sausage meat."

Folk origins. Slavia, *Národní písně,* Series 2, part 4, 275). Words from Jodie Mikula and His Orchestra, "Wheelbarrow," *A Toast to Czech Music* (Ennis: 1985), LP.

Two sets of lyrics to "Wheelbarrow Polka" are generally known in Texas, both attached to the same melody, a lively polka. The Joe Patek Orchestra of Shiner, a town in the south-central part of the state, recorded the first two verses of the first version in the late 1940s. The Patek 78 rpm was reissued on an Arhoolie compilation CD in 1993.[1] The second set of lyrics was recorded by the Jodie Mikula Orchestra, a storied family ensemble from Ennis, a North Texas town near Dallas. The Mikula "Já mám trakař novej" was included on the band's 1985 LP, *A Toast to Czech Music*, reissued on a Rounder compilation CD in 1994.[2]

The first verses of both versions descended from songs included in old Czech folk collections. The first, which uses the Slovak word *tragač* for wheelbarrow, is from the ethnographic region of eastern Moravia called Valašsko (Wallachia). This is one of the Moravian areas from which many Texas Czechs emigrated. The compiler of the songbook was a teacher in Visovice, about ten miles southwest of Vsetín.[3] A first verse similar to that of the second version was published in a Czech songbook in 1879. The song was found in the small village of Vonšov, on the eastern border of Bohemia and Germany. It was transcribed by one of the members of Slavia, a folklore collecting and literary society.[4] Both songs have since gained more verses.

Like the oil salesman in "Wheelbarrow," street peddlers who sold their wares were necessary parts of the economy in both rural and urban life, particularly in preindustrial times. As one writer explains, "Some peasants, especially those in certain poor, unfruitful districts which had long been unable to support their population, had for generations been accustomed to setting out on foot either to follow a wandering trade or to sell certain wares."[5] Another example of a street peddler can be found in "Dráteník" (Song 19), the song in this book about an itinerant wire worker who sells his ability to repair clay pots. While at work, the peddlers usually announced their wares or their repair abilities by means of short, recognizable street cries. These street cries are grouped within the category of work songs, and many have been studied by scholars.[6]

Even though both "Wheelbarrow" and "Tinker" evoke the market atmosphere of the street, neither is a street cry. Instead, they are both lyrical songs that describe and express feelings about everyday activities, songs that are sung after the day's work is done.[7] "Wheelbarrow" is an excellent example of a lyrical song. Both versions known in the state elevate the sturdy hand-pushed cart, praise the attributes of good oil, describe details of everyday life, and entertain with lighthearted lyrics that sometimes veer into playful double meaning.

John and Mark Dujka sang all four verses of the first version on their 1999 CD, *The Tradition Continues*.[8] Czech and Then Some of Ennis included "Wheelbarrow," with mostly the words to the second version, on their third CD called *The Easy Life*, recorded in 2001.[9] Wence and Helen Shimek of Hallettsville sang four verses, combining two verses of each set of lyrics, on their 1984 cassette tape, *More Polkas and Waltzes*.[10] The Ennis Czech Boys performed the second version at the 2016 South Texas Sausage and Polka Fest in Hallettsville.[11]

25. Já ráda tancuju *I Love to Dance*

Já ráda tancuju

1. Někomu jen ta píseň stačí,
aby se cítil ještě mladší.
Muzika když spustí zvesela,
každému náladu hned udělá.
Když začnou trumpety tu moji,
hned se mi každá bolest zhojí.
Nejdu spát domů až ráno v pět,
když zahrajou na klarinet.
Chorus:
Hrajte! Já ráda tancuju.
Možná že zítra snad
už tady nebudu.
A proto hrajte!
Já chci být veselá,
když na mě láska má zapoměla.

I Love to Dance

1. For some people it takes just a song
to make them feel still younger.
When the music starts joyfully,
everyone gets into a good mood.
When the trumpets start my song,
my every pain is immediately healed.
I don't go to sleep at home until five in the morning
when they play on the clarinet.
Chorus:
Play! I love to dance.
Maybe tomorrow
I will no longer be here.
And so, play!
I want to be happy
when my love has forgotten me.

2. Na našem dvorku pěkně hráli.
Na mě se do okénka smáli.
Hráli mě písničku nejsladší,
kterou mám na tom světě nejradší.
Smutně jsem při ní zaplakala
a mého mládí litovala,
které mi uvadlo jak ten květ
a nikdy se nevrátí zpět.

2. In our courtyard they played nicely.
They smiled at me through the window.
They played me the sweetest song
which I like best in the world.
I cried to it with sadness
and I regretted my youth
which wilted like that flower
and never will return.

From "Já ráda tancuju, I Love to Dance," words by Vašek (Václav) Zeman, music by Jaromír Vejvoda, arranged by Vaclav F. Fisher (Chicago: Vitak-Elsnic, 1941), used with permission by Vitak-Elsnic Company, a Division of Music Publishers of America, LLC.

"Já ráda tancuju," an upbeat polka that praises the healing power of dance and music, was published in Prague in 1937 and in 1941 by Vitak-Elsnic of Chicago. The music was written by Jaromír Vejvoda, and the words by Vašek (Václav) Zeman, who also collaborated on over thirty other songs, including "Škoda lásky," known as "Beer Barrel Polka" in English. After the Soviet-backed Communist Party took control of the Czechoslovakian government in 1948, Zeman fled to Canada. Vejvoda continued to live near Prague, where he and his family operated a restaurant. The new government censors changed some of Zeman's lyrics for having a "pessimistic" outlook. The second and third lines of the chorus to "Já ráda tancuju," for example, were changed from "Maybe tomorrow I will no longer be here" to "Play my song that I love so much!"[1]

"I Love to Dance," with the uncensored lyrics, is one of the songs Vrazels' Polka Band of Buckholts performed at the 1976 Festival of American Folklife in Washington, D.C.[2] The festival was a special twelve-week showcase of folk talent from across the country during America's bicentennial celebrations. The Gil Baca Orchestra of Houston was the first of three Texas Czech polka bands to perform at the annual Washington folklife festival. They played at the first one, in 1967.[3] Mark Halata and Texavia of Houston performed in 2008.[4]

Texas bands typically play the popular trio, or chorus, of "I Love to Dance." The Vrazels included the song this way on their LP called *Vrazel's Polka Band Performing in Washington, D.C.*, a live recording of their 1976 festival performance.[5] Tony Janak's Polka Band of Yoakum included "I Love to Dance" on its fortieth anniversary CD, which is a reissue of selected recordings the band made between 1963 and 1997.[6] Al Vanek and Michael Snapka of the Ennis Czech Harvesters sang a duet of "I Love to Dance" on their 1980 LP.[7] Mark Halata and Texavia included "I Love to Dance" on their 2003 CD, *Moon over Moravia,* reissued on a Texas Polka Music Museum CD.[8] The Choral Group of SPJST Lodge 88 in Houston, a choir of about forty singers accompanied by an orchestra of twenty instrumentalists, released "Já ráda tancuju" on their LP from 1978 entitled *Czech Folksongs.*[9] The Vlk Sisters of Dallas included the song on their self-titled 1978 LP.[10]

26. Julajda/Julida *Julayda; Džulajda; Župajda*

Julida

1. Ten panský kočí má modré oči.
   On se mně vyptal, kde já spím v noci.
   Chorus:
   Julida, Julida, já tě mám ráda,
   Julida, Julida, já tě ráda mám.

2. A já spím sama na naši půdě.
   Žádný tam za mnou vylézt nemůže.

3. Čtyři tam vlezli, jeden tam zůstal,
   Jak jsi se, Pepíčku, jak jsi se vyspal?

4. Já jsem se vyspal, ale jen málo.
   Mně se tam něco hezkého zdálo.

5. Půlnoc odbyla, lampička zhasla.
   Andulka povzdychla, postýlka praskla.

6. Počkej, Pepíčku, až se to sleze.
   Zaplatíš postýlku, babu i kněze.

Julida

1. That coachman has blue eyes.
   He asked me where I sleep at night.
   Chorus:
   Julida, Julida, I love you.
   Julida, Julida, I love you.

2. I sleep alone in our attic.
   No one can climb up to me.

3. Four climb up there, one remained.
   How, Joey, how well did you sleep?

4. I slept, but only a little.
   I had a nice dream there.

5. Midnight passed, the lamp burnt out.
   Annie sighed, the bed broke.

6. Just you wait, Joey, when they get together.
   You'll pay for the bed, the midwife, and the priest.

From "Julida Polka," words and music by Andrew Grill, arranged by Joseph P. Elsnic, (Chicago: Vitak-Elsnic, 1941), used with permission by Vitak-Elsnic Company, a Division of Music Publishers of America, LLC.

The song American polka lovers know as "Julida," or sometimes "Julajda,"[1] "Julayda,"[2] or "Džulajda,"[3] also exists in similar form in the Czech Republic under the title "Župajda."[4] "Župajda" likely evolved from an earlier Prague song, perhaps the one mentioned by Karel Čapek in his 1925 essay "Songs of the People of Prague."[5] That early version, for which Čapek does not provide a name, has bawdy lyrics about a flirtatious coachman with blue eyes and several boys who try to climb into a girl's sleeping loft. The first two verses he quotes are a near match for those of our American "Julida."

In the modern Czech version, the word župajda[6] is a nonsense word, filling out the song's line with an emphatic, funny, repetitive sound element. These types of nonsense words and syllables are common in songs and are sometimes called nonlexical vocables. A well-known example in English is the "fa la la la la" of the Christmas carol "Deck the Halls." The American version took the nonsense sound and transformed it into "Julida," a different spelling and now the name of a girl. In 1951, Frankie Yankovic and His Yanks of Cleveland recorded Walt Solek's English words with the title "My Girl Friend Julayda."[7] Texas musician Carl Finch of Denton's Brave Combo sings the lyrics "I'm sure you've heard of our gal Julida."[8]

In December of 1940, Vitak-Elsnic Music Company of Chicago published what became Andrew Grill's popular orchestral arrangement of "Julida Polka," and a month later they put out a piano solo with the six Czech verses in this book. Adolph Hofner and His Orchestra of San Antonio produced an enthusiastic rendition in 1948 with the first five Czech verses, accented by the hot piano playing of Charlie Poss, on the band's 78 rpm record called *Julida Polka.*[9] It was rereleased on the Arhoolie CD *South Texas Swing.* In Texas, "Julida" is also known as "Julajda," its Czech spelling. Frank Migl's Orchestra of the small Texas community of Novohrad released "Julajda (Julida) Polka" on a Humming Bird 78, probably in the late 1940s, with Migl on Czech vocals. It was rereleased on the first volume of Schulenburg's Texas Polka Music Museum's "Bands of Texas" series, compilation CDs that pay tribute to Texas polka music.[10]

The 1981 Brave Combo recording of "Julida Polka" with English lyrics was used on the soundtrack of Les Blank's 1984 polka documentary *In Heaven There Is No Beer?*[11] And for another interpretation of the title, in 1997 a British record company released radio recordings from about 1952 of country music great Hank Thompson and the Brazos Valley Boys. One of the cuts featured the band's pianist Gil Baca, a well-known Texas polka musician, singing "Julida" in Czech, under the title "Uvalde Polka."[12]

27. Kajdu *Ztratila jsem kajdu; I Lost My Vest*

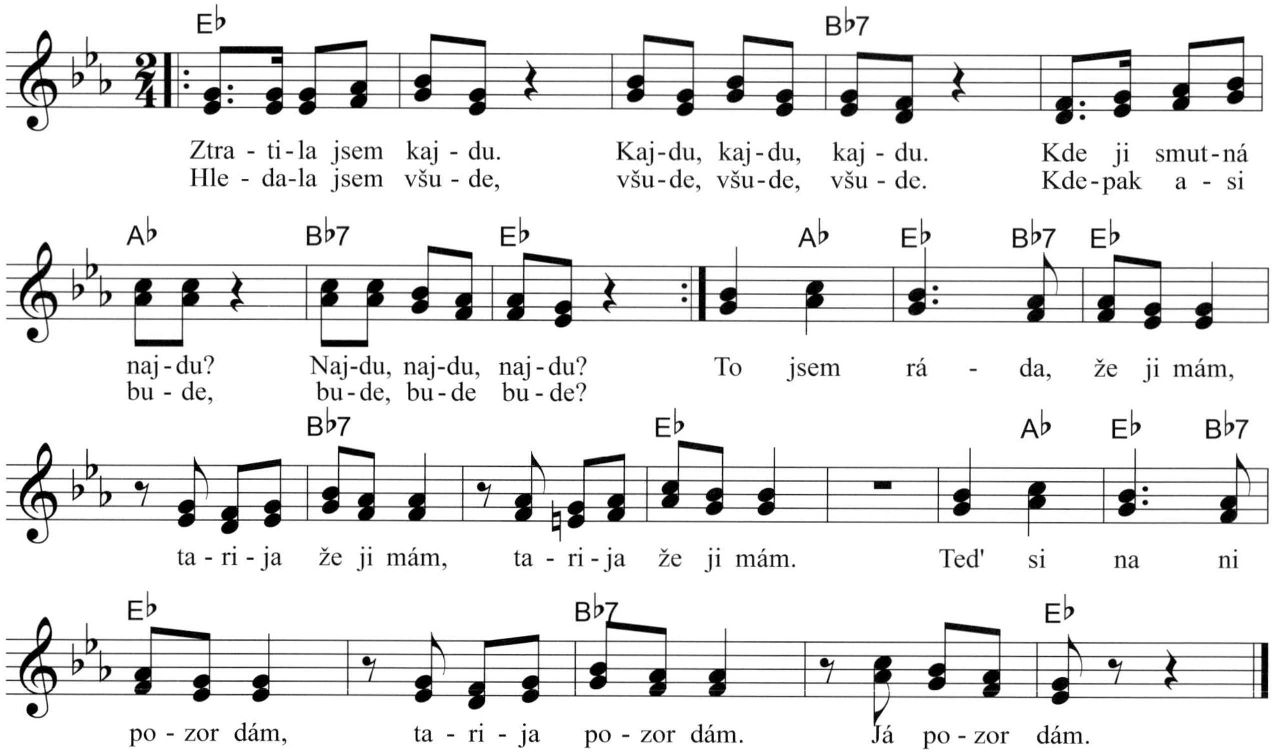

Kajdu

1. Ztratila jsem kajdu,
kajdu, kajdu, kajdu.
Kde ji smutná najdu,
najdu, najdu, najdu?
Hledala jsem všude.
Všude, všude, všude.
Kdepak asi bude,
bude, bude bude?
Chorus:
To jsem ráda, že ji mám,
ta-ri-ja že ji mám, ta-ri-ja že ji mám.
Ted' si na ni pozor dám,
ta-ri-ja pozor dám. Já pozor dám.

The Vest

1. I lost my vest,
vest, vest, vest.
Where will I, sad me, find it,
find it, find it, find it?
I looked everywhere,
everywhere, everywhere, everywhere.
Where might it be,
it be, it be, it be?
Chorus:
I'm glad that I have it.
Ta-ri-ja have it, ta-ri-ja have it.
Now, I'll be more careful with it,
ta-ri-ja careful with it. I'll be careful with it.

2. Ztratila jsem kajdu,
kajdu, kajdu, kajdu.
Kde ji smutná najdu,
najdu, najdu, najdu?
Najdu já ji v lese,
v lese, v lese, v lese.
Myslivec ji nese,
nese, nese, nese.

2. I lost my vest,
vest, vest, vest.
Where will I, sad me, find it,
find it, find it, find it?
I will find it in the woods,
the woods, the woods, the woods.
A hunter is carrying it,
carrying it, carrying it, carrying it.

Folk origins. Jindřich, *Jindřichův Chodský zpěvník*, song no. 243. Words and music from George Koudelka, Flatonia, Texas.

"Ztratila jsem kajdu," often simply called "Kajdu," is one of the fourteen hundred tunes and four thousand song texts collected in the Chodsko region of western Bohemia by the teacher and folklorist Jindřich Jindřich (1876–1967).[1] Jindřich was born in the region and returned there after leaving for university studies. He taught school in Domažlice, a town known for its preservation of traditional folk culture, bagpipe music, and historic architecture. Jindřich published eight volumes of folk songs between 1926 and 1955.[2]

The song had appeared in several publications before Jindřich notated and published it in one of his many songbooks. Most of the lyrics were quoted, for example, in an 1890 Czech-German phraseological dictionary by František Štěpán Kott, a secondary school teacher and celebrated linguist from Prague. Kott studied common language phrases and idioms and often included folk songs among his documented examples in the multiple dictionaries he published between 1879 and 1893.[3]

"Kajdu," sometimes called "I Lost My Vest," is both an energetic dance number and a great song to sing in a group. The six-note melody is easy to learn, and the chorus is repetitive and employs the nonsense word "ta-ri-ja," a string of syllables that are fun to say. The lyrics are light and humorous with repeated words, such as the four repetitions of the words "kajdu," "najdu," "všude," and "bude" in the first verse. One way to get a group to perform the song together is for a leader to sing the verse line and have the group respond with the repeated words.

The East Bernard Czech Singers included both verses of "Kajdu Polka" on their 1997 cassette tape, *Around the Moon*.[4] One of the singers, Martha Viktorin, also set sacred lyrics to the "Kajdu" melody, giving the song the title "We Are One in Spirit." This practice of adapting secular polka songs for sacred purposes became somewhat common in the 1970s when several Catholic churches in the United States began to celebrate Mass with the inclusion of folk and popular music, including polka. The tunes were familiar, and the lyrics were new and appropriate for the occasion. Polka Masses began to be performed in Texas in the mid-1990s, first brought to the state by Julius Tupa, founder of *Texas Polka News*.[5]

Chris Rybak of Hallettsville sings the first verse and chorus of "Kydu Polka" on his 1994 cassette tape, *I Love to Polka*.[6] The Dancehall Boys of Austin and Taylor, with John Ondrusek on vocals, included "Kajdu Polka" on their 1995 CD, *Behind the Blacksmith Shop*.[7] Vrazels' Polka Band of Buckholts included "Kajdu Polka" on *It's Polka Party Time*, their 1996 CD that they also reissued on the 2002 CD *Greatest Hits Volume 2*.[8] Czech and Then Some of Ennis celebrated its ten-year anniversary in 2007 with the release of the CD *A Tribute: 10 Years of Polka Music*, which included "Kajdu Polka."[9] The Taylor Czech Chorus included "Stratila jsem Kajdu (I Lost My Vest)" on its 2007 CD, *Songs of Our Heritage*.[10] The Texas Legacy Czech Band of Houston, successor to the Bobby Jones Band, included "Kajdu Polka" on its first recording, a self-titled CD released in 2008.[11]

28. Kde domov můj? *Where Is My Home?*

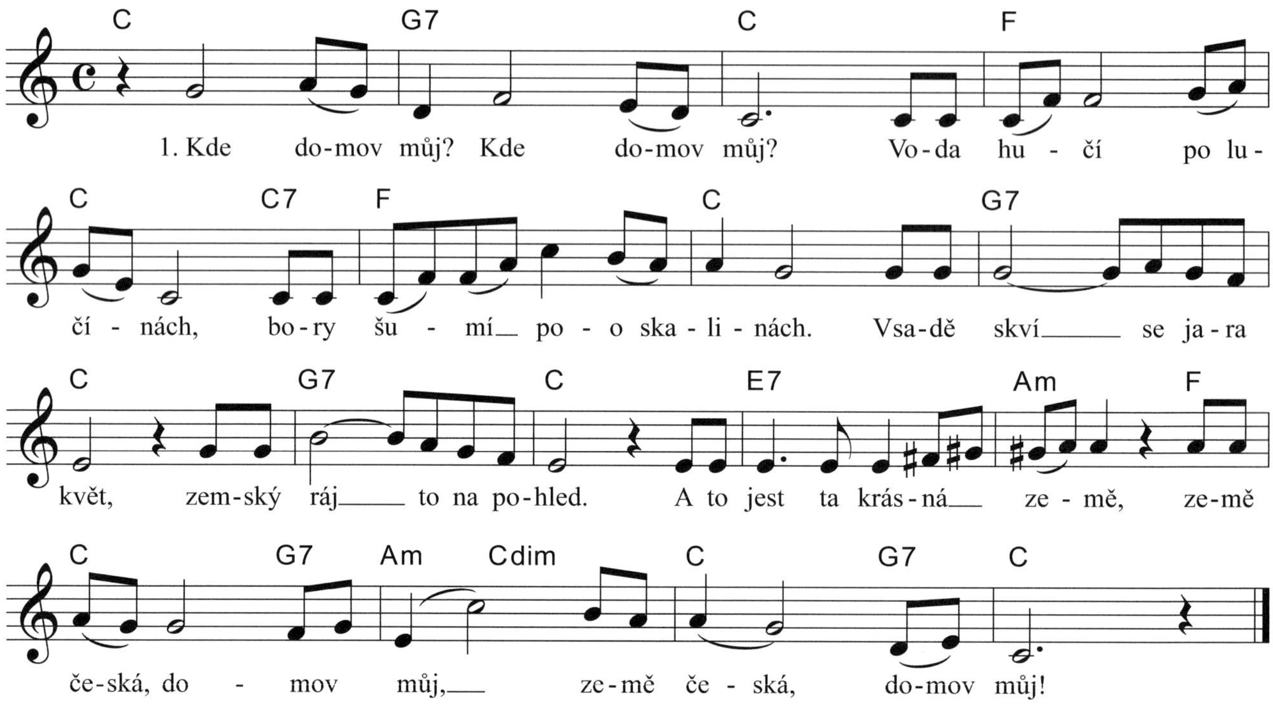

Kde domov můj?

1. Kde domov můj? Kde domov můj?
Voda hučí po lučínách,
bory šumí po skalinách.
V sadě skví se jara květ,
zemský ráj to na pohled.
A to jest ta krásná země,
země česká, domov můj,
země česká, domov můj!

2. Kde domov můj? Kde domov můj?
V kraji znáš-li bohumilém
duše útlé v těle čilém,
mysl jasnou, vznik a zdar,
A tu sílu vzdoru zmar.
To je Čechů slavné plémě,
mezi Čechy, domov můj,
mezi Čechy, domov můj!

Where Is My Home?

1. Where is my home? Where is my home?
Water roars through the meadows,
pines rustle through the cliff rocks.
Spring flowers adorn the garden,
an earthly paradise to the eyes.
And this is that beautiful land,
the Czech land, my home,
the Czech land, my home!

2. Where is my home? Where is my home?
If, in the heavenly land, you have met
slender souls in an agile body,
of clear mind, vigorous and prospering,
and with a strength that frustrates all defiance.
That is the glorious nation of Czechs,
among the Czechs, my home,
among the Czechs, my home!

Words by Josef Kajetán Tyl, music by František Škroup, from *Fidlovačka,* first performed in Prague, 1834.

The first verse of this wistful song that begins with a question is the national anthem of the Czech Republic.[1] Shortly after the formation of the independent nation of Czechoslovakia, the first verse was adopted as half of the new country's two-song anthem. "Kde domov můj?" represented the Czechs, and "Nad Tatrou sa blýska" (It's Lightning over the Tatras), the Slovaks.[2] In 1992, when the Czechs and the Slovaks broke up to form two separate republics, often referred to as the Velvet Divorce for its peaceful proceedings, the national anthem split as well.

"Kde domov můj?" was first performed in the comic operetta *Fidlovačka*, which premiered in 1834 at the Estates Theater in Prague.[3] A *fidlovačka* is a cobbler's tool, and the operetta, with text by Josef Tyl and music by František Škroup, was named after a spring festival commemorating a successful eighteenth-century strike of Prague shoemakers.[4]

The Czech journalist Milena Jesenká, whose name was immortalized in Franz Kafka's book *Letters to Milena,* described hearing "Kde domov můj?" while at a performance of *Fidlovačka* during World War I. She said it was not yet an official anthem back then but rather a well-known national song. But when the song started, a man sitting in front of her suddenly and quietly began to stand. "I don't know what he wanted to express," she continued, "but the act was as if to honor the Czech song." Soon everyone in the theater was standing and singing along. "Kde domov můj?" she went on, "was not a song against anyone, but for something. It did not wish for anybody's destruction, but for our continued existence. It is not a warrior song, but a song of our Czech home, that land without anything grandiose about its countryside, a land of hills and hillocks, . . . a land of fragrant boundaries between fields and tranquil little streams. The land where we are at home."[5]

Even before its official designation as part of Czechoslovakia's national anthem, "Kde domov můj?" has been abundantly available in Czech-language songbooks on both sides of the ocean. In the lyric collection *Česko-americký zpěvník* published in Houston in 1916, for example, it appears at the beginning of the book.[6] It is first in Rev. Vincent Pisek's *Twenty-Two Bohemian Folk-Songs*, published in 1912 in New York, a book found in a number of early Texas Czech households.[7]

There is a Texas version of the song. Sean Gallup, in his book *Journeys into Czech-Moravian Texas,* included the lyrics dictated to him in 1994 by Rose and August Konvicka of Moravia, Texas.[8] Used with permission from Texas A&M University Press.

1. Kde domov můj, kde domov můj?
Kde se rodí kukuřice
a bavelna ještě více,
kde ten sladký melas
je a špeku nechybuje.
A to je ta krásná země,
zem texaská, domov můj,
zem texaská, domov můj.

2. Kde domov můj, kde domov můj?
Školy máme vystaveny,
aji spolky založeny,
moravské i anglické.
Sláva nám vždycky roste.
A to je ta krásná země,
zem Texaská, domov můj,
zem Texaská, domov můj.

1. Where is my home, where is my home?
Where corn sprouts
and cotton even more,
where there's sweet molasses
and bacon isn't lacking.
And this is that beautiful country,
the land of Texas, my home,
the land of Texas, my home.

2. Where is my home, where is my home?
We've built our schools
and founded our fraternals,
Moravian and English.
Our glory always grows.
And this is that beautiful country,
the land of Texas, my home,
the land of Texas, my home.

29. Kdybych byla ptáčkem *If I Were a Bird; If I Was a Bird*

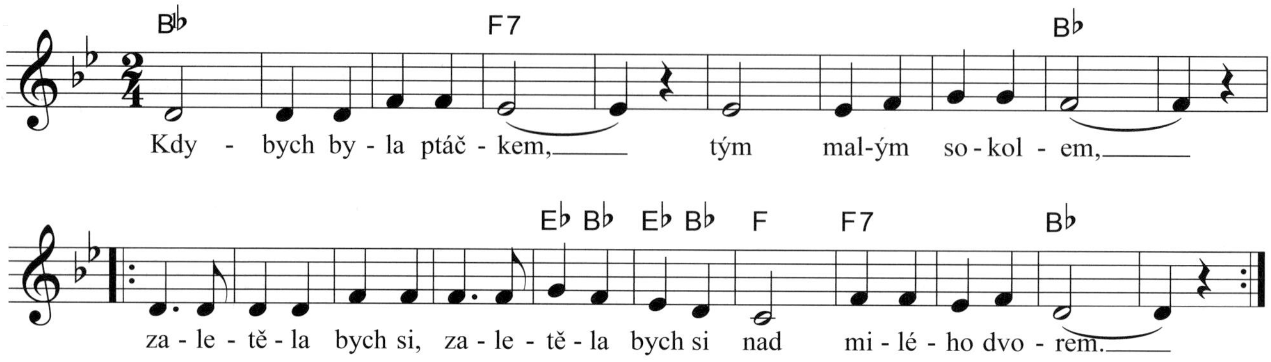

Kdybych byla ptáčkem

1. Kdybych byla ptáčkem,
tým malým sokolem,
zaletěla bych si, zaletěla bych si
nad milého dvorem.

2. Nad milého dvorem
nad jeho maštalí.
Podívala bych se, podívala bych se,
co chlapci dělají.

3. Jeden koně češe,
druhý obrok nese,
třetí nejmilejší, ze všech nejkrásnější,
psaníčko jí píše.

4. Komu ty, můj milý,
psaníčko si píšeš?
Tobě, moje milá, tobě, moje milá,
že už moje budeš.

If I Were a Bird

1. If I were a little bird,
a little falcon,
I would fly, I would fly
over my dear one's yard.

2. Over my dear one's yard,
over his stable,
I would take a look at, I would look at
what the boys are doing.

3. One combs the horse,
another carries feed,
the third, the dearest and most handsome,
writes the most beautiful love letter to her.

4. To whom, my dear,
are you writing this letter?
To you, my dear, to you, my dear,
so that you will be mine.

Folk origins. Sušil, *Moravské národní písně*, 515, and Bartoš and Janáček, *Kytice z národních písní moravských*, 70. Words from Bartoš and Janáček. Music from Rudy Kurtz Orchestra, "Kdybych byla ptáčkem" (Waco, TX: Humming Bird 182-A, late 1940s–early 1950s), 78 rpm.

Many variants of "Kdybych byla ptáčkem" were found by nineteenth-century Czech folklorists. The lyrics known in Texas are, with minor word changes, the same as those published by František Sušil and František Bartoš, both prolific collectors of Moravian folk songs. The four verses are from Lidečko, a village in the Vsetín district of Moravia, an area of heavy emigration to Texas.[1] They tell a story about a young woman who imagines that she is a falcon who flies "over my dear one's yard." She can see three boys there, all busy doing something. One is combing a horse, another is carrying feed, and the third—her boyfriend—is writing a letter to her.

The last verse brings the song to a happy ending. The girl asks the boy, "To whom, my dear, are you writing this letter?" He answers, "To you, my dear, so that you will be mine." Bartoš himself seemed to be carried away with contentment when he wrote about the meaning of these lyrics in 1903: "The blissful feeling of happy lovers is beautifully illustrated in this song."[2]

The farmyard and happy lovers are replaced by a battlefield and separated lovers in additional lyrics published by the Dallas Czech Singers in 1985. In verse four, the letter writer is drafted into the army and does not get the girl. He tells her that since he cannot have her, she should marry his brother and in this way she will still be part of their family.[3] Verses in the Dallas book echo a theme common to two of the "Kdybych byla ptáčkem" songs collected by František Sušil and published in 1860. Sušil includes them in his section called "Songs about War." One, from Kyjov in southern Moravia, begins with lyrics like those Bartoš found. But in the fourth verse, the boy writes the girl to tell her "you will not be mine." He goes on to vividly describe what kind of life awaits him as a soldier: "My wife will be a sharp saber. She will cut through for me whenever there is a need." He further describes his saber as "sharpened on both sides. It will hack for me from Hungary to Moravia."[4]

In another army version of the song from Sušil's book, the female is not the girlfriend but rather the soldier's mother. Sušil found this one in Valašské Klobouky, again part of the Moravian region where many of the Texas Czechs emigrated from. In these lyrics, the mother says if she were a bird, "I would fly into the field above the whole army so that I can see what my dear one is doing." The song ends with a benediction: "The Blessed Mary will protect us, you, my son, at war, and me, sad at home."[5]

The song is known in Texas as "If I Were a Bird" or "If I Was a Bird." The Rudy Kurtz Orchestra from Shiner, with Kurtz singing the first three verses, recorded the song in the late 1940s or early 1950s.[6] Kurtz's handwritten notation of the melody is on display in a binder called "Musicians Notebook" in the Kalich House Music Museum at the Texas Czech Heritage and Cultural Center in La Grange. Vrazels' Polka Band from Buckholts recorded "If I Were a Bird" about 1966, and it became the signature song of Anton, one of the two Vrazel brothers.[7] John and Frank Majek of the Corpus Christi Leo Majek Orchestra, sang a duet on their 1960s album *Polka and Waltz*.[8] Ray Baca of Fayetteville released "If I Was a Bird" on his band's first LP called *Ray Baca's Polka Band*.[9] The Red Ravens of El Campo recorded "If I Were a Bird" in 1977; it was reissued on a compilation CD titled *Texas Bohemia* in 1994.[10] More recent recordings include the 2005 CD *Polkas for Everyone* by Czech and Then Some of Ennis,[11] a 2008 CD called *New Sounds* by the Lazy Farmers of Bellville,[12] and a 2012 CD called *Keepin' Tradition Alive* by the Incredible Music Makers of Praha.[13]

30. Když já libě spím *Dreamland Waltz*

Když já libě spím

1. Když já libě spím, máš mě nechat spát.
   Když se probudím, máš mě milovat.
2. Na ten dnešní den měl jsem libý sen.
   Spatřil jsem tebe v krásné zahradě.
3. V krásné zahradě, v líbezném sadě
   mezi růžemi jsme se bavili.
4. Měsíček milé, sad ten osvětlil
   a tvou milou tvář libě ozářil.
5. Tvá modrá očka, překrasná byla.
   Jak hvězda jitřní, tak se třpytila.

When I Sweetly Sleep

1. When I sweetly sleep, you must let me sleep.
   When I wake up, you must love me.
2. On this very day I had a lovely dream.
   I caught sight of you in a beautiful garden.
3. In a beautiful garden, in a delightful orchard,
   among the roses we enjoyed ourselves.
4. The dear little moon kindly lit up that orchard
   and lovingly shined on your dear face.
5. Your sweet blue eyes were exquisite.
   Like the morning star, that's how they sparkled.

Broadside origins. Words to verses 1–2 and music from "Když já libě spím, In Dreamland," arranged for piano and voice by A. L. Maresh (Cleveland: Maresh Music, 1908); words to verses 3–5 from KJT, *Sbírka českých písní*, 77.

"Když já libě spím," a beautiful love song, was arranged for piano and voice by A. L. Maresh and published by his Cleveland music company in 1908. Maresh was born in Cleveland in 1877 to Czech immigrant parents and began composing music at the age of sixteen. In 1896, he opened a music store in his parents' home, from which he sold instruments and European sheet music. In 1906, he was able to move to a business location. By this time he had already composed and arranged "hundreds of pieces of Bohemian popular music," according to Victor Greene in *A Passion for Polka,* his study of American ethnic music.[1]

Maresh may have learned "Když já libě spím" from the sheet music he imported and sold in his store. In the 1870s, it was published as a *kramářský tisk* (broadside print) by Jan Rippl in Jihlava, a town on the Bohemian-Moravian border.[2] A later arrangement of the song, published in

Prague by Jan Spurný sometime in the 1870s, was reviewed in an 1880 Czech journal in rapturous terms, praising it as "the miraculous child of Marie Grundová: 'Když já libě spím, máš mne nechat spát.'"[3] As an importer, Maresh may have had access to these early published versions. But however he first learned the song, copies of his arrangement can still be found in collections of Czech American polka musicians.

The Maresh "Když já libě spím" has two verses, which are the words most commonly sung in Texas. These verses appear as the first two in this songbook; the other three became part of the song at some point and can be found in the 1960s lyric book published by the Katolická jednota Texaská (Catholic Union of Texas, or KJT). Adolph Hofner and His Texans of San Antonio recorded the song for Bluebird Records in a Dallas session on February 13, 1940.[4] A 78 rpm was released as "Dis ja liebe spim," a phonetic rendering of the Czech title, and reissued on CD by Arhoolie in 1994. Hofner and his brother Emil sing a duet on the first three verses, enhanced by Adolph's crooning vocal lead and Emil's ethereal steel guitar solo and fills.[5]

Another early recording was "Dreamland Waltz" by the Joe Patek Orchestra of Shiner, a 78 rpm probably released in the late 1940s. It was reissued on a CD called *Joe Patek Orchestra: The 78s*, produced by Lee Roy Matocha of Fayetteville. Joe and Jerome Patek sing the first two verses as a duet, Jerome singing his signature high harmony. [6] The Leo Majek Orchestra of Corpus Christi released "Dream Waltz" in the mid-1960s on its first album. John and Frank Majek sang a duet on three verses, the same ones the Hofners sang.[7] The Pavelka Orchestra of Robstown released "Dreamland Waltz" on an LP in 1977, with Benny Pavelka providing the vocal and Mike Pavelka humming a lovely wordless harmony.[8] The Ennis Czech Boys released "Dreamland" on their 2016 CD, *Cheers to 10 Years*.[9]

31. Když jsme opustili Shiner/Prahu *Shiner Song; Praha Polka*

Když jsme opustili Shiner/Prahu

1. Když jsme opustili Shiner/Prahu,
   slunce svítilo.
   Piva bylo dosti,
   a jídla do sytosti.
   Když jsme opustili Shiner/Prahu,
   slunce svítilo.

2. Když jsme opustili pivovar,
   bečka byla prázdná.
   A my jsme popíjeli,
   a dobře jsme se měli.
   Když jsme opustili pivovar,
   bečka byla prázdná.

When We Left Shiner/Praha

1. When we left Shiner/Praha,
   the sun was shining.
   There was plenty of beer,
   and food to fill us.
   When we left Shiner/Praha,
   the sun was shining.

2. When we left the brewery,
   the keg was empty.
   We drank well
   and we had a good time.
   When we left the brewery,
   the keg was empty.

Unknown origins. Words and music from Joe Patek Orchestra, "Shiner Song" (San Antonio: Martin M103, late 1940s), 78 rpm, used with permission; reissued on *Texas-Czech, Bohemian, and Moravian Bands* (Arhoolie Folkloric 7026, 1993), CD.

This flexible and generous song is hard to pin down. Irena Přibylová, who wrote about it for a 2014 Czech symposium on world music held near Brno, said the origin of the song "remains to this day a mystery." She went on to say that Czech Americans insist it comes from the old country, but those who live in the old country know it from old American recordings. Přibylová goes on to speculate, possibly in jest, that the song may have been created during the Czechoslavic Ethnographic Exhibition in Prague, held during the summer of 1895.[1] This exhibition of folk culture, which attracted two million local and foreign visitors, was on the same grand scope as the multiple world's fairs of the nineteenth century.[2]

One of the many music ensembles that played during the exhibition was an eighteen-member band from Chicago led by J. Holeček, according to Přibylová. The band performed classical and folk songs and participated in a number of processions through Prague. This all occurred within the crush of patriotic and enthusiastic crowds who indulged in what Přibylová describes as some "truly dissipated beer-drinking." She wonders if the general ebullient atmosphere may have inspired the visiting band to write the good-natured "Když jsme opustili Prahu," either while in Prague or on the boat headed back to America.[3]

Another Czech music scholar, Lubomír Tyllner, pointed out in a 2015 interview with John Novak that the melody of "Když jsme opustili Prahu" sounds like the Czech folk song called "Zdálo se mně, má panenko" (I Had a Dream, My Darling).[4] It was a favorite of Tomáš Masaryk, founding president of the 1918 independent nation of Czechoslovakia.[5]

The Texas polka collector and musician George Koudelka of Flatonia wonders if the song came to Texas by way of the Six Fat Dutchmen, a popular polka band from New Ulm, Minnesota, for whom the German-Czech "Dutchman" style of polka music was named. The Six Fat Dutchmen, who toured widely, came to Texas several times. One report says they "established a record for weekly attendance at the Mraz Ballroom in Houston sometime in the 1940s."[6] Koudelka has a 1946 recording of the band's 78 rpm called "Praha Polka," with lyrics that begin with the familiar "Když jsme opustili Prahu." The record provides an additional clue by naming the composer or arranger of the song as B. Leopold, the name written under the song title, though it is not clear who B. Leopold is.[7]

Leaving the origin question behind, it is safe to say that "Když jsme opustili Prahu" was definitely known in Texas in the early 1940s. Adolph Hofner and His Bohemians, as they were known at the time, recorded the song for Columbia Records at a 1942 session in Hollywood. It was released as a 78 rpm under the title "Dis Syme Odpustik Prahu" and featured Walter Kleypas on accordion. In 2010, the British Archive of Country Music reissued the session on the CD *Swing with the Music*. Adolph Hofner and His Orchestra recorded it for Imperial in about 1949 as "Shiner Song," though they continued to sing "Prahu" in the lyrics. This second cut, featuring fiddle, was reissued on the Arhoolie CD *Texas-Czech, Bohemian, and Moravian Bands*.[8] In 1950, the band changed its name to Adolph Hofner and the Pearl Wranglers when the Pearl Brewing Company of San Antonio became their radio sponsor.

One of Pearl's rivals was Shiner Beer, brewed by the Spoetzl brewing company of Shiner, a town about ten miles from the Hofners' hometown of Moulton. Shiner Beer was a long-time sponsor of the Joe Patek Orchestra. The Patek band recorded "Shiner Song" on the Martin label, also in the late 1940s. They most definitely sang the word "Shiner" on the recording. Their brass-heavy version was rereleased on that same Arhoolie CD called *Texas-Czech, Bohemian, and Moravian Bands*. Chris Strachwitz, who founded Arhoolie Records in 1960, interviewed Joe Patek in about 1966. Strachwitz asked Patek where the "Shiner Song" came from, and Patek replied, "That's kind of song comes from Europe but we just give it the name, you see. . . . We sing about Shiner sun when we left Shiner, what the sun was shining and then another verse is that was at the brewery and it was plenty to drink and plenty to eat."[9]

"Shiner Song" is the fight song of both Shiner High School and Saints Cyril and Methodius Catholic School in Shiner. The Patek version was named one of the one hundred best state songs by *Texas Monthly* in 2004. The

Texas Polka Music Association designated it an "All Time Favorite Song" in 1995. Whether the lyrics say "Shiner" or "Prahu," it is played by most polka bands in the state and sung by most of the choirs. "Když jsme opustili Prahu" even made its way to the Czech Republic, where it was recorded, with the Texas lyrics and in a style reminiscent of Adolph Hofner, by the singer Honza Vyčítal and his band Staří zavináči in 1991.[10]

32. Kolíne, Kolíne

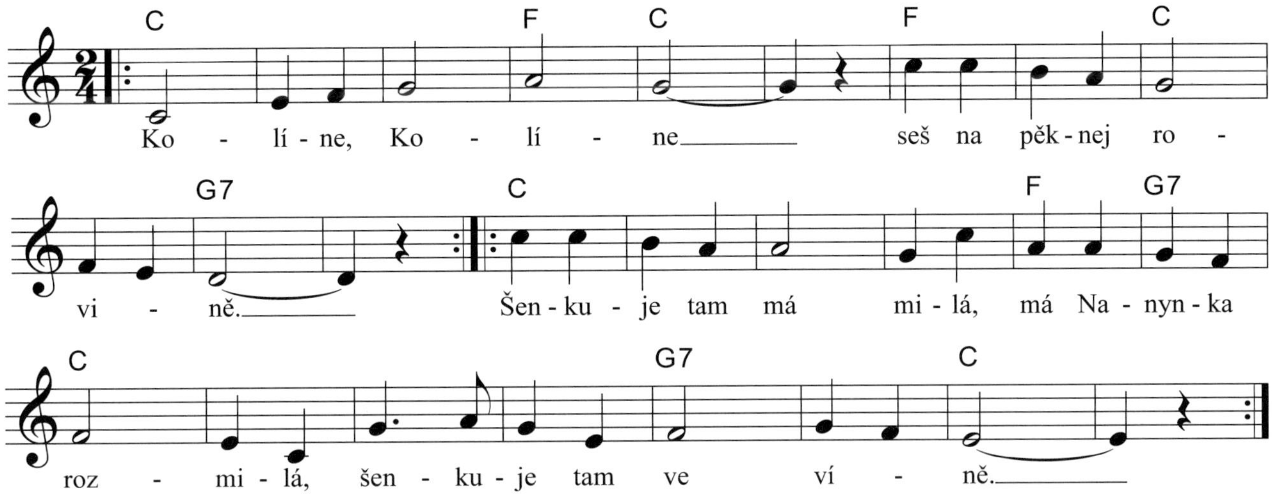

Kolíne, Kolíne (Novotný)

1. Kolíne, Kolíne,
   seš na pěknej rovině.
   Šenkuje tam má milá,
   má Nanynka rozmilá,
   šenkuje tam ve víně.

2. Přišel tam hošíček,
   ten její milovníček.
   Dal si nalejt vína,
   pořád nad ním dřímá,
   sed si za stoleček.

3. Nesed' a nedřímej,
   radši vína nalejvej,
   aby lidi neřekli,
   a na nás to nesmekli,
   že jseš ty můj milej.

4. Já jsem k vám nepřišel
   vína nalejvati,
   ale já jdu pro lásku,
   malovaný obrázku,
   tebe milovati.

Kolín, Kolín (Novotný)

1. Kolín, Kolín,
   you stand in a pretty plain.
   My beloved is tending bar there,
   my lovely Annie,
   she is serving in the winery.

2. A young man arrived there,
   he was her beloved.
   Some wine was served to him,
   he keeps dozing off over it
   and sat down at the table.

3. Don't sit down and don't sleep.
   It's better to pour some wine
   so that people don't say
   and make fun of us,
   that you are my sweetheart.

4. I didn't come to you
   to pour wine.
   But I am coming for love,
   a beautiful painting,
   to love you.

Kolíne, Kolíne (Kmoch)

1. Kolíne, Kolíne,
stojíš v pěkné rovině.
Šenkuje tam má milá,
má panenka rozmilá,
šenkuje tam ve víně.

2. Přišel tam Pepíček,
měl na stranu klobouček.
Dal si nalejt máz piva
a při tom si zazpívá,
Kolínečku, Kolíne.

3. Hradečku, Hradečku,
seš na pěkném kopečku,
tam jsem prožil svoje mládí
mezi svými kamarády
při plzeňském pivečku.

Kolín, Kolín (Kmoch)

1. Kolín, Kolín,
you stand in a pretty plain.
My beloved is serving there,
my lovely doll,
she is serving in the winery.

2. Joey arrived there
with his lopsided hat at his side.
He had a beer
while singing
sweet Kolín, Kolín.

3. Hradečku, Hradečku,
you are on a pretty hill,
there I spent my youth
among our friends
drinking Pilsner beer.

Folk origins. Novotný words from Novotný, *Libické písně*, 42; Kmoch verses from Kapusta, *Dechové kapely*, 151–52. Music from "Kolíne, Kolíne, Polka s Textem," František Kmoch (Chicago: Georgi and Vitak, 1910s).

Kolín is a town situated about fifty miles east of Prague on the Elbe River. In 1757, during the Seven Years' War, the Austrian and Prussian armies fought a bloody battle near the town of Kolín. The Austrians won and kept the Czech lands intact and within their realm. The boundaries the victory established closely align with the boundaries of the present-day Czech Republic. But the battle also left over 20,000 casualties.[1] The song "Kolíne, Kolíne," collected in the first half of the 1800s by the priest and folklorist František Sušil, memorializes the dead. "Kolíne, Kolíne, in the pretty plain," the song begins in a haunting minor key, "many of your sons will die." Five more verses go on to describe the grief caused by the deaths of these soldiers.[2] This Sušil version of the song entered the realm of art music with composer Leoš Janáček's arrangement of it.[3]

Václav Juda Novotný, another Czech folklorist, published a different "Kolíne, Kolíne" at the beginning of the twentieth century. He heard the song in the town of Libice, about ten miles north of Kolín, and published it in his 1901 collection of fifty folk songs called *Libické písně* (Songs of Libice).[4] This one has a march-like melody and is in a major key. Except for the first line that describes the pretty plain, the lyrics are different from the ones collected by Sušil and do not mention the battle of Kolín at all. Instead they tell the story of a man who seems to be returning to Kolín after an absence. He goes to visit his beloved at her workplace.

The Novotný song was used by František Kmoch in his band arrangement, published in Prague in 1906.[5] Kmoch was born near Kolín in 1848. He studied in Prague and returned home to teach and also to perform music. He became bandleader for the politically active Sokol athletic club in Kolín soon after he began teaching. He married, started a music school, led and toured widely with the accomplished Kolín concert band, and wrote many popular marches and dance pieces. He lived in Kolín his whole life and died there in 1912. The town still holds a brass band festival in his name every year.[6] For his famous "Kolíne, Kolíne" march, Kmoch used the first verse and the lively Libice tune collected by Novotný. But Kmoch changed the lyrics after the first verse. In his second verse, the young man ignores his sweetheart, drinks a beer, and joins a rousing sing-along, a toast to "sweet Kolín." In the third verse, Kmoch incorporates another famous battle site, one that occurred in 1866 near the town of Hradec Králóve, about fifty miles west of Kolín. This verse also ends in a toast.[7]

The Kmoch brass band arrangement doubles as a rousing polka, and it has been inspiring dancers for many years in Texas. Bands often play the entire Kmoch arrangement. Some sing the Novotný words, some the Kmoch, and some a mix of the two. The Adolph Migl Orchestra of Novohrad, a farming community in Fayette County named for the Bohemian town of the same name, made an early Texas recording of "Kolíne, Kolíne," in 1947 or 1948.[8] The band played the whole march and sang two verses. The Texas Czech Folk Singers of Dallas recorded the long version of "Kolíne, Kolíne" on a cassette tape with accordion accompaniment.[9] The Dujka Brothers of Brenham also recorded the full march version and sang the first two Kmoch verses.[10] Houston's SPJST Lodge 88 choir and orchestra gave the march a full sound—with about forty singers and twenty instrumentalists—on their 1978 LP, *Czech Folksongs.*[11]

33. Krásná Amerika *Beautiful America*

Krásná Amerika

Krásná, to je krásná,
to je krásná Amerika.

1. V Americe sú slepice,
ty nesu vejce jak čepice.

2. V Americe tam je hej,
tam z pítka teče petrolej.

3. V Americe sú děvčata,
hezké jsou jako poupata.

4. V Americe to je blaze,
tam teče pivo po podlaze.

5. Proto se všichni sejdeme,
do Ameriky pojedeme.

Beautiful America

Beautiful, it is beautiful,
it is beautiful America.

1. In America are hens,
they lay eggs as big as caps.

2. In America it is fun,
there petroleum flows from the spigot.

3. In America are girls
as pretty as flower buds.

4. In America it is pleasant,
there beer flows onto the floor.

5. That is why we will all get together,
we'll go to America.

English Lyrics

Beautiful, there's a beautiful,
there's a beautiful America.

1. That is why we're bound away,
We'll be going on our way.

2. Where we know are beautiful girls
just like beautiful shining pearls.

3. Where the boys will be drinking,
at the girls they'll be winking.

4. There we'll find our dear sweetheart,
one we'll love with all our heart.

Unknown origins. Words from Bartoš and Bartoš, *Spivejme pisničky*, 188–89. Music from Joe Patek Orchestra, "Beautiful America" (Waco, TX: Humming Bird 103, late 1940s), 78 rpm, used with permission. English lyrics by Ray Krenek, from Ray Krenek and His Orchestra, "Beautiful America" (Rosenberg, TX: FBC 105, 1949), 78 rpm, used with permission.

"Krásná Amerika" is one of many immigrant comic songs about an earthly paradise that chronicled the nineteenth-century mass migration of Europeans who sought refuge in the New World.[1] The exaggerated expectations that the verses describe—free-flowing beer, eggs the size of caps—poke fun at the high hopes immigrants had for a better life. Some of the humorous words also have a satirical bite that conveys an undercurrent of skepticism about extravagant claims for the opportunities one could find in America. Such hyperbole was employed by agents who sold ship tickets and land and handed out misleading information about places that wanted settlers, like the state of Texas. A commemorative book published by St. Mary's Parish in Praha includes this story about Veronika Kulak from Frenštát, a town in the Moravian region. Veronika arrived at the Galveston port in 1873 with her younger sister. The two teenage girls had seen advertising material that promoted immigration to America. Many years later, in a history of the Praha parish, Veronika's daughter related what her mother and aunt told her about the promotional material they had seen.

"They saw posters with a pretty little girl dressed in a beautiful pink lacy dress with a big bow for the sash, and lacy pink bonnet with a long ribbon tied under her chin. The words on the poster told them something like: 'Come to America, where life is so grand. The hardest work that you might have to do all day long is pick something that looks like white roses.'" The charming work description referred to the sweaty, back-breaking job of picking cotton! Nevertheless, Veronika thrived in her new home. She married Jon Vaněk, who emigrated from a Moravian village a few miles from her own. Together they raised twelve children, all baptized in the Praha Church.[2]

"Krásná Amerika" is fondly regarded in Texas, so much so that the mild bite of the song's humor gave way to sweet playfulness and sincerity in the hands of Texas lyricists. Ray Krenek of Wallis recounted in a 2002 interview that he and his father, Edward, wrote lyrics in Czech, German, and English.[3] Their English lyrics, reprinted here, envision a better life but describe it in simpler and more realistic terms. The Kreneks tell of young men who dream of flirting and falling in love in America. Another set of English lyrics, by Adolph Hofner, describes immigrants who have made a successful move and have already settled down. They report that they are "happy to be, to work, to plant, to know that we're free."

The orchestras of both Ray Krenek and Joe Patek made early recordings. "Krásná Amerika," a 78 rpm by the Ray Krenek Orchestra with the Czech lyrics, was possibly the first, according to George Koudelka of Flatonia, who played drums with Adolph Hofner for many years. It was recorded in the legendary Houston studio of Gold Star Records sometime in the mid-to-late 1940s.[4] The Krenek Orchestra also released its English version, first on Krenek's own FBC Records in 1949 and reissued shortly thereafter by Humming Bird, another early independent recording company with headquarters in Waco.[5]

Joe Patek Orchestra recorded "Beautiful America" with the Czech lyrics. It was released by Humming Bird around the late 1940s and in 1993 was included on the Arhoolie compilation CD called *Texas-Czech, Bohemian, and Moravian Bands*.[6] Adolph Hofner and the Pearl Wranglers recorded their western swing version of "Beautiful America" for Sarg Records, yet another fabled independent Texas recording label, located in the town of Luling. The Hofner song, with both Czech and Adolph's English lyrics, was released in 1959 as a 45 rpm. It was rereleased in 1994 on a German compilation CD of Texas Czech music called *Texas Bohemia*.[7]

34. Letěla husička *Little Goose*

Letěla husička

1. Letěla husička, letěla zvysoka.
 Nemohla doletět, spadla do potoka,
 spadla do potoka.

2. Spadla do potoka, vodičku vypila
 a to na znamení, že jsi mne nechtěla,
 že jsi mne nechtěla.

The Little Goose Flew

1. The little goose flew, she flew from above.
 She couldn't fly on, she fell into the creek,
 she fell into the creek.

2. She fell into the creek, she drank up the water
 and this as a sign that you didn't want me,
 that you didn't want me.

Folk origins. Erben, *Pjsně národnj w Čechách*, 1:198, and *Nápěvy prostonárodních písní českých*, 88–89. Words and music from Jimmy Brosch and His Happy Country Boys, "Little Goose," *Believe It or Not* (Houston: Guide G-1001, 1967 or 1968), LP.

The Bohemian poet and folklorist Karel Jaromír Erben published "Letěla husička" in 1842 as a two-verse folk text. Erben's words tell of a little goose who was flying, fell into the creek, and then drank up all the water to keep the innkeeper from watering down the beer.[1] Except for the beer ending, these words are familiar to many Texans as a polka called "Little Goose." In the Texas telling, the goose's appearance, fall, and drinking of the water are a sign, a prediction for the future. The boy who witnesses this startling scene considers it a bad omen. He takes it to mean that he is not wanted.

Erben separately published two melodies for this text in 1861.[2] The first melody, a triple-time folk dance called a *rejdovák*, became widely familiar through its inclusion in the "Česká beseda," a popular national dance.[3] The second melody is the lively polka known in Texas.

"Little Goose" is only one of several Czech folk and popular songs that are unified by the presence of a flying goose, not a domestic goose but a wild one. The goose flies alone over scenes of human concerns, and its aberrant appearance affects the people below in some way. One, called "Husička dívoka" (Wild Goose), is about a wild goose who drinks only the clean water from the creek and leaves the dirty behind.[4] Another tells the story of a little goose who falls into the creek, shot down by a hunter. She cries for her poor children, left alone without their mother.[5]

A third example is about a little goose who flies over a courtyard. The goose's appearance prompts the girl to tell the boy that they cannot become involved. She says that his family does not approve of her because she is poor. The priest and folklorist František Sušil collected this version in the Lichnov area of northeastern Moravia, probably in the 1850s. Vrazels' Polka Band of Buckholts includes a Sušil verse in their 1969 recording of "Little Goose." The additional verse goes: "I would want you, my folks won't give me to you because your family is above us, is above us."[6]

Bačova Česka Kapela of Fayetteville recorded "Letěla husička" for Columbia Records in 1930, released as a 78.[7] Jimmy Brosch and His Happy Country Boys of Houston brought out their rendition on *Believe It or Not,* their LP from 1967 or 1968.[8] The Leo Majek Orchestra of Corpus Christi included "Little Goose Polka" on its second album, released in the late 1960s, with John and Frank Majek on vocals.[9] Ellinger Combo included the song on its 1968 LP called *From Ellinger with Love.*[10] Johnny Mensik and Orchestra of Ennis released "Little Goose Polka" on their 1972 LP, *Required of Us a Song,* with Mensik on vocals that combine the hunter verse with the Brosch verses.[11] The Dujka Brothers of Brenham included the song on their 2011 CD, *25 Years Making Tracks.*[12]

35. Lístečku dubový *Oaken Leaf*

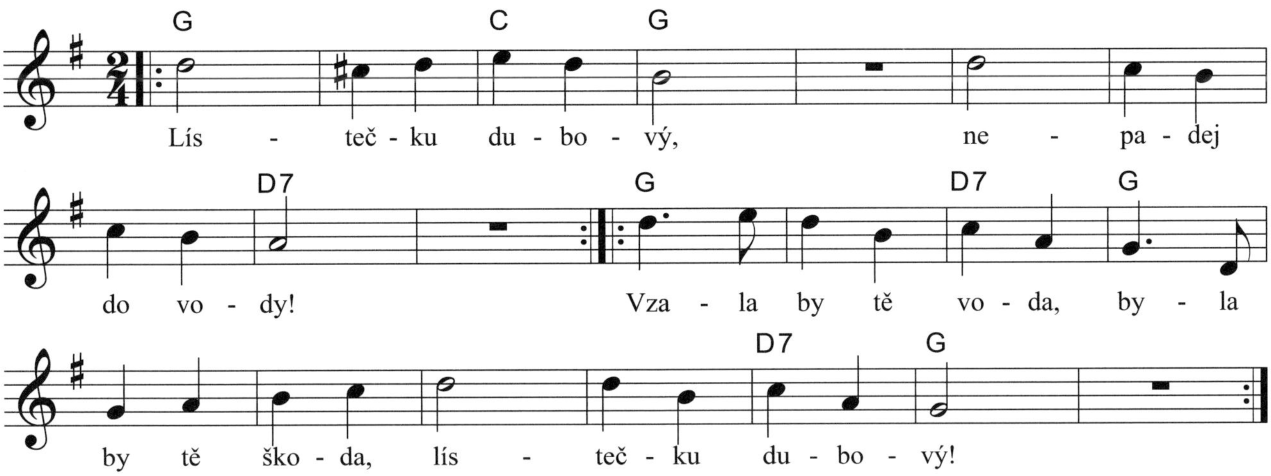

Lístečku dubový

1. Lístečku dubový
   nepadej do vody!
   Vzala by tě voda
   byla by tě škoda,
   lístečku dubový!

2. Až rozum dostanem,
   milovat přestanem.
   Nebudem se ženit,
   za pannami chodit,
   zůstanem svobodní.

Little Oak Leaf

1. Little oak leaf,
   don't fall into the water.
   If the water should take you,
   it would be a pity,
   little oak leaf.

2. When we get some sense,
   we will stop loving.
   We won't get married,
   we won't visit girls,
   we will stay single.

Folk origins. Holas, *České národní písně a tance*, 4:101–2. Verses 1 and 3 and music from "Lístečku dubový (Oh! Oaken Leaf)," arranged for piano and voice by Louis Vitak (Chicago: Georgi and Vitak, 1915).

The lyrics to "Lístečku dubový" begin with an exhortation to a little oak leaf not to fall into the water and be carried away. This image from nature—of fighting against inevitable seasonal decline—is placed in juxtaposition to the human affairs of the second verse, where young men announce that they will not get married, they will stay single.

The song was based on a waltz collected in the central region of Bohemia and published in Prague in 1909. The words to the folk waltz begin with the little oak leaf image and then predict that the boys will not get married but will stay single and visit the girls, that the war will take the boys and their freedom away.[1] Until 1918, when Czechoslovakia became an independent nation, the pairing of the oak leaf with military service would have been a familiar one for Czechs serving in the Habsburg army. From at least the eighteenth century it was the custom for Habsburg soldiers to wear a sprig of oak leaves in their helmets as a *Feldzeichen* (field sign), in Czech called *polní označení*. One military historian describes the oak leaf as "synonymous with Habsburg service."[2]

The waltz collected in Bohemia was arranged by Louis Vitak of Chicago, with revised but similar lyrics and melody, and published by Georgi and Vitak in 1915 for piano and voice. The last verse of Vitak's lyrics describe the excitement of war and one soldier's plan to rejoin his girl when he returns home, but this is not one of the verses typically performed in Texas and not included with the two in this book. The song is almost always played in the state as a polka. A homemade Baca band book from the 1930s contains the alto saxophone part of a "Listečku dubovy" march arrangement by Louis Vitak and published by Vitak-Elsnic of Chicago, though the publication date is not included.[3]

The Joe Patek Orchestra of Shiner released "Oaken Leaves" on a self-titled album in the late 1960s with Joe and his brother Jerome singing a duet on the first verse.[4] Lee Roy Matocha Orchestra of Fayetteville released "Oaken Leaf Polka," in about the late 1960s, on its LP entitled *By Special Request*, with Matocha singing the first verse.[5] "Oaken Leaf Polka," with two vocal verses, was released by the Ellinger Combo on its circa 1970s album.[6] Czech Harvesters of Ennis included verse 1 of "Oak Leaf" on their 1994 album.[7] The East Bernard Czech Singers included two verses of "Oaken Leaf Polka" as part of a medley on their 2000 CD.[8]

36. Lodička malá *Dreamboat Waltz*

Lodička malá

1. Na břehu malá lodička stojí,
 pojd' má panenko, sednem si do ní.
 Poplujem dál a dál, v zelený háj a háj,
 poplujem dál v zelený háj.

2. Poplujem spolu v zelené lesy,
 kde slavík zpívá si svoje plesy.
 Poplujem dál a dál, v zelený háj a háj,
 poplujem dál v zelený háj.

3. Tak jako slavík píseň si zpíval,
 tak Jeník svoji milenku líbal.
 Na rety rudě líbal ji víc a víc,
 milence láskou hoří líc.

4. Lod'ka je malá, vesla jsou krátký,
 pojd' má milenko, poplujem zpátky.
 Poplujem dál a dál, v zelený háj a háj,
 poplujem dál v manželský ráj.

The Little Boat

1. On the shore there is a little boat,
 come, my doll, let's sit down in it.
 We'll sail onward into the green grove,
 we'll sail onward into the green grove.

2. We'll sail together into the green woods
 where the nightingale sings his exultation.
 We'll sail onward into the green grove,
 we'll sail onward into the green grove.

3. Just as the nightingale sang his song
 so did Johnny kiss his sweetheart.
 On her red lips he kissed her more and more,
 her cheeks burned with love.

4. The boat is small, the oars are short,
 come, my darling, we'll sail back.
 We'll sail farther and farther into the green grove,
 we'll sail farther into married bliss.

English lyrics

Down by the river our dream boat is waiting,
so come to me, dear, our ship will be sailing.
We'll sail to our dream land where dreams will all come true,
let's sail and sail to the land of dreams.

Unknown origins. Czech words and music from "Lodička Malá Waltz (My Dream Boat)," arranged for piano and voice by Joseph P. Elsnic (Chicago: Vitak-Elsnic, 1943), used with permission by Vitak-Elsnic Company, a Division of Music Publishers of America, LLC. English lyrics by Ray Krenek, from "My Dream Boat Waltz," *Top Hit Tunes: Ray Krenek and His Orchestra* (Brenham, TX: Gold-Sun 102, 2006), CD, used with permission.

The waltz "Lodička malá," arranged by Joseph Elsnic and published in 1943 by his Chicago music publishing company Vitak-Elsnic, is based on a Czech song of unknown origins called "My pluli dál a dál" (We Sailed On and On).[1] The words of the Elsnic arrangement describe a married couple's passionate love for each other. The words of the Czech song "My pluli dál a dál" describe a passion for nature—for the joys of drifting in a small boat through the green woods and the rippling water, watching the fish at play.

"My pluli dál a dál," with its singable tune and outdoor theme, became part of a popular post–World War I Czech genre of songs that drew upon American influences. After the end of the war, American support for the newly independent Czechoslovakia led to the young nation's exposure to American ideas and culture. Among these was an influx of films and novels about the American West that helped inspire a growing number of Czech outdoor organizations that appealed to young people. These included clubs formed around scouting, camping, and boating, as well as the more free-form *trampské hnutí* (tramping movement), among others.[2] Music and group singing, a regular part of weekend campouts or other nature outings, led to the development of a campfire style and shared body of songs.[3] The East Bernard Czech Singers, a seven-member female choral group from near Houston, included a dreamy rendition of "My pluli dál a dál" on their 1988 cassette called *Czech Listening and Dancing Favorites*.[4]

Most Texas Czechs know and perform the Elsnic arrangement of the song, but the Ray Krenek English lyrics are also known. The Ray Krenek Orchestra released a 78 rpm of "My Dream Boat Waltz" in 1949 under the FBC, or Fort Bend County, record label, which Krenek partially owned. The vocals are English lyrics written by Ray and sung by the trio of Ray, his brother Linhart, and Birdie Hilsher.[5] The Red Ravens of El Campo included both the Elsnic Czech and the Krenek English lyrics on their CD called *Back Porch Music*.[6] The Praha Brothers of Temple did the same on their self-titled CD released in 2003.[7]

Other Texas recordings, all with Elsnic lyrics only, include a 1972 LP by Jimmy Brosch and His Happy Country Boys of Houston, *You Ask for It,* with vocal solo by Vincent Garcia.[8] Texas Legacy Czech Band of Houston released the song on their 2009 CD, *The Legacy Continues,* with vocals by Mike Gest and Randy Cernosek.[9] Czech and Then Some of Ennis included "Dreamboat Waltz" on their twentieth-anniversary CD, *Getting Better with Age*, released in 2017.[10]

37. Louka zelená *Green Meadow Waltz*

Louka zelená

1. Louka zelená neposekaná (neposečená),
   roste na ní kvítí.
   Kdo chce holku mít, musí za ní jít,
   když měsíček svítí.
   Chorus:
   Na té louce, na palouce,
   jak se ta travička seče lehce (pěkně leskne).

2. Já jsem holku měl, já jsem za ní šel,
   když měsíček vyšel.
   Ona nespala, na mě čekala,
   až jsem tam k ní přišel.

3. Stála u dveří, jedla večeři,
   já měl veliký hlad.
   Chtěl jsem kousíček za pár hubiček,
   ona nechtěla dát.

Green Meadow

1. A green meadow, uncut,
   flowers grow on it.
   He who wants to have a girl must go to her
   when the moon is shining.
   Chorus:
   On the meadow, on the green,
   how easy it is to cut the grass (how nicely it shines).

2. I had a girl, I went to her
   when the moon came out.
   She was not sleeping, she was waiting for me
   until I came there to her.

3. She stood by the door, she was eating dinner,
   I was very hungry.
   I wanted a bit of food for a couple of kisses,
   she did not want to give them.

4. Nechci hubičky, jsi moc maličký,
řekla Mařenka má.
Na to máme čas, až je párek z nás,
raděj promluv s mamá.

4. I don't want kisses, you are too short,
said my Mary.
We have time for that when we are a couple,
you'd better talk to Mom.

Folk origins. Slavia, *Národní písně*, Series 2, part 1, 7. Words and music from "Louka zelená," arranged for piano and voice by Louis Vitak (Chicago: Georgi and Vitak, 1917). Alternate words (in parentheses) from Adolph Hofner and His Orchestra, "Green Meadow Waltz" (Imperial 1140, 1947), 78 rpm.

"Louka zelená" begins with a simple image—an uncut meadow where the flowers grow. Fairy tales, like folk songs, use this kind of straight-forward description. There are few details, and the reader, or listener, is invited into an unexplained world. On top of this spare image comes a pronouncement—if a boy wants a girl, he must go to her when the moon is shining. Our young boy does as he is told. He goes to his girl when the moon comes out and finds that she is waiting for him. The supernatural spell wanes, however, when she refuses his offer of kisses. Things come back to earth when she tells him that he is too short, that when they are a couple they will have "time for that."

The words to the first verse were published in a Czech folk song collection in 1877. They were collected in the Proseč region of Bohemia, about one hundred miles east of Prague, by members of Slavia, a literary society.[1] Years later, in 1940, in Rosebud, Texas, the folklorist William Owens collected another version of the song.[2] The version Owens found in Texas had been arranged by Louis Vitak and published in 1917 by Georgi and Vitak of Chicago. Texans usually sing the first two verses only, and many singers substitute the words in parentheses for the original Vitak text.

"Louka zelená" was first recorded in Texas by Bačova Česká Kapela at a 1929 recording session in San Antonio.[3] Ray, a member of this original Baca Band, recorded the song about 1950 with his own band, the Ray Baca Orchestra. This 78 rpm was released by FBC, or Fort Bend County, based in Rosenberg, under the title "Green Meadow Waltz," and then rereleased by Humming Bird of Waco shortly thereafter.[4] One more recording was made by the Bacas, this one an instrumental by Ray's son Gil Baca and His Orchestra. Ray plays the hammered dulcimer on the recording, an LP called *Polkas and Waltzes* that was released in 1967.[5]

At least two other early recordings were made, both released as 78s and more recently included on compilation CDs. Adolph Hofner and His Orchestra recorded a slow swing version in 1947, released by Imperial, that was reissued in 1993 on the Arhoolie CD *Texas-Czech, Bohemian, and Moravian Bands*.[6] The rousing brass version by the Joe Patek Orchestra of Shiner, originally released by the Martin label of Waco in about 1949, was later reissued on *Joe Patek Orchestra: The 78s*.[7] Czech Heritage Singers of Galveston, under the direction of Rev. Paul Chovanec, recorded three verses of "Louka zelená" for their 1981 self-titled LP.[8] Three generations of the Hodde musical family performed on the Fritz Hodde and the Fabulous Six 2008 CD, which includes "Green Meadow." The vocal duet was sung by Arthur Palla and Fritz's son, Scott Hodde, while Scott's son, Brandon, played drums.[9]

38. Moon over Moravia

Moon over Moravia

Chorus:

Moon over Moravia, stars sparkle and shine.
Music plays in Moravia. Waltz with me darling tonight.

1. The fields are all plowed, my work is all done,
it's time for a cold beer and a whole lot of fun.
We'll join our friends at the old country store,
nine-fifty-seven leads right to the door.

Words and music by Mark Hermes and Daniel Klapuch, Moravian Moon Publishing, ASCAP, and John Dujka, At the Dance Music, BMI, used with permission.

2. The accordion sings in three-quarter time,
lovers are dancing with stars in their eyes.
Twirling around on that old dance floor,
this is what nights like this are made for.
Czech Chorus
Nad Moravou hvědičky, a měsic svití.
Hraje muzika v hospodě, má milá se mnou tančí.

The Lavaca County farming community of Moravia is one of the early Czech settlements in Texas; the first immigrants arrived there in the 1870s. Moravia Store, located on Farm-to-Market Road 957, has served the community since 1881. That is when early pioneers Ignác Jalůfka and Jakub Holub first moved a building onto what was then an undeveloped road. In 1889, Jalůfka built a new structure on the site—a combination store, saloon, and dance hall.[1] The same building serves the same purpose today and inspired this waltz with bilingual lyrics.

One evening in 1999, when the harvest moon lit up the sky, Daniel Klapuch and Mark Hermes sat in the store, jotting down ideas on a paper napkin. The two men, both of whom have family ties to Moravia, were trying to come up with a song to capture the beauty of the evening and their feelings for the store and the community. They showed a draft of the song to the musician John Dujka, who also has family ties to Moravia. Dujka suggested melodic changes and urged them to add a portion of the song in Czech. They contacted Martha Viktorin of East Bernard, one of the East Bernard Czech Singers, who created a rhyming Czech translation of the chorus.[2] The Dujka Brothers, in 2001, were the first to record "Moon over Moravia."[3]

The song was enthusiastically received in the Texas Czech community. Mark Halata of Houston, whose ancestors settled in Moravia and where Mark and his family have a second home, recorded it with his band Texavia in 2003.[4] The Red Ravens of El Campo, another polka band with ties to Moravia, recorded it in 2004.[5] Mark Hermes of Hallettsville, one of the songwriters, recorded it with his band the Czechaholics in 2007.[6] The Vrazels of Buckholts, with no known kinship ties but plenty of friends in Moravia, recorded the song in 2007.[7]

In a 2016 story in the monthly *Texas Polka News*, the editor Gary E. McKee describes the song's popularity this way: "In a backwards compliment, a musician told Daniel [songwriter Daniel Klapuch] that he sure liked singing 'Moon over Moravia' but at an all-day music event he had to sing it SIX times to satisfy the dancing crowd."[8]

39. Muziky, muziky

Muziky, muziky

1. Muziky, muziky, vy pěkně hrajete,
   vy jste mě ze spaní probudily.

2. Já jsem se nevyspal, děvče jsem nedostal,
   toho jste muziky, samy vinny.

3. Když jsem šel od milé, klekání zvonili,
   kukačka na dubu zakukala.

4. Kukačko, nekukej, já jsem dnes mrzutej,
   má milá se na mně rozhněvala.

5. To jsi se, Jeníčku, pro málo rozhněval,
   že jsem tě nevyšla vyprovodit.

6. Byla již noc tmavá, já jsem se ven bála,
   vždyť já ti to mohu vynahradit.

Musicians, Musicians

1. Musicians, musicians, you play nicely,
   you awoke me from my sleep.

2. I didn't sleep, I didn't get a girl,
   of this you, musicians, are alone to blame.

3. When I left my darling, the evening bells chimed.
   A cuckoo in the oak sang "cuckoo."

4. Cuckoo, don't sing "cuckoo," I am grouchy today.
   My darling is cross with me.

5. Johnny, you got angry over such a little thing,
   because I didn't go outside to see you off.

6. It was already a dark night. I was afraid,
   but I can make it up to you.

Folk origins. Sládek, *Trocnovské písně I*, 27, and Plicka, *Český zpěvník*, 166–67. Words to verses 1–2 and music from "Muziky, Muziky, Pochod," by František Kmoch (Chicago: Georgi and Vitak, 1910s); verses 3–6 from KJT, *Sbírka českých písní*, 6–7.

"Muziky, muziky," an early František Kmoch piece, is one of six of his marches in this songbook. In a number of his enduringly popular compositions for brass bands, Kmoch inserted a Czech folk song as the trio of the piece. The lyrics of the trios were meant to be sung and, because the songs he inserted were either well known or easy to learn, the audience often joined in.

"Muziky, muziky" appears in several folk collections as a waltz.[1] Kmoch's trio melody is the same as the waltz but is rhythmically a two-step, suitable for both marching and dancing the polka. This is another example of how he helped shape the European military march into something with specific meaning for Czechs. These polka-marches were very popular. The sheet music for "Muziky, muziky," for example, first published in the Czech capital of Prague in 1891, sold over 120,000 copies.[2]

The melody and lyrics to the folk song "Muziky, muziky" came from the Bohemian town of České Budějovice, about one hundred miles due south of Prague.[3] The lyrics tell of a spat between two young lovers that is set against an aurally rich background that includes band music, bells that chime in the evening, and a cuckoo that sings while sitting on the branch of an oak tree. These village and bird sounds from an old folk song even today evoke the everyday intimacy of life. "Muziky" is known in Texas both in its full march form and in its trio form, as a lyrical song. Sometimes an additional section from the march is added as an instrumental, as shown in the notation. Typically one or two verses are sung.

The Leo Majek Orchestra of Corpus Christi plays the trio only and sings the first two verses.[4] The Lee Roy Matocha Orchestra and Kovanda's Czech Band, both of Fayetteville, perform the full Kmoch composition and sing the first verse.[5] The Shiner Hobo Band plays the long form as an instrumental version on their 2004 CD.[6] The Ennis Czech Boys sing the first two verses of "Music, Music Polka" on their 2016 CD, *Cheers to 10 Years!*[7]

The name "Muziky, muziky" also graces the stage of the Sanford Schmidt Amphitheater on the grounds of the Texas Czech Heritage and Cultural Center just outside La Grange. The center was established in 1997, and one of its features is the amphitheater, an outdoor theater that overlooks the lower Colorado River. Besides this grand stage, the center also has a combination museum, library, and banquet hall, completed in 2009. The extensive grounds include a Czech village with several historic houses and cabins, a general store and *hospoda* (pub), an early SPJST lodge building, a sawmill, log crib, large barn, smoke house, music museum, newspaper museum, and a Polka Lovers Club of Texas museum.[8]

40. Na naší půdě straší *Haunted Garret; Boogie Bear*

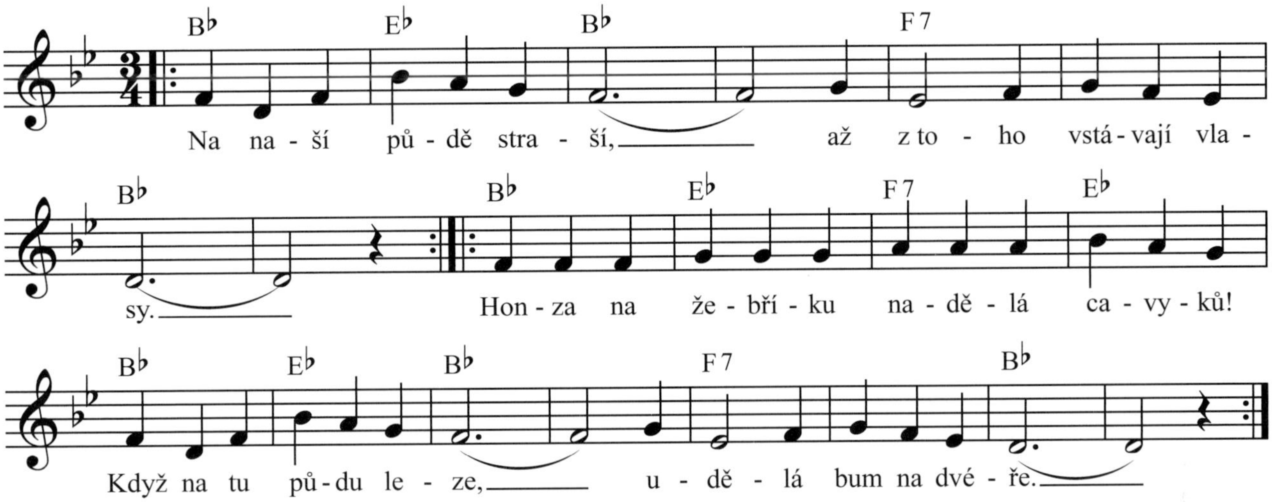

Na naší půdě straší

1. Na naší půdě straší,
   až z toho vstávají vlasy.
   Honza na žebříku nadělá cavyků.
   Když na tu půde leze,
   udělá bum na dvéře.

2. Matka jí říkávala,
   aby si vdovce vzala.
   Vdovec že nepije, svou ženu nebije.
   Tak jako každý fláma,
   flámuje až do rána.

3. Když jsem já praštil z vojnou
   namluvil jsem si kojnou.
   Koupil jsem jí prsten po prestnu, postel,
   postýlku malovanou,
   aby hajala se mnou.

4. Vdavky budem mít panské.
   Pít budem jen šampanské.
   On nic neprohloupí, když radio koupí.
   A pak každou chviličku
   budem pít ze škopíčku.

In Our Haunted Attic

1. In our haunted attic
   your hair will stand on end.
   Johnny on the ladder messes around.
   When he climbs up the ladder,
   he'll make a thump on the door.

2. Mother would tell her
   to marry a widower.
   A widower doesn't drink, doesn't beat his wife.
   Like every scoundrel,
   he goofs off till morning.

3. When I returned from the war
   I spoke to a wet nurse.
   I bought her ring after ring, a bed,
   a painted cot,
   so that she would sleep with me.

4. We'll have a noble wedding.
   We'll drink only champagne.
   He won't do anything silly if he buys a radio.
   And then every moment
   we'll drink from a bucket.

Unknown origins. Words and music from "Na naší půdě straší," arranged for voice and piano by Louis Vitak (Chicago: Vitak-Elsnic, 1928).

"Na naší půdě straší" is a Czech song of unknown origins arranged by Louis Vitak and published in 1928 by Vitak-Elsnic of Chicago. Victor Records had already recorded the song a couple of years earlier by Bohemian vocalist and accordion player Václav Albrecht of Chicago, a prolific recording artist during the 1920s.[1]

A catchy waltz with humorous and earthy lyrics, the song begins as a ghost story, makes a couple of detours, and ends up as a robust drinking song. The first recording in Texas was probably the 78 rpm made by the Julius Dietert Orchestra, a German band from Seguin that played both German and Czech music. The orchestra released an instrumental of "Haunted Garret Waltz" on the flip side of "Red Raven Polka" in the late 1940s.[2] Alfred Vrazel of Vrazels' Polka Band of Buckholts remembers hearing the song in 1957 at the Bill Mraz Ballroom in Houston when he walked in to drop off an audition tape. He said Jimmy Brosch was playing, and added, "I still remember the song—Paul Machac was singing the 'Haunted Garret Waltz.'"[3]

Ray Krenek of Wallis may have given the song one of the titles known in Texas. Krenek released his version, titled "It's a Boogie Bear Upstairs," on his orchestra's LP *Top Hit Tunes* from the 1960s.[4] Wence and Helen Shimek of Hallettsville, early promoters of the Hallettsville Polka and Sausage Festival,[5] sang a duet of "Boogie Bear" on their recording *Wence and Helen,* a cassette tape from 1984.[6] Lee Roy Matocha of Fayetteville included "Boogie Bear Waltz" on his late 1960s LP, *By Special Request.*[7] More recordings, all under the title "Haunted Garret Waltz," are from 1987 by Jerry Haisler and the Melody 5 of Temple,[8] from the year 2000 by the East Bernard Singers,[9] and from 2016, a YouTube video of the Ennis Czech Boys performing at the Polka and Sausage Festival in Hallettsville.[10]

41. Na rozloučenou *Farewell March; Farewell Polka*

Music from "Na rozloučenou," arranged for orchestra by Louis Vitak (Chicago: Vitak-Elsnic, 1927), used with permission by Vitak-Elsnic Company, a Division of Music Publishers of America, LLC.

"Na rozloučenou" or "Farewell March," the only song without words in this book, is included because of the role it plays in the Texas Czech wedding reception, a custom of great importance within this group of celebration-loving people. The song is often played for the grand march that opens the wedding dance. It became the standard music sometime between the two world wars, according to the musician George Jurecka of Weimar.[1] The sheet music first became available through Vitak-Elsnic in 1927. But other music is sometimes used as well, such as popular American band marches. For big crowds or lengthy choreography, the band may play a medley of polkas or a combination of a march and several other songs.

A lead couple guides the wedding party and all willing guests in a pattern that ends with the newlyweds in the middle of a circle, dancing their first dance as married people. Glenn Darilek of La Marque, who went to many weddings as a young boy, said he remembers it working this way: "All you had to do was shuffle your feet to the music and follow the person in front of you."[2] The grand march—besides forcing celebrants to work off some of the fabulous food served at Czech weddings—provides a participatory and playful way for the group to accept and welcome the newlyweds into the life of the community.

Margie and Alan Hanslik of Hallettsville are seasoned leaders of wedding grand marches. Since 1965 they have led about fifty grand marches for family and friends. Some of these included over one hundred couples, and some were for smaller groups. Margie started participating in marches as a small child, growing up in the Schulenburg area and going to numerous Czech weddings. She particularly remembers her oldest sister's wedding that took place in 1952. The ceremony was in their local Catholic church at 8 o'clock in the morning. Following the ceremony, all the guests went to the SPJST hall for the day-long, two-meal reception with continual access to multiple beer kegs. There was a lunch that started with the traditional chicken noodle soup, gift opening in the afternoon, and an evening meal with sausage, beef stew, and an abundance of other dishes. Then it was time for the dance. According to Margie, the traditional wedding dance always started with the grand march and ended at midnight with "Svatební píseň" (Song 54), the ceremonial song to remove the bride's veil.[3]

The Henry Brosch Orchestra of Praha recorded "Farewell March," released by Sarg Records of Luling, sometime in the 1950s or 1960s. When a live band is not available, the recording is one of several used to accompany grand marches today and is admired for its tempo, which clocks at about 108 beats per minute.[4] Other recordings include two that feature the cimbalom, or hammered dulcimer. Gil Baca and Band recorded "Farewell Polka" on the LP *Baca's Style Music* in the 1970s, with Gil's father, Ray, playing a dulcimer solo on the trio.[5] Ray Krenek and His Orchestra included "Wedding March" on the 2008 CD *15 Top Hit Tunes Featuring Ray on His Dulcimer.*[6] Chris Rybak of Hallettsville recorded a whole CD called *Grand March* that includes his continual forty-five-minute arrangement of grand march music. It incorporates "Farewell Polka" as well as many popular Czech and English-language songs.[7]

42. Naše Káča pláče *Snowflower Polka*

Naše Káča pláče

1. Naše Káča pláče, co je jí?
   Ukradli jí sukni zloději.
   Ukradli jí sukni, střevíce,
   naše Káča pláče velice.
   Sukýnku, střevíce, ukradli je obě dvě.
   Sukýnku, střevíce, Káče pláče velice.

2. Když ta Káča nám tak plakala,
   dali jsme jí druhou sukýnku,
   sukýnku novou a střevíce.
   Už ta Káča nám tak nepláče.
   Sukýnku, střevíce, dali jsme jí obě dvě.
   Sukýnku, střevíce, už nám Káča nepláče.

Our Katy Is Crying

1. Our Katy is crying, what has happened to her?
   Thieves have stolen her skirt.
   Thieves have stolen her skirt and shoes.
   Our Katy is crying very hard.
   Skirt and shoes, they stole both.
   Shirt and shoes, Katy is crying very hard.

2. When Katy cried to us,
   we gave her another skirt,
   a new skirt and shoes.
   Katy isn't crying to us anymore.
   Skirt and shoes, we gave both to her.
   Skirt and shoes, Katy isn't crying to us anymore.

Folk origins. Erben, *Prostonárodní české písně a říkadla* (1864), 264. Words from KJT, *Sbírka českých písní*, 112. Music (trio only) from "Naše Káča pláče," arranged for piano with words by Louis Vitak (Chicago: Georgi and Vitak, circa 1910s).

In his 1864 folk song collection, Karel Jaromír Erben published two versions of the song about poor Kača, who is crying and cannot be consoled.[1] In both versions, she is crying because thieves have stolen her skirt and shoes. In the second version, she is crying not only because thieves have stolen her skirt and shoes but also because the theft has left her with nothing to wear to an event where there will be music and soldiers. The thieves are never identified.

"Naše Káča pláče" acquired the English title "Snow Flower," an alternate name, when it was included on the 1914 Frank Tryner arrangement for orchestra published by the Chicago firm of Georgi and Vitak.[2] Whoopee John Wilfahrt, the Minnesota German musician who helped popularize the "Dutchman" style of polka, a style also played in Texas, recorded an instrumental of "Snow Flower Polka" on a 78 rpm in 1930.[3] An early Texas instrumental version was recorded on a 78 rpm by the Joe Patek Orchestra of Shiner, under the title "Snowflower Polka," probably in the 1950s.[4]

The lyrics most known in the state begin like those in the Vitak piano arrangement. But in the second verse, Katy gets new shoes and a skirt and stops crying. The Vrazels' Polka Band from Buckholts included "Snowflower Polka" on one of their early LPs, in about 1966.[5] The Lee Roy Matocha Orchestra of Fayetteville released "Snowflower Polka" with vocals on a 45 in the 1960s.[6] The City Polka Boys of Houston included the song on their album from about 1973 recorded live at a Dallas dance hall.[7] Fritz Hodde and the Fabulous Six of Hutto released "Snow Flower Polka" on their 1998 CD, *Standing Tall.*[8] The Shiner Hobo Band recorded "Snow Flower Polka" for two CDs, both as instrumentals. The first is a 1992 field recording made by Thomas Meinecke for the German label Trikont. On this CD, called *Texas Bohemia,* Meinecke catches the music as well as the enthusiasm of the crowd. The Hobos later recorded the song for their 2007 CD, *Frankie and Johnny, Hobo Style.*[9]

43. Nemelem *Grinders Polka*

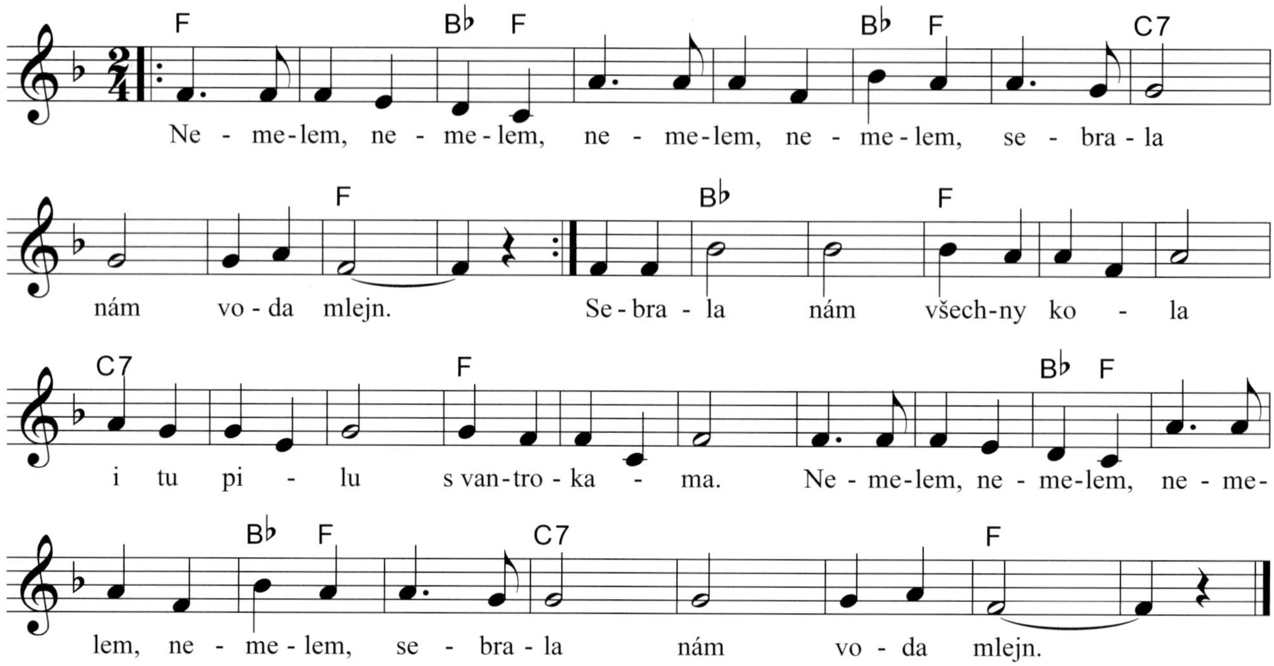

Nemelem

1. Nemelem, nemelem,
nemelem, nemelem,
sebrala nám voda mlejn.
Sebrala nám všechny kola
i tu pilu s vantrokama.

2. Nepijem, nepijem,
nepijem, nepijem,
vyteklo nám pivo ven,
vytekly nám všechny sudy,
teď musíme sušit huby.

3. Jen ty jsi, jen ty jsi,
jen ty jsi, jen ty jsi,
má panenko, vzpomeň si,
vzpomeň sobě na ty časy,
když jsme spolu husy pásli.

We're Not Milling

1. We're not milling, we're not milling,
we're not milling, we're not milling,
the water broke the mill.
It broke all of the wheels
and the saw with the flumes.

2. We're not drinking, we're not drinking,
we're not drinking, we're not drinking,
our beer has leaked out.
All of our barrels have leaked out,
now our mouths are dry.

3. Just you, just you,
just you, just you,
my doll, remember,
remember the times
when we herded the geese together.

Words for verse 1 and music from "Nemelem, Pochod," by Jan Čermák, arranged for piano and voice by Louis Vitak (Chicago: Georgi and Vitak, 1916). Words for verses 2–3 from KJT, *Sbírka českých písní*, 58–59.

"Nemelem" was written by a bandleader and music teacher, Jan Čermák (1867–1935) of Vysoké Mýto, a town about one hundred miles east of Prague. Founded in the thirteenth century, Vysoké Mýto attracts visitors with its preserved buildings and monuments as well as its natural surroundings. Čermák spent most of his life in the town and is particularly remembered for teaching music to school-aged children. He organized and conducted a youth orchestra from about 1904, an endeavor that taught music to hundreds of young people from the town and surrounding area. After Čermák's death in 1935, the orchestra was taken over by his son Josef. Since 1992, an annual national competition for young male and female brass musicians held in the town, called Čermákovo Vysoké Mýto, has honored both men.[1]

Two different Chicago music companies, Georgi and Vitak and Aloysius J. Turek, brought out "Nemelem" sheet music in 1916. They each credit Jan Čermák as composer.[2] Like a number of other songs in this book, it is a polka that doubles as a drinking song. The usual English title is "Grinders Polka."

The setting seems to be someplace jovial, perhaps a pub, where a group of people have gathered. They begin to sing that they are not working at the mill because the water has broken it. In the second verse, they explain that they are not drinking because all the beer is gone, it has "leaked out" of the barrels. In the third verse, they seem to be explaining all this to "my doll," possibly a wife or sweetheart who has come to find her missing companion. At this point, they abruptly change the subject and remind her of fond memories, "when we herded the geese together."

The lyrics took on a different meaning during the World War II Nazi occupation of Czechoslovakia. Svatava Jakobson and Alan Lomax, two folklorists, worked together to develop a book of folk songs for use by Voice of America to help rally support for the Allies. Lomax, a Texan, worked for the Library of Congress, the sponsor of the project. Jakobson, who much later moved to Austin, where she taught Czech at the University of Texas, was instrumental in choosing songs for inclusion in the book. During one interview, she spoke to a Czech national who suggested "Nemelem" be included. He said: "Czechs sing it among themselves as a sort of incentive for sabotage at work. The sense of the text is, 'We don't do any work because everything has been taken from us.'"[3]

The first Texas recording was made by Bačova Česka Kapela (Baca Czech Band) of Fayetteville during a session in San Antonio on August 28, 1935. The 78 rpm record was released by Vocalion, with credit given to J. Čermák as composer.[4] The Bacas sang the first verse only, as a duet. In 1967 a second Baca band, under direction of Gil Baca, recorded "Nemelem." Gil's father, Ray Baca, veteran of the first Baca band and master of the hammered dulcimer, played on the recording. Ray also sang a lively rendition of the first verse as part of a trio with Vernon Drozd and Gene Lichnovsky.[5] Vrazels' Polka Band of Buckholts included "Grinders Polka" on their first album, recorded about 1965.[6]

The University of Texas Czech Singers, on their 1977 album *Czechoslovakian Folksongs*, sang all three verses accompanied by the accordionist Robert Ermis.[7] Some years later, in 2007, the Taylor Czech Chorus included two verses on their CD *Songs of Our Heritage*.[8] A few more representative recordings are Lee Roy Matocha on his late 1970s album called *Lee Roy Is Back Again*;[9] City Polka Boys of Houston on their 1997 CD, *The Okruhliks*;[10] the Shiner Hobo Band on their 2004 CD, *Ještě jednou* (*One More Time*);[11] and Mark Halata and Texavia of Houston on their 2018 CD called *Live at Moravia Store*.[12]

44. Okolo měsíce *Around the Moon*

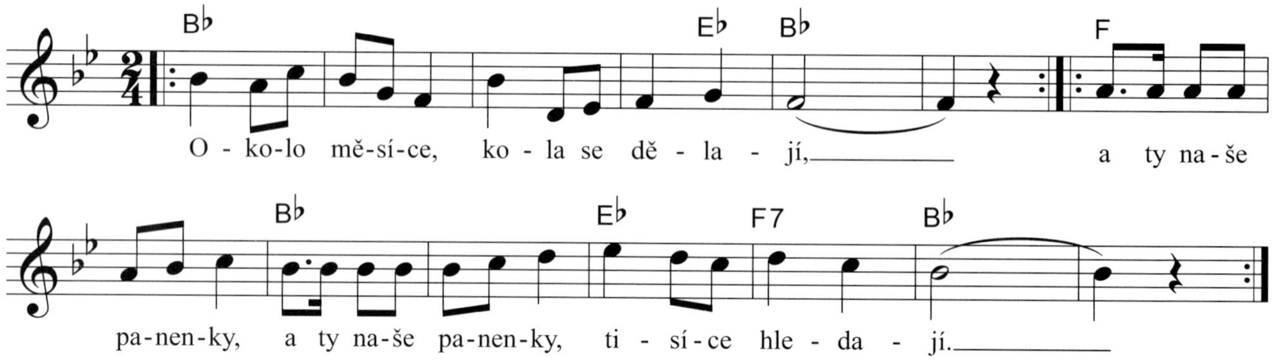

Okolo měsíce

1. Okolo měsíce kola se dělají,
   a ty naše panenky, a ty naše panenky,
   tisíce hledají.

2. Tisíce hledají, samy nic nemají.
   Jen ty jedny šatečky, jen ty jedny šatečky,
   co na sobě mají.

3. V pátek je vyperou, v sobotu naškrobí,
   v neděli na ulici, v neděli na ulici,
   parádu dělají.

Around the Moon

1. Around the moon circles are forming,
   and these our young women, and these our young women,
   they're looking for thousands.

2. They're looking for thousands, they themselves have nothing,
   only these dresses, only these dresses
   they are wearing.

3. On Friday they wash them, on Saturday they starch them,
   on Sundays on the street, on Sundays on the street,
   they parade around.

University Czech Singers' Version

1. Okolo měsíca kola se dělajú,
   a ti naši mládenci, a ti naši mládenci
   peníze nemajú.

2. Peníze nemajú, všade je hledajú,
   len ty jedny gaťata, len ty jedny gaťata,
   co na sobě majú.

1. Around the moon circles are forming,
   and these our young men, and these our young men,
   they have no money.

2. They have no money, they are looking everywhere for it,
   only these trousers, only these trousers,
   the ones they are wearing.

English Lyrics

Ring, ring around the moon, there's gonna be a change.
Let the music play all day, rainy weather's on its way,
there's gonna be a change.

Words and music (trio only) from "Okolo Měsíce Polka" (Chicago: Georgi and Vitak, 1910s). University Czech Singers lyrics from song sheet "Český Klub, Universita Texasu" (Czech Club, University of Texas), circa 1980s. English lyrics, origins unknown.

To illustrate how embedded "Okolo měsíce" is in Czech culture, it appears in the seminal Czech novel *The Good Soldier Švejk*. In the story, an army chaplain drunkenly blurts out the song as Švejk attempts, with great difficulty, to escort him home. The dark comic satire, written by Jaroslav Hašek, chronicles the adventures of a Czech soldier who was drafted into the Austrian army during World War I, as Hašek himself was.[1]

The Czech lyrics describe the desires of penniless young people for an unobtainable abundance. The women search for "thousands," something grand and out of reach. The men look everywhere for money. The men want trousers, the women want dresses, but they all have only the clothes they are wearing. In reality, the women wash their dresses on Friday, starch them on Saturday, and wear them on Sunday.

The first set of lyrics is well known in Texas. The second set is a version brought to Texas by Josef Roštinský, a visiting professor of Slavic Languages at the University of Texas at Austin from 1977 to 1978. The words are similar to those published in a collection of Moravian songs by František Bartoš and Leoš Janáček in 1901.[2] While in Austin, Roštinský taught members of the University Czech Singers, a student folk choir. He used this opportunity to introduce his students to Czech folk music that was from the Moravian region of the country, which is where most Texas Czechs emigrated from.[3] The lyrics are documented on the choir's 1977 album called *Czechoslovakian Folksongs* as well as on its song sheets.[4]

The English lyrics, of unknown origins,[5] describe a different kind of abundance, one that Texas farmers know well. A familiar saying, "Ring around the moon means rain soon," describes a lunar occurrence that many people believe predicts a rain or snow storm, usually a big one. The ring around the moon, a spectacular event on a clear night, occurs when a layer of cold air in the upper atmosphere causes ice crystals to form. The ice crystals refract, or bend, the moonlight and cause it to focus into a ring.

Columbia Records recorded Fayetteville's Bačova Česka Kapela (Baca's Czech Orchestra) performing "Okolo měsíce" in a San Antonio session on August 28, 1935. The Bacas played a 1913 orchestral arrangement by F. Tryner, which was published by Georgi and Vitak of Chicago, later known as Vitak-Elsnic.[6] The Bacas sang the first verse. The Jodie Mikula Orchestra of Ennis, which celebrated its fifty-year anniversary in 2017, performed the first two verses in a lively dance version.[7] Fritz Hodde and the Fabulous Six of Hutto sang two Czech verses and the English verse on their 1998 CD. The Fabulous Six celebrated their fifty-year anniversary in 2018.[8] The East Bernard Czech Singers performed and recorded several albums from 1986–2000. "Okolo měsíce," with the first two verses of the Czech lyrics followed by the English verse, appears on their 2000 CD *Our Best to You*.[9] Czech Melody Masters of Taylor and Austin sang all three Czech verses on their 2000 CD, *Czech Melody Masters Play Old Tyme Radio Favorites*.[10]

45. Opice *Monkey Polka*

Opice

1. Slyšte, lidičky, tuto novinu,
   a jak říkal švec za jeho vinu.
   Jiného ševce hanil velice.
   Ach, to dělá opice!
   Chorus:
   Na bále se opil,
   pohoršení tropil.
   Domů se ubíral,
   celý svět proklínal.
   Přišel domů s brášky,
   snědl tři slanečky.
   Ach, to dělá opice!

Monkey

1. Listen, folks, to this news
   of how the shoemaker told of his shame.
   He greatly blamed another shoemaker.
   Oh, the monkey does that!
   Chorus:
   In the dance hall he got drunk,
   he caused a scandal.
   He went home,
   he cursed the whole world.
   He came home with his brothers,
   he ate three sardines.
   Oh, the monkey does that!

2. Do sednice vlez jak nějaký vrah,
začal ženu bit, až z něho byl strach.
Naposled mlatil hrnce a číše.
Ach, to dělá opice!

3. Nastudil se, švec zle se roztonal,
dýchačku dostal, žadného neznal.
Jeho přátele, ti mu běželi,
bychom ho ještě uzřeli.

4. Pohřeb šefce byl velice smutný,
na něj se sešli všecky ty klepny.
Okolo rakvi tři zas děvečky,
v rukách nesly slanečky.

5. Muzikantův sbor za rakví vrzal,
na rakev padlo přemnoho slz.
Ze všech naříká žena nejvíce.
"Ach, to dělá opice!"

2. Into the room he crept like some kind of murderer,
he started to beat his wife, causing terror.
In the end he beat pots and bowls.
Oh, the monkey does that!

3. The cobbler got a cold, became violently ill,
he got a lung disease, knew nobody.
His friends, they ran to him,
so we could still see him.

4. The shoemaker's funeral was very sad.
All the gossipers attended.
Around the coffin again three girls,
they carry sardines in their hands.

5. The musician's choir sang behind the coffin.
Upon the coffin lots of tears fell.
Above everything the woman cries the most.
"Oh, the monkey does that!"

Folk origins. Přibylová, "'Když jsme opustili Prahu,'" 37. Words from Bartoš and Bartoš, *Spivejme pisničky*, 71–72. Music from Victor Caka and the Polka Timers, "Monkey Polka" (San Antonio: TNT 5069, circa 1960s), 45 rpm.

In 2014, Irena Přibylová, who teaches English and American Studies at Masaryk University in Brno, wrote about Czech songs she heard on the radio in Texas during a visit to the state. One of the songs she discusses is "Opice." She says the melody comes from a Prague song called "Cvočkář Danda" (Danda the Nail Maker),[1] an early twentieth-century imitation of a broadside murder ballad. The Prague song tells the story of a nail maker who spends the evening in a pub and is murdered by two villains on his way home. The words to "Opice," the song known in Texas, tell a different sensational story, this one about a shoemaker, an ill-behaved, abusive drunkard, who also dies in the end.

Both "Cvočkář Danda" and "Opice" are parodies of a traditional style of popular music that was widely found in Europe starting in the sixteenth century. The lyrics, usually of a religious, heroic, or sensational character, were printed and sold at markets and fairs, often by the author, who also performed them. The British called these songs broadside ballads; the Czechs referred to them as *kramářská písně*, a phrase related to the Czech word *krámář* (shopkeeper).[2] Before newspapers, these ballads were a way for people to learn about dramatic events, such as "murders, disasters, and wars."[3] In the late nineteenth century, after newspapers became widespread, the style of the *kramářská píseň* was sometimes imitated and used in an exaggerated way for humorous entertainment.[4]

The Czech word *opice* means "monkey," and the word *opilec* means "drunkard," so the title is a pun. The two words did not grow out of the same source, and they share no meaning, but their spoken sound is similar. The lyrics go to great lengths to make a symbolic or metaphorical connection between the two mammals—the monkey and the drunkard—and it is true that both are well known for getting into trouble. But even when the plot descends into chaos, it describes the way it feels to be caught in an out-of-control situation. The lyrics make sense, in other words, within the elastic rules of comedy.

The words known in Texas were recorded by the concertina player and polka bandleader Roman Rezac of Lonsdale, Minnesota. "Opice" is the first cut on the orchestra's album called *Old Time Czech Style,* a 1960s LP from the Minnesota record company Pleasant Peasant. Rezac and his wife, Christine, enjoyed spending winters in Texas, where they became acquainted with some of the state's polka players and where Rezac also played with a three-piece band.[5]

Victor Caka of Shiner, a musician and well-known accordion technician, made a wonderful recording of all five verses of "Opice" in the late 1960s. It was released as a 45 by the San Antonio independent record label TNT, which stands for Tanner 'N Texas.[6] Vrazels' Polka Band released an instrumental about 1965 on their first LP, self-titled *Vrazels' Polka Band.*[7] The Bill Mraz Orchestra of Houston included the first verse and chorus on their 1960s LP, *Swing and Sway the Oompah Way.*[8] The Red Ravens of El Campo included the first verse and chorus on *Polka Better,* their cassette tape from 1981.[9] The Ennis Czech Boys performed the first two and last verse of "Monkey Polka" on their 2016 CD, *Cheers to 10 Years.*[10] The Czechaholics of La Grange included two verses on their 2017 CD, *Certified P.O.L.K.A.*[11] The Jodie Mikula Orchestra of Ennis recorded a spirited rendition of the first two and last verses of "Opice" for their 1993 CD, *Klobase Polka.*[12]

46. Pivo červené *Red Beer Polka; Trávo, trávo*

Pivo červené

1. Trávo, trávo, trávo zelená!
Kdo tě bude trávo, žít,
až já budu v hrobě hnít?
Trávo, trávo, trávo zelená!

2. Pivo, pivo, pivo červené!
Kdo tě bude pivo pít,
až já budu v hrobě hnít?
Pivo, pivo, pivo červené!

3. Bratři, bratři! Vy budete pít!
Kdo ho ale bude pít,
až i vy budete hnít?
Bratři, bratři! Kdo ho bude pít?

4. Pak ho budou naši kluci pít!
Ti zas budou kluky mít,
ti též budou pivo pít.
Pivo, ty se věčně budeš pít!

5. Děvče, děvče, děvče rozmilé!
Kdo tě bude milovat,
až já budu v hrobě spát?
Děvče, děvče, děvče rozmilé!

Red Beer

1. Grass, grass, green grass!
Who will mow you, grass,
when I am rotting in the grave?
Grass, grass, green grass!

2. Beer, beer, red beer!
Who will drink you, beer,
when I am rotting in the grave?
Beer, beer, red beer!

3. Brothers, brothers! You will drink!
But who will drink it,
when even you are rotting?
Brothers, brothers! Who will drink it?

4. Then our boys will drink it!
They also will have boys,
and those too will drink beer.
Beer, you will be drunk forever!

5. Girl, girl, beloved girl!
Who will love you
when I am sleeping in the grave?
Girl, girl, beloved girl!

Folk origins. Words from Erben, *Pjsně národnj w Čechách*, 2:10–11. Music from Erben, *Nápěvy prostonárodních písní českých*, 169–70.

An early version of the words to the Czech folk song "Pivo červené" was published in 1825.[1] The lyrics in this book come from the 1843 publication by the Bohemian folklorist Karel Jaromír Erben; the melody is from his 1861 collection of tunes. The song, which appears in his section on drinking songs, is a rousing anthem that proclaims beer to be eternal.[2]

The song has been in America since at least the 1880s, when it was included in a lyric booklet published by August Geringer of Chicago.[3] Geringer's Czech-language publications, including newspapers, novels, cookbooks, and political tracts espousing freethinking ideas, were widespread among early Czech American immigrants.[4] The Czech Heritage Museum and Genealogy Center in Temple preserves some of these artifacts donated by Texas Czechs.

The five verses consist of questions and answers. The first question is addressed to the green grass: Who will mow you when I rot in the grave? The second asks a similar question of beer: Who will drink you? By the fourth verse, the song spins out into eternity—the sons of the beer drinkers will drink the beer, as well as their sons, and in this way beer drinking will go on forever. The rowdy song ends quietly, with a plaintive question addressed to a beloved girl.

A variant of the song can be found in the 1860 collection of the Moravian priest and folklorist František Sušil. The lyrics are titled "Loučení se rekrutovo" (The Recruit's Farewell) and appear in Sušil's chapter on soldier songs. The tune is in a minor key and sets a quiet frame of mind. The lyrics begin with a young man cutting hay with a scythe: "Grass, grass, green grass! the cold dew falls on you. Who will mow you, grass, when I'm wearing a sword?" The fifth and final verse addresses the man's sweetheart: "Anka dearest, you were my delight. Who will you love when your boyfriend is in the war?"[5] The two versions stand in contrast: the one Erben collected is a hearty and irreverent sing-along, whereas the one from Sušil is a contemplative soldier's lament. They both, however, end with the same question.

In Texas, "Red Beer Polka" is decidedly a drinking song. The first recording in the state features vocals on only the second verse, the one about beer. Adolph Pavlas and His Bohemians of Schulenburg recorded "Pivo červené" in San Antonio for Vocalion Records in 1937.[6] Another recording that spotlights the lone beer verse is on a compilation CD featuring all the bands that played at the 1999 New Braunfels Polka Fest, an annual event in the historic Texas town established in 1845 by German immigrants. The Bohemian Dutchmen played and sang the beer verse in German, beginning with the words *Bier, bier* (Beer, beer).[7] A lively dance-hall rendition of "Red Beer Polka" was recorded by the Dancehall Boys in 1997 at Beyersville SPJST near Taylor.[8] The vocal duet leads with the "pivo červené" verse and follows with the verse about the eternal life of beer. The long-lived Ray Krenek and His Orchestra recorded its last CD in 2008. One of the songs included Ray's reimagined "Pivo červené," to which he gave the title "Yellow Beer Polka." Ray supplied the bilingual lyrics and also livened the accompaniment with his hammered dulcimer playing. The English words were sung by Ray's son Chris, and the German words by Duwayne Engelhardt.[9]

47. Pod našima okny *Under Our Windows*

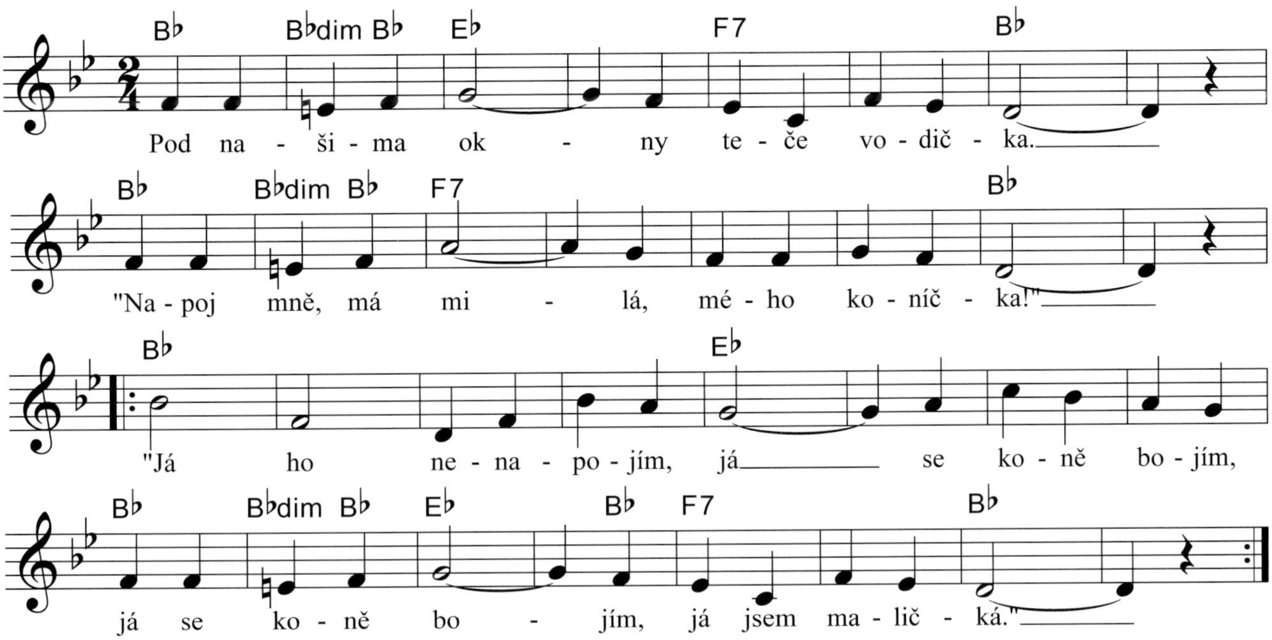

Pod našima okny

1. Pod našima okny teče vodička.
Napoj mně, má milá, mého koníčka!
"Já ho nenapojím, já se koně bojím,
já se koně bojím, já jsem maličká."

2. Pod našima okny roste oliva.
Pověz mně, má milá, kdo k vám chodívá?
"K nám žádný nechodí, mně se každý bojí,
mně se každý bojí, že jsem chudobná."

3. Pod našima okny roste z růže květ.
Pověz mně, má milá, proč tě mrzí svět?
"Mně svět nic nemrzí, mně jen srdce bolí,
mně jen srdce bolí, plakala bych hned!"

Under Our Windows

1. Under our windows water flows.
My dear, give my horse a drink of water!
"I will not, I'm afraid of the horse,
I'm afraid of the horse, I'm little."

2. Under our windows grows an olive tree.
Tell me, my dear, who comes to visit you?
"No one comes to us, everybody is afraid of me,
everybody is afraid of me because I'm poor."

3. Under our windows a flower grows from the rosebush.
Tell me, my dear, why does the world trouble you?
"The world doesn't trouble me, it's just that my heart aches,
my heart aches, I could cry right now!"

Folk origins. Erben, *Pjsně národnj w Čechách*, 1:55–56, and Novotný, *Libické písně*, 72–73. Words from Svoboda, *Věnec lípový*, 126. Music (trio only) from "Pod Našima Okny" by František Kmoch, arranged by Louis Vitak (Chicago: Georgi and Vitak, 1913).

Several songs in this book tell stories about young people who fall in love but whose parents do not allow them to marry because of the unequal economic status of their families. In "Pod našima okny," a young woman reveals her feelings about her impoverished circumstances to a passing stranger who asks her to water his horse. She tells him that she is afraid to water his big horse, because she is small. When he asks about her callers, she tells him that no one comes to visit her family and that no one calls on her. They fear her, she says, because "I am poor."

The Bohemian folklorist Karel Jaromír Erben first published these three verses in the 1842 edition of his monumental folk song collection.[1] The song, well known in the Czech Republic and also in Slovakia, has several variants of both the lyrics and the melody. Many children learn the song in school, and bands and choirs often perform it.[2]

The melody that is widespread in the United States is one of fifty songs published by Václav Novotný in his 1901 songbook called *Libické písně,* meaning "Songs of Libice."[3] In the book, the song is called "Okolo Libice" (Around Libice) because that is how the first verse begins. But after those two words, the rest of the verse and also the third verse are the same as in this songbook. A woman named Anna Majorová taught Novotný this version of the song, one she had sung in her youth. Majorová had learned many songs in the 1840s and 1850s while growing up in the town of Libice nad Cidlinou, about forty miles west of Prague. After Novotný had written down sixty songs that she sang for him, he expressed admiration for her good memory. She said, "That's nothing; what I've forgotten you can see by this story" and proceeded to tell him that one Sunday afternoon, when she and her cousin were young, she sang while her cousin counted up how many songs she knew. They stopped at three hundred.[4]

"Okolo Libice" is one of the songs included in "Czech Folklore in Texas," the 1942 University of Texas master's thesis written by Olga Pazdral, a schoolteacher from West. Pazdral and her students collected songs, stories, proverbs, lullabies, children's poetry, riddles, games, and other folklore from Czech families in the area. Pazdral also included a Slovak version of "Pod našima okny," called "Pod tím našim okenečkem," in the thesis. For these two songs, which share several verses, she credits her source as the popular 1912 bilingual Czech-English songbook *Twenty-Two Bohemian Folk-Songs.*[5]

"Pod našima okny" was also used by František Kmoch as the trio of one of his well-known marches. A few years after Novotný published *Libické písně,* the Chicago music firm of Georgi and Vitak published "Pod našima okny-Pochod." It became a favorite among polka lovers in America.[6] Adolph Pavlas and His Bohemians of Schulenburg recorded the full march and one verse of the trio for Vocalion in 1937.[7] The Joe Patek Orchestra of Shiner recorded the full march as well as all three verses on a 45 in the late 1950s.[8] The East Bernard Czech Singers recorded the full march, two Czech verses, and one verse in English on their 1997 cassette tape titled *Around the Moon.*[9] The Leo Majek Orchestra of Corpus Christi included a verse of "Under the Window Polka" on its *Polka and Waltz* LP, released about the mid-1960s.[10] The Tony Janak Orchestra of Yoakum sang two verses on its 1997 *Heart of Texas Polkaland.*"[11]

48. Pode mlejnem *At the Mill; Below the Mill*

Pode mlejnem

1. Pode mlejnem, nade mlejnem,
husy se pasou (perou), husy se pasou,
husy se pasou.
Vem Jeníčku, vem flintičku,
zastřel některou, zastřel některou,
zastřel některou.

2. Já ty husy nezastřelím,
ty já dobře znám, ty já dobře znám,
ty já dobře znám.
Jsou to husy mé Mařenky (panímámy),
kam já chodívám, kam já chodívám,
kam já chodívám.

3. Jsou to husy popelavý,
drobnýho peří, drobnýho peří,
drobnýho peří.
Vzkázala mi má panenka,
že mi nevěří, že mi nevěří,
že mi nevěří.

Below the Mill

1. Below the mill, above the mill,
geese are grazing (fighting), geese are grazing,
geese are grazing.
Take, Johnny, take your gun.
Shoot one, shoot one,
shoot one.

2. I will not shoot those geese,
I know them well, I know them well,
I know them well.
These are geese of my Mary (the mistress),
where I go, where I go,
where I go.

3. They are ash-gray geese,
of tiny feathers, of tiny feathers,
of tiny feathers.
My darling let me know
that she doesn't believe me, doesn't believe me,
doesn't believe me.

Folk origins. Erben, *Prostonárodní české písně a říkadla* (1864), 115–16, and Sládek, *Náš poklad*, 127. Words to verse 1 and music from "Pode mlejnem pochod," by František Kmoch (Chicago: Georgi and Vitak, circa 1910); verse 2 from KJT, *Sbírka českých písní*, 19; verse 3 from Sládek, *Náš poklad*, 127. Alternate words (in parentheses) from Erben, *Prostonárodní české písně a říkadla* (1864), 115–16.

"Pode mlejnem" is one of František Kmoch's popular brass band marches that uses a Czech folk song for the trio, or the lyrical section of the march. The song, in many variants, was collected by folklorists in central and western Bohemia during the nineteenth century. Karel Jaromír Erben published words in his 1864 book of folk songs that are like those we know in Texas today.[1] When František Kmoch composed his march in the early twentieth century, he used the Erben lyrics, with few changes, but gave the song a new melody. The Prague music company Urbánek and Sons published the Kmoch sheet music in 1906.[2]

Erben's version of the lyrics have the geese fighting ("se perou") rather than grazing, and Jeníček is on his way to talk to the mistress, the *panímámy*, someone who has authority over him, rather than to Mařenka, presumably a friend. Other versions in Texas use the word *panenky*, meaning "doll." or "lassie."[3] Geese were certainly a part of rural life in both the Czech lands and in Texas where the immigrants settled. Domesticated geese were dependable watch animals, sending up a racket whenever anyone or anything came near. They also provided food for the table, feathers for pillows, and feathers to fill the warm bed comforter that many Czechs in Texas still call *peřina* or its diminutive, *peřinka*.

Earlier bands usually played the entire march, which includes several sections. The band book used by the Baca Orchestra of Fayetteville in the 1930s, for example, contains sheet music for the full arrangement.[4] The earliest Texas recording of the Kmoch march was by Adolph Pavlas and His Bohemians at a San Antonio recording session on November 9, 1937. The band played the full composition, and the vocal duet on the trio was provided by bandleader Julius "Adolph" Pavlas and saxophonist Charlie Rainosek.[5] During its brief but fondly remembered existence, the band was also known as Adolf and the Gold Chain Bohemians, named after the flour brand of their radio sponsor, Universal Mills of San Antonio.

A 78 rpm record by the Joe Patek Orchestra of Shiner also has a lively rendition of the full arrangement, including a vocal duet by brothers Joe and Jerome Patek.[6] A more recent recording of the full march is on a CD released in 2000 by Czech Melody Masters of Taylor and Austin called *Czech Melody Masters Play Old Tyme Radio Favorites*. This CD was dedicated to the memory of the musician Adolph Hofner of San Antonio, who died that same year.[7] Later recordings, featuring the trio only, include CDs by Mark Halata of Houston, 2001,[8] and the Czechaholics of La Grange, 2007.[9]

49. Ráno, raníčko *Good Morning Polka*

Ráno, raníčko

1. Zítra ráno, ráno, raníčko,
dříve nežli vyjde sluníčko,
dám si ještě hrát, to na důkaz,
že mám tě rád.

2. Až se zase jednou sejdeme,
potom už se nerozejdeme,
budeš jenom mou, já navždy dám,
ti lásku svou.
Chorus:
Dnes naposled pojd' jen ke mně blíž,
jak rád tě děvče mám, ty dobře víš.
Dnes naposled svou lásku mi dej,
pak na mě holčičko, holčičko jen vzpomínej.

Morning, Dear Morning

1. Tomorrow morning, morning, dear morning,
before the sun rises,
I will ask them to play music again, as proof
that I love you.

2. When we meet once more,
then we won't part again.
You will be only mine, I will forever give
you my love.
Chorus:
Today for the last time, come closer to me.
How I love you, girl, you know this well.
Today for the last time give me your love,
then dear girl, dear girl, just remember me.

From "Ráno, Raníčko, Dnes naposled, Polka," words and music by Václav Bláha, arranged by Vaclav F. Fisher (Chicago: Vitak-Elsnic, 1940), used with permission by Vitak-Elsnic Company, a Division of Music Publishers of America, LLC.

"Ráno, raníčko" is widely known in Texas as "Good Morning Polka." Both the Czech and American publishers of the sheet music use the title "Ráno, raníčko" as well as the first words of the trio, "Dnes naposled" (Today for the Last Time) as an alternate title. The song, by the musician and prolific songwriter Václav Bláha, was published in Prague about 1938[1] and then in Chicago in 1940. Unlike many of Bláha's lyrics, "Ráno, raníčko" does not dwell on the rural folk themes that he so often used to help tell a story. But Bláha does reference an old folk song in the lyrics, subtly evoking the listener's memories.[2]

The first two lines of "Ráno, raníčko" can be found in the well-known song "Černé oči" (Black Eyes), which was published in the 1827 book of Slavic folk songs collected by František Čelakovský.[3] "Černé oči" can also be found in an 1842 collection by Karel Jaromír Erben and in many popular Czech songbooks, including those for children,[4] as well as heard on recordings such as one released in

1992 called *The Oldest Collections of Czech Folk Songs.*[5] Often sung as a lullaby, "Černé oči" starts with a verse that goes "Black eyes, go to sleep, but you must get up in the morning." The song continues "Morning, morning, dear morning, before the sun rises." In the rest of "Černé oči," the sun comes out and a woman goes to market. She brings back news that a war is on and soon all the young men will be taken away.

The story told in "Ráno, raníčko," which evokes this morning image, gives an intimate glimpse of a couple's last few hours before the man is scheduled to depart. Where he is going is never revealed, but the beginning of the second verse, "When we meet once more," shows his intention, or at least his hope, to return. Because the story line is so lightly sketched, the lyrics are open to imagination. The music, an upbeat polka, adds a note of optimism for the couple's future.

Frank Migl's Orchestra of Hallettsville recorded the full arrangement, with vocals on the chorus, for an early 78 rpm record issued by Humming Bird, an independent Texas label that recorded a number of Czech bands as well as other ethnic groups in the state.[6] Leroy Rybak's Swinging Orchestra of Hallettsville brought out a cassette tape with an instrumental "Good Morning" probably in the mid 1980s.[7] Ray Zapletal and His Music Masters of Ennis included "Rano Ranicko" on their mid-1960s LP entitled *Bluebonnet Czech,"* with Zapletal singing the chorus.[8] The Bay City Dutchmen included "Rano Ranicko Polka," a rollicking instrumental, on their LP *TV Polka Time.* According to the liner notes, the song was one of many polkas they played during their Sunday afternoon appearances on *Polka Party*, a show broadcast on KZTV in Corpus Christi during the 1970s.[9]

50. Rostú, rostú, rostú *Corn Cockle Polka*

Rostú, rostú, rostú

1. Rostú, rostú, rostú
   konopě za cestú
   a sú pěkně zelené.
   Mezi něma leží
   synek polámaný,
   volá vody studené.

2. První psaní napsal,
   svému otci poslal,
   aby mu vody podal.
   Otec pilně oral,
   pilně doorával,
   voděnky mu nepodal.

It's Growing, It's Growing, It's Growing

1. It's growing, it's growing, it's growing,
   hemp across the path
   and it's nicely green.
   Among it lies
   an injured boy.
   He calls for cold water.

2. The first letter he wrote
   he sent to his father
   so that he would give him some water.
   The father was plowing diligently,
   he diligently was finishing up his plowing.
   He didn't hand him any water.

3. Druhé psání napsal,
svéj maměnce poslal,
aby mu vody dala.
Ona kúdel přadla
a len dopřádala,
voděnky mu nedala.

4. Třetí psaní napsal
svojéj miléj poslal,
aby mu vody dala.
Ona zlatem šila,
stříbrem vyšívala,
voděnky mu podala.

5. O lepší je, lepší
moja nejmilejší
nežli celá rodina.
Ona zlatem šila,
stříbrem vyšívala,
voděnky mi podala.

3. The second letter he wrote
he sent to his mother
so that she would give him some water.
She was spinning cotton
and was nearly finished.
She didn't hand him any water.

4. The third letter he wrote
he sent to his beloved
so that she would give him some water.
She was sewing with gold,
embroidering with silver.
She handed him some water.

5. Better, better is
my beloved
than my whole family.
She was sewing with gold,
embroidering with silver,
she brought me water.

Folk origins. Erben, *Pjsně národnj w Čechách*, 1:96; Sušil, *Moravské národní písně*, 326–27, 329; and F. Bartoš, *Nové národní písně moravské*, 79–80. Words to verses 1–2 and 5, and music from Jimmy Brosch and His Happy Country Boys, "Corn Cockle Polka" (Houston: Guide 101, 1967), 45 rpm, used with permission. Words to verses 3–4 from František Bartoš, *Nové národní písně moravské*, 79–80.

In Texas, this beloved song is usually called by its English title, "Corn Cockle Polka." The title refers to a weed native to Europe that spread to grain fields in the United States and southern Canada.[1] The song was introduced into the repertory by the fiddler and saxophonist Jimmy Brosch, who grew up in Praha in Fayette County. He eventually moved about one hundred miles due east to Houston, where he, his wife, Lucy, and their four children settled. A busy polka musician for forty-six years who also worked as a railroad switchman, he worked on the book *Jimmy Brosch Remembers Twenty Legendary Texas Czech Polka Bands* after he retired. Theresa Cernoch Parker, at that time the owner and publisher of the *Texas Polka News*, did the writing; Brosch told the stories; and they conducted musician interviews together. In the chapter on his own band, the Happy Country Boys, Brosch tells the story of how "Corn Cockle Polka" came about.[2]

Brosch says that back in the 1940s, he and his uncle, a butcher for their local meat club, used to deliver meat every Friday to Firasek's Store in Praha. "The men would be sitting around drinking beer and their wives would be singing all kinds of Czech songs," Brosch says in the book. He was struck by one song in particular that he describes as a "very slow song, a funeral march." About twenty years later, Brosch still remembered the melody—an aunt used to hum it all the time—and he decided to have his band learn it. He played the song for them, but the band members thought it was too slow. He rearranged it, gave it a polka beat, shortened the lyrics, and this time the band liked it and so did audiences.[3]

Jimmy Brosch and His Happy Country Boys recorded "Rostú, rostú, rostú" in 1967, the band's first time in a studio. The song needed an English title, and a young son of one of the musicians suggested "Corn Cockle Polka." Under that catchy title, it was released as a 45 and was an immediate hit in Texas, but orders for the record also came in from all over the country. "Corn Cockle Polka" was recognized in 1996 by the Texas Polka Music Association as one of two "All Time Favorite Songs," the other being "Shiner Song" (Song 31) by the Joe Patek Orchestra.[4]

The song that Brosch remembers the women singing at Firasek's Store is an old Moravian folk "counting" song. Many melodies have attached to the lyrics over the years, and some are indeed slow and solemn.[5] The word *rostú* is in a Moravian dialect, as are other words in the lyrics, and several variants of the song can be found in the early major folk-song collections.[6] One of the variants from the central Haná region of Moravia, collected and published in 1842 by František Sušil, is part of the Moravian *beseda*, a stylized suite of folk dances similar to the Czech *beseda*.[7] The Moravian composer Leoš Janáček arranged a short piano version of this Haná variant under the title "Konopě," meaning "hemp."[8] "Rostú, rostú, rostú" has a rich and storied history that only adds to the pleasure of hearing it performed in a wonderful arrangement made in Texas.

Many Czech bands in the state have recorded "Corn Cockle Polka" or have likely played it at some point. You can hear Jimmy Brosch and His Happy Country Boys perform their exuberant 1967 version on the CD that accompanies Brosch's book.[9] Another typically energetic performance was recorded by the German documentarian Thomas Meinecke when he visited Texas to learn about Bohemian, Moravian, and German bands in the state. One of his field recordings captured a 1992 jam session in Hallettsville that included Vrazels' Polka Band of Buckholts, the Leo Majek Orchestra of Corpus Christi, and the Bobby Jones Czech Band of Wharton, all playing their hearts out on "Corn Cockle Polka" while the crowd shouted approval.[10]

51. Sirotek *Orphan Waltz*

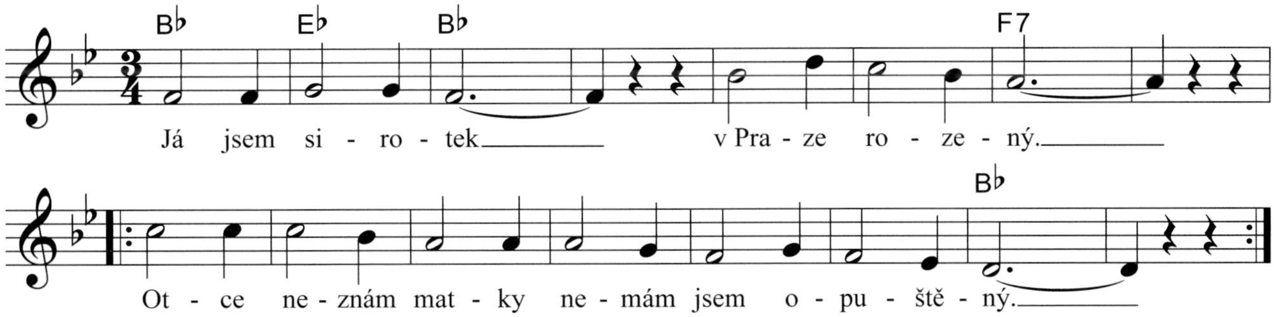

Sirotek

1. Já jsem sirotek v Praze rozený.
   Otce neznám, matky nemám,
   jsem opuštěný.

2. Otče, otče můj, kam's dal rozum svůj?
   Zanechal's zde sirotečka,
   zkazil's život můj.

3. Matko, máti má, proč's mě zrodila?
   Neměla jsi citu lásky
   pro svého syna?

4. Ta porodnice co v Praze stojí,
   jest tam dítek na tisíce.
   Otce neznají.

5. Syn jde do boje a tam bojuje.
   Pláčou pro něj rodičové.
   Pro mě nikdo ne.

6. Nyní umírám, na vás vzpomínám.
   Bez lásky jsem na svět přišel,
   bez ní umírám.

Orphan

1. I am an orphan, born in Prague.
   I don't know my father, I have no mothers,
   I am abandoned.

2. Father, father mine, did you lose your mind?
   You left a little orphan here,
   you ruined my life.

3. Mother, mother mine, why did you give birth to me?
   Didn't you have any loving feeling
   for your son?

4. That maternity hospital that stands in Prague,
   there are children by the thousands there.
   They don't know their fathers.

5. A son goes into battle, and fights there.
   His parents cry for him.
   No one cries for me.

6. Now I am dying, I am remembering you.
   Without love I came into the world,
   without it I am dying.

Folk origins. Pletka and Karbusický, *Písně lidu pražského*, 27. Words and music from Joe Patek Orchestra, "Sirotek-Waltz (Orphan)" (Rosenberg, TX: FBC Records, FBC 121–2, 1949), 78 rpm, used with permission.

The Czech writer Karel Čapek (1890–1938) identified "Já jsem sirotek" as an urban folk song in his 1925 essay "Písně lidu pražského" (Songs of the People of Prague). According to Čapek, these songs of the city developed after the 1848 abolishment of *robota,* the compulsory unpaid labor required of serfs. When this last vestige of feudalism was abolished, country people who had been tied to the land began to move to cities in search of work.[1] The essay was republished as an introduction to a 1966 songbook also called *Písně lidu pražského.* The book includes words and music of songs Čapek discusses, including three verses of the venerable "Sirotek."[2]

Prague songs rose from within this new urban population of working people. Some of the songs had older village origins, and some were written by unknown singers and songwriters around themes relevant to the new surroundings. The lyrics often show an intimacy with the city and mention specific places, like the Prague maternity hospital in "Sirotek." In the 1930s, emerging popular song styles of the interwar years began to relegate these nineteenth-century urban folk songs to the past, but many are still known in the Czech Republic, where they are often performed as sing-alongs.[3]

In the United States, "Sirotek," subtitled "The Orphan," was arranged for piano and voice and published in 1913 by A. L. Maresh, the owner of Maresh Music Co. of Cleveland. Maresh's version has three verses.[4] Louis Vitak, of Vitak-Elsnic Music Co. in Chicago, published his arrangement with an additional two verses in 1924.[5] The first three verses of the Maresh and Vitak versions are similar to one another, and both the Maresh and Vitak words appear in several Texas lyric books.[6]

The lyrics most known in the state, however, are the six verses that were introduced by the Joe Patek Orchestra of Shiner. The first three verses of the Patek lyrics closely follow the three verses included in the songbook *Písně lidu pražského* (Songs of the People of Prague). The Patek "Sirotek" was first released in 1949, by FBC Records of Rosenberg, and then reissued, probably that same year, by Humming Bird of Waco.[7] The Patek band's uninhibited brass core, the playful fills of its syncopated piano, and the searing vocal duet with its high lonesome harmony gives this early rendition of "Sirotek" astonishing emotional power. A contemporary reissue of this historic recording would be a welcome event.

In the early 1970s, the Lee Roy Matocha Orchestra of Fayetteville recorded "Orphan Waltz," a cut released on the band's album *Something Old, Something New.* Matocha later released an undated live recording made in Ennis on a 2002 compilation CD. Matocha sings all six Patek verses as a solo vocalist on both recordings.[8] The Dancehall Boys of Austin and Taylor, now the Czech Melody Masters, included "Orphan" on their 1996 CD, *The Dancehall Boys Live.* The bandleader John Ondrusek sings the first three and last Patek verses on this live recording made at a fiftieth wedding anniversary dance in New Taiton, a community southwest of Houston.[9] Vrazels' Polka Band of Buckholts also sang the first three and last Patek verses on the band's fiftieth-anniversary CD titled *Golden Sounds,* released in 2003.[10] The Shiner Hobo Band included verses 1–3 and verse 5 on their 2004 CD, *Ještě jednou (One More Time).*[11]

52. Šla Nanynka do zelí *Annie in the Cabbage Patch*

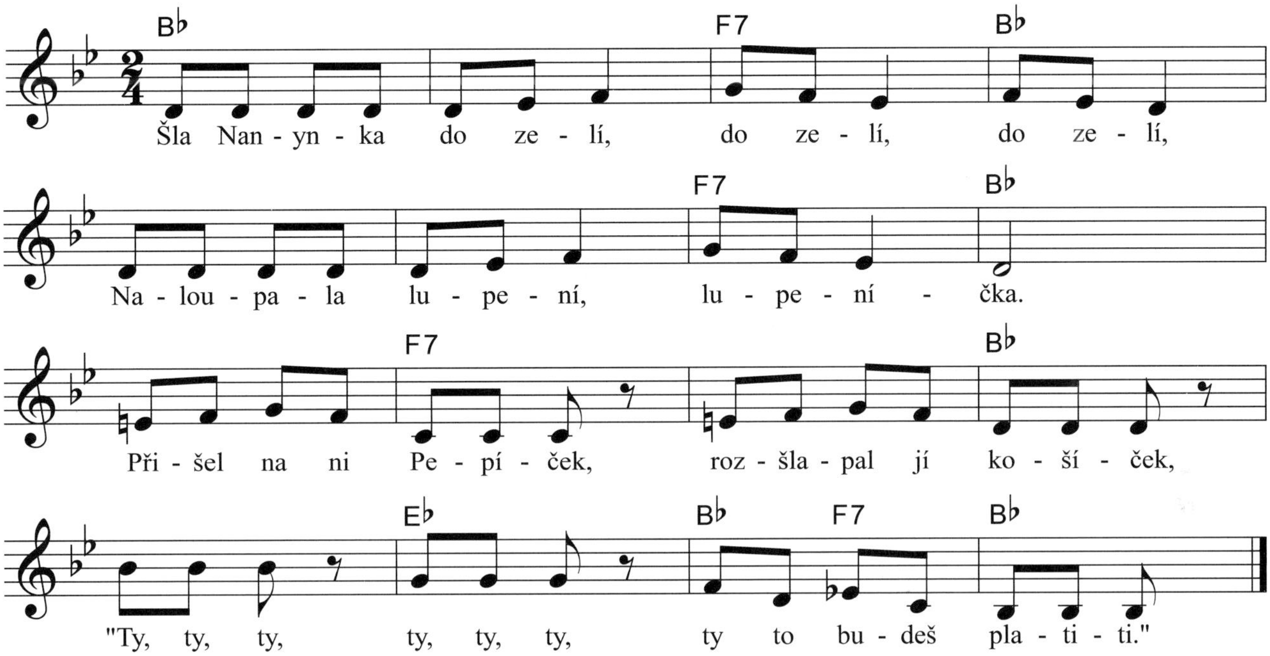

Šla Nanynka do zelí

1. Šla Nanynka do zelí,
do zelí, do zelí;
natrhala lupení,
lupeníčka.
Přišel na ni Pepíček,
rozšlapal jí košíček.
"Ty, ty, ty, ty, ty, ty,
ty to budeš platiti."

2. Já to platit nebudu,
nebudu, nebudu;
radši se dám na vojnu,
na vojničku.
Na vojnu se nedávej,
truc rodičům nedělej.
Ty, ty, ty, ty, ty, ty,
ty to musíš platiti.

Annie Went to the Cabbage Patch

1. Annie went to the cabbage patch,
cabbage patch, cabbage patch.
She harvested little cabbage leaves,
little cabbage leaves.
Joey came up to her
and stamped her basket.
"You, you, you, you, you, you,
you will pay for this."

2. I will not pay for it,
I won't, I won't;
I would rather join the army,
join the army.
Don't join the army,
don't defy your parents.
"You, you, you, you, you, you,
you must pay for this."

English Lyrics

1. To the garden Annie went,
   Annie went, Annie went;
   cutting cabbage her intent,
   her intention.
   Joey followed mischief bound,
   stamped her basket in the ground.
   Oh! Oh! Oh! Naughty Joe!
   Pay for this before you go.

2. You will get no pay from me,
   not from me, not from me.
   Rather I'd a soldier be,
   soldier become.
   Don't be such a spiteful lad,
   that would make your parents sad.
   No! No! No! Naughty Joe!
   Pay for this before you go.

Folk origins. Erben, *Nápěvy prostonárodních písní českých*, 121, and *Prostonárodní české písně a říkadla* (1864), 269. Czech and English words and music from "Šla Nanynka do zelí," Pisek, *Twenty-Two Bohemian Folk-Songs*, 38–39.

The charming tune to "Šla Nanynka do zelí" was published in Karel Erben's 1861 book of melodies to Czech folk songs. He published these lyrics two years later in his 1864 collection of Czech songs and rhymes.[1] It became widely known as the foot-stomping last number of the popular Czech *beseda*, a ballroom dance that was first performed in Prague in 1862.[2]

The quadrille-like *beseda* combines folk dances from several Czech regions with an accompanying arrangement of Czech folk songs. The *beseda* has been danced in Texas since at least the early 1900s. A 1976 memoir by John Staša in the SPJST newspaper *Věstník* describes a 1911 *beseda* group that rehearsed in an empty rent house on a farm near Buckholts. A dance instructor and a violinist came from nearby Temple every Sunday to teach the four young couples.[3]

The *beseda* still appears regularly at festivals and fairs and is taught in various youth groups associated with fraternal and heritage organizations. At the 2016 Caldwell Kolache Festival, for example, thirty-two youngsters performed the dance "in front of a huge crowd." A photograph shows the girls with headdresses of flower garlands wearing red skirts, white puffy-sleeved blouses, and aprons. The boys have white shirts, red vests embellished with gold ribbon, and black scarves around their necks.[4]

Folk costumes, though not originally intrinsic to the dance, are now an integral part of it. The traditional Czech *kroje* (folk costumes) have been modified by Texans but still display lively color, embroidery, ribbons, lace, and other decorative features. Svatava Jakobson, an influential Czech professor at the University of Texas at Austin in the 1960s and 1970s, admired the way Texans personalized the folk costume. She was particularly taken with the intricate bouquet of bluebonnets embroidered on the back of bandleader Gil Baca's vest. She observed him as his band was about to start playing on the town square of Crosby in the early 1980s.[5] In an article on Texas Czech ethnic identity, the linguist Lida Dutkova-Cope says the care and attention people give to creating their folk costumes shows that belonging to the group is both "pleasurable and meaningful."[6]

"Šla Nanynka do zelí" is a favorite with children. The typical children's movements are described by West high school teacher Olga Pazdral in her 1942 master's thesis, "Czech Folklore in Texas." "Children often join hands and dance in a circle as they sing it," she writes. "During the tenth and twelfth bars each child stamps his feet, and during the concluding bars each one shakes his finger threateningly at another child in the circle."[7]

The Gil Baca Orchestra of Fayetteville included "Annie in the Cabbage Patch" on an album from the 1970s entitled *Gil Baca and Band Play Baca's Style Music*. Their arrangement supplements the "Annie" verse with a chorus from "Baruška" and features Ray Baca on hammered dulcimer.[8] Ray Krenek was also featured playing hammered dulcimer on the song on his band's 2008 CD.[9] The Lee Ilse Orchestra of La Grange, with Lee Roy Matocha on vocals, released the song on a 45 rpm in the early 1960s; like Baca's arrangement, it ends with a "Baruška" chorus.[10] Another recording, this one with the two Czech verses as well as the English lyrics, was released by the Dujka Brothers of Brenham in 1999.[11]

53. Spadl lístek z javora *Falling Leaf; Falling Leaves; Fallen Leaf Waltz*

Spadl lístek z javora

1. Spadl lístek z javora,
   padl na nás na oba.
   Pojd' má milá, pojd' a doprovod' mě
   až do našeho dvora.

2. A já s tebou nepůjdu,
   protože tvá nebudu.
   Ty jsi synek bohatých rodičů,
   já mám jenom chudobu.

3. Nic si z toho nedělej,
   že já jsem tak bohatej.
   Přijdu večer k tvému okénečku,
   dám ti sladkou hubičku.

A Leaf Fell from the Maple

1. A leaf fell from a maple tree,
   it fell on us both.
   Come, my dear, come and accompany me
   up to our courtyard.

2. And I will not go with you
   because I will not be yours.
   You are the son of rich parents,
   I have only poverty.

3. Do not worry at all
   that I am so rich.
   I will come this evening to your window,
   I will give you a sweet kiss.

Words to verses 1–2 and music from "Spadl lístek z javora" by Sláva Mach, arranged by Joseph P. Elsnic (Chicago: Vitak-Elsnic, 1941), used with permission by Vitak-Elsnic Company, a Division of Music Publishers of America, LLC. Words to verse 3 from KJT, *Sbírka českých písní*, 60.

"Spadl lístek z javora," with the English title "Falling Leaf Waltz," was published in 1941 by Chicago's Vitak-Elsnic Music Co. in an arrangement by Joseph P. Elsnic. The haunting tune and lyrics were written by Pravoslav (Sláva) Mach, a composer and dance band musician who was born in Kladno, about twenty miles west of Prague. Mach studied music in Prague as a young man and remained there the rest of his life, part of the city's energetic film and musical theater scene.[1]

"Spadl lístek z javora" echoes the lyrics of a Moravian folk song called "Listečku z javora" (Leaf from the Maple) that opens with a maple leaf falling in a courtyard.[2] The song known in Texas as "Falling Leaf" opens with a maple leaf falling on two people. The lyrics take the form of a dialogue between two people and address the theme of economic inequality and its effect on romantic relationships. The boy asks the girl to accompany him to his courtyard, but she refuses, telling him she cannot because he is rich and she is poor. In the third verse, known in Texas but not part of the Vitak-Elsnic version, the boy persists in his pursuit, though to what end is not revealed.

The City Polka Boys of Houston, renamed Texas Sound Check in 2000, included "Falling Leaves Waltz" on their 1980s LP entitled *Cookin' Texas Music*. Their bandleader Benny Okruhlik said he learned it from a songbook that was given to him by an audience member when the band played a dance at the popular Martinez Hall in San Antonio.[3] Brothers John and Mark Dujka sing "Fallen Leaf Waltz" as a duet on one of their early CDs, from 1992, called *Out behind the Barn*.[4] The accordionist Chris Rybak's solo cassette tape *I Love to Polka*, released in 1994 when he was still a teenager, includes "Falling Leaves Waltz."[5] Czech and Then Some of Ennis, an influential band long involved with the town's yearly National Polka Fest, included "Falling Leaf Waltz" on their 2005 CD, *Polkas for Everyone*. David Slovak on lead and Danny Zapletal on harmony sing all three verses as a duet.[6]

On its 2004 CD, *Ještě jednou (One More Time)*, the Shiner Hobo Band included the first two verses of "Falling Leaves Waltz." The large and popular Hobo Band was first organized by local musicians in the Shiner area who were returning from service after World War I and wanted to play music again. The toilet plunger as bandleader baton was first introduced in 1936, a tradition still in place. The Hobos marched and played at many events, bolstered by a keg of beer regularly provided by Kosmas Spoetzl, the owner of Shiner's Spoetzl Brewery. The band slowly disbanded in the 1950s but reorganized in 1986 for the Texas Sesquicentennial celebrations, apparently attracted by the brewery's renewed offer to provide regular kegs for performances.[7]

54. Svatební píseň *Wedding Song; Unveiling Song*

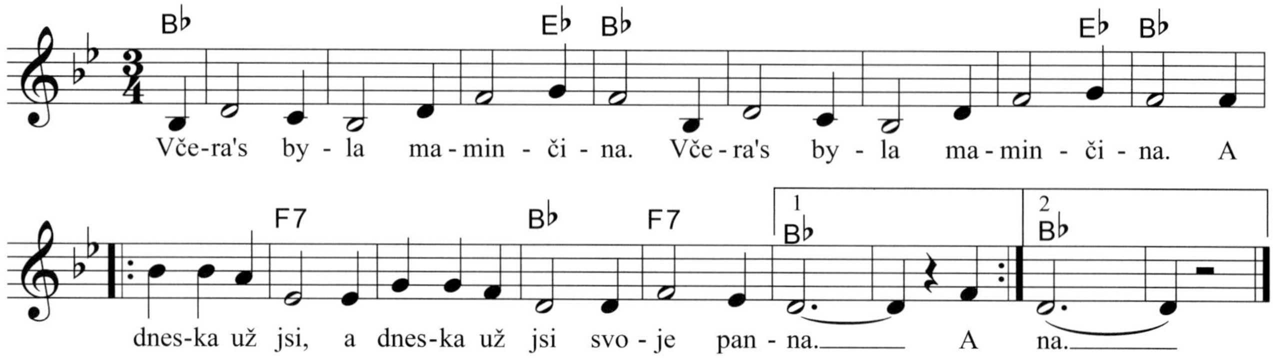

Svatební píseň

1. Včera's byla maminčina
a dneska už jsi, a dneska už jsi,
svoje panna.

2. Včera's měla bílé šaty
a dneska už máš, a dneska už máš,
samé láty.

3. Včera's měla bílý věnec
a dneska už máš, a dneska už máš,
černý čepec.

4. Nechtěla jsem, musela jsem
před oltář kleknůt, ručičky zepnůt,
plakala jsem.

5. Dej nevěsto, dej nám piva
by ti Pán Bůh dal, by ti Pán Bůl dal
za rok syna.

6. Dej ženichu, dej nám ještě
by ti Pán Bůh dal, by ti Pán Bůh dal
za dva děvče.

Wedding Song

1. Yesterday you were your mother's
and today you are, today you are
your own woman.

2. Yesterday you had a white dress
and today you have, today you have
only rags.

3. Yesterday you had a white garland
and today you have, today you have
a black cap.

4. I didn't want to but I had to
kneel at the altar and clasp my hands,
I cried.

5. Give, bride, give us beer
so that God will grant you, so that God will grant you
a son in a year.

6. Give, groom, give us more
so that God will grant you, so that God will grant you
a girl in two years.

Folk origins. Polášek and Kubeša, *Vałaské pěsničky II*, 32–33. Words from Bartoš and Bartoš, *Spivejme pisničky*, 68. Music from Jimmy Brosch and His Happy Country Boys, "Wedding Waltz," *Believe It or Not* (Houston: Guide LP-1001, 1968), LP.

Collections of Czech folk music include many wedding songs. "Svatební píseň," a wedding song that is widespread in Texas, was published in a 1940 book called *Valaské pěsničky,* a collection of 150 folk songs from the Wallachian region of northeastern Moravia. The words and music had been notated in 1899 by the folklorist Matouš Václavek. It was taught to him by a fifty-nine-year-old singer from Vidče, a village not far from Rožnov nad Radhoštěm, a town in northeastern Moravia.[1]

A drawing of the 1861 wedding procession of Josef and Františka Laštovica that took place in Hostýn near Ellinger, Texas, can be seen at the Fayetteville Area Heritage Museum.[2] The drawing depicts a crowd of revelers riding horses alongside a large hill. There are wonderful details in this early image of Czech Texas. The wedding party is headed for a small frame church that sits on top of the hill. The women wear elaborate headdresses, and some of the men wear a type of hat typical of those worn by Moravian men at that time. The bottles two men are waving over their heads possibly contain a homemade plum brandy popular with Moravians called *slivovice.* One man on horseback fires a pistol into the air. A small dog walks along with the procession, and several children watch it go by. True to the portrayal in the drawing, Czech weddings can be legendary affairs, and some of the traditions associated with early ones persist to this day.

The capping ceremony, called čepení in Czech, is a widespread, traditional Slavic wedding ritual. Usually late at night during a wedding celebration, the women of the village sing a song while removing the bride's veil and replacing it with an embroidered cap. This headdress symbolizes her new status as a married woman.[3]

The capping ceremony was also widespread in Texas, though it is now performed much less than it used to be. In Texas, a cloth "field" bonnet, the kind farm women used to wear, substitutes for the more dainty Moravian cap. The bride or both the bride and groom sit in the middle of the hall where the festivities are being held. Women replace the bride's veil with a bonnet while singing "Svatební píseň," or the polka band hired for the dance performs the song. The ceremony is usually exaggerated and played for laughs. The bonnet might be old and ratty, or made of black fabric, as verse 3 of the lyrics describes the cap. The groom is often given a beat-up straw hat, or a cowboy hat. Sometimes a beer is thrust into his hand while the bride gets a baby doll or even a live baby to hold.[4]

The song was first recorded in Texas as part of a folklore project by William Owens in the late 1930s. It is preserved in the archives at Texas A&M University, where Owens taught English. He was also a folklorist who traveled throughout Texas recording songs in many languages that were part of the rich cultural heritage of the state. Ethel Jecmenek, a Czech woman he met in Rosebud in the Temple area, sang this song for him. He says she called it "Zašovu" in Czech, and in English she called it "A Song Sung at a Wedding." The lyrics she sang refer to Zašová, a Moravian village located near Rožnov, where her family had come from. Most of her verses are like those notated by Václavek, the Moravian folklorist.[5]

A much longer version of the song, seventeen verses in all, is in the possession of Eileen Rosipal, a member of the Taylor Czech Chorus. Rosipal learned the song from her mother, Mary Kajs Sladecek of Corn Hill, a farming community in Williamson County. She remembers that her mother's lyrics were handwritten on a piece of paper and that they sang the Czech verses at weddings in the late 1950s and in both Czech and English in the late 1960s. They passed out song sheets so everybody could join in.[6] The Taylor Czech Chorus sang all seventeen Czech verses for their 2018 CD, *Still . . . Carrying On the Tradition.*[7]

One final version was collected at a wedding in Granger in 1991. Kevin Hannan, then a graduate student in Slavic languages and linguistics at the University of Texas at Austin, attended the wedding and wrote about it later in an article published in *Věstník,* the popular weekly newspaper of the SPJST. "At midnight," he wrote, "there was a pause in the music and it was announced that a special event would take place in the middle of the hall. A chair was brought out for the young bride and a crowd assembled around her. A group of women began to remove the bride's veil while the people surrounding her broke out in song."The song, of course," he wrote, "was 'Svatební píseň.'"[8]

All these versions of the "Wedding Song"—and there are even more—use the same melody that was found in Moravia. With a few word changes, the basic core of the lyrics, those focused on the removal of the bride's veil, can be found in all of them. Most also include subsequent toasts to the bride and groom. This is the way the lyrics are presented in this songbook, and they also match the first four verses as performed by Jimmy Brosch and His Happy Country Boys on their 1968 LP, *Believe It or Not.*[9] This song has long been treasured by the Texas Czech community and deserves continued care, protection, and performance.

55. Švestková alej *Prune Song*

Švestková alej

1. Za naší vesnicí na hlavní silnici
bosenský rostou švestky, bajó!
S Ančou jsme hlídali, švestky jsme jídali,
bejvalo to moc hezký.
Vždycky jsme seděli vedle sebe,
na hvězdy čučeli a na nebe,
a ted'ko sám a sám na všecko vzpomínám,
chtěl bych být blízko tebe.
Chorus:
V tej naší aleji
švestky se válejí.
Já dneska nehlídám, já dneska nehlídám,
oči mně pálejí.
(Kdybych já holku měl,
já bych si za ní šel,
dal bych jí hubičku na její tvářičku,
žádný by nevěděl.)

2. Za naší vesnicí na hlavní silnici
švestky jsou jako pěsti, bajó!
Anča nic neřekla, ode mě utekla,
ted' nemám žádné štěstí.
Andula s jiným ted' švestky hlídá,
už naše povidla neuhlídá,
dřív tady hvězdičky vídali věcičky
o tom se nepovídá.

3. Za naší vesnicí, na hlavní silnici
švestky jsou očesaný, bajó!
Šaty mám v almaře a s jinou na faře
máme to podepsaný.
Snad až se ožením zapomenu,
pak ti to, Andulo, připomenu,
co jsi to provedla, že jsi mě podvedla.
Švestky ted' nemaj cenu.

Plum Alley

1. Outside of our town on the main road
grow Bosnian plums, they do!
Annie and I guarded them and ate them,
it used to be really nice.
We always sat next to each other,
and gazed at the stars and the sky.
And now all alone I remember everything,
I would like to be close to you.
Chorus:
In that lane of ours
the plums roll about.
Today I'm not guarding them, today I'm not guarding them,
my eyes are burning me.
(If I had a girl
I would go to see her.
I would give her a kiss on her sweet cheek,
No one would know.)

2. Outside of our town on the main road
the plums are as big as your fist, they are!
Annie didn't say anything, she ran off from me.
Now I don't have any happiness,
Annie now guards plums with someone else,
she won't be able to protect our plum jam.
Before, the little stars saw every little thing that went on here
but we don't talk about it.

3. Outside of our town on the main road
plums have been harvested, they have!
My clothes are in the wardrobe, and I am
engaged to another girl in our parish.
Perhaps after I am married I will forget.
Then, Annie, I will remind you of
what you did to me, that you deceived me.
Plums now are worthless.

From "Švestková alej, Prune Song," arranged for piano and voice by Joseph P. Elsnic (Chicago: Vitak-Elsnic, 1937), used with permission by Vitak-Elsnic Company, a Division of Music Publishers of America, LLC. Second half of chorus (in parentheses) from KJT, *Sbírka českých písní*, 15.

"Švestková alej" is from an operetta called *Veličenstvo v plavkách* (*Majesty in a Swimsuit*). It premiered in Prague between the two world wars, in the late 1920s, during what is considered a golden age of Czech musical theater. *Majesty in a Swimsuit* featured songs written by several different songwriters, one of whom was Jaroslav (Jarka) Mottl (1900–86), the composer of "Švestková alej."[1] The song was published in Prague by Jos. Šváb in 1930.

Jarka Mottl was a Prague native and self-taught musician who was comfortable in many different styles. He first published tramping songs, the music endemic to the back-to-nature youth movement that began in the 1920s and was partially inspired by the mythology of the American West. His songwriting also crossed over into popular, cabaret, operetta, and film music.[2] "Švestková alej" is well known in America as "Prune Song," which refers to plums in their dried form. But Mottl's lyrics focus on the fresh fruit of the plum trees that have been grown for centuries in orchards and also on both sides of many alleys and lanes in the Czech Republic.[3]

In the song, a boy tells the story of his relationship with Annie, a romance that began in early autumn during the plum harvest. The ripening stages of plums serve as a metaphor for the growth and decline of their love. When the plums were growing, the two were sweethearts, and together they guarded them and ate the fresh fruit while gazing at the stars and the sky. When the plums were the size of fists, Annie ran off and found someone else. He says she no longer tends their *povidla*, a concentrated plum jam that requires constant stirring, long cooking, and is often made outside. By verse 3, the plum harvest is over, the boy is engaged to another girl in the parish, and he hopes to forget Annie. But he wonders if she will live to regret her actions. For him, the experience has spoiled his taste for plums.[4]

Columbia Records released a 78 rpm record of "Švestková alej" by Romy Gosz and His Bohemian Orchestra of Wisconsin in 1933, reported to have sold around 100,000 copies.[5] In Texas, Bačova Česka Kapela (Baca Czech Band) of Fayetteville recorded the song in 1935 at a San Antonio session. It was released as a Vocalion 78.[6] Both the Gosz and the Baca versions were largely instrumental, though both included vocals on the chorus. The chorus at this point consisted of the original first four lines, which were then repeated.

By 1939, when the Texas A&M English professor and folklorist William A. Owens made a field recording of the song in Texas, he documented additional lyrics for the second half of the chorus.[7] Though the added lyrics fit somewhat awkwardly into the storyline, they can shorten the song. The chorus, with these additional lyrics, can be heard on a 1942 Columbia recording of "Švestková alej (Prune Song)" by Adolph Hofner and His San Antonians.[8] English lyrics, which delightfully poke fun at the usual conventions of the cheating song, were also added to the chorus at some point. The title for the English lyrics is "We Left Our Wives at Home." Some of the lines go "we left our wives with some other guys," "we left our skirts with some other shirts," and "hope they had a very good time."

Many bands and choral groups in Texas know and have recorded the song, and these variations can be found within their arrangements. One example is by Kovanda's Czech Band of Fayetteville. They released their version in 1999, which includes the first two Czech verses and the expanded Czech chorus.[9] Another example is by Julius Tupa, founder of *Texas Polka News*. Tupa and his band Sagebrush of Houston recorded "Prune Song" in the 1970s. Their rendition includes the Czech chorus as well as the English lyrics, the latter sung by what sounds like the whole band. The slide guitar, electric guitar, and fiddle all wail on solos, while the piano and rest of the rhythm section keep this popular song swinging.[10]

56. U studánky seděla *At the Spring*

U studánky seděla

1. U studánky seděla,
do voděnky hleděla.
Spatřila malou rybičku,
jak polykala vodičku.

2. Rybičko, tys němá tvář,
já slyšela, že kouzla znáš.
Ty víš, co trápí srdce mé,
ty víš, kde můj miláček je.

3. Miláček se odebral,
mě nešťastnou zanechal.
Až on se z ciziny vrátí,
on večery mně ukrátí.

4. Sbohem, sbohem, milko má,
mně zůstane láska tvá.
Až budu v dálné cizině,
bude tvé štěstí spanilé.
(budu jen myslet na tebe.)

At the Spring She Sat

1. At the cold spring she sat,
into the water she gazed.
She caught sight of a small fish
as it gulped the water.

2. Little fish, you are a mute creature,
I heard that you knew magic.
You know what tortures my heart,
you know where my darling is.

3. My darling went away,
he left me unhappy.
When he returns from abroad
he will shorten my evenings.

4. Good bye, good bye, my dear,
I will keep your love.
Even when I am far away in a foreign land
your happiness will be beautiful.
(I will think only of you.)

Unknown origins. Words to verses 1, 3, 4 and music from "U studánky seděla, neb Zlatá Rybka, valčík s textem" (At the Spring She Sat, or Gold Fish, waltz with text), arranged by Louis Vitak (Chicago: Georgi and Vitak, 1915). Words to verse 2 and alternate ending to verse 4 (in parentheses) from KJT, *Sbírka českých písní*, 10.

"U studánky seděla," origins unknown,[1] is a popular waltz told from the perspective of a woman left behind when her sweetheart leaves for a foreign land, possibly to serve in the military. The song opens with a woman sitting beside a spring, gazing into the water. She sees a small fish and asks it for news of her boyfriend. In the last verse, the fish delivers a sweet message to her from her faraway love. A popular version known in the Czech Republic ends on a gloomier note—the fish advises her to forget her boyfriend because he already has another girl.[2] Sheet music of the song was released in 1915, arranged by Louis Vitak of Georgi and Vitak Music Company of Chicago.

Also known as "At the Spring," the song is well known in the Texas Czech community and can be found in many local lyric books and song sheets.[3] Its melody can also be heard in a polka Mass. Martha Viktorin wrote English lyrics to fit the melody and included the song, titled "We Offer Thanks," in the polka Mass she compiled for Holy Cross Catholic Church of East Bernard. The parish is in a farming community about thirty miles east of the Houston outskirts.[4] The Taylor Czech Chorus, on one of its CDs, sings verses of both "U studánky seděla" and Viktorin's "We Offer Thanks" as a medley. The recording was made at a concert the chorus presented at the Taylor Brethren Church in 2005.[5]

To further show how this song plays a part in the everyday lives of Texas Czechs, it was in the repertory of the Moulton All-Girl Polka Band. The Polka Band was part of the elementary school music program in Moulton. It was first organized in 1987 by the music educator and Moulton High School band director George Koudelka. The All-Girl Polka Band's ten members were twelve years old at the time they and the high school band recorded music for a late-1980s CD. The girls' version of "At the Spring Waltz" is one of the songs included on the recording.[6]

Adolph Hofner and His Bohemians of San Antonio recorded an early western swing version of the song during their 1942 Hollywood recording session, released as a 78 rpm by Columbia Records. The smooth interplay of Emil Hofner's steel guitar, Walter Kleypas's accordion, and Adolph's vocals creates a little magic of its own, evoking the smoothness of a fish gliding through water.[7] The Joe Patek Orchestra of Shiner recorded a 78 for the Humming Bird label, later reissued on a compilation CD.[8] Another recording, this one from 1973, was made by the Ellinger Combo, a band from the community of Ellinger that lies about midway between San Antonio and Houston. The combo's version, first released by Houston's Guide Records, is included on the compilation CD called *Texas Bohemia*, released in 1994 by Trikont, a German independent record label.[9]

More recent recordings are by Mark Halata and Texavia of Houston on their 2007 CD, *Amerika*. The accordionist Halata is joined on vocals by Jeff and Bruce Brosch.[10] The Moravians, a group of seven high school friends from Ennis, played their first gig at a school talent show in 1997. They won and never stopped playing. "U Studanky Waltz" is included on their 2013 CD, *Czech Spirit Will Live On*.[11]

57. Veselá bída *Happy Go Lucky; Strašidlo*

Veselá bída

Introduction:
My jsem ta veselá bída.
Veselá, veselá bída.

1. Když se všechni oženili,
já se dneska ožením.
Ženu pošlu do roboty,
sám si lehnu do peřin.

2. Seděla jsem na pavlači,
přišlo na mě strašidlo.
Mělo boty a kalhoty,
na mě se moc tlačilo.

3. Vem košilku mezi zuby;
dělej na mě bububů.
Kdyby se tě všichni báli,
já se tě bát nebudu.
Chorus:
Šup sem, šup tam,
nám už je to všecko jedno.
Šup sem, šup tam,
nám už je to pryč.

Happy Misery

Introduction:
We are that happy misery.
Happy, happy misery.

1. Since everybody's gotten married
today I'll marry, too.
I will send my woman off to work,
I'll lie down in the featherbed by myself.

2. I sat down on a porch,
a scarecrow came up to me.
It had shoes and pants,
it pushed me around.

3. Take my shirt between your teeth,
say "boo-boo-boo" to me.
Even if everyone else is afraid of you,
I won't be afraid.
Chorus:
Jump here, jump there,
it's all the same to us.
Jump here, jump there,
everything is gone.

Words and music from "Veselá Bída," arranged by Louis Vitak (Chicago: Georgi and Vitak, 1924); verse 1, line 1, and chorus, line 4, from Dennis Svatek, Taylor, Texas.

"Veselá bída," with its miscellany of impudent boasts, has a perfect match in the jaunty tune of its polka. Also known in Texas by the names "Strašidlo" or "Strashidlo" and "Happy Go Lucky Polka," it is a compilation of brags. The carefree narrator claims that since everyone else is married, he, too, will get married. He will send his bride out to work while he lolls in bed. He takes a walk and is pushed around by a scarecrow but responds by making fun of it: "Say 'boo-boo-boo' to me." The Texas version of "Veselá bída" descended from the 1924 arrangement by Louis Vitak and is a patchwork of fragments from older texts.[1] At its core is a well-known bawdy song commonly sung by Czech soldiers during World War I, which reflected the absurd situation of Czechs fighting a war for their Austrian rulers: "Jump here, jump there, it's all the same to us."[2]

"Veselá bída" was first recorded by Adolf and the Boys of Schulenburg at a San Antonio session in 1937.[3] The group is also known in the state as Adolf Pavlas and the Gold Chain Bohemians because of the popularity of their 1930s radio program. The show was sponsored by Fort Worth's Universal Mills and its Gold Chain brand of flour. The recordings of the band left a big impression on Texas polka musicians because of the high skill level of its players and the inventiveness of its arrangements. Tuba and bass player Mike Gest of Houston especially compliments the band's recording of "Happy Go Lucky Polka." He points out its underlying "horse clopping" rhythm, the "beautiful three-part harmony" of the singers, and the opening drum solo. "A drum solo," Gest says. "No one was doing that at the time."[4]

Adolph and Emil Hofner of San Antonio recorded the song twice, and both versions have been reissued on CDs. The first, with Czech lyrics, was a 78 in 1947 for Imperial Records.[5] The second, with English lyrics, was recorded in Nashville in 1955. It was released on an album of nine songs as part of a Decca series of long-playing albums called *Country and Western Dance-O-Rama*.[6] A 1955 *Billboard* ad lists the bands for the series. The first four albums feature Milton Brown and His Brownies, Bob Wills and His Texas Playboys, Spade Cooley and His Buckle-Busters, and Adolph Hofner and His San Antonians, all masters of western swing.[7]

One other recording is by the Czech Heritage Singers, a Houston-Galveston area choral group founded in 1974 and led by Fr. Paul Chovanec. They first met to prepare a program for the annual Sts. Cyril and Methodius Heritage Day, a Houston festival hosted annually by the city's Czech, Polish, and Ukranian communities. "Veselá bída" is on the group's 1977 album.[8]

58. Vstávej, má milá *Arise, My Darling; Pretty Dancing Girl*

Vstávej, má milá

1. Vstávej, má milá, už je den bílý.
   Půjdeme do háje trhat květiny.
   Půjdeme do háje trhat květiny.

2. Já bych vstávala, hlava mě bolí,
   Vem bílý šáteček a zavaž mně ji.
   Vem bílý šáteček a zavaž mně ji.

3. Když jsem tě počal, hlavu vázati,
   ty si mně počala hned umírati,
   ty si mně počala hned umírati.

4. Já neumírám, já jen vomdlévám,
   pro tebe, synáčku, že chodíš jinam,
   pro tebe, synáčku, že chodíš jinam.

Arise, My Darling

1. Arise, my darling, the day is already here.
   We'll go to the meadow and pick flowers.
   We'll go to the meadow and pick flowers.

2. I would get up, but I have a headache.
   Get a white scarf and tie it around my head.
   Get a white scarf and tie it around my head.

3. When I began to tie your head,
   you began to die right away,
   you began to die right away.

4. I am not dying, I am only fainting
   for you, son, because you go somewhere else,
   for you, son, because you go somewhere else.

English Lyrics (Pretty Dancing Girl)

1. Pretty dancing girl, moving gracefully,
   how I long for one dance,
   won't you dance with me?

2. Pretty dancing girl, with your tossing curls,
   set my heart all awhirl,
   pretty dancing girl.

Folk origins. Erben, *Prostonárodní české písně a říkadla* (1864), 400, and Slavia, *Národní písně,* Series 2, part 4, 110. Words to verses 1–2 and music from "Vstávej má milá pochod," arranged by Louis Vitak for piano and voice (Chicago: Georgi and Vitak, circa 1915); words to verses 3–4 from Slavia, *Národní písně,* Series 2, part 4, 110. English words from "Pretty Dancing Girl," by Bernie Roberts (Chicago: Vitak-Elsnic, 1964), used with permission by Vitak-Elsnic Company, a Division of Music Publishers of America, LLC.

Sheet music for "Vstávej, má milá," a Czech folk song from southern Bohemia, was published in the early 1900s by the Chicago music company Georgi and Vitak in an arrangement by Louis Vitak. Though similar lyrics had been documented in 1864 by Karel Jaromír Erben, the lyrics in the Vitak arrangement are most like those published in 1879 by Slavia, a Prague literary and oratory society whose members collected and published several books of folk songs, tales, and rhymes.[1] Whether deliberate or not, the trio melody bears a striking resemblance to an aria from *Martha,* a popular opera by the German composer Friedrich von Flotow that premiered in Vienna in 1847.[2] The aria in its later Italian form, "M'appari" (Like a Dream), became known in the United States in the early 1900s, bolstered by the Italian tenor Enrico Caruso's popular performances and recordings.[3]

Adolph and the Boys of Schulenburg were the first in Texas to release a record of the song. They recorded the full Vitak arrangement of "Vstávej, má milá" at a session in San Antonio in 1937. The group included the first two verses on the trio.[4] Charlie Adamcik and the Polka Tones of Dallas included "Arise, My Darling" on their self-titled mid-1960s LP. Cathey and Patricia Adamcik, daughters of the bandleader, sing the first two verses.[5] By the time Vernon Drozd and the Texas Brass of Houston recorded the song in 1969, the tune had acquired additional English lyrics written by Bernie Roberts under the title "Pretty Dancing Girl." On the Texas Brass recording, the vocalist Brian McWhirter sings a verse in English and one in Czech while the pianist Gene Lichnovsky plays a spirited accompaniment.[6] Their bandleader Drozd, a legendary performer who soars on the recording's saxophone and clarinet solos, grew up in the farming community of Moravia and also spent years in Houston playing with the Ray Baca Orchestra.[7]

Brave Combo of Denton, who sometimes refers to its Grammy-award-winning music as "nuclear polka," released the song twice, in 1987 and again in 1998 for their Grammy-nominated CD *Polka Party.* The bandleader Carl Finch sings the English verses and one Czech verse on both recordings.[8] Tony Janak's Polka Band of Yoakum includes four Czech verses on its "Arise My Darling." The Janak rendition is in waltz time. It appears on their fortieth-anniversary compilation CD, a collection of "most requested" songs recorded by the band between 1963 and 1997.[9]

"Vstávej, má milá" has been recorded by many other Texas bands and choral groups. The tune can be heard with sacred lyrics written by Martha Viktorin of East Bernard. "Here We Gather, Lord," is one of the hymns included in the polka Mass that Viktorin compiled in 2000 for Holy Cross Catholic Church in East Bernard.[10]

59. Vzpomínka na Cameron *Memories of Cameron*

Vzpomínka na Cameron

Chorus:
Vzpomínka věčná na Cameron zbejvá,
jen všech ten čas, tak jen, tak rychle ubejvá.

1. Když mladý hošík na vojnu musí jít,
a se svou matičkou se musí rozloučit.

2. Když mladý hošík z vojny se navrátí,
přijde k své matičce, a líbá jí na tváři.

Memories of Cameron

Chorus:
An eternal memory of Cameron remains,
only that the time is so quickly running out.

1. When a young boy must go to war,
he must say goodbye to his mother.

2. When a young boy returns from the war,
he walks up to his mother and kisses her on the cheek.

Words and music by John and Rosie Majek. From Leo Majek Orchestra, "Memories of Cameron," *Songs from the Heart* (Corpus Christi: Majek Recording Studio, circa 1980s), cassette tape, used with permission.

The lovely, haunting waltz "Vzpomínka na Cameron" was written in the 1940s by John Majek and his mother, Rosie, matriarch of the Majek family. Rosie's seven children, including John, grew up on the family farm near Cameron, in Milam County, before the Majek family relocated to Corpus Christi in 1940. Five of her six sons served in World War II, and all five safely returned home.[1]

"Vzpomínka na Cameron" was first recorded when the Leo Majek Orchestra, under the direction of Leo Sr., played a live performance on the *Czech Melody Hour* of Temple radio station KTEM. The show was broadcast on Labor Day weekend, 1952. The song was captured on tape by an avid listener and longtime Czech language teacher, Calvin Chervenka. Some years later, after Calvin's death, his nephew Glen Chervenka was going through his uncle's belongings and came across the tape. Glen gave the recording to Alfred Vrazel, whose family had been longtime friends of the Majeks. Alfred made a copy of the song for Jerry Majek, son of the songwriter John and present bandleader of the Majek Orchestra.[2]

In a recent interview, Jerry said the song known now is shorter than the one on the tape, a concession made by the Majek Orchestra to the standard length of popular songs. The Majek recording most known in Texas is from about the 1980s and features Frank and John Majek on a vocal duet; the two began playing as teenagers under the direction of their father, Leo Sr. By the time of this recording, the Majek Orchestra included four of Leo and Rosie's sons, two grandsons, the wife of one of the grandsons, and a great-grandson. It was released as a cassette tape and reissued in 2011 on the CD *Jimmy Brosch Remembers Twenty Legendary Texas Czech Polka Bands*.[3] The words and music in this book come from that recording.

Also known by the English title "Memories of Cameron," the song is a sentimental favorite in Texas and is one of the numbers performed in large jam sessions or when several bands are playing the same event, such as a church picnic or a battle dance. Vrazels' Polka Band of Buckholts recorded "Memories of Cameron Waltz" in 1978 on their *Silver Anniversary Sounds* LP.[4] Jerry Haisler and the Melody Five of nearby Temple also recorded the song in 1978, with vocal by Alice Sulak, on their LP *For the First Time*.[5] The Czech Harvesters of Ennis recorded "Memories of Cameron Waltz" on their 1980 LP, *A Gathering of Friends*. The vocalists Al Vanek and Michael Snapka added their own English version of the chorus.[6] A recent recording is a 2016 CD called *Where It Began* by a young band with deep polka roots in the state, called the All Around Czechs, based in the town of West.[7]

60. Z vojny; Slavíček *From the War; Mockingbird*

Z vojny; Slavíček

1. Slavíček je malý ptáček, chytit se nedá.
Proto vždycky na vysokém stromě sedává.
O půlnoci zazpívá.
Má panenka ta jest má,
ona vždycky ve svém srdci na mě vzpomíná.

2. Adie má nejmilejší, s tebou se loučím.
Pánu Bohu a rodičce tebe poručím.
Nemůžu s tebou bývat,
musím pryč mašírovat.
Pro svobodu a vlast svojú musím bojovat.

From the War; Nightingale

1. The nightingale is a small bird, he's impossible to catch.
That's why he always sits in a tall tree.
At midnight he sings.
My girl is mine,
she always in her heart remembers me.

2 *Adieu my dearest.* I am saying goodbye.
To God and your parents I entrust you.
I cannot be with you,
I must march away.
For freedom and my homeland I must fight.

Folk origins. Erben, *Pjsně národnj w Čechách*, 1:128–29. Words from Jimmy Brosch and His Happy Country Boys, "Mocking Bird," *Believe It or Not* (Houston: Guide LP-1001, 1967 or 1968), LP, used with permission. Music from "Z vojny (From War)," arranged for voice and piano by Louis Vitak (Chicago: Georgi and Vitak, 1913).

This song tells of a man bidding his sweetheart farewell as he marches off to war. But first he evokes the image of a small bird who sings at midnight and is impossible to catch. In Czech, *slavík* or the diminutive *slavíček* means nightingale. In Texas, where there are no nightingales, the words came to mean mockingbird as well.

Nightingales are birds of the Old World, where they are frequently evoked in poetry and considered melancholic and virtuosic singers, but these nightingales are not to be found in the Americas.[1] Mockingbirds are New World birds that would have been unfamiliar to new immigrants to Texas. Like male nightingales, male mockingbirds are prodigious singers and often sing at night during mating season. But unlike nightingales, mockingbirds "mock" or mimic sounds from the environment around them.[2] The meaning of the lyrics can shift in interesting ways depending on which bird comes to the listener's mind.

Another name for this song is “Z vojny” or “From War.” It was arranged by Louis Vitak, and his several-part arrangement was published under that title by Georgi and Vitak in 1913.[3] The Rudy Kurtz Orchestra of Shiner recorded an instrumental “From the War” in the late 1940s or early 1950s, released by Humming Bird of Waco as a 78 rpm record.[4] The Kurtz Orchestra plays the full Vitak arrangement. The score in this book includes the whole arrangement, but most Texas bands have shortened the piece. All the bands mentioned below play and sing the song, either one or two verses, and sometimes add a section from the long piece as an instrumental.

A recording by Jimmy Brosch and His Happy Country Boys in the late 1960s featured the two verses reprinted here. On their LP *Believe It or Not,* guitarist Paul Machac sings the verses on “Mocking Bird.” Mark Halata and Texavia also include both verses on their 2018 CD, *Live at Moravia Store.* Halata sings the first, and the Texavia drummer Greg Machac sings the same second verse that his father, Paul, sang on the earlier Brosch album, with bassist Mike Gest adding a harmony vocal.[5] Fritz Hodde and the Fabulous Six of Pflugerville have “Mockingbird Waltz,” first verse only, on their 1998 CD, *Standing Tall.*[6] The Shiner Hobo Band likewise includes the first verse of “Mockingbird Waltz” on their CD *Ještě jednou (One More Time)* in 2004.[7] The Red Ravens of El Campo recorded both verses on their 2004 CD, *Havin' Fun.*[8]

61. Zahučely hory *Roaring Mountains*

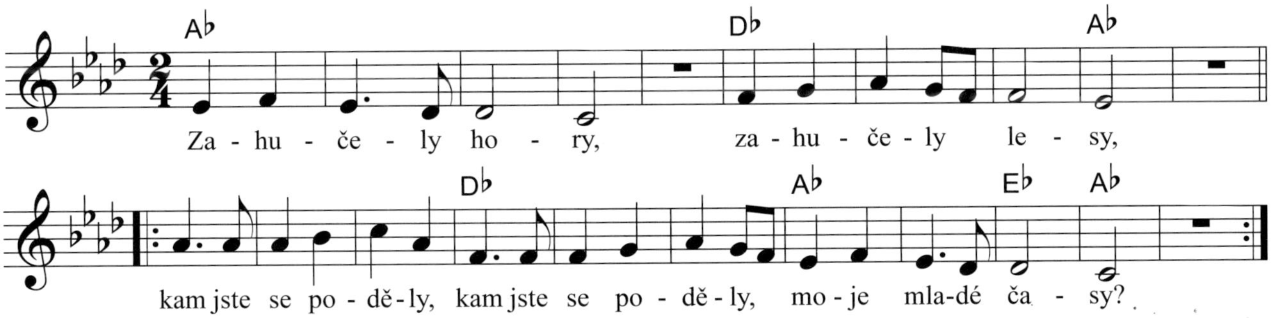

Zahučely hory

1. Zahučely hory, zahučely lesy,
   kam jste se poděly, kam jste se poděly,
   moje mladé časy?

2. Moje mladé časy neužily krásy,
   moje mladá léta, moje mladá léta
   neužila světa.

3. Mladost, moje mladost, jak jsem tě utratil,
   jako bych byl kámen, jako bych byl kámen
   do voděnky hodil.

4. Ještě se ten kámen ve vodě obrátí,
   ale moje mladost, ale moje mladost,
   nikdy se nevrátí.

The Mountains Roared

1. The mountains roared, the forests roared,
   what has become of you, what has become of you,
   my young days?

2. My young days did not enjoy beauty,
   my young years, my young years
   did not enjoy the world.

3. Youth, my youth, how I wasted you,
   as if I threw away, as if I threw away a stone
   in the water.

4. The stone in the water will still turn over,
   but my youth, but my youth,
   it will never return.

Folk origins. Kollár, *Národnié zpiewanky*, 69; Jungmann, *Slowesnost*, 492; Sušil, *Moravské národní písně*, 351; and Erben, *Nápěvy prostonárodních písní českých*, tune 352. Words and music from "Zahučely hory" (trio only), arranged by Louis Vitak (Chicago: Georgi and Vitak, 1918).

"Zahučely hory," an old lament shared by the Czechs, Slovaks, and Poles of Central Europe, exists as "Roaring Mountains" in Texas where it is performed as an up-tempo polka. The lyrics tell of the loss of youth: the mountains and forests are roaring because the singer's young years are gone forever, thrown away like a stone into water. The landscape evoked by the song reflects the prominence of mountains in the borderlands shared by Poland, Slovakia, and Moravia, where the song was first collected and is still sung. Indeed, in the Czech Republic, "Zahučely hory" is often performed at the funerals of foresters.[1]

An early version of these lyrics was published by Jan Kollár in his 1834 collection of Slovak folk songs.[2] A Czech version was published in 1845 by the linguist Josef Jungmann as part of his project to reinvigorate the written Czech language.[3] The Moravian folklorist and priest František Sušil published another version in 1860, partly in a Moravian dialect, with one of the two most common melodies that are still attached to the song, a slow lament in a minor key.[4] The melody known in Texas is quite the opposite. It is a polka variant of the tune published by the Bohemian writer and folklore collector Karel Jaromír Erben in 1861.[5] In a recent book, the folklorist James P. Leary includes the song in Polish from a 1941 field recording made in Wisconsin with yet another melody.[6] "Zahučely hory" is an old song that belongs to many people; its roar echoes the shock felt by successive generations as each faces loss and the passage of time.

The song has long been part of the Czech choral tradition. Its most famous arrangement, from 1864, is by Pavel Křížkovský using the words and melody from Sušil. Křížkovský was a priest, choirmaster, and composer who taught at the school of the Abbey of St. Thomas in Brno, the major city in Moravia. There he oversaw the musical education of the important Moravian composer Leoš Janáček, who entered the abbey school at age eleven. The Křížkovský choral arrangement was published many times, starting in 1883, and continues to be a popular piece.[7] John J. Karas, a speaker at the 1986 Texas Czech Music Symposium that took place in College Station, gave a lecture-recital on the music of Křížkovský. During his presentation, Karas sang a solo version of "Zahučaly hory" and pointed out that the song "is sung even here in Texas to this day."[8]

"Roaring Mountains" is popular in Texas. Two of the choirs that have recorded it are the Czech Singers of Victoria[9] and the SPJST Lodge 88 Choral Group of Houston, backed up by the lodge orchestra.[10] The Johnnie Holub Polka Band of Schulenburg released one of the first recordings in 1967, reissued on CD in 2013. The song was also released in 2013 on a CD called *Holub Polka Band: Younger Generation,* the band managed by Johnnie's son, John Holub Jr. of Columbus.[11]

The Pavelka Orchestra of Robstown has a heartfelt rendition on its LP *From Sunny South Texas*, likely recorded between 1968 and 1975.[12] John and Frank Majek of the Leo Majek Orchestra of Corpus Christi sing a lovely duet on their album *Dance*, from the late 1960s.[13] Two more recordings from the 1960s–1970s are by Vrazels' Polka Band of Buckholts[14] and the Bill Mraz Orchestra of Houston.[15] In 2003, Mark Halata and Texavia of Houston released the song, with two verses sung by Halata and Bruce Brosch, on their CD *Moon over Moravia.*[16]

NOTES

Introduction

1. Machann and Mendl, *Krásná Amerika,* 40.
2. Hewitt, "Czechs in Texas," 43–47; Machann and Mendl, *Krásná Amerika,* 30, 32.
3. Gallup, *Journeys into Czech-Moravian Texas,* 4.
4. Gallup, *Journeys into Czech-Moravian Texas,* 3–4; Dravillas, "Czech Culture in Fayette County, Texas," 24; Machann and Mendl, *Krásná Amerika,* 258; Eckert, *Stones on the Prairie,* 87–88.
5. Machann and Mendl, *Krásná Amerika,* 105, 110n5; Dutkova, "Texas Czech," 143–45; Dravillas, "Czech Culture in Fayette County, Texas," 23.
6. Eckert, *Stones on the Prairie,* 17–18.
7. C. Keil, A. V. Keil, and Blau, *Polka Happiness,* 13–14.
8. Leary, "Czech Polka Styles in the U.S.," 80–82; Leary, "Czech-American Polka Music in Wisconsin," 37–39.
9. Sayer, *The Coasts of Bohemia,* 50, 13–14.
10. Kouba and Volek, "A Historical Survey of Czech Music 2," 54; Štěpánek and Karásek, *An Outline of Czech and Slovak Music, Part I,* 34–37; Krader, "Bohemia, Moravia, and Slovakia," 178–82.
11. Spottswood, *Ethnic Music on Records,* 2:608. The recording was reissued on *Texas-Czech, Bohemian, and Moravian Bands* (Arhoolie Folklyric CD-7026, 1993), CD.
12. Simonett, *The Accordion in the Americas,* 19, 23.
13. Opekar, "Dechovka," 192.
14. Eckert, *Stones on the Prairie,* 168.
15. Markl and Karbusický, "Bohemian Folk Music," 25–29.
16. Kapusta, *Dechové kapely,* 33–63.
17. Greene, *A Passion for Polka,* 50–51.

Chapter I: Music and the Texas Czech Community

1. Blau and March, *Polka Heartland,* 33.
2. Peña, *Texas-Mexican Conjunto,* 21–22.
3. Casey, *Dance Across Texas,* 14.
4. Blau and March, *Polka Heartland,* 37.
5. Blau and March, *Polka Heartland,* 37.
6. Keil, Keil, and Blau, *Polka Happiness,* 14–15; J. S. Griffith, "Waila," 190–92.
7. Brands, *Lone Star Nation,* 91–92; Cat Spring Agricultural Society, *The Cat Spring Story,* "Introduction"; Hewitt, "Czechs in Texas," 46, 54–55.
8. Newcomb Jr., *The Indians of Texas,* 362.
9. Meinig, *Imperial Texas,* 50–54; Machann and Mendl, *Krásná Amerika,* 209, 216; Grider, "Wends"; C. F. Griffith, "Czech and Polish Music in Texas," 175–76.
10. The letter of Friedrich Ernst in 1832 to friends back home was published in an Oldenburg newspaper as well as a book describing travels in Texas. See Jordan, *German Seed in Texas Soil,* 40–41.
11. Eckert, *Stones on the Prairie,* 61–63, 79.
12. Eckert, *Stones on the Prairie,* 61–62, 84.
13. Hewitt, "Czechs in Texas," 61–71.
14. Eckert, *Stones on the Prairie,* 74.
15. Hewitt, "Czechs in Texas," 68.
16. Machann and Mendl, *Krásna Amerika,* 161; Sitton and Utley, *From Can See to Can't,* 24; Koudelka, "History of Texas Polka Music," 2.
17. One Czech who did participate in the Texas Revolution was Frederick Lemsky, a musician who played fife in the Texas Army band during the Texans' victorious battle at San Jacinto, April 21, 1836. See Spell, *Music in Texas,* 24–26.
18. Hewitt, "Czechs in Texas," 73–74.
19. Machann and Mendl, *Krásná Amerika,* 35–38; Hewitt, "Czechs in Texas," 81, 94, 102.
20. Meinig, *Imperial Texas,* 54.
21. Hewitt, "Czechs in Texas," 103.
22. Machann and Mendl, *Krásná Amerika,*110; Dravillas, "Czech Culture in Fayette County, Texas," 23.
23. Dravillas, "Czech Culture in Fayette County, Texas," 65–66; Heinsohn, "First Catholic Church in Fayette County"; Eckert, *Stones on the Prairie,* 147–53; Machann and Mendl, *Krásná Amerika,* 86–88, 110–11; Cope and Hopkins, *Centennial of Czech Studies,* 34.
24. Maly, *This Church at Wesley,* 11–12, 17–18; Hewitt, "Czechs in Texas," 217–20; Machann and Mendl, *Krásná Amerika,* 86, 116–17.
25. Machann and Mendl, *Krásná Amerika,* 87, 178–81.
26. Eckert, *Stones on the Prairie,* 184.
27. Eckert, *Stones on the Prairie,* 184–99; Eckert, "The Years of *Svoboda,*" 63–74; Machann and Mendl, *Krásná Amerika,* 182–83, 273.
28. Eckert, *Stones on the Prairie,* 184; Machann and Mendl, *Krásná Amerika,* 272–73; Herman, "Final Days?"
29. Hazen and Hazen, *The Music Men,* 4, 8.
30. *La Grange Journal,* May 5, 1880, 3.
31. *La Grange Journal,* April 19, 1883, 3.

32. *La Grange Journal*, September 9, 1886, 3.
33. Hudson and Maresh, *Czech Pioneers of the Southwest*, 316; Baca, *Baca's Musical History*, 4.
34. Baca, *Baca's Musical History*, 2, 7, 10–11; Parker and Brosch, *Jimmy Brosch Remembers*, 182; Gil Baca Orchestra, *Polkas and Waltzes* (Houston: Kermit Records KB-1200, 1967), LP liner notes; Mikus, "Baca Family Musical History," 14; Greene, *A Passion for Polka*, 24.
35. Johnston, "The Cimbál (Cimbalom) and Folk Music," 98–101; Mikus, "Baca Family Musical History," 15; Baca, *Baca's Musical History*, 16. The Baca dulcimer is part of the collection of the Fayetteville Area Heritage Museum.
36. Baca, *Baca's Musical History*, 14; Machann and Mendl, *Krásná Amerika*, 159–60; Mikus, "Baca Family Musical History," 14–15.
37. Greene, *A Passion for Polka*, 143–44; Brown, "Baca Band and Orchestra," 19–20; Hartman, *History of Texas Music*, 113–14; Národní Svaz Českých Katolíků v Texas, *Naše dějiny*, 158–59; Gössel and Šír, *Bohemia on Records*, 83–85.
38. Baca, *Baca's Musical History*, 34; Baca's Czech Band (Bacova Ceska Kapela), *Baca's First Recordings* (Houston: Kermit Records, no date), LP liner notes. The LP, which reissued twelve recordings from the 1929–35 sessions, used the photograph on its cover.
39. Baca, *Baca's Musical History*, 43; Mikus, "Baca Family Musical History," 15–16; Brown, "The Baca Band and Orchestra," 20.
40. McKee, "Al Sulak," 4–6; Parker and Brosch, *Jimmy Brosch Remembers*, 129–30; Thomas Durnin, email to Barton, August 22, 2018, quoting article on Ray Krenek Orchestra in *Sealy News*, September 20, 1956; Ray Krenek, interview by Barton and Novak, November 21, 2002, Sealy, TX; Freddie Krc, emails to Barton, December 6, 2019; Joe Ray Krenek, phone conversation with Barton, January 9, 2020.
41. McKee, "Al Sulak," 4–6; Parker and Brosch, *Jimmy Brosch Remembers*, 129–31; Freddie Krc, phone conversation with Barton, December 9, 2019; Ray Krenek, interview by Barton and Novak, November 21, 2002, Sealy, TX.
42. Jecmenek, "Ilse's Orchestra and Lee Ilse Orchestra," 477.
43. Parker and Brosch, *Jimmy Brosch Remembers*, 103.
44. Simonett, *Accordion in the Americas*, 19, 23.
45. Heinsohn, "Ondrej Gallia's Store."
46. Parker and Brosch, *Jimmy Brosch Remembers*, 111–12; McKee, "Polka by the Bay," 5; Ahlers, "The Leo Majek Orchestra."
47. Texas Czech Heritage and Cultural Center, "Leo Majek Orchestra," La Grange: December 5, 2015. According to the program, the Rosie Majek quote was from a story by Madeleine Greene in a 1961 issue of *Věstník*, the weekly newspaper of the SPJST.
48. Texas Czech Heritage and Cultural Center, "Leo Majek Orchestra," La Grange: December 5, 2015; Parker and Brosch, *Jimmy Brosch Remembers*, 112–18; Martha Ann Majek email to Barton, June 25, 2020.
49. Kolar, "Early Czech Dance Halls in Texas," 4.
50. Lotto, *Fayette County*, 403–4.
51. Jurecka, *Dance Band Experience*,14; Heinsohn, "The Peter Family of Dubina, Texas"; Folkins, *Texas Dance Halls*, 49–50.
52. Stacy Labaj, interviews with Mr. and Mrs. Joe Rosacky and Mrs. Emilie Batla, 1963–75, Stacy Mikulencak Labaj and Ben A. Merrick Papers, 1929–1997, Briscoe Center for American History, University of Texas, Austin.
53. Kolar, "Early Czech Dance Halls in Texas," 5–6; Morris, *A History of the SPJST*, 4–15, 168–69; Hewitt, "Czechs in Texas," 151–58.
54. Kolar, "Early Czech Dance Halls in Texas," 5–6; Morris, *A History of the SPJST*, 163–64.
55. Texas Historical Commission, Texas Historical Landmark "Buckholts SPJST Lodge Hall," 600 East SH 36, Buckholts, 2008; Kolar, "Early Czech Dance Halls in Texas," 4.
56. Kolar, "Early Czech Dance Halls in Texas," 11; Hewitt, "Czechs in Texas," 169–71.
57. KJT #35, "About."
58. Laznovsky, "Sokols in Texas," 10–11; Sokol Ennis, "Our History."
59. National Polka Festival, "History."
60. Machann, "Country-Western Music," 4.
61. Hewitt, "Czechs in Texas," 257.
62. Hewitt, "Czechs in Texas," 307. For a roster of those who served, see Buňata, *Památník Čechoslováků*, 166–85.
63. Hudson and Maresh, *Czech Pioneers of the Southwest*, 358–65; Hewitt, "Czechs in Texas," 304–7; Machann and Mendl, *Krásná Amerika*, 60–66, 230–31.
64. Hudson and Maresh, *Czech Pioneers of the Southwest*, 358–65; Hewitt, "Czechs in Texas," 304–7; Machann and Mendl, *Krásná Amerika*, 60–66, 230–31.
65. Hudson and Maresh, *Czech Pioneers of the Southwest*, 358–65; Hewitt, "Czechs in Texas," 304–7; Machann and Mendl, *Krásná Amerika*, 60–66, 230–31.
66. *La Grange Journal* 40, no. 33 (August 14, 1919), quoted in Baca, *Baca's Musical History*, 24–25; Mikus, "Baca Family Musical History," 15.
67. Hazen and Hazen, *The Music Men*, 191.
68. Hazen and Hazen, *The Music Men*, 191.
69. Baca Orchestra, *Baca's Music Book*, contains sheet music published by Vitak-Elsnic and Joseph Jiran, both music companies then located in Chicago, as well as a few pieces arranged by band member I. J. Baca. It is part of the collection of the Texas Czech Heritage Museum and Genealogy Center, Temple, TX.
70. Greene, *A Passion for Polka*, 47.

71. Greene, *A Passion for Polka*, 47–48.
72. Greene, *A Passion for Polka*, 48–56, 248; Gössel and Šír, *Bohemia on Records*, 30–32, 42–44, 67–68.
73. Hazen and Hazen, *The Music Men*, 191; Malone, *Country Music USA*, 34.
74. Greene, *A Passion for Polka*, 70–71.
75. Greene, *A Passion for Polka*, 72–73.
76. Spottswood, *Ethnic Music on Records*, 1: xv.
77. Greene, *A Passion for Polka*, 73.
78. Spottswood, *Ethnic Music on Records*, 2:612–17. See also Greene, *A Passion for Polka*, 75–76.
79. Roy, "'Race Records' and 'Hillbilly Music,'" 275.
80. Hickinbotham, "Recording Industry"; see also Malone, *Country Music USA*, 38–39.
81. Spottswood, *Ethnic Music on Records*, 2:608–9.
82. Spottswood, *Ethnic Music on Records*, 2:601–2. The band is also known by the name Adolf and the Gold Chain Bohemians, headed by Julius "Adolf" Pavlas of Engle, Fayette County, Texas. See Parker and Brosch, *Jimmy Brosch Remembers*, 64.
83. Spottswood, *Ethnic Music on Records*, 2:657.
84. Spottswood, *Ethnic Music on Records*, 2:635–36; Russell and Pinson, *Country Music Records*, 430–31, 742.
85. Malone, *Country Music USA*, 94.
86. Greene, *A Passion for Polka*, 122.
87. Craig, "'The Farmer's Friend,'" 330–31.
88. Malone, *Country Music USA*, 33–34.
89. Baca, *Baca's Musical History*, 28.
90. Skrabanek, *We're Czechs*, 81.
91. Koudelka, "Adolf and the Boys"; Parker and Brosch, *Jimmy Brosch Remembers*, 63–74.
92. Koudelka, "Adolf and the Boys."
93. Koudelka, "Adolf and the Boys"; Parker and Brosch, *Jimmy Brosch Remembers*, 66, 70–71.
94. Greene, *A Passion for Polka*, 127–35.
95. Machann and Mendl, *Krásná Amerika*, 81, 173–74; Blaha, "SPJST Lodge Texaska Orlice," 72.
96. Machann and Mendl, *Krásná Amerika*, 164; Sitton and Utley, *From Can See to Can't*, 260–61; Malone, *Country Music USA*, 177–78.
97. Strachwitz, "Joe Patek Interview," quote from introductory material to interview.
98. Parker and Brosch, *Jimmy Brosch Remembers*, 47–54.
99. Strachwitz, "Joe Patek Interview."
100. Meewes, "Czech Mates," 31; DeKunder, "Patek, Joe," 241.
101. Parker and Brosch, *Jimmy Brosch Remembers*, 50.
102. Leary, "Czech Polka Styles in the U.S.," 85.
103. Meinecke, *Texas Bohemia*,18.
104. Strachwitz, "Joe Patek Interview."
105. Strachwitz, "Joe Patek Interview."
106. Rubin, "Review of Texas-Czech, Bohemian, and Moravian Bands."
107. Rubin, "Review of Texas-Czech, Bohemian, and Moravian Bands."
108. Parker and Brosch, *Jimmy Brosch Remembers*, 52.
109. Parker and Brosch, *Jimmy Brosch Remembers*, 193–200; Russell, *Country Music Originals*, 215–16; Strachwitz, "Adolph Hofner Interview" and "Adolph Hofner and His Texans"; Malone, *Country Music USA*, 152–53; *Adolph Hofner and the Pearl Wranglers*, CD liner notes.
110. Malone, *Country Music USA*, 152.
111. Strachwitz, "Adolph Hofner Interview."
112. Russell and Pinson, *Country Music Records*, 430–31; Parker and Brosch, *Jimmy Brosch Remembers*, 195–96; Greene, *A Passion for Polka*, 148–49; *Adolph Hofner and the Pearl Wranglers*, CD liner notes.
113. Russell, *Country Music Originals*, 216.
114. Russell, *Country Music Originals*, 216; Parker and Brosch, *Jimmy Brosch Remembers*, 197.
115. Russell, "Adolph Hofner: Spinning Old Europe's Folk Music."
116. Greene, *A Passion for Polka*, 148.
117. Parker and Brosch, *Jimmy Brosch Remembers*, 151–53.
118. Parker and Brosch, *Jimmy Brosch Remembers*, 151–53, 159–60.
119. Parker and Br osch, *Jimmy Brosch Remembers*, 153–54, 157–59; Glenn, "A Houston Tradition Dies in Polka-Hall Fire."
120. Russell, "Lee Roy Matocha."
121. Meiners, "The Lee Roy Matocha Band," 479.
122. Parker and Brosch, *Jimmy Brosch Remembers*, 101–2. The radio shows are listed on Matocha's business card, circa 1990s.
123. Bragg, "Polka Player's Heart," 3.
124. Svatek, "Lee Roy Matocha."
125. Parker and Brosch, *Jimmy Brosch Remembers*, 102.
126. Parker and Brosch, *Jimmy Brosch Remembers*, 103–4, 107; Bragg, "Polka Player's Heart"; Texas Czech Heritage and Cultural Center, "The Lee Roy Matocha Orchestra."
127. Parker and Brosch, *Jimmy Brosch Remembers*, 1–12; McKee and Parker, "Vrazels: Playing for Our Friends," 4–7; Alfred Vrazel interview by Barton and Novak, Buckholts, Texas, August 29, 2013.
128. McKee and Parker, "Vrazels: Playing for Our Friends," 4–7; Texas Czech Heritage and Cultural Center, "Vrazels' Polka Band, 1953–2008."
129. Parker and Brosch, *Jimmy Brosch Remembers*, 11; "Alfred Vrazel Show Extended," *Texas Polka News*, 12; Parker, "Alfred Vrazel," 5.
130. Dooley, "The Vrazels Polka Band Have Retired after 55 Years."
131. McKee, "Hi, Alice!," 3, 8–9; Folkins, *Texas Dance Halls*, 125, 133; Wheeler, "Save the Last Dance for Alice"; Jerry Haisler, phone conversation with Barton, February 12, 2020.

132. Jerry Haisler and the Melody 5, *For the First Time,* LP liner notes; Folkins, *Texas Dance Halls,* 125; Jerry Haisler and the Melody 5, "Bio."
133. Haisler, filmed remarks delivered at Texas Dance Hall Preservation tribute to Alice Sulak.
134. Haisler, filmed remarks delivered at Texas Dance Hall Preservation tribute to Alice Sulak; quote from McKee, "Hi, Alice!," 3.
135. Deb Fleming, executive director, Texas Dance Hall Preservation, emails to Barton, January 13–14, 2020.
136. Eckert, "Language Change," 206; Cope, "Texas Czech Legacy Project," 101.
137. Machann and Mendl, *Krásná Amerika,* 235.
138. Parker, "Church Picnics 2019 (Updated 7/10/19)."
139. Orsak, "158th Prazska Pout."
140. National Polka Festival, "History" and "Bands/Music."
141. Westfest, "About" and "Attractions."
142. Twitchell, "Kolache Festival This Saturday in Caldwell."
143. Cope, "Texas Czech Legacy Project," 102.
144. Machann and Mendl, *Krásná Amerika,* 95.
145. KJT, Katolická jednota Texaská, *Sbírka českých pisni.* Interviews with Lorenda Polasek of the KJT state office in La Grange and phone interview with Ed Goerig by Barton, June 5, 2014. KJZT stands for Katolická jednota žen Texaských (Catholic Women's Union of Texas).
146. Bartoš and Bartoš, *Spivejme pisničky.* Phone interviews by Barton with Nica Pyron, August 3, 2018; and with Nica Pyron and Gracie Hatten, April 6, 2020.
147. Schindler, *Písničky České: Czech Folk Song Collection,* ix–x.
148. Schindler, *Písničky České: Czech Folk Song Collection,* xi–xii.
149. Chervenka, "History of the Dallas Czech Singers (DCS)," 243–47.
150. Parker, "About Texas Polka News."
151. Chandler, "Publisher's Note," 2.
152. Everett, "Corey Mikula."
153. Edgell, "Polka Pride."
154. McKee, "The Hodde Trilogy."
155. Salivarová, "Czech Folk Songs," 132.

Chapter II. Czech Folk and Popular Songs

1. Clapham et al., "Czech Republic."
2. Clapham et al., "Czech Republic."
3. Kotek, *Dějiny české populární hudby a zpěvu do roku 1918,* 47.
4. Tyrrell, *Czech Opera,* 65.
5. Kotek, *Dějiny české populární hudby a zpěvu do roku 1918,* 54.
6. Kotek, *Dějiny české populární hudby a zpěvu do roku 1918,* 33.
7. Porter et al., "Ballad."
8. Kotek, *Dějiny české populární hudby a zpěvu do roku 1918,* 19.
9. Kotek, *Dějiny české populární hudby a zpěvu do roku 1918,* 19.
10. Kotek, *Dějiny české populární hudby a zpěvu do roku 1918,* 41.
11. Tyllner, *Tradiční hudba,* 71.
12. Tyllner, *Tradiční hudba,* 71.
13. Kotek, *Dějiny české populární hudby a zpěvu do roku 1918,* 37.
14. Kotek, *Dějiny české populární hudby a zpěvu do roku 1918,* 41.
15. Kotek, *Dějiny české populární hudby a zpěvu do roku 1918,* 45.
16. Tyllner, *Tradiční hudba,* 72.
17. Karbusický, *Mezi lidovou písní a šlágrem,* 105.
18. Karbusický, *Mezi lidovou písní a šlágrem,* 105.
19. "Pololidová píseň" (Half-folk Song), in Brouček and Jeřábek, *Lidová kultura,* 772.
20. "Pololidová píseň," 772.
21. Karbusický, *Mezi lidovou písní a šlágrem,* 105; Kotek, *Dějiny české populární hudby a zpěvu do roku 1918,* 128.
22. Karbusický, *Mezi lidovou písní a šlágrem,* 105.
23. Černušák, Lamb, and Tyrrell, "Polka."
24. Zíbrt, *Jak se kdy v Čechách tancovalo,* 334.
25. Zíbrt, *Jak se kdy v Čechách tancovalo,* 334.
26. Zíbrt, *Jak se kdy v Čechách tancovalo,* 335.
27. Černušák, Lamb, and Tyrrell, "Polka."
28. Černušák, Lamb, and Tyrrell, "Polka."
29. Černušák, Lamb, and Tyrrell, "Polka."
30. Černušák, Lamb, and Tyrrell, "Polka."
31. Strobel, "Polka."
32. Strobel, "Polka."
33. Stavělová, "The Polka versus the Waltz," 104.
34. Strobel, "Polka."
35. From the Czech National Museum. Used with permission.
36. Stavělová, "The Polka versus the Waltz," 94.
37. Stavělová, "The Polka versus the Waltz," 94.
38. Kapusta, *Dechové kapely,* 22.
39. Kapusta, *Dechové kapely,* 23.
40. Kapusta, *Dechové kapely,* 137.
41. "Lidovka," in Brouček and Jeřábek, *Lidová kultura,* 497.
42. "Lidovka," in Brouček and Jeřábek, *Lidová kultura,* 497.
43. "Lidovka," in Brouček and Jeřábek, *Lidová kultura,* 497; my translation.
44. Kotek, *Dějiny české populární hudby a zpěvu 1918–1968,* 24.
45. Kotek, *Dějiny české populární hudby a zpěvu 1918–1968,* 25.
46. Greene, *A Passion for Polka,* 138.
47. Koukal, *Dechovka,* 134.
48. Koukal, *Dechovka,* 79.

49. Koukal, *Dechovka*, 141.
50. Koukal, *Dechovka*, 143.
51. Koukal, *Dechovka*, 219.

Chapter III. Czech Songs in Texas

1. *A já sám*

1. Seidel, *Národ v písni,* 315.
2. Erben, *Prostonárodní české písně a říkadla* (1864), 415.
3. Erben, *Prostonárodní české písně a říkadla* (1864), 415.
4. Novotný, *Bechyňské písně,* 53.
5. Rehrig, *Heritage Encyclopedia of Band Music*, 1:424.
6. Czech and Then Some, "A Ja Sam Polka," *A Tribute: 10 Years of Polka Music* (Ennis, TX, 2007), CD; Danny Zapletal interview by Barton and Novak, Ennis, TX, June 6, 2014; Zapletal and Barton emails, November 10, 2015.
7. Parker, "Alfred Vrazel," 7.
8. Vrazels' Polka Band, "All by Myself," *Golden Sounds* (Buckholts, TX: VPB 518, 2003), CD.
9. Taylor Czech Chorus, "A já sám," *Songs of Our Heritage* (Taylor, TX, 2007), CD.
10. Brave Combo, "A Ja Sam," *Let's Kiss: 25th Anniversary Album* (Denton: Dentone Records, 2004), CD. Hernandez was the Brave Combo bassist from 1985 to 2007.

2. *Aj, lučka, lučka*

1. Atherton, *Oblíbené písně,* 1–3.
2. Roberts, *From Good King Wenceslas,* 90–91.
3. Atherton, *Oblibené písně,* dedication page.
4. Hašek, *The Good Soldier Švejk.*
5. Joe Patek Orchestra, "Oh! Meadow!" (San Antonio: TNT 5064, 1963), 45 rpm.
6. Jodie Mikula Orchestra, "Meadow Polka," *From the Good Old Days* (Ennis, TX, 1973), LP.
7. Dujka Brothers, "Old Meadow Polka," *Shining Up Old Favorites* (Brenham, TX: JED Musical Prod., 2008), CD.
8. All Around Czechs, "Green Meadow Polka," *Where It Began* (West, TX, 2016), CD.

3. *Andulko šafářova*

1. Novotný, *Bechyňské písně,* "Úvod" (Introduction), i–iv.
2. In Czech, a woman's last name often ends with *-ová,* with the accent, or *čárka*, over the "á." Words that end with *-ova* with no accent over the "a," however, do not serve the same grammatical function. In the case of the title "Andulko šafářova," šafář, which means "foreman," is transformed into the possessive adjective šafářova, meaning "of the foreman" or "foreman's." Thanks to Lida Cope, director of the Texas Czech Legacy Project, for helping sort this out; Lida Cope emails to Frances Barton, February 16–20, 2017.
3. Frank Kmoch, "Andulko šafářova polka" (Caretaker's Annie), arranged by Joseph P. Elsnic (Chicago: Vitak-Elsnic, 1942).
4. Kapusta, *Dechové kapely*, 159.
5. Spottswood, *Ethnic Music on Records*, 2:608.
6. Baca Orchestra, "Annie the Farmer's Daughter March," *Bača's First Recordings* (Houston: Kermit Records, no date), compilation LP of reissued recordings.
7. Johnston, "Neroztavili se," 33.
8. Ray Krenek and His Orchestra, "Happy Annie," *Top Hit Tunes* (Wallis: Gold-Sun LP-101, late 1960s), LP.
9. SPJST Lodge 88 Choral Group and Orchestra, "Andulko Šafářová," *Czech Folksongs* (Houston: Guide LP-1050, 1978), LP.
10. Lee Roy Matocha Orchestra, "Annie the Foreman Polka," *Red Hot and Rolling* (Houston: Julius Tupa RVS Studios, 1982), cassette tape.

4. *Baruška*

1. Greene, *A Passion for Polka,* 56 and 269n33.
2. "Barbara Polka," arranged by A. Grill (Chicago: Joseph Jiran, 1914); "Barbara (Baruška)," arranged by Karel M. Coufal (Chicago: Aloysius J. Turek, 1916); "Barbara Polka (Baruška)," by F. Kovářík (Chicago: Georgi and Vitak, 191?). The Georgi and Vitak date estimate is from the catalog of the Vitak-Elsnic Collection housed at Bowling Green State University, Bowling Green, Ohio.
3. *Databáze národních autorit NK ČR,* "Kovářík, František, 1858–1936."
4. Kotek, *Dějiny české populární hudby a zpěvu 1918–1968,* 17, 203.
5. Adolph Hofner and His Bohemians, "Baruška Polka" (Columbia 391-F, 1942), 78 rpm.
6. Adolph Hofner and His Orchestra, "Barbara Polka" (Imperial IF-75 8027-A, no date), 78 rpm.
7. Baca, *Baca's Musical History,* 31–32; emails between Gary E. McKee and Barton, January 19–22, 2018.
8. Benny Brosh and His Orchestra, "Barbara Polka" (Waco: Humming Bird 160, circa 1950), 78 rpm.
9. Czech Heritage Singers, "Baruška," *The Czech Heritage Singers* (Houston: Rampart Recording, 1981), LP.
10. Ray Zapletal and His Music Masters Orchestra, "Barbara Polka," 1960s, reissued on *Texas Czech* (Omaha: Polka Cassettes of Nebraska, 2010), CD.
11. Julius Tupa, "Barbara Polka," *Songs I'll Always Remember* (Houston: Guide LP-1010, circa 1970s), LP.

5. *Bolí, bolí*

1. Jeff Brosch phone interview by Barton, February 6, 2018; email exchange on March 6, 2018. See also Parker and Brosch, *Jimmy Brosch Remembers,* 24.

2. Pazdral, "Czech Folklore in Texas," 232; Erben, "A já vždycky," in *Prostonárodní české písně a říkadla* (1864), 232.
3. Jimmy Brosch and His Country Boys, "Bolí, bolí" (Houston: Guide, circa 1968), 45 rpm.
4. Ray Krenek Orchestra, "Headache Waltz," *15 Top Tunes Featuring Ray on His Dulcimer* (Houston: Southwest Recordings, 2008), CD.
5. Leo Majek Orchestra, "Headache Waltz," *Polka and Waltz* (Corpus Christi: Majek Stereo LP-100, mid-1960s), LP.
6. Lee Roy Matocha Orchestra, "Headache Waltz," *By Special Request* (Fayetteville, TX: Lee Records LP#5, late 1960s), LP.
7. Ray Zapletal and His Music Masters, "Headache Waltz," *Bluebonnet Czech"* (Ennis, TX: circa mid-1960s), LP.
8. Dujka Brothers, "Headache Waltz (Boli, Boli)," *Grandpa's List* (Brenham, TX: JED Musical Prod., 2001), CD of reissued recordings.
9. Czech and Then Some, "Headache Waltz," *Play Old Time Music* (Ennis, TX, 2012), CD.
10. Czech Melody Masters, "Headache Waltz," *Czech, Please* (Austin: CMM Records CMM-004, 2015), CD.

6. Brána malovaná

1. Erben, *Pjsné národnj w Čechách,* 1:208.
2. Pletka, *Pisničky Josefa Švejka,* 152. See also Hašek, *The Good Soldier Švejk,* 472. The Czech novel was first published in 1921–23.
3. Ferdinand Sládek, *Náš poklad,* 1:26.
4. Library of Congress, "Image 61 of the Alan Lomax Collection, Manuscripts, Freedom Songs of the United Nations, 1943."
5. Red Ravens, "Garden Gate Polka," *Polka Better* (El Campo, TX, 1981), cassette tape.
6. Wence and Helen Shimek and the All Star Sounds, "Painted Gate," *Wence and Helen Present More Polkas and Waltzes* (Hallettsville, TX: WS-1003, 1984), cassette tape.
7. Mark Halata and Texavia, "Painted Gate Polka," *Moon over Moravia* (Webster, TX, 2003), CD.
8. Leroy Rybak's Swinging Orchestra, "Painted Gate Polka," *Polka and Waltz Classics* (Hallettsville, TX: CLR-2316, 2006), CD.
9. Vrazels' Polka Band, "Painted Gate Polka," *Greatest Hits, Vol. 2* (Buckholts, TX: VPB-517, 2002), CD.
10. Taylor Czech Chorus, "Malovaná brána," *Still . . . Carrying On the Tradition* (Taylor, TX, 2018), CD.

7. Červená a bílá

1. "Červený, bílý," in Erben, *Prostonárodní české písně a říkadla* (1864), 140. The text is as follows: "Červeny bíly, to se mně líbí, červeny bíly to já mám rád: červeny tvářičky, a bíly ručičky, hezoučky děvče to já mám rád!" (Red white, I like that, red white I love that: red cheeks, and white hands, a beautiful girl, I love that!).
2. "Červenobílí," in Slavia Praha general game program for the 2012–13 season; Roberts, "fotbal" and "Sparta/Slavia," *From Good King Wenceslas,* 44, 158.
3. Roberts, "lev," *From Good King Wenceslas,* 91; Derek Sayer, *The Coasts of Bohemia,* 340n71; Jezek, "The Origin and Evolution of the Czech Flag."
4. "Červená a bílá," arranged by Anton Grill (Chicago: Joseph Jiran, 1921); recording at Library of Congress, accessed October 8, 2020, www.loc.gov/item/jukebox-61234/.
5. Bačova Česka Kapela, "Červená a bílá" (Columbia 165-F, 1930), 78 rpm; see Spottswood, *Ethnic Music on Records,* 2:608.
6. Gary D. Krupala, email to Frances Barton, January 31, 2018.
7. Bill Mraz Orchestra, "Red and White Waltz," *Festival Album* (Houston: Mraz LP 501, 1950s), LP.
8. Lee Roy Matocha, "Red and White," *Let's Dance with Lee Roy* (Fayetteville, TX: Lee LP-1, mid-1960s), LP. Alfred Vrazel interview by Barton and Novak, Buckholts, August 29, 2013.
9. East Bernard Czech Singers, "Red and White Waltz," *Our Best to You* (East Bernard, TX, 2000), CD.
10. Lazy Farmers, "Red and White," *New Sounds* (Bellville, TX, 2008), CD.
11. Czech Melody Masters, "Red and White Waltz," *Czech, Please* (Austin: CMM Records CMM-004, 2015), CD.

8. Červená růžičko

1. Erben, *Pjsně národnj w Čechách,* 1:90–91.
2. Vycpálek, "Vozičko v písni," 217.
3. *Česko-americký zpěvník* (circa 1880s), 43.
4. Harry Czarnek and the Texas Dutchmen, *Red Rose Polka* (Houston: TAP L0018, 1975), LP liner notes; *Věstník,* February 11, 1976, 29.
5. Vrazels' Polka Band, "Red Rose Polka," *Performing in Washington, D.C.* (Buckholts, TX: VPB 110, 1976), LP.
6. Bill Mraz Orchestra, "Red Rose Polka," *Polka Heritage—Made Famous* (Houston: Guide 1046, 1977), LP.
7. Joe Patek Orchestra, "Red Rose Polka," *The Magic of Joe Patek* (Houston: Guide LP-1044, 1970s), LP.
8. Mark Halata and Texavia, "Red Rose Polka," *Amerika* (Webster, TX, 2007), CD.
9. The Moravians, "Red Rose Polka," *Czech Spirit Will Live On* (Ennis, TX, 2013), CD.

9. Červená růžičko

1. Karbusický, *Mezi lidovou písní a šlágrem,* 17–18.
2. Erben, *Pjsně národnj w Čechách,* 1:90–91.
3. Slavia, *Národní pohádky,* Series 1, part 2, 31–33.

4. KJT, *Sbírka českých písní,* 106–7; Schindler, *Písničky České,* 174.
5. "Red Rose Waltz," *From the Good Old Days* (Ennis, TX, 1973), LP.
6. McKee, "Mikulas Celebrate 50 Years of Making Happy Music," 4–5; Parker and Brosch, *Jimmy Brosch Remembers,* 55–62; and "Jodie Mikula Orchestra Carries on a Family Tradition," 7.
7. Joe Patek Orchestra, "Red Rose Waltz," *The Magic of Joe Patek* (Houston: Guide LP-1044, 1970s), LP.
8. Dujka Brothers, "Red Rose Waltz," *The Tradition Continues* (Brenham, TX: JED Musical Prod., 1999), CD.
9. Czechmates, "Red Rose Waltz," *20th Anniversary Live* (Dallas, 1993), cassette tape.
10. Lee Roy Matocha Orchestra, "Red Rose Waltz," *The King of Polka* (Houston: Guide LP-1041, mid-1970s), LP.

10. Červené víno, bílé koláče

1. De Goeij, "How Czech Wine Got Its Terroir Back."
2. The Slovak "Víno sem, víno tam" has the same tune as the Texas song and some of the same words. See https://pesnicky.orava.sk/noty?view=song&id=882, accessed August 2, 2019.
3. Tyrrell, *Janáček: Years of a Life,* 1:14–15.
4. The word *mašina* (the nominative form) is in Jonáš, *Slovník česko-anglický,* 185.
5. Bícha, "Karel Jonas of Racine," 129.
6. Skrabanek, *We're Czechs,* 99–100.
7. Joe Patek Orchestra, "Red Wine Polka" (San Antonio: TNT, late 1950s), 45 rpm.
8. Vrazels' Polka Band, "Red Wine Polka" (San Antonio: TNT, circa 1959), 45 rpm.
9. Telstars, "Red Wine Polka," *The New World of Polka* (Houston, Guide LP-1019, 1970s), LP; McKee, "It Was Never a Job," 6–9.
10. Czechaholics, "Red Wine Polka," *Certified P.O.L.K.A.* (Brenham, TX: JED Musical Prod., 2017), CD.

11. Červený šáteček

1. F. Bartoš, *Národní písně moravské,* 2:878; Erben, *Prostonárodní české písně a říkadla* (1886), 241–42.
2. Geary, *Folk Dances of Czecho Slovakia,* 26.
3. Vožda, *Hanácká beseda.*
4. George Koudelka, interview by Barton and Novak, Flatonia, Texas, December 29, 2004.
5. Chervenka, "The Czechs in Review," 21.
6. Adolph Hofner and His San Antonians, "Cerveny satachek," recorded for Columbia Records in 1942; issued on *Swing with the Music* (Dover: British Archive of Country Music, 2010), CD. See also Spottswood, *Ethnic Music on Records,* 2:636.
7. Frank Migl and His Orchestra, "Red Handkerchief Waltz" (Houston: Humming Bird 161-B, circa 1950–1953), 78 rpm; Parker and Brosch, *Jimmy Brosch Remembers,* 145.
8. Joe Patek's Orchestra, "Red Handkerchief" (San Antonio: TNT-5014, circa 1950s), 45 rpm.
9. Harry Czarnek and the Texas Dutchmen, "Red Handkerchief," *A Polka Picnic* (Houston: Guide-1022, circa 1970s), LP.
10. Donnie Wavra Orchestra, "Red Handkerchief," *25 Years* (New Ulm, TX, 1997), LP.
11. Shiner Hobo Band, "Red Handkerchief Waltz," *Frankie and Johnny* (Shiner, TX, 2007), CD.

12. Česká písnička

1. Koukal, *Dechovka,* 56–73.
2. Interview with George Koudelka by Barton and Novak, Flatonia, December 29, 2004.
3. Mikulencak, "A Narrative History," 12–18.
4. Brown, "The Baca Band and Orchestra," 19–20; Spottswood, *Ethnic Music on Records,* 2:609; Bačova Česka Kapela, "Pisnička Česká" (Song of Bohemia; Columbia SA 2348, 1935), 78 rpm.
5. Kovanda's Czech Band, "Our Czech Song," *Our Czech Music* (Fayetteville, TX: KCB 103, 1994), cassette tape.
6. East Bernard Czech Singers, "Our Czech Songs," *Czech Songs We Treasure* (East Bernard, TX, 1992), cassette tape.
7. Taylor Czech Chorus, "Pisnicka Ceska," *Songs of Our Heritage* (Taylor, TX, 2007), CD.
8. Chris Rybak, "Song of Bohemia," *Let's Have a Party* (Hallettsville, TX, 1996), CD.
9. Czech and Then Some, "Song of the Czechs," *Polkas for Everyone* (Ennis, TX, 2005), CD.

13. Cestička k Mayrovce

1. "Hornický skanzen Mayrau ve Vinařicích" (Mayrau Open-Air Mining Museum in Vinařice).
2. Koukal, *Dechovka,* 112; Kotek, *Dějiny české populární hudby a zpěvu 1918–1968,* 103–5.
3. Gössel, *Kamarádi, dolů sfárejme! Nahrávky z let 1929–1952,* CD liner notes. All the songs on the CD are mining songs, including the Ctibor/Poupě "Cestička k Mayrovce." The CD is one of a series of historic reissues from Supraphon called *Historie psaná šelakem* (History written by recordings).
4. Rhinehart, *A Way of Work,* 3, 93–94. The percentage of Czech miners figure is from historian Josef Barton, email to Frances Barton, August 29, 2019.
5. Buňata, *Pamatník Čechoslováků,* 157; Machann and Mendl, *Krásná Amerika,* 51.
6. Rhinehart, *A Way of Work,* 106, 110–12.
7. Vrazels' Polka Band, "Path to Moravia," *Performing in Washington D.C.* (Buckholts, TX: Cen-Tex Records VPB-101, circa 1976), CD.

8. Joe Patek Orchestra, "Road to Moravia," *The Magic of Joe Patek* (Houston: Guide LP-1044, 1970s), LP.
9. Czech and Then Some, "Path to Moravia," *Polkas for Everyone* (Ennis, TX, 2005), CD.
10. Mark Halata and Texavia, "Path to Moravia," *Texavia* (Webster, TX, 2001), CD, and *Live at Moravia Store* (Webster, TX, 2018), CD.
11. Taylor Czech Chorus, "Cestička k Mayrovce," *Still . . . Carrying on the Tradition* (Holland, TX: Awesome Works Recording, 2018), CD.

14. Chaloupky pod horami

1. Holý, *The Little Czech*, 157; Roberts, *From Good King Wenceslas*, 25–26.
2. Kotek, *Dějiny české populární hudby a zpěvu 1918–1968*, 181–82.
3. Kotek, *Dějiny české populární hudby a zpěvu 1918–1968*, 181.
4. SPJST Lodge 88 Choral Group and Orchestra, "Chaloupky pod horami," *Czech Folksongs* (Houston: Guide 1050, 1978), LP.
5. Harry Czarnek and the Texas Dutchmen, "Cottages under the Mountains," *Polka Hit Parade* (Houston: Camwood Records and Tapes 103, mid-1980s), cassette tape.
6. Travelers, "Cottages Under the Mountains," *Old Time Classics* (Columbus, TX, 1992), CD. Interview with George Koudelka by Barton and Novak, December 29, 2004, and letter from Koudelka to Barton, January 10, 2005.
7. Lee Ilse Orchestra, "Cottage under the Mountains" (La Grange: Bess Records BS-102-A, early 1960s), 45 rpm.

15. Co jste hasiči?

1. Bytel and Baierl, *Druhý výběr z lidových písní*, 68; Langhanse, *Krásná pasačka*, 13.
2. Roberts, *From Good King Wenceslas*, 147; Kroupa, "Poslední rum."
3. Zetka's Polka Band, "Fire Brigade," *On Fire with Zetka's Polka Band* (El Campo, TX, 1994), cassette tape.
4. Vrazels' Polka Band, "Fire Brigade," *Golden Sounds: 50th Anniversary* (Buckholts, TX: VPB-518, 2003), CD.
5. Shiner Hobo Band, "Fire Brigade Polka," *Ještě jednou (One More Time*; Shiner, TX, 2004), CD.
6. Dujka Brothers, "Fire Brigade Polka," *Grandpa's List: The Best of the Dujka Brothers, Vol. 2* (Brenham, TX: JED Musical Prod., 2001), CD.

16. Co ten ptáček jarabáček

1. Sušil, *Moravské národní písně*, 216.
2. Myers, *Ethnomusicology*, 179.
3. Greene, *A Passion for Polka*, 50. For the Czech publishing history of "Jarabáček," see Kapusta, *Dechové kapely*, 159.
4. "Jarabáček" (Bird of Spring), by František Kmoch, arranged by Louis Vitak (Chicago: Georgi and Vitak, 194?).
5. Round Top Brass Band, "Bird of Spring March," *Presenting the Round Top Brass Band* (Round Top, TX, 1981), LP; George Koudelka letter to Frances Barton, December 12, 2017.
6. Wence Shimek and the All Star Sounds, "Jerabacek: The Bird," *You Asked for It* (Hallettsville, TX, 1982), LP.
7. Gene Lichnovsky, "Jarabacek (Bird of Spring) March," *Gene Lichnovsky: Piano Solos, Polkas, Waltzes, Marches* (Houston: CD-1-GL, circa 2010), CD.

17. Čtyři koně

1. Erben, *Pjsně národnj w Čechách*, 3:14–15; Sušil, *Moravské národní písně* (1860), 712; F. Bartoš, *Národní písně moravské*, 1:103. The Sušil and Bartoš spelling of the song title is "Štyry koně."
2. Bradáč, *Plzeňské písně*, 70.
3. *Hřebíček* is a folk name for carnation. See *Slovník spisovného jazyka českého*.
4. Joe Patek Orchestra, "Four Horses" (San Antonio: TNT 5064, 1963), 45 rpm.
5. Leo Majek Orchestra, "Four Horses" (Corpus Christi: Majek Records 114A, circa mid-1960s), 45 rpm.
6. Rudy Kurtz Orchestra, "Four Horses Waltz," TNT 5042, 1964, 45 rpm reissued on *Jimmy Brosch Remembers* (Katy, TX, 2011), CD.
7. Czech Harvesters, "Four Horses Waltz," *Tenth Anniversary* (Dallas: CH-30188, 1988), cassette tape.
8. Czechaholics, "Four Horses," *Spreadin' the Tradition* (Brenham, TX: JED Musical Prod., 2006), CD.

18. Dobrú noc, milko má

1. Interview with Matthew Strmiska by Barton and Novak, Austin, August 8, 2013.
2. Phone interview with Alfred Vrazel by Barton, November 13, 2019.
3. "Piseň o Milce pro mládenecký jakož i pro panenský stav," 1855, a *kramářský tisk* (broadside print) held by Regionální muzeum ve Vysokém Mýtě-Knihovna (Library of the Regional Museum in Vysoké Mýto), is described in its catalog by the first line of the song: "Dobrou noc, dobrou noc Milko má, Dobrou noc ti vinšuji."
4. Eppinger, Havlíček, and Pazdírek, *Pějme píseň dokola*, 1:42.
5. Red Ravens, "Good Night My Darling," *Polka Better* (El Campo, TX, 1981), cassette tape
6. Ellinger Combo, "Good Night My Darling Waltz," *A Little Bit of the Best* (Ellinger, TX, 1984), LP.
7. Bobby Jones Czech Band, "Good Night My Darling," Houston, SPJST Lodge 88 Splash Day, mid-1980s, live recording.

8. Ennis Czech Boys, "Good Night My Darling Waltz," *Cheers to 10 Years* (Ennis, TX, 2016), CD.

19. Dráteník

1. Roucek, *Slavonic Encyclopaedia,* 936.
2. Newmarch, *The Music of Czechoslovakia,* 52–53; Tyrrell, *Czech Opera,* 63.
3. Karbusický, "The Experience of the Indexical Sign," 37.
4. Interview with the ethnomusicologist Lubomír Tyllner by Novak, Prague, CZ, May 2015.
5. Bačova Česka Kapela, "Drateník (Tinker) Polka" (Okeh 17359; Columbia 193-F), both 78 rpm. See Spottswood, *Ethnic Music on Records,* 2:608.
6. Ray Krenek and His Orchestra, "Tinker Polka," *Top Hit Tunes* (Sealy, TX: Gold Sun-102, 2006), CD.
7. Shiner Hobo Band, "Tinker Polka," *Frankie and Johnny Hobo Style* (Shiner, TX, 2007), CD.
8. Joe Patek Orchestra, "Tinker Polka," reissued on *Joe Patek: The 78s* (Fayetteville, TX, circa 2002), CD.
9. Dancehall Boys, "Tinker Polka," *An Evening in Dubina* (Taylor, TX: CMM Records CD5/A, 1998), CD.
10. Czechaholics, "Tinker Polka," *Cause for Celebration* (Brenham, TX: JED Musical Prod. CZ1005, 2014), CD.
11. Lee Roy Matocha Orchestra, "Tinker Polka," reissued on *Muziky, Muziky* (Fayetteville, TX, 2002), CD.
12. Leo Majek Orchestra, "Tinker Polka," *Memories* (Corpus Christi: circa 1992), cassette tape.

20. Haj, husičky, haj

1. F. Bartoš, *Naše děti,* 198, 200–1.
2. Salzmann and Scheufler, *Komárov,* 74.
3. Merrick (né Mikulenčak), "Mikulencak-Zarsky Family History," chapter 3, 14–15.
4. Svoboda, *Věnec lípový,* 175–76. The book belonged to Josef Bartoň, who emigrated in 1904 from Hodslavice, Moravia, and settled in Granger.
5. Salzmann and Scheufler, *Komárov,* 111.
6. Václav Bláha and His Orchestra, "Haj, husičky, haj," arranged by Alois Čuma (Prague: Ultraphon B 14877, 1946), 78 rpm. The American recording is Frank Linhart a jeho Orchestra, vocal chorus by Česko-Americké Kvartet, "Haj husičky haj" (Columbia 318-F, 1925), 78 rpm; accessed August 6, 2018, https://archive.org/details/78_haj-husicky-haj-shepherd-maid-polka_frank-linhart-a-jeho-orchestra-cesko-americke_gbia0001789a.
7. Vrazels' Polka Band, "Gander Polka (Haj, husičky, haj)," *Polka Sounds from the Country* (Buckholts, TX: VPB 106, circa 1970), LP.
8. Harry Czarnek and the Texas Dutchmen, "Haj, husičky, haj," *Red Rose Polka* (Houston: TAP L0018, 1975), LP.
9. Kovanda's Czech Band, "Haj, Husicky, Haj," *Authentic Czech Polka and Waltz Music* (Omaha, NE: Video-Tape Prod., 1999), CD.
10. East Bernard Czech Singers, "At the Mill/Gander/Little Goose Medley," *Czech Listening and Dancing Favorites* (East Bernard, TX, 1988), cassette tape.

21. Hastrman

1. Holub and Kopečný, *Etymologický slovník jazyka* českého, 120–21; and Machek, *Etymologický slovník jazyka českého,* 162.
2. Pazdral, "Czech Folklore in Texas," 38–46; Gallup, *Journeys into Czech-Moravian Texas,* 22.
3. Cheek, *Rusalka,* 10; Tyrrell, *Czech Opera,* 149–52.
4. Slavia, *Národní pohádky,* Series 1, part 2, 39.
5. Lubomír Tyllner, interview by John Novak, Prague, CZ, May 2015.
6. Machek, *Etymologický slovník jazyka českého,* 176; Poldauf, *Comprehensive Czech-English Dictionary,* 204.
7. Wence and Helen Shimek and the All Star Sounds, "Hasterman," *Presents More Polkas and Waltzes* (Hallettsville, TX: WS-1003, 1984), cassette tape.
8. Jodie Mikula Orchestra, "Hastrman," A *Toast to Czech Music* (Ennis, TX, 1985), LP.
9. Jerry Haisler and the Melody 5, "Hasterman Waltz," *Jerry Haisler and the Melody 5, Volume 3* (Temple, TX, 1987), cassette tape.
10. Lee Roy Matocha Orchestra, "Hastrman Waltz," *By Popular Demand* (Fayetteville, TX, 1987), LP.
11. Leroy Rybak's Swinging Orchestra, "Hasterman," *Don't Mess with Texas Polkas and Waltzes* (Hallettsville, TX: LR-1001, circa 1980s), cassette tape.
12. Fritz Hodde and the Fabulous Six, "Hastrman," *40 Years* (Hutto, TX, 2003), CD.
13. Mark Halata and Texavia, "Hasterman," *Moon over Moravia* (Webster, TX, 2003), CD.
14. Czechaholics, "Hastrman (Water Sprite) Waltz," *Cause for Celebration* (Brenham, TX: JED Musical Prod., 2014), CD.

22. Hledám galánečku

1. Rejzek, *Český Etymologický Slovník,* 182.
2. F. Bartoš, *Dialektologie moravská,* 461; Institute of the Czech Language, *Český jazykový atlas,* 82–83.
3. Two examples are *Praha tančí: Písničky z let 1945–1955* (Prague dance: Songs from 1945–1955; Prague: Supraphon, 1986), LP; *V hospodě: Original Czech Pub Songs II* (Prague: Master Music, 2001), CD.
4. Gary E. McKee email to Barton, March 28, 2019.
5. Johnny Mensik and Orchestra, "Looking for My Sweetheart," *Required of Us a Song* (Dallas: USR 3181, 1972), LP.

6. Lee Roy Matocha Orchestra, "Looking for My Sweetheart," *Lee Roy Is Back Again* (Houston: Guide LP-1026, early 1970s), LP; Joe Patek Orchestra, "Looking for My Sweetheart," *Shiner Gold* (Houston: Guide LP-1037, early 1970s), LP.
7. University Czech Singers, *Czechoslovakian Folksongs* (Houston: EMPAC-1212, 1977), LP; Roger Kolar emails to Barton, March 2–4, 2018.
8. Czech Melody Masters, "Looking for My Sweetheart," *Czech Melody Masters Play Old Tyme Radio Favorites* (Taylor, TX: CMM-001, 2000), CD.

23. *Hora Shinerská*

1. Bureau of Economic Geology, University of Texas at Austin, "Physiographic Map of Texas."
2. Renfro, *Shine On: 1909–2009*, 25, 38, 80–83. According to the book, Kosmos Spoetzl leased the brewery in 1914 and bought it in 1915.
3. Joe Patek Orchestra, "Shiner Beer Polka" (Rosenberg, TX: FBC Records 122-1, 1949), 78 rpm.
4. Lee Roy Matocha, "Texas Special," *The Country Boy Is Back* (Houston: Guide 1049, 1970s), LP.
5. Vrazels' Polka Band, "Hills of Shiner," *On the Road* (Buckholts, TX: VPB-112, 1981), LP.
6. Dujka Brothers, "Hill of Shiner," *The Tradition Continues* (Brenham, TX: JED Musical Prod., 1999), CD.
7. Czechaholics, "Hills of Shiner Polka," *Ještě jednou (One More Time*; Brenham, TX, 2007), CD.

24. *Já mám tragač nový*

1. Joe Patek Orchestra, "Wheel Barrow Polka" (San Antonio: Martin M104, circa 1949), 78 rpm.
2. Jodie Mikula Orchestra, "Wheelbarrow," *A Toast to Czech Music* (Ennis, TX, 1985), LP.
3. Peck, *Valašské národní písně*, 36.
4. Slavia, *Národní písně*, Series 2, part 4, 275; Tyrrell, *Czech Opera*, 151.
5. Roucek, *Slavonic Encyclopaedia*, 936.
6. See Tykač, "Kočující obchodníci," 370–75; and Karbusický, "The Experience of the Indexical Sign," 35–37.
7. Nettl, *Folk and Traditional Music*, 92–93.
8. Dujka Brothers, "Wheelbarrow Polka," *The Tradition Continues* (Brenham, TX: JMD Music Prod., 1999), CD.
9. Czech and Then Some, "Wheelbarrow," *The Easy Life* (Ennis, TX: CATS-3, 2001), CD.
10. Wence and Helen Shimek and the All Star Sounds, "Wheel Barrow," *Presents More Polkas and Waltzes* (Hallettsville, TX: WS 1003, 1984), cassette tape.
11. Ennis Czech Boys, "Wheelbarrow Polka," video of appearance at South Texas Sausage and Polka Fest, March 20, 2016, https://www.youtube.com/watch?v=kGtXCDQcEXs.

25. *Já ráda tancuju*

1. Koukal, *Dechovka*, 102–3, 106.
2. Interview with Alfred Vrazel by Barton and Novak, Buckholts, August 29, 2013.
3. Baca, *Baca's Musical History*, 41–43.
4. Interview with Mark Halata by Barton and Novak, Moravia, August 10, 2013.
5. Vrazels' Polka Band, "I Love to Dance," *Performing in Washington, D.C.* (Buckholts, TX: Cen-Tex Records, VPB 110, 1976), LP.
6. Tony Janak's Polka Band, "I Love to Dance," *40 Year Anniversary 2003* (Yoakum, TX, 2003), CD.
7. Czech Harvesters, "I Love to Dance," *A Gathering of Favorites* (Dallas: Rainbow Sound, R-2678, 1980), LP.
8. Mark Halata and Texavia, "I Love to Dance," *Moon over Moravia* (Webster, TX, 2003), CD.
9. SPJST Lodge 88 Choral Group and Orchestra, "Já ráda tancuju," *Czech Folksongs* (Houston: Guide 1050, 1978), LP.
10. The Vlk Sisters, "Já ráda tancuju," *The Vlk Sisters* (Dallas, 1978), LP.

26. *Julajda/Julida*

1. Edward Królikowski and His Orchestra, "Julajda (Julida) Polka (arr. A. Grill)," instrumental, (Columbia 18715-F, 1942), 78 rpm; Spottswood, *Ethnic Music on Records*, 2:741–42.
2. Walter Solek, "My Girl Friend Julayda Polka" (Harmonia: H-1174A, circa 1948), 78 rpm.
3. Viktor Česky Kapela, "Džulajda Polka," arranged by Carl Weiss (RCA Victor Int'l Series 25–2002-A, Bohemian, no date), 78 rpm; "Džulajda," *Souvenirs from Prague: Famous Czech Tunes of Golden 30s* (Apon 2481, circa 1950s), LP.
4. František Horký, Šramlíček, "Župajda," *V Hospodě: Nejrozvernější lidovky* (In the pub: The buffooniest popular songs; B.M.S. MM0112-2, 2001), CD reissue of Czech LP, no date.
5. Čapek, "Písně lidu pražského," 7. See also Opekar, "Staropražská písnička," 754. Čapek's essay was reprinted in Pletka and Karbusický, *Písně lidu pražského.*
6. "Župajda" can be found in several songs in the novel by Jaroslav Hašek, *Osudy dobrého vojáka Švejka za světové války*, 148, 166.
7. Frankie Yankovic and His Yanks, "My Girl Friend Julayda" (Columbia 39116, 1951), 78 rpm; see Dolgan, *America's Polka King*, 208.
8. Brave Combo, "Julida," *Music for Squares* (Denton: Four Dots FD-1005, 1961), LP.
9. Adolph Hofner and His Orchestra, *Julida Polka* (Imperial 8020-A, 1948), 78 rpm.
10. Frank Migl's Orchestra, "Julajda (Julida) Polka" (Houston: Humming Bird 158-A, circa late 1940s), 78 rpm.

11. Blank, *In Heaven There Is No Beer?,* documentary film.
12. "Uvalde Polka," *Hank Thompson: Sounds of the Brazos Valley,* radio broadcasts, circa 1952 (UK: Country Routes RFD CD-19, 1997), CD.

27. *Kajdu*

1. Jindřichová, "Chodské lidové písně," xix, attachment 13.
2. Jindřichová, "Chodské lidové písně," 13–16. See also Jindřich, *Jindřichův Chodský zpěvník*, song no. 243.
3. Kott, *Česko-německý slovník*, 548.
4. East Bernard Czech Singers, "Kajdu Polka," *Around the Moon* (East Bernard, TX: EBCS-1006, 1997), cassette tape.
5. Walser, "The Polka Mass," 183; McKee, "Worshipping More Vigorously," 6–7.
6. Chris Rybak, "Kydu Polka," *I Love to Polka* (Hallettsville, TX, 1994), cassette tape.
7. Dancehall Boys, "I Lost My Vest," *Behind the Blacksmith Shop* (Austin: 1995), CD.
8. Vrazels' Polka Band, "Kajdu Polka," *It's Polka Party Time* (Buckholts, TX: VPB-515CD, 1996), CD.
9. Czech and Then Some, "Kajdu Polka," *A Tribute: 10 Years of Polka Music* (Ennis, TX, 2007), CD.
10. Taylor Czech Chorus, "Stratila jsem Kajdu (I Lost My Vest)," *Songs of Our Heritage* (Taylor, TX, 2007), CD.
11. Texas Legacy Czech Band, "Kajdu Polka," *Texas Legacy Czech Band* (Houston, 2008), CD.

28. *Kde domov můj?*

1. Macura, "Where Is My Home?," 3–7, offers an interesting discussion of the song. This essay first appeared in a Macura collection called *Masarykovy boty* (Masaryk's shoes; Prague: Pražská imaginace, 1993).
2. Janko Matúška wrote the lyrics to "Nad Tatrou sa blýska" in 1844 when he was a twenty-three-year-old student. He used the Tatras, the highest mountain range of the Carpathians, to symbolize a free Slovak homeland. He set the words to the folk melody "*Kopala studienku*" (She Dug a Well). The song is now the anthem of the Slovak Republic.
3. Josef Kajetán Tyl (1808–56) was a dramatist, writer, and director of the Estates Theater. František Škroup (1801–62) was a composer whose opera *Drateník* is often credited as being the first in the Czech language.
4. Síglová, "The Fidlovačka Fest"; Sayer, *The Coasts of Bohemia*, 26, 73.
5. Milena Jesenká's article is quoted in Sayer, *The Coasts of Bohemia*, 226–27; translation from Sayer. Her article first appeared as "O umění zůstat stát" (On the art of standing), 1939, 205–6.
6. *Česko-americký zpěvník* (1916), 6.
7. Pisek, *Twenty-Two Bohemian Folk-Songs*, 7–9.
8. Gallup, *Journeys into Czech-Moravian Texas*, 85.

29. *Kdybych byla ptáčkem*

1. F. Bartoš and Janáček, *Kytice z národních písní moravských*, 70.
2. F. Bartoš, *Sto lidových písní československých*, 92–93.
3. Schindler, *Písničky české*, 18.
4. Sušil, *Moravské národní písně*, 579.
5. Sušil, *Moravské národní písně*, 581.
6. Rudy Kurtz Orchestra, "Kdybych byla ptáčkem" (Waco: Humming Bird 182-A, late 1940s or early 1950s), 78 rpm.
7. Vrazels' Polka Band, "If I Were a Bird," *Dancin' Time* (Austin: Austin Custom Records, VPB 102, circa 1966), LP.
8. Leo Majek Orchestra, "If I Were a Bird," *Polka and Waltz* (Corpus Christi: Majek LP-100, mid-1960s), LP.
9. Ray Baca, "If I Was a Bird," *Ray Baca's Polka Band* (Fayetteville, TX: Baca Records 4248, no date), LP.
10. Red Ravens, "If I Were a Bird," reissued on *Texas Bohemia* (Hamburg: Trikont US-0201, 1994), compilation CD.
11. Czech and Then Some, "If I Was a Bird," *Polkas for* Everyone (Ennis, TX, 2005), CD.
12. Lazy Farmers, "If I Were a Bird," *New Sounds* (Bellville, TX, 2008), CD.
13. Incredible Music Makers, "If I Were a Bird," *Keepin' the Tradition Alive* (Praha, 2012), CD.

30. *Když já libě spím*

1. Greene, *A Passion for Polka*, 55–56. See also Gössel and Šír, *Bohemia on Records*, 67–68.
2. "Vesely zpěv pod názvem: Libý sen," 1870?, a *kramářský tisk* (broadside print) held by Moravská zemská knihovna (Moravian Regional Library), Brno, is described in its catalog by the first line of the song: "Když já libě spím, máš mně nechat spát."
3. Pokorný, "Poesie posledních čtrnácte dni," 54.
4. Russell and Pinson, *Country Music Records*, 430–31.
5. Adolph Hofner and His Texans, "Dis ja liebe spim" (Bluebird B-8463, 1940), 78 rpm; reissued on *South Texas Swing* (Arhoolie Folklyric CD-7029, 1994), CD. Producer Chris Strachwitz, in the liner notes for the Arhoolie release, speculates that the 1940 Bluebird 78 had limited release "based on the rarity of those discs."
6. Joe Patek Orchestra, "Dreamland Waltz," *Joe Patek Orchestra: The 78s* (Fayetteville, TX, circa 2000), CD.
7. Leo Majek Orchestra, "Dream Waltz," *Polkas and Waltzes* (Corpus Christi: Majek LP 100, mid-1960s), LP.
8. Pavelka Orchestra, "Dreamland Waltz," *The Pavelka's New Sound* (Houston: EMPAC 1213, 1977), LP.
9. Ennis Czech Boys, "Dreamland," *Cheers to 10 Years* (Ennis, TX, 2016), CD.

31. Když jsme opustili Shiner/Prahu

1. Přibylová, "'Když jsme opustili Prahu,'" 33.
2. Filipová, "Peasants on Display," 16.
3. Přibylová, "'Když jsme opustili Prahu,'" 33.
4. Lubomír Tyllner, interview by John Novak, Prague, May 2015.
5. Tomáš Masaryk, the founding president of Czechoslovakia, served in that office from 1918 to 1935. He died in 1937. The folk song "Zdálo se mně, má panenko" was published in Václav J. Novotný, *Řečické písně*, 19–20. A memorable recording was made by Czech refugees-in-exile Jarmila Novotná and Jan Masaryk (son of Tomáš), who lived in New York City during World War II, for an album called *Songs of Lidice* (RCA Victor, 1942). The recording was banned under the Nazis and then the Soviets but was finally released in 1992, three years after the end of Soviet rule, as *České písně a árie* (Czech Songs and Arias; Prague: Supraphon, 1992), CD.
6. Greene, *A Passion for Polka*, 156.
7. Letter from George Koudelka, Flatonia, TX, to Frances Barton, February 23, 2009. Six Fat Dutchmen, *Praha Polka* (RCA Victor 20–6127, 1946), 78 rpm, in Koudelka's possession.
8. Russell and Pinson, *Country Music Records*, 430–31; Adolph Hofner and His Bohemians, "Dis syme odpustik Prahu (Farewell to Prague)" (Columbia, Co 321-F, 1942), 78 rpm; Adolph Hofner and His Orchestra, "Shiner Song" (Imperial 1149, circa 1949), 78 rpm.
9. Joe Patek's Orchestra, "Shiner Song" (San Antonio: Martin M103, late 1940s), 78 rpm; Chris Strachwitz, "Joe Patek Interview."
10. McCord and Morthland, "The 100 Best Texas Songs"; Honza Vyčítal a Staří zavináči, "Když jsme opustili Prahu" (Prague: Multisonic 31 0100–2, 1992), CD.

32. Kolíne, Kolíne

1. Polišenský, *History of Czechoslovakia in Outline*, 80.
2. Sušil, *Moravské národní písně*, 585. Three of Sušil's verses also appear in Erben with a different melody, *Prostonárodní české písně a říkadla* (1886), 521.
3. "Kolíne, Kolíne" can be heard on a recording of folk music arranged by Leoš Janáček called *Moravian Folk Poetry in Songs*, Iva Bittová and the Škampa Quartet (Prague: Supraphon, 2004), CD.
4. Novotný, *Libické písně*, "Uvod" (Introduction) and 42.
5. Kapusta, *Dechové kapely*, 150–52, 160.
6. Greene, *A Passion for Polka*, 50–51. See also Rehrig, *Heritage Encyclopedia of Band Music*, 1:411–12.
7. Kapusta, *Dechové kapely*, 150–52.
8. Adolph Migl Orchestra, "Kolíne, Kolíne Polka" (Waco: Humming Bird, late 1940s), 78 rpm; reissued on *Jimmy Brosch Remembers* (Katy, TX, 2011), CD.
9. Norbert Blazek and the Texas Czech Folk Singers, "Koline, Koline," *Zazpivajme si* (Dallas, 1970s or 1980s), cassette tape.
10. Dujka Brothers, "Koline, Koline Polka," *Grandpa's List* (Brenham, TX: JED Musical Prod., 2001), CD.
11. SPJST Lodge 88 Choral Group and Orchestra, "Kolíne, Kolíne," *Czech Folksongs* (Houston: Guide 1050), 1978.

33. Krásná Amerika

1. Rammel, *Nowhere in America*, 18–20; Greene, *A Singing Ambivalence*, 26–27, 46–47.
2. Praha Centennial Book Committee, *Assumption of the Blessed Virgin Mary Catholic Church*, 138–39.
3. Ray Krenek interview by Barton and Novak, November 21, 2002, Sealy, TX.
4. Ray Krenek Orchestra, "Krásná Amerika" (Houston: Gold Star 813, mid-to-late 1940s), 78 rpm; George Koudelka note to Frances Barton, August 17, 2015.
5. Ray Krenek Orchestra, "Beautiful America" (Rosenberg, TX: FBC 105, 1949), 78 rpm; reissued (Waco: Humming Bird 105, late 1940s), 78 rpm.
6. Joe Patek Orchestra, "Krasna Amerika (Beautiful America)" (Waco: Humming Bird 103, late 1940s), 78 rpm.
7. Adolph Hofner and the Pearl Wranglers, "Krasna Amerika" (Luling: Sarg 169-45, 1959), 45 rpm.

34. Letěla husička

1. Erben, *Pjsně národnj w Čechách*, 1:198.
2. Erben, *Nápěvy prostonárodnich písní českých*, 88–89, song nos. 345–46.
3. One example of the "Česká beseda" sheet music that was available in the United States is "Beseda: Český Národní Tanec," by Ferdinand Heller, arranged by A. L. Maresh (Cleveland: Maresh Music Co., 1911).
4. Čelakovský, *Slowanské národní písně*, 1:53–54.
5. Erben, *Prostonárodní České písně a říkadla* (1864), 396.
6. Sušil, *Moravské národní písně*, 386; Vrazels' Polka Band, "Little Goose Polka," *Favorites* (Buckholts, TX: Cen-Tex Records VPB-105, 1969), LP.
7. Bačova Česka Kapela, "Letela Husička Pochod Polka" (Columbia CO 168-F, 1930), 78 rpm; see Spottswood, *Ethnic Music on Records*, 2:608.
8. Jimmy Brosch and His Happy Country Boys, "Little Goose," *Believe It or Not* (Houston: Guide LP-1001, 1967 or 1968), LP; and (Houston: Makko Records, 1967 or 1968), 45 rpm.
9. Leo Majek Orchestra, "Little Goose Polka," *Dance* (Corpus Christi: Majek Stereo LP-101, late 1960s), LP.
10. Ellinger Combo, "Little Goose Polka," *From Ellinger with Love* (Houston: Guide 1004, 1968), LP.

11. Johnny Mensik and Orchestra, "Little Goose Polka," *Required of Us a Song* (Ennis, TX: USR 3181, 1972), LP.
12. Dujka Brothers, "Little Goose Polka," *25 Years Making Tracks* (Brenham, TX: JMD 1010, 2011), CD.

35. Lístečku dubový

1. Holas, *České národní písně a tance,* 4:101–2; "Lístečku dubovy" (Prague: Mojmír Urbánek, 1909).
2. Bassett, *For God and Kaiser,* 117, 187.
3. "Lístečku dubový," arranged for piano and voice by Louis Vitak (Chicago: Georgi and Vitak, 1915); Baca Orchestra, "Baca's Music Book: Music for Alto Saxophone," 1930s, part of the collection of the Czech Heritage Museum and Genealogy Center, Temple, Texas.
4. Joe Patek Orchestra, "Oaken Leaves," *Joe Patek and His Orchestra* (San Antonio: TNT LP-3008, circa 1960s), LP.
5. Lee Roy Matocha Orchestra, "Oaken Leaf Polka," *By Special Request* (Fayetteville, TX: Lee LP #5, circa 1960s), LP.
6. Ellinger Combo, "Oaken Leaf Polka," *The Ellinger Combo Returns* (Houston: Guide LP-1012, circa 1970s), LP.
7. The Czech Harvesters, "Oak Leaf," *Squeezin' and Fiddlin'* (Dallas: CH 40194, 1994), LP.
8. East Bernard Czech Singers, "All By Myself/Oaken Leaf Polka Medley," *Our Best to You* (East Bernard, TX, 2000), CD.

36. Lodička malá

1. Langhanse, *Krásná pasačka,* 63.
2. Pohunek, "A Century of Czech Tramping," 19–22.
3. Beil, *Skautský zpěvník,* 46.
4. East Bernard Singers, "We Sailed On and On (My Pluli dal a dal)," *Czech Listening and Dancing Favorites* (East Bernard, TX: E.B.C.S.1003, 1988), cassette tape.
5. Ray Krenek Orchestra, "My Dream Boat Waltz" (Rosenberg, TX: FBC-111.2, 1949), 78 rpm.
6. Red Ravens, "Dream Boat Waltz," *Back Porch Music* (El Campo, TX, 2003), CD.
7. Praha Brothers, "Dreamboat Waltz," *Praha Bros.* (Temple, TX, 2003), CD.
8. Jimmy Brosch and His Happy Country Boys, "Dreamboat," *You Ask for It* (Houston: Guide LP-1011, 1972 or 1973), LP.
9. Texas Legacy Czech Band, "Dreamboat Waltz," *The Legacy Continues* (Houston, 2009), CD.
10. Czech and Then Some, "Dreamboat Waltz," *Getting Better With Age* (Ennis, TX, 2017), CD.

37. Louka zelená

1. Slavia, *Národní písně,* Series 2, part 1, 7.
2. Owens, *Tell Me a Story, Sing Me a Song,* 217–18. The recording is part of the William A. Owens Papers, Cushing Memorial Library and Archives, Texas A&M University.
3. Bačova Česká Kapela, "Louka zelená-Valčík" (Okeh Records 17359 and Columbia 193-F, 1929), 78 rpm. See Spottswood, *Ethnic Music on Records,* 2:608.
4. Ray Baca Orchestra, "Green Meadow Waltz" (Rosenberg, TX: FBC Records 130, circa 1949), 78 rpm.
5. Gil Baca Orchestra, "Green Meadow," *Polkas and Waltzes* (Houston: Kermit Records KB-1202, 1967), LP.
6. Adolph Hofner and his Orchestra, "Green Meadow Waltz" (Imperial 1140, 1947), 78 rpm.
7. Joe Petek's [*sic*] Orchestra, "Louka Zelena Waltz" (Waco: Martin M104–2, circa 1949), 78 rpm.
8. Czech Heritage Singers, "Louka zelená," *The Czech Heritage Singers* (Houston: Rampart Recording, 1981), LP.
9. Fritz Hodde and the Fabulous Six, "Green Meadow Waltz," *Holding Things Together* (Hutto, TX, 2008), CD.

38. Moon over Moravia

1. Národní Svaz *Českých Katolíků* v Texas, *Naše dějiny,* 312–13; Texas Historical Commission, "Moravia General Store" and "Site of Moravia School" historical markers.
2. McKee, "Accordions Play in 3/4 Time," 4–5, and "Moon Over Moravia Store Shines On!," 3, 8–10; Vesely, "Songwriter Hits Sweet Notes in Czech Style," 11.
3. Dujka Brothers, "Moon over Moravia," *Grandpa's List* (Brenham, TX: JED Musical Prod., 2001), CD.
4. Mark Halata and Texavia, "Moon over Moravia," *Moon over Moravia* (Houston, 2003), CD.
5. Red Ravens, "Moon over Moravia," *Havin' Fun* (El Campo, TX, 2004), CD.
6. Czechaholics, "Moon over Moravia," *Ještě jednou (One More Time*; Brenham, TX, 2007), CD.
7. Vrazels' Polka Band, "Moon over Moravia, "*Songs from Now and Then* (Buckholts, TX: VPB 521, 2007), CD.
8. McKee, "Accordions Play in 3/4 Time," 4.

39. Muziky, muziky

1. See Plicka, *Český zpěvník,* 166–67; Sládek, *Trocnovské písně I,* 27.
2. Kapusta, *Dechové kapely,* 131, 161.
3. Plicka, *Český zpěvník,* 166–67.
4. Leo Majek Orchestra, "Music, Music Polka," *Dance* (Corpus Christi: Majek Stereo LP-101, late 1960s), LP.
5. Lee Roy Matocha Orchestra, "Muziky! Muziky!" on *Muziky! Muziky!* (Fayetteville, TX, 2002), CD; Kovanda's Czech Band, "Music, Music Polka," *Music of the Homeland* (Omaha, NE: Czech Polka and Waltz Video-Tape Prod. Co., 1999), CD.
6. Shiner Hobo Band, "Music, Music Polka," *Ještě jednou (One More Time*; Shiner, TX, 2004), CD.
7. Ennis Czech Boys, "Music, Music, Polka," *Cheers to 10 Years!* (Ennis, TX, 2016), CD.

8. Texas Czech Heritage and Cultural Center, "Texas Czech Village."

40. Na naší půdě straší

1. Václav Albrecht, "Na naší půdě straší (Our Attic Is Haunted)" (Victor 79116, 1926), 78 rpm; see Spottswood, *Ethnic Music on Records*, 2:606. On pages 602–8, Spottswood lists 180 songs recorded by Albrecht from 1922 to 1932.
2. Julius Dietert Orchestra, "Haunted Garret Waltz" (San Antonio: Martin 100, circa late 1940s), 78 rpm.
3. Parker and Brosch, *Jimmy Brosch Remembers*, 154.
4. Ray Krenek and His Orchestra, "Boogie Bear," *Top Hit Tunes* (Wallis: Gold-Sun LP 101, late 1960s), LP.
5. Parker and Brosch, *Jimmy Brosch Remembers*, 40.
6. Wence Shimek and the All Star Sounds, "Boogie Bear," *Wence and Helen* (Hallettsville, TX: WS 1003, 1984), cassette tape.
7. Lee Roy Matocha, "Boogie Bear Waltz," *By Special Request* (Fayetteville, TX: Lee LP 5, circa 1960s), LP.
8. Jerry Haisler and the Melody 5, "Haunted Garret Waltz," *Jerry Haisler and the Melody 5, Volume 3* (Temple, TX, 1987), cassette tape.
9. East Bernard Czech Singers, "Haunted Garret Waltz," *Our Best to You* (East Bernard, TX, 2000), CD.
10. Ennis Czech Boys, "Haunted Garrett Waltz," 2016 South Texas Polka and Sausage Fest, Hallettsville.

41. Na rozloučenou

1. Jurecka, *The Dance Band Experience*, 17–18. Jurecka provides a detailed description of wedding march choreography.
2. Darilek, "Recollections on Texas Czech Weddings," 3, 6.
3. Margie Hanslik phone interview by Frances Barton, August 21, 2018. The unveiling song, called "Svatební píseň," is one of the songs in this book.
4. Henry Brosch Orchestra, "Farewell March," reissued on *Jimmy Brosch's Collection* (Houston, 2000), CD. George Koudelka interview by Frances Barton, Schulenburg, July 30, 2017. To get an idea of the range of tempos, the Romy Gosz recording of "Farewell Polka," from about 1938, is 120 beats per minute.
5. Gil Baca and Band, "Farewell Polka," *Bača's Style Music* (Houston: Kermit Records KB-1202, circa early 1970s), LP.
6. Ray Krenek and His Orchestra, "Wedding March," *15 Top Hit Tunes Featuring Ray on His Dulcimer* (Houston: Southwest Recordings, 2008), CD.
7. Chris Rybak, *Grand March* (Hallettsville, TX, 2009), CD.

42. Naše Káča pláče

1. Erben, *Prostonárodni české písně a říkadla* (1864), 264.
2. "Naše Kača pláče," English title "Snow Flower Polka," arranged by F. Tryner (Chicago: Georgi and Vitak, 1914).
3. Whoopee John Wilfahrt, "Snow Flower Polka" (Vocalion Records 15904, 1930), 78 rpm.
4. Joe Patek Orchestra, "Snowflower Polka" (Waco: Humming Bird 159-A, circa 1950s), 78 rpm.
5. Vrazels' Polka Band, "Snowflower Polka," *Dancing Time* (Austin: Austin Custom Records, VPB 102, circa 1966), LP.
6. Lee Roy Matocha Orchestra, "Snowflower Polka" (Houston: Allstar A7312, 1960s), 45 rpm.
7. City Polka Boys, "Snow Flower Polka," *Live from WFLA: The City Polka Boys* (Houston: circa 1973), LP. The City Polka Boys changed their name in 2000 to Texas Sound Check.
8. Fritz Hodde and the Fabulous Six, "Snow Flower Polka," *Standing Tall* (Austin: Austin Recording Studios, 1998), CD.
9. Shiner Hobo Band, "Snow Flower Polka," *Texas Bohemia* (Hamburg: Trikont US-0201, 1994) CD; and *Frankie and Johnny Hobo Style* (Fayetteville, TX, 2007), CD.

43. Nemelem

1. Kotek, *Dějiny české populární hudby a zpěvu 1918–1968*, 42; "Jan Čermák," *Vysokomýtský zpravodaj*.
2. "Nemelem pochod," by J. Čermák, arranged for piano and vocal by Louis Vitak (Chicago: Georgi and Vitak, 1916); "Nemelem pochod," J. Čermák, arranged for piano and vocal by Karel M. Coufal (Chicago: Aloysius J. Turek, 1916).
3. Jakobson, "Czechoslovak Section."
4. Bačova Česka Kapela, "Nemelem" (Vocalion 15915, 1935), 78 rpm. See Spottswood, *Ethnic Music on Records*, 2:609.
5. Gil Baca and His Orchestra, "Nemelem," *Polkas and Waltzes* (Houston: Kermit Records KB-1200, 1967) LP.
6. Vrazels' Polka Band, "Grinders Polka," *Vrazels' Polka Band* (Austin: Austin Custom Records VPB 101, circa 1965), LP.
7. University Czech Singers, "Nemelem, Nemelem," *Czechoslovakian Folksongs* (Houston: EMPAC-1212, 1977), LP.
8. Taylor Czech Chorus, "Nemelem," *Songs of Our Heritage* (Taylor, TX, 2007), CD.
9. Lee Roy Matocha Orchestra, "Grinders Polka," *Lee Roy Is Back Again* (Houston: Guide LP-1026, late 1970s), LP.
10. City Polka Boys, "Grinders Polka," *The Okruhliks* (Houston: CPB106, 1997), CD.
11. Shiner Hobo Band, "Grinders Polka," *Ještě jednou (One More Time*; Shiner, TX, 2004), CD.
12. Mark Halata and Texavia, "Nemelem," *Live at Moravia Store* (Webster, TX, 2018), CD.

44. Okolo měsíce

1. Hašek, *The Good Soldier Švejk*, 113.
2. F. Bartoš and Janáček, *Národní písně moravské*, 931.
3. Roštinský, "The Moravian Folk Song," 44–49; Smith, "Memories about the University of Texas Czech Club," 49.
4. University Czech Singers, "Okolo měsíca," *Czechoslovakian Folksongs* (Houston: EMPAC-1212, 1977), LP.

5. The English lyrics can also be found in the liner notes for *Deep Polka: Dance Music from the Midwest* (Smithsonian Folkways Recordings, SFW 40088, 1998), CD.
6. Bačova Česka Kapela, "Okolo mesice" (Vocalion 15940, Columbia 261-F, 1935), 78 rpm; reissued on *Texas-Czech, Bohemian, and Moravian Bands* (Arhoolie CD-7026, 1993), CD; Spottswood, *Ethnic Music on Records*, 2:609.
7. Jodie Mikula Orchestra, "Around the Moon," *Play Me a Polka: Tex-Czech Polkas* (Rounder Records 6029, 1994), compilation CD.
8. Fritz Hodde and the Fabulous Six, "Around the Moon Polka," *Standing Tall* (Pflugerville, TX, 1998), CD.
9. East Bernard Czech Singers, "Around the Moon (Okolo měsíce)," *Our Best to You* (East Bernard, TX, 2000), CD.
10. Czech Melody Masters, "Around the Moon," *Play Old Tyme Radio Favorites* (Taylor, TX: CMM-001, 2000), CD.

45. Opice

1. Přibylová, "'Když jsme opustili Prahu,'" 37.
2. Fronek, *Anglicko-český, česko-anglický slovník*, 795.
3. Opekar, "Kramářská píseň," 445.
4. Opekar, "Kramářská píseň," 445.
5. White Funeral Homes, Lonsdale, Minnesota, "Roman E. Rezac, 1917–2010, obituary."
6. Victor Caka and the Polka Timers, "Monkey Polka" (San Antonio: TNT 5069, circa 1960s), 45 rpm.
7. Vrazels' Polka Band, "Monkey Polka," *Vrazels' Polka Band* (Austin: Austin Custom Records VPB-101, circa 1965), LP.
8. Bill Mraz Orchestra, "Monkey Polka," *Swing and Sway the Oompah Way* (Houston: Mraz 506, circa 1960s), LP.
9. Red Ravens, "Monkey Polka," *Polka Better* (El Campo, TX, 1981), cassette tape.
10. Ennis Czech Boys, "Monkey Polka," *Cheers to 10 Years* (Ennis, TX, 2016), CD.
11. Czechaholics, "Monkey Polka," *Certified P.O.L.K.A.* (Brenham, TX: JED Musical Prod., 2017), CD.
12. Jodie Mikula Orchestra, "Monkey Polka," *Klobase Polka* (Ennis, TX, 1993), CD.

46. Pivo červené

1. Čelakovský, *Slowanské národnj pjsně*, 2:23–24.
2. Erben, *Pjsně národnj w Čechach*, 2:10–11; and Erben, *Nápěvy prostonárodních písní českých*, 169–70.
3. *Česko-americký zpěvník* (circa 1880s), 112–13.
4. Jan Habernicht, *History of Czechs in America*, 394–95. See also Machann and Mendl, *Krásná Amerika*, 187.
5. Sušil, *Moravské národní písně*, 601.
6. Adolph Pavlas and His Bohemians, "Pívo Červene (Red Beer)" (Vocalion 15966, 1937), 78 rpm; see Spottswood, *Ethnic Music on Records*, 2:602.
7. Bohemian Dutchmen, "Red Beer Polka," *The Best of the 4th Annual New Braunfels Polka Fest—Live* (New Braunfels: PBL1001CD, 1999), CD.
8. Dancehall Boys, "Red Beer Polka," *Back to Moravia* (Taylor, TX: CMM Records CMM-3, 1997), CD.
9. Ray Krenek and His Orchestra, "Yellow Beer Polka," *15 Top Hit Tunes Featuring Ray on His Dulcimer* (Houston: Southwest Recordings, 2008), CD.

47. Pod našima okny

1. Erben, *Pjsně národnj w Čechách*, 1:55–56.
2. Svobodová and Polívka, *Písnička I*, 108. This elementary music textbook contains three different melodies for the song as well as three different sets of lyrics, though some of the verses overlap.
3. Novotný, *Libické písně*, 72–73.
4. Novotný, *Libické písně*, 72–73; also see "Úvod" (Introduction) at the beginning of the songbook.
5. Pazdral, "Czech Folklore in Texas," 18–19. Pazdral's source for these two songs can be found in Pisek, *Twenty-Two Bohemian Folk-Songs*, 28–30, 32–33.
6. "Pod nasima okny," by František Kmoch, arranged for piano with text by Louis Vitak, included in *Bohemian Dance Album No. 1* (Chicago: Georgi and Vitak, 1913). See also Greene, *A Passion for Polka*, 54; Blau and March, *Polka Heartland*, 46.
7. Adolph Pavlas and His Bohemians, "Pod našima okny" (Vocalion 15979, 1937), 78 rpm.
8. Joe Patek Orchestra, "Under Our Windows Polka" (San Antonio: TNT 5020A, circa 1955–59), 45 rpm.
9. East Bernard Czech Singers, "Underneath Our Windows," *Around the Moon* (East Bernard, TX, 1997), cassette tape.
10. Leo Majek Orchestra, "Under the Window Polka," *Polka and Waltz* (Corpus Christi: Majek Stereo LP-100, circa mid-1960s), LP.
11. Tony Janak Orchestra, "Under the Windows," *Heart of Texas Polkaland* (Yoakum, TX, 1997), cassette tape.

48. Pode mlejnem

1. Erben, *Prostonárodní české písně a říkadla* (1864), 115–16.
2. Kapusta, *Dechové kapely*, 162.
3. Schindler, *Písničky České*, 33.
4. Baca Orchestra, "Baca's Music Book: Music for Alto Saxophone," 1930s, part of the collection of the Czech Heritage Museum and Genealogy Center, Temple, TX.
5. Adolph (Pavlas) and His Bohemians, "Pode mlejnem (At the Mill) Polka" (Vocalion 15968 and Columbia 274-F), 78 rpm; see Spottswood, *Ethnic Music on Records*, 2:602. The vocalists sing the Erben words.
6. Joe Patek Orchestra, "At the Mill March (Pode mlejnem-pochod)" (Waco: Humming Bird 170-A, 1951), 78 rpm;

reissued on *Américan Polka* (San Antonio: Eagle Music Prod. LSCD-8017, 2001), CD.

7. Czech Melody Masters, "At the Mill," *Old Tyme Radio Favorites* (Taylor, TX: CMM-001, 2000), CD.
8. Mark Halata and Texavia, "At the Mill Polka," *Texavia* (Webster, TX, 2001), CD.
9. Czechaholics, "At the Mill Polka," *Ještě jednou (One More Time;* Brenham, TX: JED Musical Prod. CZE1002, 2007), CD.

49. Ráno, raníčko

1. "Ráno, raníčko," words and music by Václav Bláha (Prague: František Kovářík, 1938).
2. For more on fragments of early songs reappearing in later songs, see Malone, *Country Music USA*, 44–45.
3. Čelakovský, *Slowanské národnj pjsně*, 3:73.
4. "Černé oči" appears in Erben, *Pjsně národnj w čechách*, 1:165. Two children's collections that include the song are Svobodová and Polívka, *Písnička I*, 29; and Landry and Cron, *Let's Sing in English*, 2:54–55.
5. *Nejstarší sbírky českých lidových písní* (The oldest collections of Czech folk songs; Prague: Supraphon 11 1293–2, 1992), CD.
6. Frank Migl's Orchestra, "Good Morning Polka" (Houston: Humming Bird 163-A, circa 1950s), 78 rpm.
7. Leroy Rybak's Swinging Orchestra, "Good Morning," *Don't Mess with Texas Polkas and Waltzes* (Hallettsville, TX: LR 1001, circa 1980s), cassette tape.
8. Ray Zapletal's Music Masters Orchestra, "Rano Ranicko (Good Morning) Polka," *Bluebonnet Czech* (Ennis, TX: circa mid-1960s), LP.
9. Bay City Dutchmen, "Rano Ranicko Polka," *TV Polka Time* (Houston: EMPAC LP-1205, 1970s), LP.

50. Rostú, rostú, rostú

1. The botanical name is *Agrostemma githago* L. (Cockle, corn cockle). The plant is a native of Europe and now also "widely established in the United States and southern Canada" in grain fields and "waste places." See Hardin and Arena, *Human Poisoning from Native and Cultivated Plants*, 73–74.
2. Parker and Brosch, *Jimmy Brosch Remembers*, 24–26.
3. Parker and Brosch, *Jimmy Brosch Remembers*, 24. See *Jimmy Brosch: My Very Last CD* (Houston, 2007), CD liner notes. The melody bears a resemblance to the Czech folk song "Kdyby tady byla taková panenka" that became popular in the 1970s with Czech tramping and bluegrass musicians.
4. Parker and Brosch, *Jimmy Brosch Remembers*, 24–26.
5. One particularly well-known recording is by the folksinger Jarmila Šulaková, reissued on *A vy páni muziganti: Folk Songs from Moravian Wallachia* (Prague: Supraphon 11 1839-2 711, 1993), CD.
6. Erben, *Pjsně národnj w Čechách*, 1:96; Sušil, *Moravské národní písně*, 326–27, 329; F. Bartoš, *Nové národní písně moravské*, 79–80.
7. The first *beseda* was the 1863 Czech *beseda* (Český národní tanec, or Czech National Dance), with music arranged by Ferdinand Heller and dance steps created by Karel Link. In 1892, Richard Kaska arranged a Moravian *beseda* in which he included "Rostú" as one of the folk songs in the suite.
8. Janáček, *Klavírní miniatury, Sešit II*, 9.
9. Jimmy Brosch and His country Boys, "Corn Cockle Polka, *Jimmy Brosch Remembers* (Katy, TX, 2011), CD.
10. Vrazels' Polka Band, Leo Majek Orchestra, Bobby Jones Czech Band, "Corn Cockle Polka," *Texas Bohemia* (Munich: Trikont US 0201, 1994), CD.

51. Sirotek

1. Čapek, "Písně lidu pražského," 9. The word "robot" was introduced into the English language by Čapek's play *R.U.R.* (Rossum's universal robots), which premiered in Prague in 1920. The word is based on *robota,* the Czech word for the compulsory unpaid labor required of serfs.
2. Pletka and Karbusický, *Písně lidu pražského,* 27.
3. Pletka and Karbusický, *Písně lidu pražského,* 27. See Opekar, "Staropražská písnička," 754–55; Karbusický, *Mezi lidovou písní a šlágrem*, 150–58.
4. "Sirotek (The Orphan)," arranged for piano and voice by A. L. Maresh (Cleveland: Maresh Music Co., 1913).
5. "Sirotek, valčik s textem," arranged for piano and voice by Louis Vitak, *Bohemian Dance Album No. 9* (Chicago: Vitak-Elsnic, 1924), 22–23.
6. KJT, *Sbírka českých písní*, 7; Bartoš and Bartoš, *Spivejme pisničky*, 88; and Schindler, *Písničky České*, 45.
7. Joe Patek Orchestra, "Sirotek-Waltz (Orphan)" (Rosenberg, TX: FBC 121–2, 1949), 78 rpm.
8. Lee Roy Matocha and His Orchestra, "Orphan Waltz," *Something Old, Something New* (Houston: Guide 1015, circa early 1970s), LP; and "Orphan Waltz," *Muziky! Muziky!* (Fayetteville, TX: circa 2002), CD.
9. Dancehall Boys, "Orphan Waltz," *The Dancehall Boys Live* (Taylor, TX: CD CMM-2, 1996), CD.
10. Vrazels' Polka Band, "Orphan Waltz," *Golden Sounds* (Buckholts, TX: VPB 518, 2003), CD.
11. Shiner Hobo Band, "Orphan Waltz," *Ještě jednou (One More Time)* (Shiner, TX, 2004), CD.

52. Šla Nanynka do zelí

1. Erben, *Prostonárodní české písně a říkadla* (1864), 269; *Nápěvy prostonárodních písní českých*, 121, melody 472. Erben's name for the girl is Andulka, and the song is indexed in his books as "Šla Andulka do zelí."

2. Kotek, *Dějiny české populární hudby a zpěvu do roku 1918,* 134.
3. Staša, "A History of the Southern District SOKOL," 19.
4. Narro, "District One Youth Beseda Dancers Perform at Kolache Festival," 21.
5. Jakobson, *Texas Czech Folk Costumes,* 2–5. The booklet accompanied an exhibit of Czech and Czech-Texas folk costumes sponsored by the Austin Czech Club and Austin Ethnic History Association, 1980s.
6. Dutkova-Cope, "Texas Czech Ethnic Identity," 659–61.
7. Pazdral, "Czech Folklore in Texas," 11.
8. Gil Baca Orchestra, "Annie in the Cabbage Patch," *Gil Baca and Band Play Baca's Style Music* (Houston: Kermit Records KB-1202, circa early 1970s), LP.
9. Ray Krenek and His Orchestra, "Annie in the Cabbage Patch," *15 Top Hit Tunes Featuring Ray on His Dulcimer* (Houston: Southwest Recordings, 2008), CD.
10. Lee Ilse Orchestra, "Annie in the Cabbage Patch" (La Grange, late 1960s), 45 rpm.
11. Dujka Brothers, "Annie in the Cabbage Patch," *The Tradition Continues* (Brenham, TX: JED Musical Prod. 105, 1999), CD.

53. *Spadl lístek z javora*

1. *Slovník české hudební kultury,* "Pravoslav Mach."
2. Sušil, "Odbytá," in *Moravské národní písně,* 319; F. Bartoš, "Lísteček z javora," in *Národní písně moravské,1,* 256. On song "fragments," see Malone, *Country Music USA,* 44–45.
3. City Polka Boys, "Falling Leaves Waltz," *Cookin' Texas Music* (Houston, 1980s), LP. Benny Okruhlik phone conversation with Frances Barton, September 4, 2018.
4. Dujka Brothers, "Fallen Leaf Waltz," *The Tradition Continues* (Brenham, TX: JMD Musical Prod. 1005, 1999), CD.
5. Chris Rybak, "Falling Leaves Waltz," *I Love to Polka* (Hallettsville, TX, 1994), cassette tape.
6. Czech and Then Some, "Falling Leaf Waltz," *Polkas for Everyone* (Ennis, TX, 2005), CD.
7. Shiner Hobo Band, "Falling Leaves Waltz," *Ještě jednou (One More Time*; Shiner, TX, 2004), CD. Band information from the liner notes.

54. *Svatební píseň*

1. Polášek and Kubeša, *Valaské pěsničky II,* 32–33.
2. A photograph of this drawing was published in Národní Svaz Českých Katolíků v Texas, *Naše dějiny,* 234.
3. Macková, "Valašská svatba," 43–44.
4. Hannan, "The Origin of the Texas Wedding Song" and "A Wedding Tradition," 92, 94, and 11–12. See also Bujnoch, *The Bujnoch Family,* 111–13; Dvoracek, *Czech Reflections,* 58; Dybala and Macik, *Generation to Generation,* 235–37.
5. Owens, *Tell Me a Story,* 213–15.
6. Eileen Rosipal, emails to Frances Barton, January 9–10, 2017.
7. Taylor Czech Chorus, "Včera's Byla," *Still . . . Carrying On the Tradition* (Taylor, TX: Awesome Works Recording, 2018), CD.
8. Hannan, "A Wedding Tradition," 11–12.
9. Jimmy Brosch and His Happy Country Boys, "Wedding Waltz," *Believe It or Not* (Houston: Guide LP-1001, 1968), LP.

55. *Švestková alej*

1. Gössel, liner notes for *Zlatý věk české operety 1928–1933,* vol. 1.
2. Kotek, *Dějiny české populární hudby a zpěvu 1918–1968,* 109.
3. Fraňková, "Czech Initiative Aims to Revive Fruit Orchards."
4. For more on "Švestková alej," see Leary, "Czech American Polka Music in Wisconsin," 41; and Leary, *Folksongs of Another America,* 341–42.
5. Roman Gosz and His Bohemian Orchestra, "Svestkova alej" (Columbia 225-F, 1933), 78 rpm; Victor Greene, *A Passion for Polka,* 166.
6. Bačova Česka Kapela, "Švestkova alej" (Vocalion 15915, 1935), 78 rpm.
7. Owens, *Tell Me a Story,* 212–13. The field recording is part of the William A. Owens Papers at Texas A&M University Cushing Memorial Library and Archives.
8. Adolph Hofner and His San Antonians, "Svestkova alej" (Columbia 321-F, 1942), 78 rpm.
9. Kovanda's Czech Band, "Švestková alej," *Authentic Polka and Waltz Music* (Omaha, NE: Czech Polka and Waltz Video-Tape Prod. Co., 1999), CD.
10. Julius Tupa and Sagebrush, "Prune Song," *Songs I'll Always Remember* (Houston: Guide LP-1010, 1970s), LP.

56. *U studánky seděla*

1. The Czech ethnomusicologist Vladimir Karbusický, in his book *Mexi lidovou písní a šlágrem,* 14–15, calls it a half-folk song from the early twentieth century.
2. Langhanse, *Krásná pasačka,* 111.
3. Besides the more widely known lyric collections and song sheets, two undated, anonymous handwritten Texas Czech lyric collections are possessed by Frances Barton. One has 8 songs, the other has 175; both include "U studánky seděla."
4. Viktorin, *Polka Mass Hymns,* 23.
5. "U Studanky Sedela, We Offer Thanks," *The Taylor Czech Chorus Presents* (Taylor, TX, 2005), CD.
6. "At the Spring Waltz," *Presenting the Moulton High School Band and Moulton All-Girl Polka Band* (Moulton: Music Department, Moulton ISD, late 1980s), CD. George Koudelka was the band director at Flatonia ISD from 1969

to 1982 and at Moulton ISD from 1982 to 1998. Information from liner notes to CD and Koudelka, "A History of Texas Polka Music," an undated manuscript possessed by Frances Barton.

7. Adolph Hofner and His Bohemians, "U studánky seděla" (Columbia 319-F, 1942), 78 rpm.
8. Joe Patek Orchestra, "Ustudansky [sic] Sedela Waltz" (Humming Bird HB125B, circa late 1940s), 78 rpm.
9. Ellinger Combo, "At the Spring Waltz," *Polka Hot Line* (Houston: Guide Records LP-1025, circa 1973), LP. Reissued on *Texas Bohemia* (Hamburg: Trikont US 0201, 1994), CD.
10. Mark Halata and Texavia, "At the Spring," *Amerika* (Webster, TX, 2007), CD.
11. The Moravians, "U Studanky Waltz," *Czech Spirit Will Live On* (Ennis, TX, 2013), CD.

57. Veselá bída

1. Erben, *Prostonárodní české písně a říkadla* (1886), 302; see also Zíbrt, *Bibliografický přehled českých národních písní*, 272.
2. Bass, "K písním lidu pražského," 20; and Vlasák, *Vojáci císařovi*, 189. The Czech soldier song is usually titled "Šup sem, šup tam."
3. Adolf and the Boys, "Veselá bida" (Vocalion 15979, 1937), 78 rpm; Spottswood, *Ethnic Music on Records*, 2:602.
4. Parker and Brosch, *Jimmy Brosch Remembers*, 68–69.
5. Adolph Hofner and His Orchestra, "Happy Go Lucky Polka" (Imperial 1141, 1947), 78 rpm.
6. "Happy Go Lucky Polka," *Adolph Hofner and His San Antonians* (Decca DL-5564, 1955), LP.
7. Ad for Decca Country and Western Dance-O-Rama series of albums, *Billboard*, October 15, 1955, 31.
8. Czech Heritage Singers, "Veselá bída," *A Bouquet of Czech Songs* (Houston: Guide 1048, 1977), LP.

58. Vstávej, má milá

1. Erben, *Prostonárodní české písně a říkadla* (1864), 400; Slavia, *Národní písně*, Series 2, part 4, 110; Tyrrell, *Czech Opera*, 151.
2. Kobbé, *The Definitive Kobbe's Opera Book*, 152–57.
3. Enrico Caruso first recorded "M'appari" for Victor on a single-sided 78 rpm record that came out in 1906, the same year Caruso sang in the New York Metropolitan Opera's production of *Martha*.
4. Adolf and the Boys, "Vstávej Má Milá (Arise My Darling)" (Vocalion 15965 and Columbia 275-F, 1937), 78 rpm. See Spottswood, *Ethnic Music on Records*, 2:602.
5. Charlie Adamcik and the Polka Tones, "Arise, My Darling," *Polkas and Waltzes* (Dallas: AD-LP-1, mid-1960s), LP.
6. Vernon Drozd and the Texas Brass, "Pretty Dancing Girl," *Vernon Drozd and the Texas Brass* (Houston: Tonka Records TLP 712, 1969), LP.
7. McKee, "Vernon Drozd: Reflecting on God's Gift," 6–7.
8. Brave Combo, "Pretty Dancing Girl," *Polkatharsis* (Rounder 9009, 1987), LP; and *Polka Party—Live and Wild* (Easydisc EDIS 7052, 1998), CD.
9. Tony Janak's Polka Band, "Arise My Darling," *40 Year Anniversary, 1963–2003* (Yoakum, TX, 2003), CD.
10. Viktorin, *Polka Mass Hymns*, no. 13.

59. Vzpomínka na Cameron

1. Parker and Brosch, *Jimmy Brosch Remembers*, 111–18; McKee, "Polka by the Bay," 4–7; phone interviews with Martha Ann and Jerry Majek, October 15, 2019, by Frances Barton.
2. Phone interviews with Alfred Vrazel, November 13, 2019, and Glen Chervenka, November 26, 2019, by Frances Barton.
3. Phone interviews with Alfred Vrazel, November 13, 2019, and Glen Chervenka, November 26, 2019, by Frances Barton. See also Leo Majek Orchestra, "Memories of Cameron," *Songs from the Heart* (Corpus Christi: circa 1980s), cassette tape liner notes.
4. Vrazels' Polka Band, "Memories of Cameron Waltz," *Silver Anniversary Sounds* (Austin: Austin Custom Records VPB-111, 1978), LP.
5. Jerry Haisler and the Melody Five, "Memories of Cameron Waltz," *For the First Time* (Temple, TX, 1978), LP.
6. Czech Harvesters, "Memories of Cameron Waltz," *A Gathering of Friends* (Dallas: Rainbow Sound R-2678, 1980), LP.
7. All Around Czechs, "Memories of Cameron," *Where It Began* (West, TX, 2016), CD.

60. Z vojny; Slavíček

1. Nightingales can be found in central and southern Europe and central Asia; in winter they migrate to northern and central Africa. See *Animal Diversity Web*, "*Luscinia megarhynochos*: common nightingale."
2. Kroodsma, *The Singing Life of Birds*, 74–75.
3. Georgi and Vitak also obtained a copyright in 1913 on *Bohemian Dance Album No. 1*, which included "Z vojny valčík" arranged for piano with text by Louis Vitak.
4. Rudy Kurtz Orchestra, "From the War" (Waco: Humming Bird HB-006, late 1940s or early 1950s), 78 rpm.
5. Jimmy Brosch and His Happy Country Boys, "Mocking Bird," *Believe It or Not* (Houston: Guide LP-1001, 1967 or 1968), LP; Mark Halata and Texavia, "Slavíček," *Live at Moravia Store* (Webster, TX, 2018), CD.
6. Fritz Hodde and the Fabulous Six, "Mockingbird Waltz," *Standing Tall* (Austin: Austin Recording Studios, 1998), CD.

7. Shiner Hobo Band, "Mockingbird Waltz," *Ještě jednou (One More Time*; Shiner, TX, 2004), CD.
8. Red Ravens, "Mockingbird Waltz," *Havin' Fun* (El Campo, TX, 2004), CD.

61. Zahučely hory

1. Interview with Zdena Kaniová by John K. Novak, Ivančice, CZ, June 2015.
2. Kollár, *Národnié zpiewanky*, 69.
3. Jungmann, *Slowesnost*, 492.
4. Sušil, *Moravské národní písně*, 402.
5. Erben, *Nápěvy prostonárodních písní českých*, 90, tune no. 352.
6. Leary, *Folksongs of Another America*, 359–60.
7. Vičarová, "Pavel Křížkovský." See also Tyrrell, *Janacek: Years of a Life*, 1:14; Novak, *The Symphonic Works of Leoš Janáček*, 32, 72.
8. Karas, "Pavel Křížkovský (1820–1885)," 72–73.
9. Czech Singers of Victoria, "Zahučely hory," *Who Will Sing the Songs?* (Victoria: 1970s–1098s), LP.
10. SPJST Lodge 88 Choral Group and Orchestra, "Zahučely hory," *Czech Folksongs* (Houston: Guide 1050, 1978), LP.
11. Johnnie Holub Polka Band, "Roaring Mountains," reissued on *Memories* (Columbus, TX, 2013), CD; and Holub Polka Band, "Roaring Mountains," *Younger Generation* (Columbus, TX, 2013), CD.
12. The Pavelka Orchestra, "Zahucely hory," *From Sunny South Texas* (Houston: EMPAC-1206, circa 1968–75), LP.
13. Leo Majek Orchestra, "Roaring Mountains," *Dance* (Corpus Christi: Majek LP-101, late 1960s), LP.
14. Vrazels' Polka Band, "Roaring Mountains," *Polkas and Waltzes* (Buckholts, TX: VPB 104, 1968), LP.
15. Bill Mraz Orchestra, "Roaring Mountains," *Your Favorite Polkas and Waltzes* (Houston: Mraz 508, 1970s), LP.
16. Mark Halata and Texavia, "Roaring Mountains," *Moon over Moravia* (Webster, TX, 2003), CD.

BIBLIOGRAPHY

Adolph Hofner and the Pearl Wranglers. Luling, TX: Sarg Records CD 101, 1998. CD liner notes.

Ahlers, John. "The Leo Majek Orchestra: Five Generations of Faith, Family, and Music." *South Texas Catholic,* December 1, 2013. https://southtexascatholic.com/news/the-leo-majek-orchestra-five-generations-of-faith-family-and-music.

"Alfred Vrazel Show Extended." *Texas Polka News* 30, no. 6 (July 2018): 12.

Animal Diversity Web. "*Luscinia megarhynchos*: common nightingale." Accessed August 25, 2019. https://animaldiversity.org/accounts/Luscinia_megarhynchos/.

Atherton, Chas. M. H. *Oblíbené písně našich hochů v Česko-Slovenské armádě v Rusku* [Favorite songs of the Čecho-Slovak Army in Russia]. New York: Jan Hus Presbyterian Church, 1921.

Baca, Cleo R. *Baca's Musical History, 1860–1978.* La Grange, TX: La Grange Journal, 1968.

Barák, Josef, Heř. Přerhof, and Josef R. Vilímek. *Hlahol: Společenský zpěvník český* [Ring out: Czech social songbook]. Prague: Jeřabek, 1861.

Bartholomew, Marshall, ed. *Songs of Yale.* New York: Schirmer, 1934.

Bartoš, Evelyn, and Aneška Bartoš. *Spivejme pisničky* [Let's sing songs]. Rosenberg, TX, 1976.

Bartoš, František. *Dialektologie moravská* [Moravian dialectology]. Brno: Matice Moravské, 1886.

———. *Národní písně moravské, v nově nasbírané* [Moravian folk songs, newly collected]. Brno: Matice moravské, 1889.

———. *Národní písně moravské nově nasbírané* [Moravian folk songs newly collected]. Vols. 1–2. Prague: Nákladem České akademie císaře Františka Josefa pro vědy, slovesnost a umění [Czech Academy of Emperor Franz Joseph for Sciences, Literature and Arts], 1899, 1901.

———. *Naše děti: Jejich život v rodině, mezi sebou a v obci, jejich poesii, zábavy, hry i práce společné* [Our children: Their life in the family, among themselves and in the community, their poetry, amusements, games, and in their work]. Prague: J. Otty, 1898.

———. *Nové národní písně moravské* [New Moravian folk songs]. Brno: Karla Winikera, 1882.

———. *Sto lidových písní československých s rozbory a výklady* [One hundred Czech-Slavic folk songs with analyses and interpretations]. Prague: J. Otto, 1903.

Bartoš, František, and Leoš Janáček. *Kytice z národních písní moravských* [Bouquet of Moravian folk songs]. Telč: E. Šolc, 1892.

Bass, Eduard. "K písním lidu pražského" [On songs of the people of Prague]. *Přítomnost* [The present] 2, no. 2 (January 22, 1925): 17–21.

Bassett, Richard. *For God and Kaiser: The Imperial Austrian Army, 1619–1918.* New Haven: Yale University Press, 2015.

Beil, Vojtěch Beil. *Skautský zpěvník: Sbírka skautských písní 1945–2014* [Scout songbook: Collection of scouting songs 1945–2014]. Brno: N.p., 2014. http://zpevnik.beil.cz/pdf/complete/zpevnik-2014-skaut.pdf.

Bícha, Karel D. "Karel Jonas of Racine: First Czech in America." *Wisconsin Magazine of History* 63, no. 2 (Winter 1979–80): 122–40.

Blaha, Albert J. "SPJST Lodge Texaska Orlice." In *History of Lee County, Texas,* ed. Mrs. James C. Killen, 71–72. Quanah, TX: NorTex Press, 1974.

Blank, Les, dir. *In Heaven There Is No Beer?* New York: Janus Films, 1984.

Blau, Dick, and Rick March. *Polka Heartland: Why the Midwest Loves to Polka.* Madison: Wisconsin Historical Society Press, 2015.

Bradáč, Jaroslav. *Plzeňské písně* [Pilsen songs], Prague: Mojmír Urbánek, 1906.

Bragg, Roy. "Polka Player's Heart Beats to 'Oom Pah Pah' Rhythm." *Houston Chronicle,* reprinted in *Seguin Gazette-Enterprise,* April 12, 1985.

Brands, H. W. *Lone Star Nation: The Epic Story of the Battle for Texas Independence.* New York: Anchor Books, 2005.

Brouček, Stanislav, and Richard Jeřábek. *Lidová kultura: Národopisná encyklopedie Čech, Moravy a Slezska* [Folk culture: An ethnographic encyclopedia of Bohemia, Moravia and Silesia]. Prague: Mladá Fronta, 2007.

Brown, Andrew. "The Baca Band and Orchestra." *The News of the Czech Center* 10, no. 3/4 (Fall/Winter 2005): 19–20.

Bujnoch, Dorothy. *The Bujnoch Family: Our Czech-American Heritage.* Yoakum, TX: Speciality Printers, 1986.

Buňata, Josef. *Památník Čechoslováků: 1618–1918* [Memorial of the Czechoslovaks]. Rosenberg, TX: Národního podniku [National Company], 1921.

Bureau of Economic Geology, University of Texas at Austin. *Physiographic Map of Texas.* Austin: 1996. http://www.beg.utexas.edu/UTopia/images/pagesizemaps/physiography.pdf.

Bytel, Antonín, and Josef Baierl. *Druhý výběr z lidových písní* [Second selection of folk songs]. Prague: Charles University, 1987.

Čapek, Karel. "Písně lidu pražského" [Songs of the people of Prague]. *Přítomnost* [The present] 2, no. 2 (January 15, 1925): 3–9.

Casey, Betty. *Dance Across Texas.* Austin: University of Texas Press, 1985.

Cat Spring Agricultural Society. *The Cat Spring Story.* San Antonio: Lone Star, 1956.

Čelakovský, František Ladislav. *Slowanské národnj pjsně* [Slavic folk songs]. Prague: J. Vetterlová z Wildenbrunu, Vol. 1, 1822; Vol. 2, 1825; and Vol. 3, 1827.

Černušák, Gracian, Andrew Lamb, and John Tyrrell. "Polka." *Grove Music Online,* 2001. Accessed October 19, 2020. https://www.oxfordmusiconline.com/grovemusic/view/10.1093/gmo/9781561592630.001.0001/omo-9781561592630-e-0000022020.

Česko-americký zpěvník. [Czech-American songbook]. Houston: *Texan,* 1916.

Česko-americký zpěvník. [Czech-American songbook]. Chicago: Aug. Geringer, circa 1880s.

Chandler, Retta Slavik. "Publisher's Note." *Texas Polka News* 32, no. 7 (September/October 2020): 2.

Cheek, Timothy. *Rusalka: A Performance Guide with Translations and Pronunciation.* Lanham, MD: Scarecrow Press, 2013.

Chervenka, Calvin. "The Czechs in Review." *Věstnik,* November 27, 1974, 21.

———. "History of the Dallas Czech Singers (DCS)." In *Písničky České: Czech Folk Song Collection,* ed. Henrietta Schindler, 243–52. Dallas: Dallas Czech Singers, 1985.

Christian Sisters Union Study Committee. *Unity of the Brethren in Texas, 1855–1966.* Taylor, TX: Unity of the Brethren, 1970.

Clapham, John, Oldřich Pukl, L. Tyllner, Karel Vetterl, Marta Toncrová, and Oskár Elschek. Revised by Jan Smaczny. "Czech Republic." 2001 *Grove Music Online.* Accessed May 25, 2019. https://www.oxfordmusiconline.com/grovemusic/view/10.1093/gmo/9781561592630.001.0001/omo-9781561592630-e-0000040479.

Cope, Lida. "Texas Czech Folk Music and Ethnic Identity." *Pragmatics* 10, no. 1 (2000): 7–37.

———. "Texas Czech Legacy Project." In *Centennial of Czech Studies at the University of Texas at Austin,* ed. Lida Cope and Mark Hopkins, 98–108. Ft. Worth: NorTex Press, 2015.

Cope, Lida, and Mark Hopkins, eds. *Centennial of Czech Studies at the University of Texas at Austin.* Ft. Worth: NorTex Press, 2015.

Craig, Steve. "'The Farmer's Friend': Radio Comes to Rural America, 1920–1927." *Journal of Radio Studies* 8, no. 2 (November 2009): 330–46.

Darilek, Glenn. "Recollections on Texas Czech Weddings." *KJT News,* June 2016, 3, 6.

Databáze národních autorit NK ČR [Datebase of National Authorities of Czech Republic]. "Kovářík, František, 1858–1936." Accessed April 8, 2018. http://ipac.svkkl.cz/arl-kl/cs/detail-kl_us_auth-p0202724-Kovarik-Frantisek-18581936/.

De Goeij, Hana. "How Czech Wine Got Its Terroir Back." *New York Times,* August 15, 2016. https://www.nytimes.com/2016/08/16/world/europe/czech-wine-moravia.html.

DeKunder, David. "Patek, Joe." In *Handbook of Texas Music,* 2nd ed., ed. Laurie E. Jasinski, 239–41. College Station: Texas A&M University Press, 2012.

Dolgan, Bob. *America's Polka King: The Real Story of Frankie Yankovic and His Music.* Cleveland: Gray and Co., 2006.

Dooley, Tara. "The Vrazels Polka Band Have Retired after 55 Years." *Houston Chronicle,* December 24, 2008. https://www.chron.com/entertainment/music/article/The-Vrazels-Polka-Band-have-retired-after-55-years-1790577.php.

Dravillas, James Brian. "Czech Culture in Fayette County, Texas." Master's thesis, University of Texas, Austin, 1998.

Dutkova, Ludmila. "Texas Czech: An Ethnolinguistic Study." PhD diss., University of Arizona, Tucson, 1998.

Dutkova-Cope, Lida. "Texas Czech Ethnic Identity: "So How Czech Are You, Really?" *Slavic and East European Journal* 47, no. 4 (Winter 2003): 648–76.

Dvoracek, Mary, ed. *Czech Reflections.* West, TX: McLennan-Hill County Czech Heritage Society, 1994.

Dybala, Barbara, and Helen Macik. *Generation to Generation: Czech Foods, Customs, and Traditions, Texas Style.* Dallas: Historical Society of the Czech Club, 1985.

Eckert, Eva. "Language Change: The Testimony of Czech Tombstone Inscriptions in Praha, Texas." In *Varieties of Czech: Studies in Czech Sociolinguistics,* ed. Eva Eckert, 189–215. Amsterdam and Atlanta: Rodopis, 1993.

———. *Stones on the Prairie: Acculturation in America.* Bloomington, IN: Slavica, 2006.

———. "The Years of *Svoboda* in the Texas Czech Community, 1880s–WWI." *Kosmas: Czechoslovak and Central European Journal* 16, no. 1 (Fall 2002): 63–78.

Edgell, Sara. "Polka Pride." *Ennis NOW Magazine,* July 2014. https://nowmagazines.com/onlineeditions/editions/714ennis.pdf.

Ennis Czech Boys. "Haunted Garrett Waltz." 2016 South Texas Polka and Sausage Fest, Hallettsville. YouTube. Accessed March 1, 2020. https://www.youtube.com/watch?v=rpYjg8wjtNM.

Eppinger, Josef, Ilja Havlíček, and Dušan Pazdírek. *Pějme píseň dokola 1* [Let's take the song around]. 3 vols. Prague: Supraphon, 1972.

Erben, Karel Jaromír. *Nápěvy prostonárodních písní českých* [Tunes of Czech folk songs]. Prague: Alois Hynek, 1861.

———. *Pjsně národnj w Čechách* [Folk songs in Bohemia]. Prague: J. Pospjšil. Vol. 1, 1842; Vol. 2, 1843; Vol. 3, 1845.

———. *Prostonárodní české písně a říkadla* [Czech folk songs and nursery rhymes]. Prague: Jaroslav Pospíšil, 1864.

———. *Prostonárodní české písně a říkadla* [Czech folk songs and nursery rhymes]. Revised and expanded ed. Prague: Alois Hynek, 1886.

Everett, Justin. "Corey Mikula: The Man Behind the Drums." *Texas Polka News* 31, no. 9 (September 2019): 15.

Fayette County History Book Committee. *Fayette County, Texas Heritage*, Vol. 1. Dallas: Curtis Media, 1996.

Filipová, Marta. "Peasants on Display: The Czechoslavic Ethnographic Exhibition of 1895." *Journal of Design History* 24, no. 1 (2011): 15–36.

Folkins, Gail. *Texas Dance Halls: A Two-Step Circuit.* Lubbock: Texas Tech University Press, 2007.

Fraňková, Ruth. "Czech Initiative Aims to Revive Fruit Orchards by Growing Trees from Seeds." Radio Prague, November 26, 2019. https://www.radio.cz/en/section/in-focus/czech-initiative-aims-to-revive-fruit-orchards-by-growing-trees-from-seeds.

Fronek, Josef. *Anglicko-český, česko-anglický slovník* [English-Czech, Czech-English dictionary]. Prague: LEDA, 1999.

Gallup, Sean N. *Journeys into Czech-Moravian Texas.* College Station: Texas A&M University Press, 1998.

Geary, Marjorie Crane. *Folk Dances of Czecho Slovakia.* New York: A. S. Barnes, 1922.

Gelnar, Jaromír. *Národní zpěvník* [Folk songbook]. Prague: Supraphon, 1982.

Glenn, Mike. "A Houston Tradition Dies in Polka-Hall Fire." *Houston Chronicle,* October 25, 2004. https://www.chron.com/news/houston-texas/article/A-Houston-tradition-dies-in-polka-hall-fire-1962825.php.

Gössel, Gabriel. *Kamarádi, dolů sfárejme! Nahrávky z let 1929–1952* [Friends? let's go on down! Recordings 1929–1952]. Prague: Supraphon, 2016. CD liner notes.

———. *Zlatý věk české operety 1928–1933* [Golden age of the Czech operetta]. Vol. 1. Prague: Supraphon, 2016. CD liner notes.

Gössel, Gabriel, and Filip Šír. *Bohemia on Records: Early Czech Sound Recordings in the United States.* Prague: National Museum, 2018.

Greene, Victor. *A Passion for Polka: Old-Time Ethnic Music in America.* Berkeley: University of California Press, 1993.

———. *A Singing Ambivalence: American Immigrants between Old World and New, 1830–1930.* Kent, OH: Kent State University Press, 2004.

Grider, Sylvia. "Wends." In *Handbook of Texas Online.* Texas State Historical Association. Last modified June 17, 2016. http://www.tshaonline.org/handbook/online/articles/plw01.

Griffith, Carolyn F. "Czech and Polish Music in Texas before World War II." In *The Roots of Texas Music,* ed. Lawrence Clayton and Joe W. Specht, 175–91. College Station: Texas A&M University Press, 2003.

Griffith, James S. "Waila." In *The Music of Multicultural America: Performance, Identity, and Community in the United States,* ed. Kip Lornell and Anne K. Rasmussen, 186–204. Jackson: University Press of Mississippi, 2016.

Habernicht, Jan. *History of Czechs in America.* Trans. Miroslav Koudelka. St. Paul: Czechoslovak Genealogical Society International, 1996; originally *Dějiny Čechův Amerických.* St. Louis: Hlas, 1910.

Haisler, Jerry. Filmed remarks delivered at Texas Dance Hall Preservation tribute to Alice Sulak. Accessed December 8, 2019. https://www.youtube.com/watch?v=NiuBqjn1SlM.

Hannan, Kevin. "The Origin of the Texas Wedding Song" and "A Wedding Tradition." *Naše rodina* [Our family] 15, no. 3 (September 2003): 92, 94, and 11–12.

Hardin, James W., and Jay M. Arena, M.D. *Human Poisoning from Native and Cultivated Plants.* 2nd ed. Durham, NC: Duke University Press, 1974.

Hartman, Gary. *The History of Texas Music.* College Station: Texas A&M University Press, 2008.

Hašek, Jaroslav. *The Good Soldier Švejk and His Fortunes in the World War.* Trans. Cecil Parrott. London: Penguin, 1974.

———. *Osudy dobrého vojáka Švejka za světové války*) [The fortunes of the good soldier Švejk during the World War]. Prague: Městská knihovna v Praze, 2011. Accessed March 11, 2020. https://web2.mlp.cz/koweb/00/03/57/67/85/svejk_3_a_4.pdf.

Hazen, Margaret Hindle, and Robert M. Hazen. *The Music Men: An Illustrated History of Brass Bands in America, 1800–1920.* Washington, DC: Smithsonian Press, 1987.

Heinsohn, Carolyn. "The First Catholic Church in Fayette County." In *Footprints of Fayette,* by Fayette County Historical Commission, December 30, 2008. http://www.fayettecountyhistory.org/footprints1.htm#first_catholic.

———. "Ondrej Gallia's Store, Mulberry, Texas—1870s." In *Footprints of Fayette County,* by Fayette County Historical Commission, December 15, 2015. www.fayettecountyhistory.org/praha.htm.

———. "The Peter Family of Dubina, Texas." In *Footprints of Fayette County,* by Fayette County Historical Commission, May 28, June 4, 11, 2013. www.fayettecountyhistory.org/footprints3.htm.

Herman, Ken. "Final Days for Texas' Last Czech-Language Newspaper?" *Austin American-Statesman,* May 6, 2018. https://www.statesman.com/news/20180506/herman-final-days-for-texas-last-czech-language-newspaper.

Hewitt, William Phillip. "The Czechs in Texas: A Study of the Immigration and the Development of Czech Ethnicity, 1850–1920." PhD diss., University of Texas at Austin, 1978.

Hickinbotham, Gary S. "Recording Industry." In *Handbook of Texas Online.* Texas State Historical Association. https://tshaonline.org/handbook/online/articles/ebro2.

Holas, Čeněk. *České národní písně a tance* [Czech folk songs and dances], Vol. 4. Prague: B. Kočího, 1909.

Holub, Josef, and František Kopečný. *Etymologický slovník jazyka českého* [Etymological dictionary of the Czech language]. Prague: Státní nakladatelství učebnic, 1952.

Holý, Ladislav. *The Little Czech and the Great Czech Nation.* Cambridge: Cambridge University Press, 1996.

"Hornický skanzen Mayrau ve Vinařicích" [Mayrau Open-Air Mining Museum in Vinařice]. Accessed July 2, 2018. http://mayrau.omk.cz/.

Hudson, Estelle, and Henry R. Maresh. *Czech Pioneers of the Southwest.* Dallas: Southwest Press, 1934.

Institute of the Czech Language. *Český jazykový atlas* [Czech linguistic atlas]. Prague: Academia, 1992.

Jakobson, Svatava. "Czechoslovak Section" in Alan Lomax Collection, Manuscripts, *Freedom Songs of the United States,* 1943. Library of Congress, Manuscript/Mixed Material. https://www.loc.gov/resource/afc2004004.ms100102.

———. *Texas Czech Folk Costumes.* Booklet. Austin: N.p., 1980s.

Janáček, Leoš. *Klavírní miniatury, Sešit II: Moravské tance* [Piano miniatures, Book II: Moravian dances]. Brno: Editio Moravia, 1995.

"Jan Čermák." *Vysokomýtský zpravodaj* [Vysoté Mýto Newsletter]. (May 2007): 1. http://obyvatel.mesto-chocen.cz/images/VMT52007.pdf.

Jecmenek, Evelyn. "Ilse's Orchestra and Lee Ilse Orchestra." In *Fayette County, Texas Heritage,* 1: 477. Fayette County History Book Committee. Dallas: Curtis Media, 1996.

Jerry Haisler and the Melody 5. "Bio." Accessed February 7, 2020. http://www.melody5.com/.

———. *For the First Time.* Temple, TX: 1978. LP liner notes.

Jesenká, Milena. "O umění zůstat stát" [On the art of standing]. *Přitomnost* [The present] 16, no. 14 (1939): 205–6.

Jezek, Zanna. "The Origin and Evolution of the Czech Flag." *Everything Czech.* April 27, 2018. www.tresbohemes.com/2018/04/the-origin-and-evolution-of-the-czech-flag/.

Jindřich, Jindřich. *Jindřichův Chodský zpěvník.* Vol. 8. Prague: Státní nakladatelství krásné literatury, hudby a umění [State publisher of beautiful literature, music and art], 1955.

Jindřichová, Hana. "Chodské lidové písně ve výuce na základních školách" [Chodsko folk songs in primary school teaching]. Master's thesis, University of West Bohemia in Pilsen, 2017.

"Jodie Mikula Orchestra Carries on a Family Tradition." *Věstnik* 84, no. 24 (June 12, 1996): 7.

Johnston, Jesse A. "The Cimbál (Cimbalom) and Folk Music in Moravian Slovakia and Valachia." *Journal of the American Musical Instrument Society* 36 (2010): 78–117.

———. "Neroztavili se: cimbál a asimilace české minority v Texasu" [Unmelted: Cimbalom and assimilation of Czech minority in Texas]. *Národopisná Revue* [Journal of Ethnology] 1 (2011): 32–41.

Jonáš, Karel. *Slovník česko-anglický s úplnou anglickou výslovností: A Bohemian and English Dictionary with Complete English Pronunciation.* 3rd ed. Chicago: F. Pancner, 1936.

Jordan, Terry G. *German Seed in Texas Soil: Immigrant Farmers in Nineteenth-Century Texas.* Austin: University of Texas Press, 1998.

Jungmann, Josef. *Slowesnost, aneb Náuka o wýmluwnosti prosaické, básnické i řečnické se sbírkau příkladů w newázané i wázané řeč* [Literature, and the study of prose, poetic, and rhetorical eloquence with a collection of examples in verse and prose]. Prague: Czech Museum, 1845.

Jurecka, George. *The Dance Band Experience of the Sigmund Jurecka Family.* Weimar, TX: Self-published, 2009.

Kafka, Franz. *Letters to Milena.* Trans. Philip Boehm. New York: Schocken Books, 1990.

Kapusta, Jan. *Dechové kapely, pochod a František Kmoch* [Brass bands, marches, and František Kmoch]. Prague: Supraphon, 1974.

Karas, John J. "Pavel Křížkovský (1820–1885)." In *Papers from Czech Music in Texas: A Sesquicentennial Symposium,* ed. Clinton Machann, 69–77. College Station, TX: Komenský Press, 1987.

Karbusický, Vladimír. "The Experience of the Indexical Sign: Jakobson and the Semiotic Phonology of Leoš Janáček." *American Journal of Semiotics* 2, no. 3 (1983): 35–58.

———. *Mezi lidovou písní a šlágrem* [Between folk song and smash hit]. Prague: Supraphon, 1968.

Keil, Charles, Angeliki V. Keil, and Dick Blau. *Polka Happiness.* Philadelphia: Temple University Press, 1992.

KJT, Katolická jednota Texaská [Catholic Union of Texas]. *Sbírka českých písní* [Collection of Czech songs]. La Grange, TX: KJT, 1960s.

KJT #35. "About." Accessed June 5, 2019. https://www.kjt35.com.

Kobbé, Gustav. *The Definitive Kobbé's Opera Book.* Edited, revised, and updated by the Earl of Harewood. New York: Putnam, 1987.

Kolar, Roger. "Early Czech Dance Halls in Texas." Austin, 1975; typed manuscript in possession of Frances Barton.

Kollár, Ján. *Národnié zpiewanky čili pjsně swětské Slowáků w Uhrách* [National songbook, or secular songs of the Slovaks in Hungary], Vol. 1. W Budjně: W Král. Universické Tiskárně [Buda: Royal University Printing House], 1834.

Kotek, Josef. *Dějiny české populární hudby a zpěvu do roku 1918* [The history of Czech popular music and singing to the year 1918]. Vol. 1. Prague: Academia Praha, 1994.

———. *Dějiny české populární hudby a zpěvu 1918–1968* [The history of Czech popular music and singing 1918–1968]. Vol. 2. Prague: Academia Praha, 1998.

Kott, František Štěpán. *Česko-německý slovník zvláště grammaticko-fraseologický, díl šestý, Dodatky A–N* [Czech-German dictionary, in particular grammatical-phraseological, Part Six, Additions to A–N]. Prague: Františka Šimáček, 1890. Accessed July 2, 2020. https://archive.org/details/eskonmeckslovnko1kottgoog/page/n553/mode/2up.

Kouba, Jaroslav, and Tomislav Volek. "A Historical Survey of Czech Music 2." https://is.muni.cz/el/1490/podzim2009/CZS33/8974387/lecture4/_48-59__4-Kouba__Volek.pdf?lang=en. In class readings for Music and the History of the Czech Lands, Brno: Masaryk University, 2009.

Koudelka, George J. "Adolf and the Boys: Schulenburg's Musical Memories of Yesteryear." *Schulenburg Sticker,* July 19, 1973.

———. "A History of Texas Polka Music." Typed manuscript, Flatonia, TX, no date, in possession of Frances Barton.

Koukal, Milan. *Dechovka: historie a současnost naší dechové hudby* [Brass: History and present of our brass music]. Prague: Slovart, 2007.

Krader, Barbara. "Bohemia, Moravia, and Slovakia." In *Ethnomusicology: Historical and Regional Studies,* ed. Helen Myers, 178–84. New York: Norton, 1993.

Kroodsma, Donald. *The Singing Life of Birds: The Art and Science of Listening to Birdsong.* Boston: Houghton Mifflin: 2005.

Kroupa, Mikuláš. "Poslední rum, po něm už jen Tuzemák" [The last rum, after it only Tuzemák]. Český rozhlas, Radio Prague International, March 10, 2002. https://www.radio.cz/cz/rubrika/ekonomika/posledni-rum-po-nem-uz-jen-tuzemak.

Labaj, Stacy, and Ben A. Marrick. Stacy Mikulencak Labaj and Ben A. Merrick Papers, 1929–1997. Briscoe Center for American History, University of Texas, Austin.

Landry, Mark, and Jan Cron, eds. *Let's Sing in English,* Vol. 2. Ostrava: Montanex, 1995.

Langhanse, Pavla. *Krásná pasačka* [Beautiful shepherdess]. Cheb: Music Cheb, 1993.

Laznovsky, Sylvia J. "Sokols in Texas." *Naše dějiny* [Our history] 4, no. 5 (September–October 1985): 10–11.

Leary, James P. "Czech American Polka Music in Wisconsin." In *The Music of Multicultural America,* eds. Kip Lornell and Anne K. Rasmussen, 33–53. Jackson: University Press of Mississippi, 2016.

———. "Czech Polka Styles in the U.S.: From America's Dairyland to the Lone Star State." In *Czech Music in Texas: A Sesquicentennial Symposium,* ed. Clinton Machann, 79–95. College Station, TX: Komenský Press, 1987.

———. *Folksongs of Another America.* Madison: University of Wisconsin Press, 2015.

Library of Congress. "Image 61 of the Alan Lomax Collection, Manuscripts, *Freedom Songs of the United Nations,* 1943." https://www.loc.gov/resource/afc2004004.ms100104/?sp=61.

Lísa, Valeš. *Slovácké a lidové písně z Uhersko Hradišt'ska* [Slavic and folk songs from Uherské hradiště]. Kroměříž: Josefa Pitharta, 1919.

Lotto, Frank. *Fayette County: Her History and Her People,* Schulenburg, TX: Published by the Author, 1902.

Machann, Clinton. "Country-Western Music and the 'Now' Sound in Texas-Czech Polka Music." *JEMF Quarterly* 19, no. 69 (Spring 1983): 3–7.

Machann, Clinton, and James W. Mendl. *Krásná Amerika: A Study of the Texas Czechs, 1851–1939.* Austin: Eakin Press, 1983.

Machek, Václav. *Etymologický slovník jazyka českého* [Etymological dictionary of the Czech language]. Prague: Czech Academy of Sciences, 1968.

Macková, Veronika. "Valašská svatba" [Wallachian wedding]. Bachelor's thesis, Charles University, Prague, 2010.

Macura, Vladimír. "Where Is My Home?" In *The Mystifications of a Nation: "The Potato Bug" and Other Essays on Czech Culture,* trans. and ed. Hana Pichová and Craig Cravens, 3–7. Madison: University of Wisconsin Press, 2010.

Malát, Jan. *Český národní poklad* [Czech national treasure]. Prague: Urbánek and Sons, 1888(?).

Malone, Bill C. *Country Music USA.* Austin: University of Texas Press, 1993.

Maly, Milton A. *This Church at Wesley.* New Ulm, TX: New Ulm Enterprise, 1996.

Markl, Jaroslav, and Vladimír Karbusický. "Bohemian Folk Music: Traditional and Contemporary Aspects." *Journal of the International Folk Music Council* 15, no. 1 (1963): 25–29.

McCord, Jeff, and John Morthland. "The 100 Best Texas Songs." *Texas Monthly,* April 2004. https://www.texasmonthly.com/articles/the-100-best-texas-songs/.

McKee, Gary E. "Accordions Play in 3/4 Time." *Texas Polka News* 28, no. 3 (April 2016): 4–5.

———. "Al Sulak: A Krenek Family Tradition." *Texas Polka News* 31, no. 5 (May 2019): 4–6.

———. "Hi, Alice!" *Texas Polka News* 30, no. 5 (June 2018): 3, 8–9.

———. "The Hodde Trilogy." *Texas Polka News* (August 2015). http://www.polkabeat.com/blog/uau3jnr7ijk1nzke9n7v1comkxfszc.

———. "It Was Never a Job." *Texas Polka News* 27, no. 12 (January 2016): 6–9.

———. "Mikulas Celebrate 50 Years of Making Happy Music." *Texas Polka News* 29, no. 3 (March 2017): 4–5.

———. "Moon Over Moravia Store Shines On!" *Texas Polka News* 31, no. 4 (April 2019): 3, 8–10.

———. "Polka by the Bay." *Texas Polka News* 31, no. 3 (March 2019): 4–7.

———. "Vernon Drozd: Reflecting on God's Gift." *Texas Polka News* (March 2015): 6–7.

———. "Worshipping More Vigorously." *Texas Polka News* 28, no. 3 (April 2016): 3, 6–7.

McKee, Gary E., and Theresa Cernoch Parker. "Vrazels: Playing for Our Friends." *Texas Polka News* 30, no. 10 (October 2018): 4–7.

Meewes, Veronica. "Czech Mates." *Texas Highways,* May 2014, 31–32.

Meinecke, Thomas. *Texas Bohemia.* Munich: Trikont, 1994. CD liner notes.

Meiners, Carolyn. "The Lee Roy Matocha Band." In *Fayette County, Texas Heritage*, 1:479. Fayette County History Book Committee. Dallas: Curtis Media, 1996.

Meinig, D. W. *Imperial Texas.* Austin: University of Texas Press, 1995.

Merrick, Ben A. (né Mikulenčak). "Mikulencak-Zarsky Family History." Dallas: Written 1979–90. Typed manuscript in possession of Frances Barton.

Mikulencak, Loretta Skrovan. "A Narrative History of the Congregation of SS Cyril and Methodius Catholic Parish, Granger Texas." Copy of manuscript in possession of Frances Barton.

Mikus, Helen Trnovsky. "The Baca Family Musical History." *Náš Český Život* [Our Czech life], 8, no. 1 (Spring 2004): 14–16.

Morris, Nick A. *A History of the SPJST: A Texas Chronicle, 1897–1980.* Temple, TX: Slavonic Benevolent Order of the State of Texas (SPJST), 1984.

Myers, Helen, ed. *Ethnomusicology: Historical and Regional Studies* (Norton/Grove Handbook in Music). New York: W. W. Norton, 1993.

Národní Svaz Českých Katolíků v Texas [National Union of Czech Catholics in Texas]. *Naše dějiny* [Our history]. Granger, TX: Našinec, 1939.

Narro, Holly. "District One Youth Beseda Dancers Perform at Kolache Festival." *Věstník* 104, no. 46 (November 30, 2016), 21.

National Polka Festival, Ennis, Texas. "History" and "Bands/Music." Accessed February 8, 2020. https://www.nationalpolkafestival.com/.

Nettl, Bruno. *Folk and Traditional Music of the Western Continents.* 3rd ed. Englewood Cliffs, NJ: Prentice Hall, 1990.

Newcomb, W. W., Jr. *The Indians of Texas: From Prehistoric to Modern Times.* Austin: University of Texas Press, 1995.

Newmarch, Rosa. *The Music of Czechoslovakia.* London: Oxford University Press, 1942.

Novak, John K. *The Symphonic Works of Leoš Janáček.* Frankfurt: Peter Lang, 2016.

Novotný, V. J. *Bechyňské písně* [Songs of Bechyňe]. Prague: F. A. Urbánek, 1900.

———. *Libické písně* [Songs of Libice]. Prague: Mojmír Urbánek, 1901.

———. *Řečické písně* [Songs of Řečice]. Prague: Hudební matice umělecké besedy, 1907.

Opekar, Aleš. "Dechovka" [Brass music]. In *Bloomsbury Encyclopedia of Popular Music of the World*, Vol. 11, *Genres: Europe,* ed. Paolo Prato and David Horn, 192–95. New York: Bloomsbury Academic, 2017.

———. "Kramářská píseň" [Shopkeepers' song]. In ibid., 445–47.

———. "Lidovka" [Folksy]. In ibid., 460–62.

———. "Staropražská písnička" [Old Prague ditty]. In ibid., 754.

Orsak, Dawn. "158th Prazska Pout." August 19, 2013. http://svacinaproject.blogspot.com/2013/08/158th-prazska-pout.html.

Owens, William A. *Tell Me a Story, Sing Me a Song.* Austin: University of Texas Press, 1983.

———. William A. Owens Papers. Cushing Memorial Library and Archives. College Station: Texas A&M University.

Painter, Joan Balejka. "Then and Now." *Cesky Stopy* 16, no. 1 (Spring 2016): 36–37.

Parker, Theresa Cernoch. "About Texas Polka News." Accessed February 9, 2020. https://www.texaspolkanews.com/about-us.

———. "Alfred Vrazel: Humble Man with a Love of Polka." *Texas Polka News* (January 14, 2015): 5–7.

———. "Church Picnics 2019 (Updated 7/10/19)." Accessed February 8, 2020. http://www.polkabeat.com/church-picnics.

Parker, Theresa Cernoch, and Jimmy Brosch. *Jimmy Brosch Remembers Twenty Legendary Texas Czech Polka Bands.* Katy, TX: BCP Enterprises, 2011.

Pazdral, Olga. "Czech Folklore in Texas." Master's thesis, University of Texas at Austin, 1942.

Peck, Eduard. *Valašské národní písně a říkadla s nápěvy do textu vřaděnými* [Wallachian folk songs and nursery rhymes with text included in the tunes]. Brno: Nákladem vlastním [published at own cost], 1884.

Peña, Manuel. *The Texas-Mexican Conjunto: History of a Working-Class Music.* Austin: University of Texas Press, 1995.

"Piseň o Milce pro mládenecký jakož i pro panenský stav" [Song about a sweetheart for the bachelor's as well as for the maiden's condition]. Litomysl: A. Augusty, 1855. Regionální muzeum ve Vysokém Mýtě - Knihovna [Library of the Regional Museum in Vysoké Mýto], catalog entry.

Pisek, Vincent, trans. and comp. *Twenty-Two Bohemian Folk-Songs.* New York: Jan Hus Bohemian Presbyterian Church, 1912.

Pletka, Václav. *Pisničky Josefa Švejka* [Songs of Josef Švejk]. Prague: Supraphon, 1968.

Pletka, Václav, and Vladimír Karbusický. *Písně lidu pražského* [Songs of the people of Prague]. Prague: Československý spisovatel, 1966.

Plicka, Karel. *Český zpěvník* [Czech songbook]. Prague: Druz stevní práce, 1949.

Pohunek, Jan. "A Century of Czech Tramping." *Folklorica: Journal of the Slavic, East European, and Eurasian Folklore Association* 16 (2011): 19–41.

Pokorný, Rudolf. "Poesie posledních čtrnácte dni: postní studie při černé kávě" [Poetry of the last fourteen days: Fasting studies over black coffee]. *Paleček* 8, no. 7 (February 14, 1880): 54.

Polášek, J. N., and A. Kubeša. *Vałaské pěsničky II* [Wallachian songs]. Brno: Knihovny Milotického Hospodáře, 1940.

Poldauf, Ivan. *Comprehensive Czech-English Dictionary/Velký česko-anglický slovník*. Čelákovice: WD Publications, 1996.

Polišenský, Josef Vincent. *History of Czechoslovakia in Outline*. London: Bohemia International, 1947.

Porter, James, Jeremy Barlow, Graham Johnson, Eric Sams, and Nicholas Temperley. "Ballad." 2001 *Grove Music Online. Accessed* May 25, 2019. https://www.oxfordmusiconline.com/grovemusic/view/10.1093/gmo/9781561592630.001.0001/omo-9781561592630-e-0000001879?rskey=nu8061&result=1.

Praha Centennial Book Committee. *Assumption of the Blessed Virgin Mary Catholic Church, Praha, Texas. Schulenburg Sticker*, 1995.

Přibylová, Irena. "'Když jsme opustili Prahu' aneb česká hudba v Texasu" [When we left Prague, or Czech music in Texas]. In *Od folkloru k world music: Svět v nás, my ve světě* [From folklore to world music: The world in us, we in the world], ed. Irena Přibylová and Lucie Uhliková, 25–42. Náměšť nad Oslavou: Městské kulturní středisko [Municipal Cultural Center], 2014.

Rammel, Hal. *Nowhere in America: The Big Rock Candy Mountain and Other Comic Utopias*. Urbana: University of Illinois Press, 1990.

Rehrig, William H. *The Heritage Encyclopedia of Band Music*. Vol. 1, *A–N*. Westerville, OH: Integrity Press, 1991.

Rejzek, Jiří. *Český Etymologický Slovník* [Czech etymological dictionary]. Prague: Voznice, 2001.

Renfro, Mike. *Shine On, 1909–2009: One Hundred Years of Shiner Beer*. Houston: Bright Sky Press, 2008.

Rhinehart, Marilyn D. *A Way of Work and a Way of Life: Coal Mining in Thurber, Texas, 1888–1926*. College Station: Texas A&M University Press, 1992.

Roberts, Andrew. *From Good King Wenceslas to the Good Soldier Švejk: A Dictionary of Czech Popular Culture*. Budapest: Central European University Press, 2005.

Roštinský, Josef. "The Moravian Folk Song: The Best Means of Preserving Czech Culture in Texas." In *Czech-Americans in Transition*, ed. Clinton Machann, 44–49. Austin: Eakin Press, 1999.

Roucek, Joseph S., ed. *Slavonic Encyclopaedia*. New York: Philosophical Library, 1949.

Roy, William G. "'Race Records' and 'Hillbilly Music': Institutional Origins of Racial Categories in the American Commercial Recording Industry." *Poetics* 32, no. 3–4 (June–August 2004): 265–79.

Rubin, Mark. "Review of Texas-Czech, Bohemian, and Moravian Bands Historic Recordings 1929–1959." Accessed July 15, 2019. http://www.markrubin.com/published/texczech.html.

Russell, Tony. "Adolph Hofner: Spinning Old Europe's Folk Music into an All-American Country Sound." *The Guardian*, June 23, 2000. https://www.theguardian.com/news/2000/jun/24/guardianobituaries3.

———. *Country Music Originals: The Legends and the Lost*. New York: Oxford University Press, 2007.

———. "Lee Roy Matocha." *The Guardian*, July 27, 2003. Accessed February 7, 2020. https://www.theguardian.com/news/2003/jul/28/guardianobituaries.artsobituaries.

Russell, Tony, and Bob Pinson. *Country Music Records: A Discography, 1921–1942*. New York: Oxford University Press, 2004.

Salivarová, Zdena. "Czech Folk Songs: A Personal View." In *Czech Music in Texas: A Sesquicentennial Symposium*, ed. Clinton Machann, 127–32. College Station, TX: Komenský Press, 1987.

Salzmann, Zdeněk, and Vladimír Scheufler. *Komárov: A Czech Farming Village*. New York: Holt, Rinehart and Winston, 1974.

Sayer, Derek. *The Coasts of Bohemia: A Czech History*. Princeton, NJ: Princeton University Press, 2000.

———. *Prague, Capital of the Twentieth Century: A Surrealist History*. Princeton, NJ: Princeton University Press, 2013.

Schindler, Henrietta, ed. *Písničky České: Czech Folk Song Collection*. Dallas: Dallas Czech Singers, 1985.

Seidel, Jan. *Národ v písni*. Prague: L. Mazáč, 1941.

Síglová, Květa. "The Fidlovačka Fest." Trans. Charles Opatmy. Český dialog/Czech Dialogue, nos. 1–2 (2007). https://www.cesky-dialog.net/clanek/2606-the-fidlovacka-fest/.

Simonett, Helena, ed. *The Accordion in the Americas: Klezmer, Polka, Tango, Zydeco, and More!*. Urbana: University of Illinois Press, 2012.

Sitton, Thad, and Dan K. Utley. *From Can See to Can't: Texas Cotton Farmers on the Southern Prairies*. Austin: University of Texas Press, 1997.

Skrabanek, Robert L. *We're Czechs*. College Station: Texas A&M University Press, 2005.

Sládek, Ferdinand. *Náš poklad* [Our treasure]. Prague: Urbánek and Sons, Vol. 1, circa 1890s.

———. *Trocnovské písně I* [Songs of Trocnov I]. Prague: Urbánek, circa 1910.

Slavia, literárni řečnický spolek [Slavia Literary Rhetorical

Society]. *Národní písně, pohádky, pověsti, říkadla, obyčeje všeobecné a zejména právní* [National songs, fairy tales, legends, nursery rhymes, customs universal and in particular legal]. Series 2, part 1. Prague: Slavia, 1877.

Slavia, literárni řečnický spolek [Slavia Literary Rhetorical Society]. *Národní písně, pohádky, pověsti, říkadla, přísloví, pořekadla, obyčeje všeobecné a zejména právní* [National songs, fairy tales, legends, nursery rhymes, proverbs, sayings, customs universal and in particular legal]. Series 2, part 4. Prague: Slavia, 1879.

Slavia, literární řečnický spolek [Slavia Literary Rhetorical Society]. *Národní pohádky, písně, hry a obyčeje* [National fairy tales, songs, games, and customs]. Series 1, part 2. Prague: Josef Vilímka, 1873.

Slovník české hudební kultury [Dictionary of Czech music culture]. "Pravoslav Mach." Brno: Institute of Musicology, Masaryk University, last modified February 16, 2006. http://www.ceskyhudebnislovnik.cz/slovnik/index.php?option=com_mdictionary&task=record.record_detail&id=6609.

Slovník spisovného jazyka českého [Dictionary of the standard Czech language]. Prague: Ústav pro jazyk český [Czech Academy of Sciences], 2011. https://ssjc.ujc.cas.cz/search.php?heslo=h%C5%99eb%C3%AD%C4%8Dek&sti=20302&where=hesla&hsubstr=no.

Smith, Woody. "Memories about the University of Texas Czech Club." In *Centennial of Czech Studies at the University of Texas at Austin,* ed. Lida Cope and Mark Hopkins, 45–49. Ft. Worth: NorTex Press, 2015.

Sokol Ennis. "Our History." Accessed June 5, 2019. https://sokolennis.com.

Spell, Lota M. *Music in Texas: A Survey of One Aspect of Cultural Progress.* Austin: N.p., 1936.

Spottswood, Richard. *Ethnic Music on Records: A Discography of Ethnic Recordings Produced in the United States, 1893 to 1942.* Vol. 1, *Western Europe,* and Vol. 2, *Slavic.* Urbana: University of Illinois Press, 1990.

Staša, John. "A History of the Southern District SOKOL." *Věstník,* November 3, 1976.

Stavělová, Daniela. "Polka jako český národní symbol" [Polka as a Czech national symbol]. *Český lid* [Czech folk] 93, no. 1 (2006): 3–26.

———. "The Polka versus the Waltz: Czech National Dances in the Political Contest of the Nineteenth Century." *Traditiones* 44, no. 2 (2015): 91–111.

Štěpánek, Vladimír, and Bohumil Karásek. *An Outline of Czech and Slovak Music, Part I.* Prague: Orbis, 1964.

Strachwitz, Chris. "Adolph Hofner and His Texans." In CD liner notes, *Adolph Hofner: South Texas Swing.* Arhoolie CD 7029, 1994.

———. "Adolph Hofner Interview." Arhoolie Foundation. Accessed February 17, 2020. https://arhoolie.org/adolph-hofner-interview/.

———. "Joe Patek Interview." Arhoolie Foundation. Accessed February 11, 2020. https://arhoolie.org/joe-patek-interview/.

Strobel, Desmond F. "Polka." In *The International Encyclopedia of Dance,* ed. Selma Jeanne Cohen and Dance Perspectives Foundation. https://www.oxfordreference.com/view/10.1093/acref/9780195173697.001.0001/acref-9780195173697.

Sušil, František. *Moravské národní písně s nápěvy do textu vřaděnými* [Moravian folk songs with melodies inserted into the texts]. Brno: Karla Winiker, 1860.

Svatek, Dennis. "Lee Roy Matocha." Post on Texas Czechs Yahoo Group, July 17, 2003.

Svoboda, Jan. *Věnec lípový* [Linden garland]. Prague: J. Rokyta, 1906.

Svobodová, Markéta, and Bohumil Polívka, eds. *Písnička I: Zpěvník pro 1: Stupeň základní školy* [The little song I: Songbook for primary school]. Prague: Ottovo nakladatelství, 1999.

Texas Czech Heritage and Cultural Center. "Texas Czech Village." Accessed March 1, 2020. czechtexas.org.

———. "The Lee Roy Matocha Orchestra." In dinner program *Honoring Texas Czech Bands of the Past.* La Grange, TX: Texas Czech Heritage and Cultural Center, November 12, 2011.

———. "Leo Majek Orchestra: Four Generations of Czech Polka Music." In dinner program *Honoring Texas Czech Bands.* La Grange: Texas Czech Heritage and Cultural Center, December 5, 2015.

———. "Vrazels' Polka Band, 1953–2008." In dinner program *Texas Czech Bands of the Past.* La Grange: Texas Czech Heritage and Cultural Center, October 9, 2010.

Texas Historical Commission. "Buckholts SPJST Lodge Hall." Texas Historical Landmark. 600 East SH 36, Buckholts, TX, 2008.

———. "Moravia General Store." Texas Historical Landmark. Moravia, TX, 1998.

———. "Site of Moravia School." Texas Historical Landmark. Moravia, TX, 1989.

Twitchell, Jenny. "Kolache Festival This Saturday in Caldwell." *The Eagle,* September 13, 2019. https://www.theeagle.com/news/local/kolache-festival-this-saturday-in-caldwell/article_e6aef158-d5b4-11e9-97a2-6b571383cbbf.html.

Tykač, Jan. "Kočující obchodníci" [Itinerant vendors]. *Český lid* 11 (1902): 370–75.

Tyllner, Lubomír. *Tradiční hudba: hledání kořenů* [Traditional music: The search for roots]. Prague: Etnologický ústav akademie věd České republiky, 2012.

Tyrrell, John. *Czech Opera*. New York: Cambridge University Press, 1989.

———. *Janáček: Years of a Life*. Vol. 1, *1854–1914: The Lonely Blackbird*. London: Faber and Faber, 2006.

Vejvoda, Zdeněk. "Folk Music, Song and Dance in Bohemia and Moravia." *Czech Music* 3 (July 2007): 14–23.

Vesely, Frances. "Songwriter Hits Sweet Notes in Czech Style." *Náš Český Život* [Our Czech life] 8, no. 3 (Winter 2004): 11.

"Vesely zpěv pod názvem: Libý sen" [Merry singing under the title: A pleasant dream]. Jjhlawě: Tisk a sklad Jána Rippla [Jihlava: Press and warehouse of Jan Rippl]. 1870. Moravská zemská knihovna (Moravian Regional Library), Brno, catalog entry.

Vičarová, Eva. "Pavel Křížkovský." In *Český hudební slovník osob a institucí* [Czech music dictionary of persons and institutions], Center for Music Lexicography, Masaryk University, last modified October 24, 2015. http://www.ceskyhudebnislovnik.cz/slovnik/index.php?option=com_mdictionary&task=record.record_detail&id=6368.

Viktorin, Martha. *Polka Mass Hymns*. East Bernard, TX: Holy Cross Catholic Church, 2000.

Vlasák, Rudolf. *Vojáci císařovi* [The emperor's soldiers]. Prague: Za svobodu [For freedom], 1932.

Vožda, Gustav. *Hanácká beseda: Národní tanec z hanáckých písní a tanců* [Hana beseda: National dance with Hana songs and dances]. Brno: Fr. Soukal, 1948.

Vycpálek, Vratislav. "Vožicko v písni." *Český lid* [Czech people] 37, no. 9/12 (1950): 213–32.

Walser, Robert. "The Polka Mass: Music of Postmodern Ethnicity." *American Music* 10, no. 2 (Summer 1992): 183–202.

Weis, Karel. *Český jih a Šumava v lidové písni* [South Bohemia and Šumava in folk song]. Vol. 9. Prague: Karel Weis, circa 1930.

Westfest, West, Texas. "About" and "Attractions." Accessed February 8, 2020. https://westfest.com/.

Wheeler, Camille. "Save the Last Dance for Alice." *Texas Co-op Power*, September 2010. https://www.texascooppower.com/travel/north-central-texas/save-the-last-dance-for-alice.

White Funeral Homes, Lonsdale, Minnesota. "Roman E. Rezac, 1917–2010, obituary." Accessed June 23, 2020. https://www.whitefuneralhomes.com/obituary/622946.

Zíbrt, Čeněk. *Bibliografický přehled českých národních písní* [Bibliographic survey of Czech national songs]. Prague: Česke akademie pro Vědy, Slovesnost a Umění [Czech Academy of Science, Art, and Literature], 1895.

———. *Jak se kdy v Čechách tancovalo: Dějiny tance v Čechách, na Moravě, ve Slezku a na Slovensku z věků nejstarších a až do nové doby*[How they once danced in the Czech lands: The history of dance in Bohemia, Moravia, Silesia and Slovakia, from the oldest of ages to the new age]. Prague: F. Šimaček, 1895.

Interviews

By Frances Barton and John Novak unless otherwise indicated

Chovanec, Rev. Paul. August 29, 2014. Houston, Texas (Barton).

Drozd, Vernon. August 13, 2013. La Grange, Texas.

Durnin, Thomas. February 2, 2014. Austin, Texas.

Halata, Mark. August 10, 2013. Moravia, Texas.

Hanslik, Margie. August 21, 2018. Phone (Barton).

Hermes, Mark. June 5, 2014. La Grange, Texas.

Hodde, Fritz. June 4, 2014. Hutto, Texas.

Kaniová, Zdena. June 2015. Ivančice, Czech Republic (Novak).

Koudelka, George. March 13, 2001, Flatonia, Texas.

———. December 29, 2004, Flatonia, Texas.

———. July 30, 2017. Schulenburg, Texas (Barton).

———. August 9, 2018. Flatonia, Texas.

Krenek, Ray. November 21, 2002. Sealy, Texas.

Paulová, Eva. May 20, 2015. Prague, Czech Republic (Novak).

Polasek, Thadious. June 5, 2014. Schulenburg, Texas.

Rybak, Chris. August 13, 2013. Hallettsville, Texas.

Sefcak, Bertha. August 22, 2003. Taylor, Texas (Barton).

Strmiska, Matthew. August 8, 2013. Austin, Texas.

Tofel, Zdeněk, and Ondřej Tofel. October 2, 2016. Koslovice, Czech Republic (Barton).

Tyllner, Lubomír. May 2015. Prague, Czech Republic (Novak).

Unruh, Jiří. October 2016. Frenštát pod Radhoštěm, Czech Republic (Barton).

Volek, Diane. June 4, 2014. Taylor, Texas.

Vrazel, Alfred. August 29, 2013. Buckholts, Texas.

Zapletal, Danny. June 6, 2014. Ennis, Texas.

DISCOGRAPHY OF TEXAS POLKA RECORDINGS CITED

Authors' Note: The number of the corresponding song in this volume appears in square brackets. Many recordings below were self-published by the bands, and information about date and place of publication and name of publisher/producer is not always available. Some dates given are estimated, with the help of several generous Texas Czech musicians. Additionally, all recordings were produced in Texas unless otherwise noted.

Adamcik, Charlie, and His Polka Tones (Dallas)

"Arise, My Darling" [Song 58]. *Polkas and Waltzes.* Dallas: AD-LP-1, mid-1960s. LP.

Adolf and the Boys, Adolf and the Bohemians, Adolph Pavlas and His Bohemians (Engle)

"Pivo Červene (Red Beer)" [Song 46]. Vocalion 15966, 1937. 78 rpm. Reissued on *Jimmy Brosch Remembers Twenty Legendary Texas Czech Polka Bands.* Katy, TX, 2011. Compilation CD.

"Pod našima okny (Under Our Windows)" [Song 47]. Vocalion 15979, 1937. 78 rpm.

"Pode mlejnem (At the Mill)" [Song 48]. Vocalion 15968 and Columbia 274-F, 1937. 78 rpm.

"Veselá bida (Happy Go Lucky)" [Song 57]. Vocalion 15979, 1937. 78 rpm.

"Vstávej Má Milá (Arise My Darling)" [Song 58]. Vocalion 15965 and Columbia 275-F, 1937. 78 rpm.

All Around Czechs (West)

"Green Meadow Polka" [Song 2]. *Where It Began.* West, TX, 2016. CD.

"Memories of Cameron" [Song 59]. *Where It Began.*

Baca Orchestra, Baca's Band and Orchestra, Bačova Česka Kapela (Fayetteville)

"Annie the Farmer's Daughter March" [Song 3]. *Bača's First Recordings.* Houston: Kermit Records, n.d. LP of reissued recordings.

"Červená a bílá" [Song 7]. Columbia 165-F, 1930. 78 rpm.

"Drateník" [Song 19]. Okeh 17359 and Columbia 193-F, 1929. 78 rpm. Reissued on *Texas-Czech, Bohemian, and Moravian Bands.* Arhoolie Folkloric 7026, 1993. CD.

"Letela Husička Pochod Polka" [Song 34]. Columbia CO 168-F, 1930. 78 rpm.

"Louka zelená" [Song 37]. Okeh Records 17359 and Columbia 193-F, 1929. 78 rpm.

"Nemelem" [Song 43]. Vocalion 15915, 1935. 78 rpm.

"Okolo mesice" [Song 44]. Vocalion 15940, Columbia 261-F, 1935. 78 rpm. Reissued on *Texas-Czech, Bohemian, and Moravian Bands.* Arhoolie Folkloric 7026, 1993. CD.

"Pisnička Česká (Song of Bohemia)" [Song 12]. Columbia SA 2348, 1935, 78 rpm. Reissued on *Texas-Czech, Bohemian, and Moravian Bands.*

"Švestkova alej" [Song 55]. Vocalion 15915, 1935. 78 rpm.

Baca, Gil, Orchestra (Fayetteville, Houston)

"Annie in the Cabbage Patch" [Song 52]. *Gil Baca and Band Play Baca's Style Music.* Houston: Kermit Records KB-1202, late 1960s. LP.

"Farewell Polka" [Song 41]. *Gil Baca and Band Play Baca's Style Music.*

"Green Meadow (Waltz)" [Song 37]. *Polkas and Waltzes.* Houston: Kermit Records KB-1200, 1967. LP.

"Nemelem" [Song 43]. *Polkas and Waltzes.*

Baca, Ray, Orchestra (Fayetteville)

"Green Meadow Waltz" [Song 37]. Rosenberg, TX: FBC Records 130, circa 1949. 78 rpm. Reissued, Waco, TX: Humming Bird Records, circa early 1950s. 78 rpm.

"If I Was a Bird" [Song 29]. *Ray Baca's Polka Band.* Fayetteville, TX: Baca Records 4248, circa 1960s. LP.

Bay City Dutchmen

"Rano Ranicko Polka" [Song 49]. *TV Polka Time.* Houston: EMPAC LP-1205, 1970s. LP.

Bohemian Dutchmen (New Braunfels)

"Red Beer Polka" [Song 46]. *The Best of the 4th Annual New Braunfels Polka Fest—Live.* New Braunfels, TX: PBL1001CD, 1999. CD.

Brave Combo (Denton)

"A Ja Sam" [Song 1]. *Let's Kiss: 25th Anniversary Album.* Denton: Dentone Records, 2004. CD.

"Julida" [Song 26]. *Music for Squares.* Denton, TX: Four Dots FD-1005, 1961. LP. Reissued on *Musical Varieties.* Rounder CD11546, 1987. CD.

"Pretty Dancing Girl" [Song 58]. *Polkatharsis.* Rounder Records 9009, 1987. LP. Also on *Polka Party—Live and Wild.* Easydisc EDIS 7052, 1998. CD.

Brosch, Henry, Orchestra (Moulton)

"Farewell March" [Song 41]. Reissued on *Jimmy Brosch's Collection: Since 1946 Music Styled for the Young and Old.* Houston, 2000. CD.

Brosch, Jimmy, and His Happy Country Boys (Houston)

"Bolí, bolí" [Song 5]. Houston: Guide, circa 1968. 45 rpm. Reissued on *Jimmy Brosch's Collection: Since 1946 Music Styled for the Young and Old.* Houston, 2000. CD.

"Corn Cockle Polka" [Song 50]. Houston: Guide 101, 1967. 45 rpm. Reissued on *Bands of Texas, Vol. 3.* Schulenburg, TX: Texas Polka Music Museum, circa 2015. Compilation CD. Reissued on *Jimmy Brosch Remembers Twenty Legendary Texas Czech Polka Bands.* Katy, TX, 2011. Compilation CD.

"Dream Boat Waltz" [Song 36]. *You Ask for It.* Houston: Guide LP-1011, ca. 1972–73. LP.

"Little Goose" [Song 34]. *Believe It or Not.* Houston: Guide LP-1001, 1967 or 1968. LP. Also on Houston: Makko Records, 1967 or 1968. 45 rpm. Reissued on *Jimmy Brosch's Collection: Since 1946 Music Styled for the Young and Old.* Houston, 2000. CD.

"Mocking Bird" [Song 60]. *Believe It or Not.* Houston: Guide LP-1001, 1967 or 1968. LP.

"Wedding Waltz" [Song 54]. *Believe It or Not.* Houston: Guide LP-1001, 1967 or 1968. LP. Reissued on *Jimmy Brosch's Collection: Since 1946 Music Styled for the Young and Old.*

Brosh, Benny, and His Orchestra (Rowena)

"Barbara Polka" [Song 4]. Waco, TX: Humming Bird 160, circa 1950. 78 rpm. Reissued on *Texas-Czech, Bohemian, and Moravian Bands.* Arhoolie, 1993. CD.

Caka, Victor, and the Polka Timers (Shiner)

"Monkey Polka" [Song 45]. San Antonio: TNT 5069, circa 1960s. 45 rpm.

City Polka Boys (Houston)

"Falling Leaves Waltz" [Song 35]. *Cookin' Texas Music.* Houston, 1980s. LP.

"Grinders Polka" [Song 43]. *The Okruhliks.* Houston: CPB-106, 1997. CD.

"Snow Flower Polka" [Song 40]. *Live from WFLA: The City Polka Boys.* Houston: circa 1973. LP.

Czarnek, Harry, and the Texas Dutchmen (Houston)

"Cottages under the Mountains" [Song 14]. *Polka Hit Parade.* Houston: Camwood Records and Tapes 103, mid-1980s. Cassette tape.

"Haj, husičky, haj" [Song 20]. *Red Rose Polka.* Houston: TAP L0018, 1975. LP.

"Red Handkerchief Waltz" [Song 11]. *A Polka Picnic.* Houston: Guide-1020, circa 1970s. LP.

"Red Rose Polka" [Song 8]. *Red Rose Polka.* Reissued on *Bands of Texas, Vol. 1.* Schulenburg, TX: Texas Polka Music Museum, circa 2010. Compilation CD.

Czechaholics (La Grange)

"Four Horses" [Song 17]. *Spreadin' the Tradition.* Brenham, TX: JED Musical Prod., 2006. CD.

"Hastrman Waltz" [Song 21]. *Cause for Celebration.* Brenham, TX: JED Musical Prod. CZ1005, 2014. CD.

"Hills of Shiner Polka" [Song 23]. *Ještě jednou (One More Time).* Brenham, TX: JED Musical Prod. CZE1002, 2007. CD.

"Monkey Polka" [Song 45]. *Certified P.O.L.K.A.* Brenham, TX: JED Musical Prod., 2017. CD.

"Moon over Moravia Waltz" [Song 38]. *Ještě jednou (One More Time).* Reissued on *Bands of Texas, Vol. 2.* Schulenburg, TX: Texas Polka Music Museum, circa 2013. Compilation CD.

"Red Wine Polka" [Song 10]. *Certified P.O.L.K.A.*

"Tinker Polka" [Song 19]. *Cause for Celebration.*

Czech and Then Some (Ennis)

"A Ja Sam Polka" [Song 1]. *A Tribute: 10 Years of Polka Music.* Ennis, TX, 2007. CD.

"Dreamboat Waltz" [Song 36]. *Getting Better with Age.* Ennis, TX, 2017. CD.

"Falling Leaf Waltz" [Song 53]. *Polkas for Everyone.* Ennis, TX, 2005. CD.

"Headache Waltz" [Song 5]. *Play Old Time Music.* Ennis, TX, 2012. CD.

"If I Was a Bird Polka" [Song 29]. *Polkas for Everyone.*

"Kajdu Polka" [Song 27]. *A Tribute: 10 Years of Polka Music.*

"Path to Moravia Waltz" [Song 13]. *Polkas for Everyone.*

"Song of the Czechs Waltz" [Song 12]. *Polkas for Everyone.*

"Wheelbarrow Polka" [Song 24]. *The Easy Life.* Ennis, TX, 2001. CD.

Czech Harvesters (Ennis)

"Four Horses Waltz" [Song 17]. *Tenth Anniversary.* Dallas: CH30188, 1988. Cassette tape.

"I Love to Dance" [Song 25]. *A Gathering of Favorites.* Dallas: Rainbow Sound R-2678, 1980. LP.

"Cameron Waltz" [Song 59]. *A Gathering of Favorites.*

"Oak Leaf" [Song 35]. *Squeezin' and Fiddlin'.* Dallas: CH 40194, 1994. CD.

Czech Heritage Singers (Galveston, La Marque, Texas City)

"Baruška" [Song 4]. *The Czech Heritage Singers.* Houston: Rampart Recording, 1981. LP.
"Louka zelená" [Song 37]. *The Czech Heritage Singers.*
"Veselá bída" [Song 57]. *A Bouquet of Czech Songs.* Houston: Guide LP1048, 1977. LP.

Czechmates (Dallas)

"Red Rose Waltz" [Song 9]. *20th Anniversary Live.* Dallas, 1993. Cassette tape.

Czech Melody Masters (Taylor, Austin)

"Around the Moon" [Song 44]. *Czech Melody Masters Play Old Tyme Radio Favorites.* Taylor, TX: CMM-001, 2000. CD.
"At the Mill" [Song 48]. *Czech Melody Masters Play Old Tyme Radio Favorites.*
"Červená a bílá" [Song 7]. *Czech, Please.* Austin: CMM Records CMM-004, 2015. CD.
"Headache Waltz" [Song 5]. *Czech, Please.*
"Looking for My Sweetheart" [Song 22]. *Czech Melody Masters Play Old Tyme Radio Favorites.* Reissued on *Bands of Texas, Vol. 4.* Schulenburg, TX: Texas Polka Music Museum, circa 2016. Compilation CD.

Czech Singers of Victoria

"Zahučely hory" [Song 61]. *Who Will Sing the Songs?* Victoria: Record 3, circa 1970s or 1980s. LP.

Dancehall Boys (Austin, Taylor)

"Dráteník" [Song 19]. *An Evening in Dubina.* Taylor, TX: CMM Records CMM-5, 1998. CD.
"Kajdu" [Song 27]. *Behind the Blacksmith Shop.* Austin: CMM Records CMM-1, 1995. CD.
"Orphan Waltz" [Song 51]. *Dancehall Boys Live.* Taylor, TX: CMM Records CMM-2, 1996. CD.
"Red Beer Polka" [Song 46]. *Back to Moravia.* Taylor, TX: CMM Records CMM-3, 1997. CD.

Dietert, Julius, Orchestra (New Braunfels)

"Haunted Garret Waltz" [Song 40]. San Antonio: Martin 100, circa late 1940s. 78 rpm.

Drozd, Vernon, and the Texas Brass (Houston)

"Pretty Dancing Girl" [Song 58]. *Vernon Drozd and the Texas Brass.* Houston: Tonka Records TLP 712, 1969. LP. Reissued as *40th Anniversary Edition.* East Bernard, TX: Rhythm Signal Records, 2009. CD.

Dujka Brothers (Brenham)

"Annie in the Cabbage Patch" [Song 52]. *The Tradition Continues: The Best of the Dujka Brothers, Vol. 1.* Brenham, TX: JED Musical Prod., 1999. CD.
"Fallen Leaf Waltz" [Song 53]. *The Tradition Continues: The Best of the Dujka Brothers, Vol. 1.*
"Fire Brigade Polka" [Song 15]. *Grandpa's List: The Best of the Dujka Brothers, Vol. 2.* Brenham, TX: JED Musical Prod., 2001. CD.
"Headache Waltz" [Song 5]. *Grandpa's List: The Best of the Dujka Brothers, Vol. 2.*
"Hill of Shiner Polka" [Song 23]. *The Tradition Continues: The Best of the Dujka Brothers, Vol. 1.*
"Koline, Koline" [Song 32]. *Grandpa's List: The Best of the Dujka Brothers, Vol. 2.*
"Little Goose Polka" [Song 34]. *25 Years Making Tracks.* Brenham, TX: JMD Music Prod. 1010, 2011. CD.
"Moon over Moravia Waltz" [Song 38]. *Grandpa's List: The Best of the Dujka Brothers, Vol. 2.*
"Old Meadow Polka" [Song 2]. *Shining Up Old Favorites.* Brenham, TX: JED Musical Prod., 2008. CD.
"Red Rose Waltz" [Song 9]. *The Tradition Continues: The Best of the Dujka Brothers, Vol. 1.*
"Red Wine Polka" [Song 10]. *The Tradition Continues: The Best of the Dujka Brothers, Vol. 1.*
"Watersprite Waltz" (Hastrman) [Song 21]. *Grandpa's List: The Best of the Dujka Brothers, Vol. 2.*
"Wheelbarrow Polka" [Song 24]. *The Tradition Continues: The Best of the Dujka Brothers, Vol. 1.*

East Bernard Czech Singers (East Bernard)

"All By Myself/Oaken Leaf Polka Medley" [Songs 1, 35]. *Our Best to You.* East Bernard, TX, 2000. CD.
"Around the Moon" [Song 44]. *Our Best to You.*
"At the Mill/Gander/Little Goose Medley" [Songs 48, 20, 34]. *Czech Listening and Dancing Favorites.* East Bernard, TX: EBCS1003, 1988. Cassette tape.
"Haunted Garret Waltz" [Song 40]. *Our Best to You.*
"Kajdu Polka" [Song 27]. *Around the Moon.* East Bernard, TX: EBCS-1006, 1997. Cassette tape.
"Our Czech Songs" [Song 12]. *Czech Songs We Treasure.* East Bernard, TX, 1992. Cassette tape.
"Red and White Waltz" [Song 7]. *Our Best to You.*
"Underneath Our Windows" [Song 47]. *Around the Moon.*
"We Sailed On and On" [Song 36]. *Czech Listening and Dancing Favorites.*

Ellinger Combo (Ellinger)

"At the Spring Waltz" [Song 56]. *Polka Hot Line.* Houston: Guide LP-1025, 1973. LP. Reissued on *Texas Bohemia.* Hamburg, TX: Trikont US-0201, 1994. CD.

"Good Night My Darling Waltz" [Song 18]. *A Little Bit of the Best.* Ellinger, TX, 1984. LP.
"Little Goose Polka" [Song 34]. *From Ellinger with Love.* Houston: Guide Records LP-1004, 1968. LP.
"Oaken Leaf Polka" [Song 35]. *The Ellinger Combo Returns.* Houston: Guide LP-1012, circa 1970s. LP.

Ennis Czech Boys (Ennis)

"Dreamland Waltz" [Song 30]. *Cheers to 10 Years!* Ennis, TX, 2016. CD.
"Good Night My Darling Waltz" [Song 18]. *Cheers to 10 Years!*
"Monkey Polka" [Song 45]. *Cheers to 10 Years!*
"Music, Music Polka" [Song 39]. *Cheers to 10 Years!*

Haisler, Jerry, and the Melody 5 (Temple)

"Hasterman Waltz" [Song 21]. *Jerry Haisler and the Melody 5, Vol. 3.* Temple, TX, 1987. Cassette tape. Reissued on *Favorites: 1978–1992.* Temple, TX, 2006. CD.
"Haunted Garret Waltz" [Song 40]. *Jerry Haisler and the Melody 5, Vol. 3.*
"Memories of Cameron Waltz" [Song 59]. *For the First Time.* Temple, TX: Big Tex ARS-JH-91078-1, 1978. LP.

Halata, Mark, and Texavia (Houston)

"At the Mill Polka" [Song 48]. *Texavia.* Webster, TX, 2001. CD.
"At the Spring" [Song 56]. *Amerika.* Webster, TX, 2007. CD.
"Hasterman" [Song 21]. *Moon over Moravia.* Webster, TX, 2003. CD.
"I Love to Dance" [Song 25]. *Moon over Moravia.* Reissued on *Bands of Texas, Vol. 1.* Schulenburg, TX: Texas Polka Music Museum, circa 2010. Compilation CD.
"Moon over Moravia" [Song 38]. *Moon over Moravia.*
"Nemelem" [Song 43]. *Live at Moravia Store.* Webster, TX, 2018. CD.
"Painted Gate Polka" [Song 6]. *Moon over Moravia.*
"Path to Moravia" [Song 13]. *Texavia.* Also on *Live at Moravia Store.*
"Red Rose Polka" [Song 8]. *Amerika.*
"Roaring Mountains" [Song 61]. *Moon over Moravia.*
"Slavíček" [Song 60]. *Live at Moravia Store.*

Hodde, Fritz, and the Fabulous Six (Hutto)

"Around the Moon Polka" [Song 44]. *Standing Tall.* Austin: Austin Recording Studios, 1998. CD.
"Green Meadow Waltz" [Song 37]. *Holding Things Together.* Hutto, TX, 2008. CD.
"Hastrman" [Song 21]. *40 Years.* Hutto, TX, 2003. CD.
"Mockingbird Waltz" [Song 60]. *Standing Tall.*
"Snow Flower Polka" [Song 42]. *Standing Tall.*

Hofner, Adolph, and His Bohemians, and His Orchestra, and His San Antonians, and His Texans, and the Pearl Wranglers (San Antonio)

"Baruška Polka" [Song 4] Columbia 391-F, 1942. 78 rpm. Reissued on *Adolph Hofner: Swing with the Music.* Dover: British Archive of Country Music, 2010. CD.
"Barbara Polka" [Song 4]. Imperial IF-75 8027-A, n.d. 78 rpm. Reissued on *Texas-Czech, Bohemian, and Moravian Bands.* Arhoolie Folkloric 7026, 1993. CD.
"Beautiful America (Krasna Amerika)" [Song 33]. Luling, TX: Sarg 169-45, 1959. 45 rpm. Reissued on *Texas Bohemia.* Munich: Trikont US-0201, 1994. CD.
"Cerveny satachek" [Song 11]. *Adolph Hofner: Swing with the Music.*
"Dis ja liebe spim" [Song 30]. Bluebird B-8463, 1940. 78 rpm. Reissued on *South Texas Swing.* Arhoolie Folklyric CD7029, 1994. CD.
"Dis syme odpustik Prahu (Farewell to Prague)" [Song 31]. Columbia Records, Co 321-F, 1942. 78 rpm. Reissued on *Adolph Hofner: Swing with the Music.*
"Green Meadow Waltz" [Song 37]. Imperial 1140, 1947. 78 rpm. Reissued on *Texas-Czech, Bohemian, and Moravian Bands.*
"Happy Go Lucky Polka" [Song 57]. *Adolph Hofner and His San Antonians.* Decca DL-5564, 1955. LP. Reissued on *Adolph Hofner: Swing with the Music.*
"Happy Go Lucky Polka" [Song 57]. Imperial 1141, 1947. 78 rpm. Reissued on *Texas-Czech, Bohemian, and Moravian Bands.*
"Julida Polka" [Song 26]. Imperial 8020-A, 1948. 78 rpm. Reissued on *South Texas Swing.*
"Shiner Song" [Song 31]. Imperial 1149, circa 1949. 78 rpm. Reissued on *Texas-Czech, Bohemian, and Moravian Bands.*
"Svestkova alej" [Song 55]. Columbia 321-F, 1942. 78 rpm. Reissued on *Adolph Hofner: Swing with the* Music.
"U studánky seděla" [Song 56]. Columbia 319-F, 1942. 78 rpm. Reissued on *Adolph Hofner: Swing With the Music.*

Holub, Johnnie, Polka Band (Schulenburg)

"Roaring Mountains" [Song 61]. Reissued on *Memories.* Columbus, TX, 2013. CD.

Holub Polka Band (Columbus)

"Roaring Mountains" [Song 61]. *Younger Generation.* Columbus, TX, 2013. CD.

Ilse, Lee, Orchestra (La Grange)

"Annie in the Cabbage Patch" [Song 52]. La Grange, TX, circa 1960s. 45 rpm.
"Cottage under the Mountains" [Song 14]. La Grange, TX: Bess Records BS-102-A, early 1960s. 45 rpm.

Incredible Music Makers (Praha)

"If I Were a Bird" [Song 29]. *Keepin' the Tradition Alive.* Praha, 2012. CD.

Janak, Tony, Polka Band (Yoakum)

"Arise My Darling" [Song 58]. *40 Year Anniversary, 1963–2003.* Yoakum, TX, 2003. CD.
"I Love to Dance" [Song 25]. *40 Year Anniversary 1963–2003.*
"Under the Windows" [Song 47]. *Heart of Texas Polkaland.* Yoakum, TX, 1997. Cassette tape.

Jones, Bobby, Polka Band (Wharton)

"Corn Cockle Polka" [Song 50]. *Texas Bohemia.* Munich: Trikont US-0201, 1994. CD.
"Good Night My Darling" [Song 18]. Houston: SPJST Lodge 88 Splash Day, mid-1980s. Live recording by Dennis Svatek.

Kovanda's Czech Band (Fayetteville)

"Haj, Husicky, Haj" [Song 20]. *Authentic Czech Polka and Waltz Music.* Omaha: Czech Polka and Waltz Video-Tape Prod., 1999. CD.
"Music, Music Polka" [Song 39]. *Music of the Homeland.* Omaha: Czech Polka and Waltz Video-Tape Prod., 1999. CD.
"Our Czech Song" [Song 12]. *Our Czech Music.* Fayetteville, TX: KCB-103, 1994. Cassette tape.
"Švestková alej" [Song 55]. *Authentic Polka and Waltz Music.*

Krenek, Ray, and His Orchestra (Wallis)

"Annie in the Cabbage Patch" [Song 52]. *15 Top Hit Tunes Featuring Ray on His Dulcimer.* Houston: Southwest Recordings, 2008. CD.
"Beautiful America" [Song 33]. Rosenberg, TX: FBC 105, 1949. 78 rpm. reissued on Waco, TX: Humming Bird 105, late 1940s. 78 rpm. Reissued on *15 Top Hit Tunes Featuring Ray on His Dulcimer.*
"It's a Boogie Bear Upstairs" [Song 40]. *Top Hit Tunes.* Wallis, TX: Gold-Sun LP-101, late 1960s. LP.
"Happy Annie" [Song 3]. *Top Hit Tunes.*
"Headache Waltz" [Song 5]. *15 Top Hit Tunes Featuring Ray on His Dulcimer.*
"Krásná Amerika" [Song 33]. Houston: Gold Star 813, mid-to-late 1940s. 78 rpm.
"My Dream Boat Waltz" [Song 36]. Rosenberg, TX: FBC 111.2, 1949. 78 rpm. Reissued on *Top Hit Tunes: Ray Krenek and His Orchestra.* Brenham, TX: JED Musical Prod., Gold Sun102, 2006. CD.
"Tinker Polka" [Song 19]. *Top Hit Tunes: Ray Krenek and His Orchestra.*
"Wedding March" [Song 54]. *15 Top Hit Tunes Featuring Ray on His Dulcimer.*
"Yellow Beer Polka" [Song 46]. *15 Top Hit Tunes Featuring Ray on His Dulcimer.*

Kurtz, Rudy, Orchestra (Shiner)

"Four Horses Waltz" [Song 17]. San Antonio: TNT 5042, 1964. 45 rpm. Reissued on *Jimmy Brosch Remembers Twenty Legendary Texas Czech Polka Bands.* Katy, TX, 2011. CD.
"From the War" [Song 60]. Waco, TX: Humming Bird HB-006, late 1940s or early 1950s. 78 rpm.
"Kdybych byla ptáčkem" [Song 29]. Waco, TX: Humming Bird 182-A, late 1940s or early 1950s. 78 rpm.

Lazy Farmers (Bellville)

"If I Were a Bird" [Song 29]. *New Sounds.* Bellville, TX, 2008. CD.
"Red and White" [Song 7]. *New Sounds.*

Lichnovsky, Gene (Houston)

"Jarabacek (Bird of Spring) March" [Song 16]. *Gene Lichnovsky: Piano Solos, Polkas, Waltzes, Marches.* Houston: CD-1-GL, circa 2010. CD.

Majek, Leo, Orchestra (Cameron, Corpus Christi)

"Corn Cockle Polka" [Song 50]. *Texas Bohemia.* Munich: Trikont US-0201, 1994. CD.
"Dream Waltz" [Song 30]. *Polka and Waltz.* Corpus Christi: Majek Stereo LP-100, circa mid- 1960s. LP.
"Four Horses" [Song 17]. Corpus Christi: Majek Records 114A, circa mid-1960s. 45 rpm.
"Headache Waltz" [Song 5]. *Polka and Waltz.*
"If I Were a Bird" [Song 29]. *Polka and Waltz.*
"Little Goose Polka" [Song 34]. *Dance.* Corpus Christi: Majek Stereo LP-101, late 1960s. LP.
"Memories of Cameron" [Song 59]. *Songs from the Heart.* Corpus Christi: Majek Recording Studio, 1980s. Cassette tape. Reissued on *Jimmy Brosch Remembers Twenty Legendary Texas Czech Polka Bands.* Katy, TX, 2011. CD.
"Music, Music Polka" [Song 39]. *Dance.*
"Roaring Mountains" [Song 61]. *Dance.*
"Tinker Polka" [Song 19]. *Memories.* Corpus Christi: Majek Recording Studio, circa 1992. Cassette tape.
"Under the Window Polka" [Song 47]. *Polka and Waltz.*

Matocha, Lee Roy, Orchestra (Fayetteville)

"Annie the Foreman Polka" [Song 3]. *Red Hot and Rolling.* Houston: Julius Tupa RVS Studios, 1982. Cassette tape.
"Boogie Bear Waltz" [Song 40]. *By Special Request.* Fayetteville, TX: Lee Records LP#5, late 1960s. LP.
"Grinders Polka" [Song 43]. *Lee Roy Is Back Again.* Houston: Guide LP-1026, late 1970s. LP.

"Hastrman Waltz" [Song 21]. *By Popular Demand.* Fayetteville, TX: LRM 1001, 1987. Cassette tape. Reissued on *By Popular Demand.* Fayetteville, TX: n.d. CD.
"Headache Waltz" [Song 5]. *By Special Request.*
"Looking for My Sweetheart" [Song 22]. *Lee Roy Is Back Again.*
"Muziky! Muziky!" [Song 39]. *Muziky! Muziky!* Fayetteville, TX, 2002. Compilation CD.
"Oaken Leaf Polka" [Song 35]. *By Special Request.*
"Orphan Waltz" [Song 51]. *Something Old, Something New.* Houston: Guide 1015, circa early 1970s. LP. Also on *Muziky! Muziky!*
"Red and White" [Song 7]. *Let's Dance with Lee Roy.* Fayetteville, TX: Lee LP-1, mid-1960s. LP.
"Red Rose Waltz" [Song 9]. *The King of Polka.* Houston: Guide LP-1041, mid-1970s. LP.
"Snowflower Polka" [Song 42]. Houston: Allstar A7312, 1960s. 45 rpm.
"Texas Special" [Song 23]. *The Country Boy Is Back.* Houston: Guide 1049, 1970s. LP.
"Tinker Polka" [Song 19]. Reissued on *Muziky! Muziky!*

Mensik, Johnny, and Orchestra (Ennis)

"Little Goose Polka" [Song 34]. *Required of Us a Song.* Dallas: USR 3181, 1972. LP.
"Looking for My Sweetheart" [Song 22]. *Required of Us a Song.*

Migl, Adolph, Orchestra (Novohrad)

"Koline, Koline Polka" [Song 32]. Waco, TX: Humming Bird, late 1940s. 78 rpm. Reissued on *Jimmy Brosch Remembers.* Katy, TX, 2011. CD.

Migl, Frank. Frank Migl's Orchestra (Hallettsville)

"Good Morning Polka" [Song 49]. Houston: Humming Bird 163-A, circa 1950s. 78 rpm.
"Julajda (Julida) Polka" [Song 26]. Houston: Humming Bird 158-A, late 1940s. 78 rpm. Reissued on *Bands of Texas, Vol. 1.* Schulenburg, TX: Texas Polka Music Museum, circa mid-2010. CD.
"Red Handkerchief Waltz" [Song 11]. Houston: Humming Bird 161-B, circa 1950–1953. 78 rpm.

Mikula, Jodie, Orchestra (Ennis)

"Around the Moon" [Song 44]. *Play Me a Polka: Tex-Czech Polkas.* Rounder Records 6029, 1994. Compilation CD.
"Hastrman" [Song 21], *A Toast to Czech Music.* Ennis, TX, 1985. LP.
"Meadow Polka" [Song 2]. *From the Good Old Days.* Ennis, TX, 1973. LP.
"Monkey Polka" [Song 45]. *Klobase Polka.* Ennis, TX, 1993. CD.
"Red Rose Waltz" [Song 9]. *From the Good Old Days.*
"Wheelbarrow" [Song 24]. *A Toast to Czech Music.* Ennis, TX, 1985. LP. Reissued on *Play Me a Polka: Tex-Czech Polkas.*

Moravians, The (Ennis)

"Red Rose Polka" [Song 8]. *Czech Spirit Will Live On.* Ennis, TX, 2013. CD.
"U Studanky Waltz" [Song 56]. *Czech Spirit Will Live On.*

Moulton All-Girl Polka Band

"At the Spring Waltz" [Song 56]. *Presenting the Moulton High School Band and Moulton All-Girl Polka Band.* Moulton, TX: Music Department, Moulton Independent School District, late 1980s. CD.

Mraz, Bill, Orchestra (Houston)

"Red and White Waltz" [Song 7]. *Festival Album.* Houston: Mraz LP 501, 1950s. LP.
"Red Rose Polka" [Song 8]. *Polka Heritage—Made Famous.* Houston: Guide 1046, 1977. LP.
"Monkey Polka" [Song 45]. *Swing and Sway the Oompah Way.* Houston: Mraz 506, circa 1960s. LP.
"Roaring Mountains" [Song 61]. *Your Favorite Polkas and Waltzes.* Houston: Mraz 508, 1970s. LP.

Patek, Joe, Orchestra (Shiner)

"At the Mill March (Pode mlejnem-pochod)" [Song 48]. Waco, TX: Humming Bird 170-A, 1951. 78 rpm. Reissued on *Américan Polka.* San Antonio: Eagle Music Prod. LSCD-8017, 2001. CD.
"Dreamland Waltz" [Song 30]. Reissued on *Joe Patek Orchestra: The 78s.* Fayetteville, TX, circa 2000. CD.
"Four Horses Waltz" [Song 17]. San Antonio: TNT 5064, 1963. 45 rpm.
"Krasna Amerika (Beautiful America)" [Song 33]. Waco, TX: Humming Bird 103, late 1940s. 78 rpm. Reissued on *Texas-Czech, Bohemian, and Moravian Bands.* Arhoolie Folkloric 7026, 1993. Compilation CD.
"Looking for My Sweetheart" [Song 22]. *Shiner Gold.* Houston: Guide LP-1037, early 1970s. LP. Reissued on *Shiner Gold and Polka Memories.* Houston: Bellaire CD1314, 1998. CD.
"Louka Zelena Waltz" [Song 37]. Waco, TX: Martin M104–2, circa 1949. 78 rpm. Reissued on *Joe Patek Orchestra: The 78s.* Fayetteville, TX: circa 2000. CD.
"Oaken Leaves" [Song 35]. *Joe Patek and His Orchestra.* San Antonio: TNT LP-3008, late 1960s. LP. Reissued on *Shiner Gold and Polka Memories.*
"Oh! Meadow" [Song 2]. San Antonio: TNT 5064, 1963. 45 rpm.
"Red Handkerchief" [Song 11]. San Antonio: TNT-5014, circa 1950s. 45 rpm.
"Red Rose Polka" [Song 8]. *The Magic of Joe Patek.* Houston: Guide LP-1044, 1970s. LP.

"Red Rose Waltz" [Song 9]. *The Magic of Joe Patek.*
"Red Wine Polka" [Song 10]. San Antonio: TNT, late 1950s. 45 rpm.
"Road to Moravia" [Song 13]. *The Magic of Joe Patek.*
"Shiner Beer Polka" [Song 23]. Rosenberg, TX: FBC Records 122-1, 1949. 78 rpm. Reissued on Waco, TX: Humming Bird, circa 1950. 78 rpm. Reissued on *Joe Patek Orchestra: The 78s.*
"Shiner Song" [Song 31]. San Antonio: Martin M103, late 1940s. 78 rpm. Reissued on *Texas-Czech, Bohemian, and Moravian Bands.* Arhoolie Folkloric 7026, 1993. Compilation CD.
"Sirotek-Waltz (Orphan)" [Song 51]. Rosenberg, TX: FBC 121–2, 1949. 78 rpm. Reissued as "Orphan Waltz (Sirotek Valcik)." Waco, TX: Humming Bird 121-B, late 1940s. 78 rpm.
"Snowflower Polka" [Song 42]. Waco, TX: Humming Bird 159-A, circa 1950s. 78 rpm.
"Tinker Polka" [Song 19]. *Joe Patek Orchestra: The 78s.*
"Under Our Windows Polka" [Song 47]. San Antonio: TNT 5020A, circa 1955–59. 45 rpm.
"Ustudansky Sedela Waltz" [Song 56]. Humming Bird HB125B, circa late 1940s. 78 rpm. Reissued on *Joe Patek Orchestra: The 78s.*
"Wheel Barrow Polka" [Song 24]. San Antonio: Martin M104, circa 1949. 78 rpm. Reissued on *Texas-Czech, Bohemian, and Moravian Bands.*

Pavelka Orchestra (Robstown)

"Dreamland Waltz" [Song 30]. *The Pavelka's New Sound.* Houston: EMPAC-1213, 1977. LP.
"Zahucely hory" [Song 61]. *From Sunny South Texas.* Houston: EMPAC-1206, circa 1968–1975. LP. Reissued on *Bands of Texas, Vol. 4.* Schulenburg, TX: Texas Polka Music Museum, circa 2016. Compilation CD.

Praha Brothers (Temple)

"Dreamboat Waltz" [Song 36]. *Praha Brothers.* Temple, TX, 2003. CD.

Red Ravens (El Campo)

"Dream Boat Waltz" [Song 36]. *Back Porch Music.* El Campo, TX, 2003. CD.
"Garden Gate Polka" [Song 6]. *Polka Better.* El Campo, TX, 1981. Cassette tape.
"Good Night My Darling" [Song 18]. *Polka Better.*
"If I Were a Bird" [Song 29]. Reissued on *Texas Bohemia.* Hamburg, TX: Trikont US-0201, 1994. Compilation CD.
"Mockingbird Waltz" [Song 60]. *Havin' Fun.* El Campo, TX, 2004. CD.
"Monkey Polka" [Song 45]. *Polka Better.*
"Moon over Moravia" [Song 38]. *Havin' Fun.*

Round Top Brass Band (Round Top)

"Bird of Spring March" [Song 16]. *Presenting the Round Top Brass Band.* Round Top, TX, 1981. LP.

Rybak, Chris (Hallettsville)

"Falling Leaves Waltz" [Song 53]. *I Love to Polka.* Hallettsville, TX, 1994. Cassette tape.
"Grand March" [Song 41]. *Grand March.* Hallettsville, TX, 2009. CD.
"Kydu Polka" [Song 27]. *I Love to Polka.*
"Song of Bohemia" [Song 12]. *Let's Have a Party.* Hallettsville, TX: CLR Studios, 1996. CD.

Rybak, Leroy. Leroy Rybak's Swinging Orchestra (Hallettsville)

"Good Morning" [Song 49]. *Don't Mess with Texas Polkas and Waltzes.* Hallettsville, TX: LR-1001, circa 1980s. Cassette tape.
"Hasterman" [Song 21]. *Don't Mess with Texas Polkas and Waltzes.*
"Painted Gate Polka" [Song 6]. *Polka and Waltz Classics.* Hallettsville, TX: CLR-2316, 2006. CD.

Shimek, Wence, Orchestra; Wence Shimek and the All Star Sounds; Wence and Helen and the All Star Sounds (Hallettsville)

"The Bird (Jerabacek) Polka" [Song 16]. *You Asked for It.* Hallettsville, TX, 1982. LP.
"Boogie Bear" [Song 40]. *Wence and Helen Present More Polkas and Waltzes.* Hallettsville, TX: WS-1003, 1984. Cassette tape.
"Hasterman" [Song 21]. *Wence and Helen Present More Polkas and Waltzes.*
"Painted Gate" [Song 6]. *Wence and Helen Present More Polkas and Waltzes.*
"Wheel Barrow" [Song 24]. *Wence and Helen Present More Polkas and Waltzes.*

Shiner Hobo Band (Shiner)

"Falling Leaves Waltz" [Song 53]. *Ještě jednou (One More Time).* Shiner, TX, 2004. CD.
"Fire Brigade Polka" [Song 15]. *Ještě jednou (One More Time).*
"Grinders Polka" [Song 43]. *Ještě jednou (One More Time).*
"Mockingbird Waltz" [Song 60]. *Ještě jednou (One More Time).*
"Music, Music Polka" [Song 39]. *Ještě jednou (One More Time).*
"Orphan Waltz" [Song 51]. *Ještě jednou (One More Time).*
"Red Handkerchief Waltz" [Song 11]. *Frankie and Johnny: Hobo Style.* Shiner, TX, 2007. CD.
"Snow Flower Polka" [Song 42]. *Texas Bohemia.* Hamburg, TX: Trikont US-0201, 1994. CD. Also on *Frankie and Johnny Hobo Style.* Shiner, TX, 2007. CD.
"Tinker Polka" [Song 19]. *Frankie and Johnny Hobo Style.*

SPJST Lodge 88 Choral Group and Orchestra (Houston)

"Andulko Šafářová" [Song 3]. *Czech Folksongs.* Houston: Guide LP-1050, 1978. LP.
"Chaloupky pod horami" [Song 14]. *Czech Folksongs.*
"Já ráda tancuju" [Song 25]. *Czech Folksongs.*
"Kolíne, Kolíne" [Song 32]. *Czech Folksongs.*
"Zahučely hory" [Song 61]. *Czech Folksongs.*

Taylor Czech Chorus (Taylor)

"A já sám" [Song 1]. *The Taylor Czech Chorus Presents.* Taylor, TX, 2007. CD.
"Cestička k Mayrovce" [Song 13]. *Still . . . Carrying On the Tradition.* Holland, TX: Awesome Works Recording, 2018. CD.
"Malovaná brána" [Song 6]. *Still . . . Carrying On the Tradition.*
"Nemelem" [Song 43]. *Songs of Our Heritage.* Taylor, TX, 2007. CD.
"Pisnicka Ceska" [Song 12]. *Songs of Our Heritage.*
"Stratila jsem Kajdu (I Lost My Vest)" [Song 27]. *Songs of Our Heritage.*
"U Studanky sedela, We Offer Thanks" [Song 56]. *The Taylor Czech Chorus Presents.*
"Včera's Byla" [Song 54]. *Still . . . Carrying On the Tradition.*

Telstars (Houston)

"Red Wine Polka" [Song 10]. *The New World of Polka.* Houston: Guide LP-1019, 1970s. LP.

Texas Czech Folk Singers (Dallas)

"Koline, Koline" [Song 32]. *Zazpivajme si.* Dallas, 1970s or 1980s. Cassette tape.

Texas Legacy Czech Band (Houston)

"Dreamboat Waltz" [Song 36]. *The Legacy Continues.* Houston, 2009. CD.
"Kajdu Polka" [Song 27]. *Texas Legacy Czech Band.* Houston, 2008. CD.

Thompson, Hank, and the Brazos Valley Boys (Waco)

"Uvalde Polka" [Song 26]. *Hank Thompson: Sounds of the Brazos Valley,* radio broadcasts, circa 1952. UK: Country Routes RFD CD-19, 1997. CD.

Travelers, The (Columbus)

"Cottages under the Mountains" [Song 14]. *Old Time Classics.* Columbus, TX, 1992. CD.

Tupa, Julius (Houston)

"Barbara Polka" [Song 4]. *Songs I'll Always Remember.* Houston: Guide LP-1010, 1970s. LP.
"Prune Song" [Song 55]. *Songs I'll Always Remember.* Reissued on *Jimmy Brosch Remembers.* Katy, TX, 2011. Compilation CD. Reissued on *Bands of Texas, Vol. 2.* Schulenburg: Texas Polka Music Museum, circa 2013. Compilation CD.

University Czech Singers (Austin)

"Hledám galánečku" [Song 22]. *Czechoslovakian Folksongs.* Houston: EMPAC-1212, 1977. LP.
"Nemelem, Nemelem" [Song 43]. *Czechoslovakian Folksongs.*
"Okolo měsíca" [Song 44]. *Czechoslovakian Folksongs.*

Vlk Sisters (Dallas)

"Ja rada tancuju" [Song 25]. *The Vlk Sisters Play and Sing Their Favorite Czech Songs.* Dallas, 1978. LP.

Vrazels' Polka Band (Buckholts)

"All by Myself" [Song 1]. *Golden Sounds: 50th Anniversary.* Buckholts, TX: VPB 518, 2003. CD. Reissued on *Jimmy Brosch Remembers.* Katy, TX, 2011. CD.
"Corn Cockle Polka" [Song 50]. *Texas Bohemia.* Munich: Trikont US-0201, 1994. CD.
"Fire Brigade Polka" [Song 15]. *Golden Sounds: 50th Anniversary.*
"Gander Polka (Haj, husičky, haj)" [Song 20]. *Polka Sounds from the Country.* Buckholts, TX: VPB 106, circa 1970. 8-track tape.
"Good Night My Darling Waltz" [Song 18]. *On the Road.* Buckholts, TX: VPB-112, 1981. LP.
"Grinders Polka" [Song 43]. *Vrazels' Polka Band.* Austin: Austin Custom Records, circa 1965. LP.
"Hills of Shiner" [Song 23]. *On the Road.* Reissued on *Greatest Hits: Vol. 2.* Buckholts, TX: VPB-517, 2002. CD.
"I Love to Dance" [Song 25]. *Performing in Washington, D.C.* Buckholts, TX: VPB 110, circa 1976. LP.
"If I Were a Bird" [Song 29]. *Dancin' Time.* Austin: Austin Custom Records, VPB 102, circa 1966. LP. Reissued on *Bands of Texas, Vol. 3.* Schulenburg, TX: Texas Polka Music Museum, circa 2015. Compilation CD.
"Kajdu Polka" [Song 27]. *It's Polka Party Time.* Buckholts, TX: VPB-515, 1996. CD. Reissued on *Greatest Hits: Vol. 2.*
"Little Goose Polka" [Song 34]. *Favorites.* Buckholts, TX: Cen-Tex Records VPB-105, 1969. LP.
"Memories of Cameron Waltz" [Song 59]. *Silver Anniversary Sounds.* Austin: Austin Custom Records VPB-111, 1978. LP.
"Monkey Polka" [Song 45]. *Vrazels' Polka Band.*
"Moon over Moravia" [Song 38]. *Songs from Now and Then.* Buckholts, TX: VPB 521, 2007. CD.
"Orphan Waltz" [Song 51]. *Golden Sounds: 50th Anniversary.*
"Painted Gate Polka" [Song 6]. Reissued on *Greatest Hits, Vol. 2.*
"Path to Moravia" [Song 13]. *Performing in Washington, D.C.*
"Red Rose Polka" [Song 8]. *Performing in Washington, D.C.*
"Red Wine Polka" [Song 10]. San Antonio: TNT, circa 1959. 45 rpm.

"Roaring Mountains" [Song 61]. *Polkas and Waltzes.* Buckholts, TX: VPB 104, 1968. LP.

"Snowflower Polka" [Song 42]. *Dancing Time.*

Wavra, Donnie, Orchestra (Columbus)

"Red Handkerchief" [Song 11]. *25 Years.* New Ulm, TX, 1997. Cassette tape.

Zapletal, Ray, and His Music Masters Orchestra (Ennis)

"Barbara Polka" [Song 4]. Reissued on *Texas Czech.* Omaha: Polka Cassettes of Nebraska, 2010. CD.

"Headache Waltz" [Song 5]. *Bluebonnet Czech.* Ennis, TX, 1960s. LP.

"Rano Ranicko (Good Morning) Polka" [Song 49]. *Bluebonnet Czech.*

Zetka's Polka Band (El Campo)

"Fire Brigade" [Song 15]. *On Fire with Zetka's Polka Band.* El Campo, TX, 1994. Cassette tape. Reissued on *Bands of Texas, Vol. 4.* Schulenburg, TX: Texas Polka Music Museum, circa 2016. CD.

SUBJECT INDEX

References to illustrations appear in italic type.

INDEX OF SONGS

References to main entries with music and lyrics appear in boldface type.